THE CRISIS OF MODERNITY

McGill-Queen's Studies in the History of Ideas
Series Editor: Philip J. Cercone

1 Problems of Cartesianism
Edited by Thomas M. Lennon, John M. Nicholas, and John W. Davis

2 The Development of the Idea of History in Antiquity
Gerald A. Press

3 Claude Buffier and Thomas Reid: Two Common-Sense Philosophers
Louise Marcil-Lacoste

4 Schiller, Hegel, and Marx: State, Society, and the Aesthetic Ideal of Ancient Greece
Philip J. Kain

5 John Case and Aristotelianism in Renaissance England
Charles B. Schmitt

6 Beyond Liberty and Property: The Process of Self-Recognition in Eighteenth-Century Political Thought
J.A.W. Gunn

7 John Toland: His Methods, Manners, and Mind
Stephen H. Daniel

8 Coleridge and the Inspired Word
Anthony John Harding

9 The Jena System, 1804–5: Logic and Metaphysics
G.W.F. Hegel
Translation edited by John W. Burbidge and George di Giovanni
Introduction and notes by H.S. Harris

10 Consent, Coercion, and Limit: The Medieval Origins of Parliamentary Democracy
Arthur P. Monahan

11 Scottish Common Sense in Germany, 1768–1800: A Contribution to the History of Critical Philosophy
Manfred Kuehn

12 Paine and Cobbett: The Transatlantic Connection
David A. Wilson

13 Descartes and the Enlightenment
Peter A. Schouls

14 Greek Scepticism: Anti-Realist Trends in Ancient Thought
Leo Groarke

15 The Irony of Theology and the Nature of Religious Thought
Donald Wiebe

16 Form and Transformation: A Study in the Philosophy of Plotinus
Frederic M. Schroeder

17 From Personal Duties towards Personal Rights: Late Medieval and Early Modern Political Thought, c. 1300–c. 1650
Arthur P. Monahan

18 The Main Philosophical Writings and the Novel *Allwill*
Friedrich Heinrich Jacobi
Translated and edited by George di Giovanni

19 Kierkegaard as Humanist: Discovering My Self
Arnold B. Come

20 Durkheim, Morals, and Modernity
W. Watts Miller

21 The Career of Toleration: John Locke, Jonas Proast, and After
Richard Vernon

22 Dialectic of Love: Platonism in Schiller's Aesthetics
David Pugh

23 History and Memory in Ancient Greece
Gordon Shrimpton

24 Kierkegaard as Theologian: Recovering My Self
Arnold B. Come

25 Enlightenment and Conservatism in Victorian Scotland: The Career of Sir Archibald Alison
Michael Michie

26 The Road to Egdon Heath: The Aesthetics of the Great in Nature
Richard Bevis

27 Jena Romanticism and Its Appropriation of Jakob Böhme: Theosophy – Hagiography – Literature
Paolo Mayer

28 Enlightenment and Community: Lessing, Abbt, Herder, and the Quest for a German Public
Benjamin W. Redekop

29 Jacob Burckhardt and the Crisis of Modernity
John R. Hinde

30 The Distant Relation: Time and Identity in Spanish-American Fiction
Eoin S. Thomson

31 Mr Simson's Knotty Case: Divinity, Politics, and Due Process in Early Eighteenth-Century Scotland
Anne Skoczylas

32 Orthodoxy and Enlightenment: George Campbell in the Eighteenth Century
Jeffrey M. Suderman

33 Contemplation and Incarnation: The Theology of Marie-Dominique Chenu
Christophe F. Potworowski

34 Democratic Legitimacy: Plural Values and Political Power
F.M. Barnard

35 Herder on Nationality, Humanity, and History
F.M. Barnard

36 Labeling People: French Scholars on Society, Race, and Empire, 1815–1849
Martin S. Staum

37 The Subaltern Appeal to Experience: Self-Identity, Late Modernity, and the Politics of Immediacy
Craig Ireland

38 The Invention of Journalism Ethics: The Path to Objectivity and Beyond
Stephen J.A. Ward

39 The Recovery of Wonder: The New Freedom and the Asceticism of Power
Kenneth L. Schmitz

40 Reason and Self-Enactment in History and Politics: Themes and Voices of Modernity
F.M. Barnard

41 The More Moderate Side of Joseph de Maistre: Views on Political Liberty and Political Economy
Cara Camcastle

42 Democratic Society and Human Needs
Jeff Noonan

43 The Circle of Rights Expands: Modern Political Thought after the Reformation, 1521 (Luther) to 1762 (Rousseau)
Arthur P. Monahan

44 The Canadian Founding: John Locke and Parliament
Janet Ajzenstat

45 Finding Freedom: Hegel's Philosophy and the Emancipation of Women
Sara MacDonald

46 When the French Tried to Be British: Party, Opposition, and the Quest for the Civil Disagreement, 1814–1848
J.A.W. Gunn

47 Under Conrad's Eyes: The Novel as Criticism
Michael John DiSanto

48 Media, Memory, and the First World War
David Williams

49 An Aristotelian Account of Induction: Creating Something from Nothing
Louis Groarke

50 Social and Political Bonds: A Mosaic of Contrast and Convergence
F.M. Barnard

51 Archives and the Event of God: The Impact of Michel Foucault on Philosophical Theology
David Galston

52 Between the Queen and the Cabby: Olympe de Gouges's *Rights of Women*
John R. Cole

53 Nature and Nurture in French Social Sciences, 1859–1914 and Beyond
Martin S. Staum

54 Public Passion: Rethinking the Grounds for Political Justice
Rebecca Kingston

55 Rethinking the Political: The Sacred, Aesthetic Politics, and the Collège de Sociologie
Simonetta Falasca-Zamponi

56 Materialist Ethics and Life-Value
Jeff Noonan

57 Hegel's *Phenomenology*: The Dialectical Justification of Philosophy's First Principles
Ardis B. Collins

58 The Social History of Ideas in Quebec, 1760–1896
Yvan Lamonde
Translated by Phyllis Aronoff and Howard Scott

59 Ideas, Concepts, and Reality
John W. Burbidge

60 The Enigma of Perception
D.L.C. Maclachlan

61 Nietzsche's Justice Naturalism in Search of an Ethics
Peter R. Sedgwick

62 The Idea of Liberty during the Age of Atlantic Revolutions, 1776–1838
Michel Ducharme
Translated by Peter Feldstein

63 From White to Yellow: The Japanese in European Racial Thought, 1300–1735
Rotem Kowner

64 The Crisis of Modernity
Augusto Del Noce
Edited and translated by Carlo Lancellotti

THE CRISIS OF MODERNITY

Augusto Del Noce

Edited and translated by
Carlo Lancellotti

McGill-Queen's University Press
Montreal & Kingston • London • Chicago

Translated with permission from
Fondazione Centro Studi Augusto Del Noce

ISBN 978-0-7735-4442-0 (cloth)
ISBN 978-0-7735-4443-7 (paper)
ISBN 978-0-7735-9673-3 (ePDF)
ISBN 978-0-7735-9674-0 (ePUB)

Legal deposit fourth quarter 2014
Bibliothèque nationale du Québec
Reprinted 2015, 2017, 2019, 2021

Printed in Canada on acid-free paper that is 100% ancient forest free (100% post-consumer recycled), processed chlorine free

The translation of this work has been funded by SEPS
Segretariato Europeo per le Pubblicazioni Scientifiche
Via Val d'Aposa 7 – 40123 Bologna – Italy
seps@seps.it – www.seps.it

Funded by the Government of Canada | Financé par le gouvernement du Canada | Canada | Canada Council for the Arts | Conseil des arts du Canada

We acknowledge the support of the Canada Council for the Arts.

Nous remercions le Conseil des arts du Canada de son soutien.

Library and Archives Canada Cataloguing in Publication

Del Noce, Augusto, 1910–1989
[Essays. Selections. English]
The crisis of modernity / Augusto Del Noce; edited and translated by Carlo Lancellotti.

(McGill-Queen's studies in the history of ideas ; 64)
Essays translated from the Italian.
Includes bibliographical references and index.
Issued in print and electronic formats.
ISBN 978-0-7735-4442-0 (bound). – ISBN 978-0-7735-4443-7 (pbk.).
ISBN 978-0-7735-9673-3 (ePDF). – ISBN 978-0-7735-9674-0 (ePUB)

1. Civilization, Modern. 2. Secularization. I. Lancellotti, Carlo, editor, translator II. Title. III. Title: Essays. Selections. English IV. Series: McGill-Queen's studies in the history of ideas; 64

CB358.D4413 2014 909.08 C2014-904355-4
C2014-904356-2

This book was typeset by Interscript in 10/12 New Baskerville.
Cover image © 2013 Olycom s.p.a. & Publifoto s.r.l.

Contents

APPENDICES

Translator's Introduction

IN HIS WRITINGS, AUGUSTO DEL NOCE quotes more than once a famous line from the preface to Hegel's *Elements of the Philosophy of Right:* "philosophy is its own time apprehended in thought."[1] Del Noce certainly disagreed with what Hegel intended to say – namely, that it is "foolish" to think "that any philosophy can transcend its contemporary world" – since he did not doubt that philosophy can achieve timeless and metahistorical truths. Nonetheless, Hegel's sentence can be used, in a different sense, to describe Del Noce's own reflection: as a form of thought deeply engaged with history. Among thinkers of his generation who shared the same classical-metaphysical orientation, Del Noce stands out for his constant effort to discern the connections between social and political developments, on one side, and philosophical and religious ideas on the other. At a time when Western academic culture was starting to be dominated by schools of thought that favoured *prepolitical* explanations – by which I mean, in a broad sense, approaches based on methods borrowed from the human sciences: economics, sociology, psychology, socio-biology, etc. – Del Noce advocated what Renzo De Felice called a *transpolitical* interpretation of contemporary history, in which people's conceptions of the world and of themselves play a significant role. This preference should not be attributed to any kind of a priori idealistic or spiritualistic bias against economic and sociological explanations of historical phenomena. It did reflect, however, Del Noce's judgment that "there is no minute detail of human life that does not reflect or, to be exact, does not 'symbolize' a general conception of life."[2]

1 Georg W.F. Hegel, *Elements of the Philosophy of Right*, ed. Allan W. Wood, trans. Hugh B. Nisbet (Cambridge: Cambridge University Press, 1991), 21.

2 Augusto Del Noce, "Revolution, *Risorgimento*, Tradition" in this volume, 49.

Del Noce's keen perception of the interplay between "the history of ideas" and "the history of facts" is one of the reasons why, twenty-five years after his death, he remains an original and engaging intellectual figure. In his native Italy he is widely regarded as one of the pre-eminent political thinkers and philosophers of the second half of last century, precisely because of his ability to reconstruct intellectual genealogies and to expose the deep metaphysical premises of social and political movements. His own lifetime (1910–1989) coincided almost exactly with the period 1914–1991 that Eric Hobsbawm called the "short twentieth century." It was marked by the two world wars and by the rise and fall of the Marxist-Leninist revolutionary dream, and of the totalitarian systems that either shared in it or opposed it. Del Noce maintained that twentieth-century history must be understood as a *philosophical history* in a specific and unique way because during that period Western culture was profoundly affected by the philosophies of history of the previous century (Idealism, Marxism, Positivism). These philosophies had become the secular, neo-gnostic surrogate of Christianity for the European educated classes after the French Revolution, and the next century put them to the practical test, bringing to light their ultimate and necessary consequences.

Del Noce himself came of age in a cultural environment dominated by neo-Idealistic philosophy: the Italian intellectual world of the late 1920s, ruled by the duumvirate of Benedetto Croce and Giovanni Gentile. They had recently fallen out because of their radically different responses to the rise of Fascism. Croce had chosen to become the moral and intellectual leader of the opposition to Mussolini, whereas Gentile had become the official philosopher of the new regime. Still, Idealistic culture was to remain the dominant intellectual force in Italy, on both sides of the political divide, until the catastrophe of the Second World War and the advent of the Marxist cultural hegemony after 1945. To Del Noce such a culture felt "totally foreign," as he had occasion to remark many years later.[3] From his mother's side, he was a descendant of an old aristocratic Catholic family from the ancient Duchy of Savoy, and he grew up in its former capital, Turin. For many centuries, this border region had been a cultural meeting point between Italy and France and had carved for itself a small but distinctive spot in the annals of philosophy. During the period before and immediately after the French Revolution, it had produced an important theologian in Cardinal Hyacinthe-Sigismond Gerdil, as well as a world-famous political thinker in Count Joseph de

3 See the interview by Massimo Borghesi and Lucio Brunelli, "Story of a Solitary Thinker," appendix A in the present volume, 265.

Maistre. In the nineteenth century it had been the home of the two major Italian philosophers of the period of the *Risorgimento*, Vincenzo Gioberti and Antonio Rosmini.

Given his background, it was only natural that, as a university student of philosophy in Turin around 1930, Del Noce would turn his attention toward France and become de facto "a 'private' student of the Sorbonne."[4] He wrote his dissertation on the religious interpretation of Descartes in the philosophy of Malebranche, and became acquainted with leading French scholars such as Étienne Gilson, Jean Laporte, and Henri Gouhier. But above all he came in contact with the works of Jacques Maritain, especially *Three Reformers* and *Integral Humanism*. For Del Noce, Maritain was, more than anything else, an example of a philosopher fully engaged with history who had developed a deep and original *non-reactionary* interpretation of the trajectory of the modern world in the light of the classical and Christian tradition. In fact, what most impressed young Del Noce was that Maritain's neo-Thomism was unafraid to challenge secular philosophy on its home turf: that ability to account for the historical development of modernity which was the major claim of the great philosophers of history of the nineteenth century: Hegel, Marx, Comte.

Del Noce's interest in the philosophical underpinnings of modern history was also a reflection of his life-long sensitivity to social and political developments. In the years immediately after his graduation, while he was working as a high school teacher in Turin, he faced the great European crisis of the 1930s. As he would write fifty years later, "Deeply rooted and ... well-founded intellectual habits made us recognize Europe as the final fruit of centuries of civilization. But now this very continent was devastated by unprecedented violence. In those years I suffered such contradiction to an extreme degree ..."[5] What was worse, "the various fashionable philosophies of that period seemed to me attempts to accommodate violence." Del Noce's intuition was confirmed "by the outcome of the Second World War and by the advance of revolutionary violence, no longer described as barbaric ... a form of thought spread that replaced the type of the philosopher with the one of the revolutionary. It absorbed ethics into politics, or denied ... that any values are absolute, since all of them are covers for class interests and the will to power." As a result of the war, large parts of the European intellectual class shifted from Idealism and historicism to Marxism. Also, many Catholics concluded that the defence of civilization against Fascist and Nazi barbarism

4 Ibid.

5 From "Violence and Modern Gnosticism" in this volume, 38.

required a reconciliation (or even a synthesis) between Christianity and Marxism. Del Noce himself was initially tempted by this idea, which seemed consistent with some aspects of the thought of Maritain. However, he felt a deep uneasiness toward Marxism on *moral* grounds because he could not accept the notion that violence is justified for the sake of the revolution.[6] This situation led him to study systematically the writings of Marx, especially Marx's youthful philosophical works, which had been discovered and published for the first time in the late 1920s.

Del Noce's study of Marx's philosophy – culminating in his 1946 essay "La 'non-filosofia' di Marx,"[7] later re-published in the book *Il problema dell'ateismo*[8] – marked a turning point in his intellectual journey. The position of the "Catholic Left" was predicated on the notion that atheism is an accessory element of Marxism, and that the core of Marx's thought is a socio-political analysis that can be separated from the "religious" aspect and used in order to fight Fascism and promote social justice. Del Noce realized that, on the contrary, all of Marx's thought is a consistent development of the radical *metaphysical* principle that *freedom requires self-creation*, and thus the rejection of all possible forms of dependence, especially dependence on God. Therefore, Del Noce came to see that in Marx "atheism ... is not the *conclusion* but rather the *precondition* of the whole system."[9] For this reason, Marx's philosophy (and not his political or economic theories) is a crucial node of Western cultural history. On one side, it is the fully consistent and irreversible endpoint of the evolution of European rationalism since Descartes. On the other, it is the origin of the idea of "total revolution" that shaped the history of the twentieth century, namely "the promise ... of a new situation of mankind in which the problem of God will no longer arise."[10] An important corollary of this idea is that ethics must be subordinated to the progress of the revolution, and not vice versa. This realization led Del Noce to reject for good the possibility of a Catholic-Communist alliance.

6 Regarding the moral starting point of Del Noce's philosophy, see again "Story of a Solitary Thinker," and also the article by Massimo Borghesi, "Augusto Del Noce: Non-Manichean Thinking," *30Days*, no. 10/11 (2009): 50–9.

7 Augusto Del Noce, "La 'non-filosofia' di Marx e il comunismo come realtà politica" [Marx's "non-philosophy" and Communism as a political reality] in *Il materialismo storico. Atti del I congresso internazionale di filosofia* [Historical materialism. Proceedings of the 1st International Conference on Philosophy] (Milan: Castellani, 1947), 357–88.

8 Augusto Del Noce, *Il problema dell'ateismo* [The problem of atheism] (Bologna: Il Mulino, 1964).

9 Augusto Del Noce, "Authority versus Power," 202, in this volume.

10 Ibid.

In the postwar years, Del Noce actively pursued his scholarly career in non-academic institutions (think-tanks, publishing houses), producing a large number of publications. In 1964, he collected some of them in his first book, *Il problema dell'ateismo,* dedicated to the trajectory of modern rationalism. In it Del Noce argues that historically the core assumption of post-Cartesian rationalism was the rejection of the *status naturae lapsae,* which over time developed into rejection of religious transcendence altogether. However, since this rejection cannot be proven, modern philosophy must justify itself as the outcome of an irreversible process of secularization; its criterion of truth is its own ability to surpass and integrate all previous forms of thought, as exemplified by the Hegelian system. Therefore, periodization of the history of philosophy becomes a crucial *theoretical* question. Neo-Idealistic philosophers downplayed the philosophical significance of atheistic thinkers like Marx and Nietzsche in order to depict the history of modernity as an organic, unitary process toward immanentism, claimed to be the philosophical fulfillment of Christianity. On the contrary, Del Noce regards atheism as a protagonist in the development of modernity, which appears at the end of every major cycle of European thought: Bruno at the end of the Renaissance, the libertines at the end of Cartesianism, de Sade at the end of the Enlightenment, Marx and Nietzsche at the end of classical German philosophy. However, a correct assessment of the role of atheism in the history of modern thought shows that it is not the necessary outcome of modernity but rather a problematic outcome, inasmuch as it does not lead to the promised fulfillment but rather to forms of nihilism. On the other hand, according to Del Noce, modernity includes a second, largely forgotten, line of development, not from Descartes to Nietzsche but from Descartes, through Vico and Pascal, to Rosmini, which does not conclude in nihilism but in the rediscovery and purification of classical metaphysical thought.

Del Noce also included in *Il problema dell'ateismo* some of his essays on Marx, in which he affirms the *philosophical* potency of Marxism, as the ultimate expression of European rationalism and the manifestation of its crisis. On the one hand, with Marxism, modern secular thought made itself a (atheistic) religion and reached the masses, thus shaping modern history as the history of the expansion of atheism. On the other, Marxism's success coincided with its decomposition: instead of producing universal liberation, it opened the way to the affluent society, "the society that succeeds in eliminating the dialectic tension that sustains the revolution by pushing alienation to the highest degree."[11] Decades before the end of

11 Del Noce, *Il problema dell'ateismo,* 314.

the Soviet Union, at a time when large segments of the Western intelligentsia still embraced Marxism as "the philosophy of our time,"[12] Del Noce understood that Marxism had been fundamentally defeated because history had refuted its fundamental metaphysical assumption, namely the revolutionary transition to the "new man." However, by infusing Western culture with historical materialism and an attitude of radical rejection of religious transcendence, Marxism had succeeded in its *pars destruens.* As Del Noce would say years later, "Marxism is the *subject* of contemporary history. More precisely, contemporary history is *at the same time* the story of its success and its failure … Marxism did realize itself, but by realizing itself *at the same time* it negated itself … Marxism succeeded in denying that values are absolute, and the nihilism that dominates the Western world reflects this 'success-failure' of Marxism."[13] Marxism paradoxically was instrumental in the rise of a new secular, relativistic, neo-bourgeois society that accepted all of Marx's metaphysical negations but rejected his religious/messianic message. Del Noce called this process a "heterogenesis of ends," meaning that Marxism was bound to produce the exact opposite outcome of what Marx intended, due to an intrinsic contradiction in its metaphysical assumptions.

In 1965 Del Noce published another major book, *Riforma cattolica e filosofia moderna*, vol. 1, *Cartesio.*[14] It was supposed to be the first in a series of monographs crowning over thirty years of work on early modern French philosophy, but Del Noce was never able to complete the other volumes. In 1964, at the age of fifty-four, he had finally succeeded in negotiating the byzantine mechanisms of the Italian academic hiring process and obtained a permanent academic position at the University of Trieste. A few years later he became a professor at the prestigious La Sapienza University of Rome, where he would spend the rest of his career. In 1966 he also agreed to edit, together with Elémire Zolla, a book series for the Borla publishing house in Turin. This series was called *Documenti di Cultura Moderna* [Documents of modern culture] and gave Del Noce the opportunity to introduce to an Italian readership many prominent contemporary authors who had been more or less ignored by the Italian cultural mainstream, such as Mircea Eliade, Simone Weil, Eric Voegelin, René Guénon, Abraham Heschel, Hans Sedlmayr, and Manuel García Pelayo.

12 A sentence by Jean-Paul Sartre, quoted by Del Noce in "Notes on Secularization and Religious Thought," 273, in this volume.

13 Borghesi and Brunelli, "Story of a Solitary Thinker," 268–9

14 Augusto Del Noce, *Riforma cattolica e filosofia moderna*, vol. 1, *Cartesio* [Catholic reformation and modern philosophy, vol. 1, Descartes] (Bologna: Il Mulino, 1965).

In the meanwhile, the 1960s brought new massive cultural and social changes. Just as the old Italian Idealistic culture had been powerless to resist the shift "from Croce to Marx" at the end of the war, Marxism itself proved powerless to stop the advent of the affluent (or "technological") society. Del Noce regarded this shift as philosophically very significant, and wrote several essays on the transformation of Western culture after the Second World War, some of which were collected in the volume *L'epoca della secolarizzazione*[15] in 1970. In his judgment the affluent society is intrinsically totalitarian and anti-traditional because its underlying philosophy is a form of radical positivism that recognizes the empirical sciences as the only valid form of knowledge. Historically, "it is the only possible bourgeois and secular answer to Marxism, and ... arises because of an intrinsic contradiction within Marxism itself ... [it] defeats Marxism in the sense that it appropriates all its negations of transcendent values, by pushing to the limit ... the aspect of Marxism that makes it a form of absolute relativism. This has the result of turning Marxism upside down into an absolute individualism, which serves the purpose of giving the technological civilization the false appearance of being a 'democracy' and the continuation of the spirit of liberalism."[16] *L'epoca della secolarizzazione* also formulates a severe critique of the progressive culture of the 1960s. Precisely because it fails to criticize Marx's metaphysical negations, Del Noce considers progressivism incapable of resisting the growing dehumanization of the technological society. He traces this failure back to an incorrect interpretation of contemporary history. After the Second World War, European intellectuals interpreted Fascism and Nazism as reactionary phenomena and identified them incorrectly with the "European past." But then, in order to exorcise the horrors of totalitarianism, "what had to be rediscovered as a truly modern attitude ... was the Enlightenment as a disposition to declare a break with the traditional structures."[17] However, this had to be an "Enlightenment after Marx" and therefore "emancipation from authority and traditions was bound to take place according to the aspect of the Enlightenment that makes negation its dominant character."[18]

The 1970s were a fruitful decade for Del Noce. As a university professor in Rome he had the opportunity to share his ideas with younger people, some of whom became disciples and collaborators. He also participated

15 Augusto Del Noce, *L'epoca della secolarizzazione* [The age of secularization] (Milan: Rusconi 1970).

16 Ibid., 91.

17 Ibid., 48.

18 Ibid., 53.

actively in the Italian cultural and political debate, giving public lectures and publishing numerous articles in various periodicals and on the editorial pages of major newspapers. In 1978 he published one of his best-known books, *Il suicidio della rivoluzione*,[19] in which he argues that the process of "decomposition" of Marxism can already be observed fully at work in the thought of Antonio Gramsci. In a scholarly tour de force Del Noce shows that Gramsci was decisively influenced by Giovanni Gentile's philosophy of the "free act." As a consequence, the Gramscian theory of hegemony, instead of leading to a Marxist revolution, is prone to becoming a tool to establish a radical liberal-bourgeois regime. Del Noce's thesis generated some controversy because in Italy in the 1970s Gramsci and Gentile were considered to be at opposite ends of the ideological spectrum: one a major icon of European Marxism, the other the official ideologue of Fascism. In *Il suicidio della rivoluzione* Del Noce argues that, actually, Gentile's philosophy and Fascism cannot be understood unless one takes into account the decisive formative role of Marxian philosophy for both Gentile and Mussolini.

In 1981 Del Noce published *Il cattolico comunista*,[20] which brought together in a single volume two studies, written several years apart, of the Italian Communist-Catholic movement after the Second World War. Del Noce remained active to the end of his life, and served a term in the Italian Senate for the Christian Democratic Party in the 1980s. Augusto Del Noce died on 30 December 1989, a few weeks after the fall of the Berlin wall had symbolically fulfilled his philosophical prophecy about the inevitable end of the "sacral period of the age of secularization."[21] His last major work was a monograph, *Giovanni Gentile*,[22] published posthumously in 1990. It was only the beginning of a steady stream of posthumous volumes collecting the many articles and essays on various topics that Del Noce had written over the years and never published in book form.[23]

• • •

19 Augusto Del Noce, *Il suicidio della rivoluzione* [The suicide of the revolution] (Milan: Rusconi, 1978).

20 Augusto Del Noce, *Il cattolico comunista* [The Communist Catholic] (Milan: Rusconi, 1981).

21 Del Noce, *L'epoca della secolarizzazione*, 116–17.

22 Augusto Del Noce, *Giovanni Gentile* (Bologna: Il Mulino, 1990).

23 For bibliographic resources, see the Del Noce Foundation's website, http://www.fondazioneaugustodelnoce.net/.

Producing the first volume ever of works by Del Noce in English requires the translator to answer a very basic question: where to start? The answer, of course, is a matter of priorities. If one were to pick Del Noce's most famous and influential book, the choice would certainly be *Il problema dell'ateismo*. For innovative, in-depth scholarship on cultural history, the choice would probably fall on his studies on Gramsci and Gentile, such as *Il suicidio della rivoluzione*. If one wished to present Del Noce as a political thinker, it would make sense to assemble in a volume his writings on the totalitarian movements of the twentieth century, with a special emphasis on Marxism-Leninism and on the interpretation of Fascism. Of course, an obvious way to introduce Del Noce to the English-speaking world would be by assembling a comprehensive anthology covering all aspects of his work; unfortunately, this is not easy to do, because Del Noce wrote about a great variety of topics and some of his most significant works are either too long or too specialized to be anthologized.

The present book is an attempt at a compromise: it is an anthology, but with a specific thematic focus. In consultation with scholars both in Italy and in the United States, I have assembled a selection of essays and lectures on the cultural history of the twentieth century, with a special emphasis on secularization and the sexual revolution. This strategy has several advantages: these topics are of interest to a broader readership who may not be otherwise interested in the history of Italian (or even European) culture; there is a large choice of texts of reasonable length; these texts are usually not overly specialized; and many of them are still very relevant to our contemporary situation and, in fact, eerily prophetic of the cultural developments of the last few decades. I should also mention that I further restricted myself to works published after 1969. This is an arbitrary dividing line, whose only justification is that in 1970 Del Noce collected his earlier works on these matters in *L'epoca della secolarizzazione*. I initially planned to include some of those essays but soon realized that the resulting book would be too long. Therefore, I decided to start with a collection of post-1969 works, hoping that in the future it would be possible to publish a complete translation of *L'epoca della secolarizzazione* by itself.

The book is divided in three parts plus an appendix. The first part offers a sample of Del Noce's ideas about European cultural history, especially his analysis of the sequence modernity-revolution-secularization and of the role of Marxism in contemporary history. By necessity, the texts in this section are neither fully homogeneous nor exhaustive: they are simply intended to quickly expose the reader to a broad range of ideas that Del Noce discussed at greater length elsewhere.

For example, the first piece, "The Idea of Modernity," is a 1981 lecture in which Del Noce presents concisely some of the theses of his 1963 book *Il problema dell'ateismo.* In particular, he discusses the axiological value of the idea of modernity and the attempt by the "philosophers of divine immanence" to purge atheism from the history of philosophy. He argues that if atheistic thinkers are given their rightful place in the history of European thought, the neo-Hegelian scheme of a unitary process from "transcendent" to "immanent" Christianity falls apart. One is then left with the familiar progression "from Descartes to Nietzsche," which ends in nihilism. Del Noce disagrees, however, with the "anti-modern" stance that regards nihilism as the unavoidable outcome of modernity. To him modernity is an "ambiguous" phenomenon, whose ambiguity can already be observed in Descartes's *Meditations on First Philosophy.* Descartes's systematic doubt differs from the libertines' doubt because it affirms the reality of freedom, which is necessarily (but problematically) a "religious" element. Del Noce is convinced that this was the origin of a second line of "modern" thought, which led to a rebirth of classical metaphysics in the French-Italian tradition, culminating in the works of Antonio Rosmini.

Nihilism as a possible outcome of modernity is the subject of the second essay, "Violence and Modern Gnosticism," also based on a lecture (from 1979). The choice of topic was probably motivated by the spasms of Marxist-inspired violence that were convulsing Italy in the late 1970s. It is a deeply autobiographical piece in which Del Noce recalls his experiences as a young man in the 1930s. According to Del Noce, the "eclipse of ethics" associated with revolutionary violence reflects "a gnostic structure of thought" that must be traced back to classical German philosophy. Neo-gnosticism played a decisive role in the process of Western secularization, which was originally a *secularization of gnosticism* inasmuch as "the 'totally other' reality … which for a gnostic lay beyond the empirical world, for a modern revolutionary lies instead in the future."[24] However, when the revolutionary dream fades away, secularized gnosticism takes a libertine form, which is accompanied by a different type of violence: the self is "experienced as a commodity" and "we reach the highest degree of reification; the reduction of people to objects becomes universal." "Making reification universal is clearly the same as denying ethics altogether, and elevating the economic dimension to an absolute … total reification … coincides with extreme greed for things (and for other people reduced to things). Therefore, violence is absolutely dominant."[25]

24 "Violence and Modern Gnosticism," 40.
25 Ibid., 45–6.

Because I did not intend Marxism per se to be the topic of the book, I did not include any of Del Noce's longer essays on Marxism (or Fascism). However, I did include the first part of a 1972 essay on "Revolution, *Risorgimento,* Tradition" in which Del Noce explores the notion of "total revolution." Starting with Rousseau and Marx, total revolution "implies the replacement of religion by politics as the source of man's liberation, since evil is a consequence of society ... and not of an original sin."[26] Del Noce discusses the "conservative" and "reactionary" responses to this "elevation of politics to religion" and finds both inadequate. Neither the conservative critique of utopia nor the reactionary "return to the past" addresses the metaphysical roots of the crisis brought about by the idea of the total revolution. In fact, "it is completely evident that 'value' is the foundation of tradition and not the other way around," and value requires that reason be able to recognize "an uncreated order, the object of non-sensitive intuition."[27] Therefore, the contemporary struggle between a revolutionary left and a conservative right is ultimately sterile because "nations can rise again only by exploring more deeply their tradition, and by criticizing the historical order from the standpoint of an ideal order."[28]

The last two pieces in the first part, "The Latent Metaphysics within Contemporary Politics" and "Secularization and Crisis of Modernity," are lectures (respectively, from 1988 and 1989, shortly before Del Noce's death) in which Del Noce summarized his "transpolitical" interpretation of twentieth-century European history. Del Noce regards Marxism as the prototype of what he calls "revolutionary thought." He uses this formula to express the fact that Marxism was not merely a political doctrine but an all-encompassing world view based on "*the rejection of every form of dependence* and thus the extinction of religion, since God is the archetype of a worldly lord. Hence, the revolution represents a transition not just from one social situation to another, but from one stage of mankind to another ... *capable of transforming human nature itself.*"[29] Revolutionary thought had first surfaced in Jacobinism during the French Revolution, and had been diagnosed as such by Joseph De Maistre. It then reached its fullest form in Marx, and, according to Del Noce, Marxism (in its Leninist reinvention) has been the protagonist of the historical period after the First World War. In fact, he argues that all other major secular political movements of the twentieth century can be understood only in

26 "Revolution, *Risorgimento,* Tradition," 51.
27 Ibid., 57.
28 Ibid., 53.
29 "The Latent Metaphysics within Contemporary Politics," 62.

reference to Marxism, either as a development (Fascism), as an inversion (Nazism), or as its decomposition (the affluent society after the Second World War). Therefore, "the history of our century represents the complete success of Marxism, in the sense that it really changed the world – and not only the part of the world where Communism succeeded … However, this complete success coincides with its complete defeat because the positions, both theoretical and concrete, that have been taken afterwards by rationalistic-secular thought are aspects of Marxism's decomposition."[30]

The second part is chronologically and thematically homogeneous: it is a group of five essays written between 1970 and 1972 on the development of Western culture after the Second World War, leading to the social and cultural transformations of the 1960s. In these pieces Del Noce writes not only as a historian of ideas but also as a cultural critic and a polemicist. In the background, we can glimpse the dramatic developments of those years: the student protests of 1968–69, the Soviet invasion of Czechoslovakia, the first rumblings of the extreme left-wing movements that would resort to terrorism in the next decade, the turmoil in the Roman Catholic Church after the Second Vatican Council. Del Noce also displays a keen awareness of the advance of the sexual revolution, which at that time was colourfully symbolized by shows like *Oh! Calcutta!* and *Hair*. To him, all these phenomena had deep philosophical significance, and already in *L'epoca della secolarizzazione* he had noted that "1968 … has been the richest year in implicit philosophy since 1945."[31] In his view, the cultural changes of the 1960s cannot be explained just in economic or sociological terms because they reflected a philosophical and cultural shift that had started in the 1950s. Del Noce describes it as a return to the mindset of the Enlightenment combined with a rediscovery of Marx, but Marx separated from his messianic-religious aspect in favour of his materialistic-relativistic aspect. Del Noce refers to this new culture in various ways: progressivism, "affluent" or "technological" or "permissive" society, etc. Here, it is the subject of three essays: "Toward a New Totalitarianism," "The Shadow of Tomorrow," and "Death of the Sacred."

I have included only the first half of "Toward a New Totalitarianism" because the second half contains some considerations about international politics that are now outdated. Del Noce identifies three inseparable aspects in the progressivist phenomenon: "scientism, eroticism,

30 "Secularization and Crisis of Modernity," 73–4.

31 Del Noce, *L'epoca della secolarizzazione*, 13.

and theology of secularization."[32] Scientism is "the 'totalitarian' conception of science, in which science is regarded as the 'only' true form of knowledge." It is the ideology of the affluent society and it is intrinsically totalitarian because it cannot rationally prove its "claim that science rules out all other forms of knowledge, and thus certain dimensions of reality which are declared to be either unknowable on non-existent." Although scientism claims to be morally neutral, it actually "includes as essential a form of morality … (the pure increase of vitality [eroticism]) which is 'absolutely contradictory' with traditional ethics."[33] In the religious domain, theological liberalism is an attempt to mimic the "horizontalism" of science, by shifting the focus of Christianity to "worldly realities."

Historically speaking, Del Noce attributes the rise of the ideology of the affluent society to the combination of two factors. First, progressivism was the result of "a crisis of anti-Fascism." This was already a thesis of *L'epoca della secolarizzazione,* and is the topic of "The Shadow of Tomorrow." Because of their bias toward the axiological value of modernity, Western intellectuals misdiagnosed Fascism and Nazism, not as secondary forms of revolutionary thought but as "reactionary phenomena." Therefore, they interpreted the horrors of the war not as a crisis of modernity itself but as a failure of the European tradition. This led them to rediscover the Enlightenment's "break with the past" and to try to reconcile it with a Westernized interpretation of Marxism. Second, secular progressivism constituted an appealing ideological weapon in the confrontation with the Soviet Union. In "The Death of the Sacred" Del Noce discusses at length why in the late 1950s several cultural trends converged on the idea "of a competition [with the USSR] taking place on the ground of a greater secularity."[34]

Del Noce's assessment of the culture of the affluent society is sharply negative: it is a form of "absolute relativism," it rejects every tradition, it reduces the human person to a "social atom," its final outcome is "systematically organized mendacity" and "universal reification." It is important to realize that Del Noce is no *laudator temporis acti.* In fact, he criticizes the new progressive mindset *for being an essentially conservative attitude,* whose goal is to "absorb and neutralize completely the idea of revolution through progressivism," thus reaching "the highest degree of bourgeois mystification."[35] The reason is that "scientism, in this extremely

32 "Toward a New Totalitarianism," 88–9.
33 Ibid., 90.
34 "The Death of the Sacred," 121.
35 Ibid., 109, 129.

expanded form that claims jurisdiction over all human realities, represents the climax of conservatism because it professes a complete relativism about values."[36] Therefore, it leads to a static society, in spite of the constant advancements of technology, ruled by an "aristocracy of industrialists, bankers, scientists, and technicians" whose task is essentially the indefinite preservation of the economic/bureaucratic *status quo ante.*

The last two essays of the second part, "The Roots of the Crisis" and "The Ascendance of Eroticism," focus on the *permissive* aspect of the "technological civilization." Consistently with his general analysis, Del Noce makes the case that the sexual revolution was not primarily a change in *moral* outlook, because the question of eroticism is first of all *metaphysical.* The idea of indissoluble monogamous marriage "was linked to the idea of *tradition,* which in turn presupposes (since *tradere* means to hand down) the idea of an objective order of unchangeable and permanent truths (the Platonic True in itself and Good in itself)."[37] Therefore, in a scientistic society "*the abolition of every meta-empirical order of truth requires that the family be dissolved.* No *merely sociological* consideration can justify keeping it."[38] Del Noce traces back the history of the permissive mindset to authors who wrote outside the academic establishment, in particular the works of Wilhelm Reich in the 1930s and the Surrealist literature immediately after the Second World War. The reason for his interest in Reich is precisely that, unlike most propagandists of the sexual revolution, he "is a thinker who understands exactly all the implications of the advancement of sexual freedom, and defines precisely all the negations that such freedom implies in the metaphysical-religious domain."[39]

The third part of the volume consists almost entirely of "Authority versus Power," a long essay from 1975 (almost a short monographic book) in which all the threads of Del Noce's reflection in the 1960s and '70s come to an organic synthesis and acquire new philosophical depth. After identifying the crisis of the idea of authority as the defining characteristic of the contemporary Western world, he traces its development across twentieth-century philosophy and culture. Whereas in the classic and humanistic tradition authority was associated with liberation from the power of sub-human instincts and arbitrary social forces, today authority is associated with repression. As a result, Western culture confuses authority and power, with disastrous consequences. On the contrary, according to Del Noce, freedom can be defended only by rediscovering the genuine meaning of authority, which is tightly linked to what he calls

36 "The Shadow of Tomorrow," 107.
37 "The Ascendance of Eroticism," 161.
38 Ibid.
39 Ibid., 165.

the "metaphysics of the primacy of being." The starting point of such metaphysics was the discovery by Greek philosophy of the idea of evidence. Evidence is the foundation and the paradigm of authority because it asks of the mind a more radical submission than could be obtained by force, but in this submission the mind finds its ultimate liberation. Vice versa, "the rejection of authority, understood in its metaphysical-religious foundation, leads instead to the fullness of 'power.' In other words, the opposition authority vs freedom … must be replaced by the opposition authority vs power, where the former has a liberating character and the latter an oppressive one. In fact, it is hard to deny … that the *real* endpoint … of the process of revolutionary liberation leads to the complete dependence of man on society."[40] In order to highlight Del Noce's diagnosis of the political aspect of the crisis of authority, I have also included in the third part the essay "A 'New' Perspective on Right and Left," written in 1970 as an introduction to the Italian translation of a debate between Jean-Marie Domenach and Thomas Molnar, which had appeared the year before in the French journal *Esprit*. Del Noce's contends that after the 1960s the Left was doomed to surrender to a conception of politics as "management technique at the service of the strongest," precisely because it accepted an incorrect metaphysical understanding of the relationship between freedom and Being.

Finally, since Del Noce is not well known to English-speaking readers, I thought it would be useful to include in an appendix a 1983 interview in which the philosopher speaks about his life and work in the context of twentieth-century history. The appendix also contains two additional essays ("Notes on Secularization and Religious Thought" and "Eric Voegelin and the Critique of the Idea of Modernity") that I had originally planned to include in the first part of the book. During the editorial process, I realized that these essays slowed down the "flow" of the volume, by being rather narrowly focused and also somewhat repetitious. Therefore, I decided to remove them from the main body of the book but to make them available in the appendix to readers who may be specifically interested in Del Noce's take on secularization theology or on the thought of Eric Voegelin.

• • •

This work was made possible by a Fellowship Research Grant from the Earhart Foundation. I would like to thank Earhart's Director of Program, Mr Montgomery Brown for his support. Support for this project also was

40 "Authority versus Power," 245.

provided by a PSC-CUNY Award, jointly funded by the Professional Staff Congress and the City University of New York, and by SEPS (Segretariato Europeo per le Pubblicazioni Scientifiche).

Next, I would like to thank all the scholars (and friends) who have encouraged and advised me on this project. In alphabetical order, I will recall Professors Massimo Borghesi, David Forte, Michael Hanby, Tobias Hoffmann, Fr Antonio Lopez, Christopher Lutz, Giovanni Maddalena, John McCarthy, Peter Simpson, David C. Schindler, and David L. Schindler. I would also like to thank Professor Andrea Caspani, who first introduced me to the works of Del Noce (and to philosophy in general) during my high-school years. Thanks to Professor Enzo Randone, president of the Fondazione Augusto Del Noce, and Ms Flavia Zuccon, the Fondazione's secretary, for their generous help. Thanks also to Professor Amanda Murphy and Ms Marina Lancellotti for their assistance in locating bibliographical references in Italy.

Last but not least, I thank my family for their love and support, including my parents, my children, and, in particular, my wife Sara, who patiently put up with many "nights with Del Noce."

PART ONE
Modernity, Revolution, Secularization

1

The Idea of Modernity

PART ONE

I will try to summarize as briefly as possible the questions posed by the idea of modernity.

1 Modern comes from *hodiernus*: first of all, the word has a chronological meaning.

2 However, when it is joined to the word "philosophy" or is turned into a substantive by introducing the idea of "modernity," it generally takes an *axiological* meaning. It indicates a "point of no return," that "today it is no longer possible."

3 This raises various questions. (a) What "is no longer possible today?" (b) By what process did the transition from the chronological to the axiological meaning take place? (c) The idea of modernity belongs in the context of a certain historical periodization. What is the role of such periodization in shaping theoretical choices? (d) Does the "critical problem" of today's philosophy – at least regarding its starting point – boil down to casting "doubt" on the usual interpretation of the "idea of modernity?"

4 The answer to (a) is simple: what is excluded is the "supernatural," religious transcendence. Why? I am inclined to define the "modernist" sense of modern philosophy as follows: "A philosophy is modern

This two-part essay was originally published as "L'idea di modernità" in the book of proceedings of the 36th Symposium of the Gallarate Center for Philosophical Studies, *Modernità: Storia e valore di un'idea* [Modernity: History and value of an idea] (Brescia: Morcelliana, 1982), 26–43. Part 1 was Del Noce's introductory remarks to the symposium, Part 2 the final lecture.

whenever it claims not to be a mere actualization of some 'virtuality' of ancient thought, or of the medieval unity of ancient and Christian thought. And when, therefore, in order to place itself within history it must affirm that we have entered a period of philosophical research marked by a sharp break with respect to the Greek and medieval periods, which are thought to have ended." That means: there was a cosmological period which corresponded to ancient philosophy, and Christian philosophy must be interpreted in opposition to it as essentially anthropological. The Middle Ages were characterized by a quest, in vain, to harmonize the Greek and Christian philosophical traditions. In order to satisfy this quest while accepting the categories of ancient thought, the Christian anthropological theme must lead to the idea of the supernatural (spirituality is fully realized only in the beyond, and the present world has meaning only in reference to a world "beyond" which transcends it). Then, the break from which "modernity" begins is the rejection of this compromise.

5 Regarding (b), consider the huge philosophical implications of the standard periodization of the history of philosophy. As Cotta[1] correctly pointed out, relocating the great "breaking point" to the beginning of modern thought, understood as a transition from childhood to maturity, from myth to criticism, implies that "the religious event of the Incarnation stops being regarded as the decisive turning point of historical existence."[2] We often hear that periodization schemes are of a "conventional" and "pedagogical" nature. *It is not true.*

6 The elimination of the supernatural can take various forms. Here I will just mention Hegelianism, which regards modern philosophy as "Christian philosophy," as Christianity expressing itself in philosophical form. It is followed by the transition "from Hegel to Nietzsche," to post- or anti-Christianity, in which atheism (understood in the strong sense that the very question of God disappears) replaces the theory of immanent divinity (in Italy this was the transition from the culture of Croce and Gentile to the secularism that followed it). The next stage highlights the irreversibility of this process and interprets it as the "crisis of the idea of modernity."

1 [TN] Sergio Cotta (1920–2007), Italian philosopher and legal scholar.

2 [TN] Sergio Cotta, "L'idea di modernità" [The idea of modernity], *Studi Cattolici* 235 (1980): 525.

7 The above definition of "modern philosophy" implies a double break with respect to classical and medieval thought. In light of this break we understand the "anti-modern" position, which does not criticize the idea of "modernity" but inverts its axiological meaning, interpreting the development of modernity as a process not toward fullness but toward nihilism. This position can take the form of Catholic medievalism (in which the process of disintegration began with medieval nominalism) or affirm the idea that the error of Western thought already started in Greek antiquity with Plato, and affects the Jewish-Christian tradition. Because these positions lack a critique of the "modernist" interpretation of the development of history, they end up being affected by the same nihilism which they correctly bring into focus.

8 Regarding (c) we must observe that today philosophers practise their trade from within this periodization scheme, which is taken as a fact. For rationalists, certainty about an irreversible historical process toward radical immanentism has replaced what for medieval thinkers was faith in revelation. Notice that for rationalists this is the only reliable certainty after historicism and the critique of evidences.

9 But is this scheme really so reliable? The history of philosophical historiography highlights the stages of development of the idea of modernity (Bayle, D'Alembert, Lessing, and so on). Above all, we must observe that the conception of historical periodization in which the idea of modernity is essential includes a few obligatory steps: (a) the Cartesian beginning of modern philosophy; (b) the idea that "nothing has been lost in the history of thought," formulated by Hegel and by various forms of Hegelianism (all the way to Gentile). What does such preservation mean? It means that the transition from divine transcendence to divine immanence does not deny the idea of God but purifies it, and is verified by this preservation.

Now, I will try to show that precisely the consideration of atheism as the ultimate outcome of rationalism, which goes hand in hand with the consideration of its optional and postulatory nature (it cannot be proved), leads us to drop the idea of a unitary process. It leads us, instead, to recognize two irreducible lines of development within the philosophy of the centuries of the so-called modern age. One goes from Descartes to Nietzsche, the other from Descartes to Rosmini, and this second line is destined to arrive at traditional metaphysical thought and refine it. Therefore, from the standpoint of the general periodization of the history of philosophy we must abandon the notion that the idea of modernity possesses an axiological character. Instead, it must be regarded as the period in which the phenomenon of atheism manifested itself and burned itself out.

PART TWO

10 I will offer just a few comments about the apparent paradox contained in the final words of the outline I proposed. I said that the consideration of atheism as the final outcome of rationalism, when rationalism is understood as negation of the possibility of the supernatural, leads to the denial of the *axiological* value attributed to the idea of modernity. From the usual perspective, modernity is regarded as the proof, provided by history, of the assertion that thought and civilization develop irreversibly from transcendence to immanence.

11 This makes clear what general conclusion I think must be reached starting from the analysis of the idea of modernity. The verdict will be that after the collapse of what I will show is the last argument that sustains his certainty, namely the ability to understand and explain history, an immanentist thinker is forced to confess that his position cannot be supported by any proof. Thus, the rationalist thinker faces Pascal's wager. Precisely when he pushes his rationalism to the limit he finds himself unable to escape the process of thought which in Pascal begins from the *pari*, the thesis that plays in the economy of Pascal's philosophy the same role that doubt plays in Descartes's thought. Of course, he may well reaffirm his position, but he will have to admit that it is a choice, that he is not obeying an irrefutable rational argument. More generally, I would say the following: at this time in the history of philosophy, the central question to which the critique of the idea of modernity leads us is a deeper understanding of Pascal's wager.

12 Please allow me to try to clarify my statements by citing myself. In my 1964 book *The Problem of Atheism*,[3] which was subtitled *The Concept of Atheism and the History of Philosophy as a Problem*, I discussed the analogy between the *modus operandi* of a medieval Christian thinker and the one of a contemporary secular thinker. The former started from sacred history, which he considered unquestionable. The latter starts from profane history and from the assertion that since the time when the new science was born – with humanism and the Renaissance as precursors – a world has come into being which rises to the dignity of a philosophical event

3 [TN] Augusto Del Noce, *Il problema dell'ateismo* [The problem of atheism] (Bologna: Il Mulino, 1964).

because it can find its justification and its self-awareness only in philosophies that break radically away from the supernatural, even if they understand the novelty of Christianity with respect to ancient thought. I added that whereas history of philosophy was born in its first great model as the historical verification of Hegelian philosophy, today, after historicism and the positivist critique of evidences, i.e., after these philosophical trends have led, consistently, to rejection of meta-historical truths, its task has become the opposite. Today, for an immanentist thinker, the criterion of historical validity of a philosophy reduces to its ability to surpass and integrate previous philosophical positions by explaining why they were born. In this sense, today's secularist philosopher not only starts, but is forced to start, from the proposition that "today it is no longer possible." This assertion is obligatory if meta-historical truths are excluded and if this exclusion is viewed as the breaking point between the present and the past of philosophy. For this reason, at that time I had already concluded that the critical problem of contemporary philosophy, at least concerning its starting point, boils down to casting doubt on the standard interpretation of the idea of modernity; or that history of philosophy as a problem must be today's formulation of the critical doubt. In other words, the first theoretical step of today's philosophy must consist in calling into question the common view of the history of philosophy, the one that says that this history, at least after Descartes, can be understood only as a process toward radical immanence. If one looks carefully, what is called into question is not only the modernist view of the history of philosophy – the view that envisions a process toward complete liberation from the mythical mentality – but also the position that is usually called anti-modernistic, which views the developments of the centuries of the modern age as a process toward catastrophe. On this matter, it is easy to point out that these two interpretations disagree only about the judgment of value, and the latter is the mirror image of the former, as Sergio Cotta nicely stated in a recent essay.[4] One should add that the anti-modern line cannot be identified without qualifications with traditionalist Catholic historiography. The Catholic philosophy of history of the nineteenth century did often regard the history of modern philosophy as a unitary process toward catastrophe, which started from medieval nominalism and continued in the three reformers – Luther, Descartes, and Rousseau – as the three originators of pantheism, atheism, and nihilism. Today, however, the anti-modern position has taken a different meaning and has become the history of a

4 [TN] Cotta, "L'idea di modernità," 524.

process of forgetfulness of being, which began with Plato and involves Christianity itself. The current anti-modern stance draws its inspiration from Nietzsche, not as the theorizer of the superman but rather as the thinker who unveiled the will to power as the soul of Western philosophy. As we shall see, the view I propose today intends to go beyond both the modern and the anti-modern position. In some way modern and anti-modern are actually twins, so that sometimes it is hard to distinguish the extreme expressions of modernity from anti-modernity. This is the case of Heidegger.

13 The philosophy of history of the nineteenth century left us as its inheritance the idea of the anthropological turning point,[5] i.e., the interpretation of the historical development of philosophy as oriented toward the radical negation of supra-historical truths or, equivalently, the idea that the general process of history can be understood only through categories developed by immanentist philosophies. According to this form of thought, acknowledging such a state of affairs means being in step with history. Secularist philosophy has shrunk and consumed itself to the point that the apparent irreversibility of such a turning point has become a starting point: today historical periodization has become decisive for theoretical thought itself. Certainly, what I will loosely call a modernist, somebody who thinks that "today it is no longer possible," does not intend to deny the factual reality that other scholars still embrace ideas from the past. Likewise, he does not intend to deny the continued existence of a great historical institution, the Catholic Church. In his view, however, the Church exhausted her civilizing task in the Middle Ages, and this is why those who have fallen behind the progress of history generally look at her, and appeal to her and to the philosophies that she uses in her own defence. But the proof of their present inadequacy lies, supposedly, in the fact that to modernity they can only oppose fruitless negations, or propose eclectic combinations with forms of thought that are not yet perfectly immanentist. Supposedly, the philosophies that present themselves, in the name of values, as modern forms of spiritualism are just instances of eclecticism. In both cases, these thinkers are said to be divided between life, which must conform to the spirit of the new age regardless of their efforts and delusions, and an outdated philosophy. Let this brief comment suffice; this view is too well known to deserve further discussion.

5 [TN] This idea is also discussed by Cotta in "L'idea di modernità," 528.

14 However, even if it may appear that today the secularist spirit has reached its broadest diffusion – to the point that we might think that a new era has begun – and even if it is a fact that many theologians have reformed their doctrines to conform to what is often called the "secular city," from the philosophical standpoint it is reasonable to ask whether we are not witnessing a reversal, so that the idea of modernity is showing its dogmatic side, and critical thinking can only be exercised against such rationalist dogmatism. Thus, we may ask whether today dogmatism does not coincide with rationalist thought. This seems to me the question that philosophical reflection now poses. In fact, this question corresponds to what I said earlier about Pascal's wager rising again.

15 Indeed, let us observe that in our century the rationalist perspective has been formulated in two very different ways. The first position, which was common when I was young, understood the process toward immanence and the essence of secularism in terms of the "death of the transcendent God," of the purification of the idea of God in divine immanence. At the time of Croce and Gentile people reasoned as follows: in the history of philosophy there was a cosmological period which corresponded to ancient thought. Christian thought must be interpreted in opposition to it as essentially anthropological. The Middle Ages were characterized by a quest, in vain, to harmonize the Greek and Christian lines of thought. In order to satisfy this quest while accepting the categories of ancient thought, the Christian anthropological theme must lead to the idea of the supernatural (spirituality is fully realized only in the beyond, and the present world has meaning only in reference to a world "beyond," which transcends it). Modernity marks a major break by fully developing the anthropological theme, so that transcendence pictured as "beyond" is replaced by transcendence within the world. Christianity continues to exist, no longer as a religion but as a philosophy. Here in Italy, Gentile never tired of repeating that the whole history of modern philosophy is a slow, gradual process toward critical awareness of this new position that the human spirit reached with Christianity, precisely as a rational development of the new truth. In fact, what else could be the meaning of the idea of the unity of philosophy and history of philosophy, on which Gentile insisted so much? Those times are far gone, you will say. But the perspective about the idea of modernity remains the same.

16 The second form of rationalism, which became prevalent after the Second World War and has been spreading ever since, speaks of the "death of God." It shifts from divine immanence to radical atheism. It

believes that the point of the matter is not to "sublate" religion into philosophy but to realize that the monotheistic God is vanishing without a trace, like the ancient divinities.[6] I believe that the first form is defenceless in front of the second. This is not the place to prove this proposition; but I think that no proof is necessary because I am sure that nobody in the audience thinks that atheism can be beaten through a restoration of the divine in terms of divine immanence; and also that nobody here doubts that by now Croce and Gentile belong irreversibly to history. Instead, now is the time to advance my argument: a critical discussion of this transition to radical atheism is also the beginning of the self-refutation of immanentism, the proof that immanentism does not rely on any evidence. This is the case because introducing atheism into the history of philosophy leads to a new and different history of philosophy, in which the notion of a unitary process of thought (in its critically rigorous developments) from Descartes to us, directed toward radical immanence, disappears. This thesis, considered in its two reciprocal and necessary aspects, is certainly unfamiliar and I had better discuss it in some detail.

17 The philosophy of divine immanence can also be called "conservative historicism." Perhaps the adjective "conservative" is superfluous because historicism is always by nature conservative. We may wonder if it negates itself as a philosophy when it stops being conservative, and if then philosophy does not become ideology, but this is a separate question. Staying with the question at hand, I wish to say that the philosophy of "immanent divinity" stays faithful to the final words of Hegel's history of philosophy: "To this point the World-spirit has come, and each stage has its own form in the true system of Philosophy; nothing is lost, all principles are preserved"[7] – except in one point: the new historicism denies that Hegel's philosophy is definitive and that it steps out of history to join the absolute. This ability to preserve the past is also supposed to be the

6 [TN] Del Noce here uses the Italian verb *inverare*, which is not easily translated into English. It means "to make true" in the sense of "preserving the truthful aspect of a theory while developing it into a higher form" and therefore is more or less analogous to Hegel's famous term *aufheben* (noun: *aufhebung*), which is usually translated in English as "to sublate" (noun: *sublation*). Elsewhere, Del Noce uses *inverare* (and corresponding noun *inveramento*) mostly to describe the contemporary attempts to "bring out the truth of Marxism." For lack of better options, throughout this book I will use *sublate/sublation* for *inverare/inveramento*, but readers should not interpret these words in an overly technical Hegelian sense.

7 [TN] Georg F.W. Hegel, *Lectures on the History of Philosophy*, trans. Elizabeth S. Haldane and Frances H. Simson (London: Kegan Paul, Trench, Trübner & Co., 1896), 546.

criterion of its *historical* truth. Now, I want to point out something that has been rarely or, to the best of my knowledge, never explicitly taken into consideration. In order to "preserve" or to present itself as true – which is the same thing, as we saw – this philosophical position must erase from the history of philosophy all atheistic episodes. It must erase them in the sense of regarding them as inchoate attempts to reclaim the value of worldly realities, but in a crudely materialistic form because they are directed against a God depicted in terms of spatial exteriority. Supposedly, atheism as materialism remains within the same naturalism that leads to the notion of God as a transcendent being. The advocates of God's transcendence and his materialistic deniers share in the same naturalism, so that both positions are surpassed by a philosophy which does not negate the divine but only its transcendence. The elders among us, who grew up at the time of Idealistic culture, know how little room was given to Marx or Nietzsche in the teaching of history of philosophy, precisely for this reason. But this did not happen only in Italy. One has only to think of the histories of philosophy by Brunschvicg[8] and by Bréhier[9] in order to realize that something very similar happened in France. And more examples could be given.

18 Now, inserting atheism into the history of philosophy leads to an extremely important observation which forces us to rethink the history of philosophy, with theoretical consequences which I will discuss. The observation is the following: the atheistic phenomenon takes place at the *final* stage, instead of the inchoative stage, of each of the three fundamental modern trends which intend to surpass religion into philosophy and thus deny the supernatural. We find it at the final stage of the philosophy of the Renaissance with libertine thought, of course considered in its higher form as *libertinage érudit*. We also find it at the end of the Enlightenment, whose distinctive characteristic was that it brought together three lines of thought that in the first half of the eighteenth century seemed to be incompatible: the libertine critique of tradition; the trends in religion and natural law that – in light of this critique – switched from a conciliatory to a revolutionary attitude; and the spirit of the new science separated from metaphysics. When this synthesis broke down, which is how the Enlightenment came to an end, libertinism continued as decadentism, the revolutionary spirit as Marxism, and the

8 [TN] Léon Brunschvicg, *Le progrès de la conscience dans la philosophie occidentale* [The progress of conscience in Western philosophy] (Paris: Alcan, 1927).

9 [TN] Émile Bréhier, *The History of Philosophy*, trans. Joseph Thomas (Chicago: University of Chicago Press, 1963).

scientistic spirit as positivism – the triad that defines today's atheism. After libertinism and the Enlightenment, let us consider the final stage of classical German philosophy, during the period from Hegel to Nietzsche. Here the trends that had been born from the Enlightenment became entangled in various ways, producing the views that are common today. They can be summarized – using formulas proposed by Max Scheler over half a century ago – as the replacement of the idea of *homo sapiens*, who is characterized by his participation in the Logos, by the idea of *homo faber*.[10] This replacement leads to the negation of the idea that there is a human nature and to the affirmation that praxis is the measure of truth – two consequences which in fact could already be found in Feuerbach and Marx. This then leads to the supremacy of power, in all its manifestations. But this is not the occasion to linger on this point, namely on the various forms taken in contemporary thought by the negation of the idea that there is a human nature.

19 Now, let us ask ourselves what is the repercussion of this insertion of atheism into the history of philosophy in a new form, precisely in connection with the question of the idea of modernity, which may seem to have little to do with it. Even if it replaces preservation by negation, atheism still intends to keep the idea that modern philosophy goes through a unitary process toward immanentism. Negation is viewed as liberation from all myths, as reduction of all philosophical positions to the historical circumstances that produced them, or to the psychological conditions of those who affirmed them. In short, atheism is supposed to result from demythologization, and to leave behind the compromise represented by the work of the philosophers of divine immanence.

But at this point we can pose the question whether this new form in which atheism is inserted in the history of philosophy may not be precisely what undermines the usual view that modern philosophy is a unitary process, by showing that it includes two irreconcilable lines of development, one from Descartes to Nietzsche and another that we can call, at least approximately, from Descartes to Rosmini, which moves toward recovering and refining traditional metaphysical and religious thought. It is also legitimate to ask if the work of destruction carried out by the first line sheds any light on the validity of the second.

20 Therefore, let us focus on the necessary stages in the standard view of modern philosophy and let us discuss how they have to be changed as a

10 [TN] See the essay "Man in History" in Max Scheler, *Philosophical Perspectives*, trans. Oscar A. Haac (Boston: Beacon Press, 1958), 65–93.

result of the new assessment of the place of atheism. According to the usual perspective, modern philosophy began when the idea of *renovatio* – which had already run through the fifteenth and sixteenth centuries, thus marking the end of the Middle Ages, and had taken two divergent forms, one as a rebirth of classical antiquity in the Renaissance and the other as a return to original Christianity in the Protestant reformation – became unlinked from the idea of *going back.* Descartes, better than any other philosopher of the eighteenth century, lent himself to become the symbol of this break with the past. He lent himself to be transfigured into the symbol of the *hero* (to use Hegel's expression) of the *decision* to trust reason, and only reason, by making the sharp break of methodical doubt. For this reason the "Cartesian novelty" used to be identified with one aspect of his thought, the rationalistic side. This chapter was then followed by another that listed Descartes's betrayals against such novelty, which were due to his will to reconcile with the past. The same will to reconcile was then attributed to the majority of subsequent philosophers (Vico, Leibniz, Kant, and so on) following a well-known template, up to the time of modernity's *temporis fructus masculus,* which was marked by the awareness that we can no longer speak of meta-historical truths, as I mentioned before.

21 As I have said, the identification of the beginning of modern philosophy with Descartes seems to be of a symbolic nature. Hence, we are tempted to abandon it, regarding it as a purely rhetorical device, and to replace it with some other beginning, in the area of the new science or in the bourgeois spirit. But actually the image of the Cartesian beginning is unavoidable and can be separated from its rhetorical transfiguration. Its true meaning can be discovered in the work of the historian who contributed more than anybody else to demolishing the myth of Descartes's rationalism – Jean Laporte. Let us listen to him: "All the various themes that will be developed, respectively, … by post-Cartesian philosophies, both those that are usually called rationalist and those that are called irrationalist, can be already found in Descartes."[11] Indeed, why is Descartes's position unique – without compare? Because every philosophy that claims to be modern in the axiological sense must necessarily refer to Descartes as its *beginner* in order to define its own historical context and be aware of its situation, and to connect intentionally to the past. As a result, such philosophies are forced to distinguish between two aspects of his thought, of which supposedly only one is true. This applies

11 Jean Laporte, *Le rationalisme de Descartes* [The rationalism of Descartes] (Paris: Presses Universitaires de France, 1945), 475–6.

to philosophies that are most opposed to each other, since Cartesian thought carries the seeds of the whole development of French spiritualism, from Malebranche to the *Philosophie de l'Esprit*,[12] and at the same time of materialism and revolutionary thought. The Cartesian beginning cannot be replaced by the rise of the new science because the Descartes that continued was not Descartes the scientist but Descartes the philosopher, who was correctly described by Lenoble[13] as an "accident" in the history of the new science. Therefore, the interpretation of the Cartesian beginning is crucial in the critique of the standard view of modern philosophy. Here, what matters most is to consider how the interpretation of Cartesian philosophy is affected by the place we assign to atheism in the history of philosophy, in this case the atheism of the libertines.

22 Descartes breaks away from both the scholastics and the libertines, and I apologize for recalling such a trivial truth. But who is his main adversary? Who can explain the inner workings of his philosophy? Now, since inserting atheism into the history of philosophy requires that we give libertine thought its proper place – recognizing it as a philosophical phenomenon and not just a transient social phenomenon – we realize that Cartesian doubt is the exact opposite of libertine doubt, which is a combination of atheism and skepticism. Libertine doubt is a type of doubt that is *produced*, that expresses within me either natural necessity or history understood also in terms of natural necessity. From the standpoint of history, it is the expression of both an enlargement of the historical-geographical horizon and a political attitude informed by the ideas of Machiavelli. Thus, it expresses a historical crisis. It is the repercussion inside consciences of an empirical reality which, by the mere fact of being real, seems to refute what tradition had taught and to bring back, in order to be understood, both Machiavelli and Paduan naturalism – which, when it is extended to the world, tends to become metaphysical skepticism and critical rationalism in the destructive sense. Now, if we look at the *Meditations*[14] we observe that Cartesian doubt is the exact opposite of libertine doubt. According to Descartes, the first certainty is

12 [TN] A twentieth-century French philosophical school of a metaphysical, spiritualist orientation. Two of its best-known exponents were Louis Lavelle (1883–1951) and René Le Senne (1882–1954).

13 [TN] Fr Robert Lenoble (1902–59), French historian of science. His remark that "Descartes est, en réalité, un accident métaphysique dans l'histoire du Mécanisme" is found in *Mersenne, ou la naissance du mécanisme* [Mersenne, or the birth of mechanicism] (Paris: Vrin, 1971), 614.

14 [TN] Descartes, *Meditations on First Philosophy*, ed. and trans. John Cottingham (Cambridge: Cambridge University Press, 1996).

that there is an *I* who *freely* doubts natural reality (i.e., deprives it of reality). Inasmuch as the I doubts freely, it is a personal and concrete subject, not a generic intellect. Inasmuch as the I is certain of its own existence, whereas natural reality is doubtful, it exists by itself, i.e., it is a substance (*res cogitans*). This "deprivation of reality" was the negation of the by-itself-ness of natural reality. In the final analysis, the affirmation that natural reality is not Being was possible because the *res cogitans* is *res cogitans Deum.*

23 It seems to me that there can be no doubt that libertine thought was the main adversary against which Descartes's essential philosophical theses took shape, even though this does not mean that we should embrace a religious interpretation of Descartes. Indeed, I devoted the second part of my book on Descartes to a study of the religious ambiguity of his thought.[15] The ambiguity is due to the fact that his critique of libertine thought is simply a photographic negative. He grants too much to his adversary by implicitly accepting that any philosophy that starts from the sensible world, either natural or historical, must necessarily conclude to that form of thought. The result is a separatism that posits that man exists apart from things and in the presence of ideas that are just his ideas. In other words, in Descartes we have at the same time the experience of freedom, which is his religious theme, and a form of separatism which coincides, if we look carefully, with the very principle of immanence that later will be developed to such a large extent in modern philosophy. I have discussed this Cartesian ambiguity, in the sense of a very peculiar combination of a religious aspect and a secular aspect, in order to show that in the initial Cartesian stage we can already discern the coexistence of the two lines of thought that I mentioned. Thus, the nature of his thought refutes the idea that modern philosophy is a unitary process toward immanentism.

24 However, in the last paragraph of my initial summary I stated that besides the line from Descartes to Nietzsche there is one from Descartes to Rosmini, which is destined to reach and to refine traditional metaphysical thought. To refine it, because atheism is the dialogical adversary that makes possible the process of purification of religious thought and enables it to avoid the danger of desiccating into formulas. A very brief discussion of this line is appropriate. The insertion of libertine thought into the history of philosophy, as the first form of atheism, not only

15 [TN] Augusto Del Noce, *Riforma cattolica e filosofia moderna*, vol. 1, Cartesio [Catholic reformation and modern philosophy, vol. 1, Descartes] (Bologna: Il Mulino, 1965).

accounts for Descartes's reflection but explains also the development of thought from Descartes to Vico, revealing a subtle continuity that goes deeper than the apparent opposition. And if Descartes is the pivotal axis, so to speak, of French philosophy, Vico plays the same role for Italian philosophy.

Well, what does Vico say in the *Conchiusione* [conclusion] of the *Scienza Nuova*?[16] He says that his work refutes the possibility of a "republic of atheists" as Bayle had described it.[17] And this is not an isolated statement because, in his work, he keeps repeating that the adversaries he is attacking are Machiavelli, Hobbes, Spinoza, Bayle, who are precisely the thinkers in whom we find harbingers, traces, or influences of the libertine world view. Let us focus on Bayle. What does his thought represent if not the decomposition of Cartesianism, the moment in which it sheds metaphysics and theology, as they had been consistently formulated by Malebranche? And even though in Bayle's case we cannot speak of libertinism – since his philosophy is the meeting point of various trends that up to that time had moved in opposite directions: Protestantism, Cartesianism, jusnaturalism,[18] libertinism – it is also certainly true that in him the decomposition of Cartesianism coincides with the resurfacing of the libertine background, in the sense that his thought seems to provide the proof that religious Cartesianism had failed to adequately address the challenge of libertine skepticism. To summarize in a formula, I think we can say that Bayle's extension of the methodical doubt to history coincides with the abandonment of doubt in the form it had taken in the *Meditations*.

But, how could this happen – and please forgive me for being too brief – if not because of the concession to the libertine way of thinking that Cartesianism had granted libertinism, albeit from a position of opposition? It did so by accepting the idea that a form of thought that starts from history must necessarily lead to skepticism (this is the meaning of what is often called Descartes's anti-historicism), to a position of split interiority in which truth can be reached only by casting doubt on natural

16 [TN] Giambattista Vico, *The New Science of Giambattista Vico*, trans. Thomas G. Bergin and Max H. Fisch (Ithaca: Cornell University Press, 1984), 419ff.

17 [TN] See Pierre Bayle, *Various Thoughts on the Occasion of a Comet*, trans. Robert C. Bartlett (Albany: SUNY Press, 2000).

18 [TN] In Italian, "giusnaturalismo" refers specifically to the effort by various early modern thinkers to reformulate the notion of natural law on purely secular, non-theological foundations, often under the inspiration of Cartesian rationalism. The best known representatives of this trend were Alberico Gentili, Johannes Althusius, and, above all, Hugo Grotius. Thomas Hobbes and John Locke are also often viewed as part of the jusnaturalist tradition.

and historical reality. Now, I think we can understand Vico as a European thinker, and also interpret his philosophy in a way that respects the letter of what he wrote, only on the condition that we view it as the correction that religious Cartesianism, and especially Malebranche's Cartesianism, needed in order to prevail over the libertine phenomenon.

25 But I also think that we could find another critique of the axiological meaning of the idea of modernity if we shifted our reflection to Kant, to his view that the ideas of God and the soul are the indispensable foundations of moral life, to the space he leaves for transcendence, and, even more generally, to his philosophy of the limitations of man, which goes against the radical solutions that characterize, in various forms, absolute immanentism. To Kant as a critic of scientism, who criticizes metaphysics in order to safeguard the truth it contains about God, freedom, and the soul.

26 The conclusion of our discussion so far is that atheism cannot defend the idea of the axiological character of modernity and push it to its farthest conclusions (as it does) except by relying covertly and without justification on the vision of history that accompanies the philosophy of divine immanence. On the other hand, it intends to be, and indeed is, the theoretical endpoint and also the criticism of that very philosophy. Thus, we return to what I said at the beginning: the discussion of the idea of modernity brings us back, after the disintegration of the idea of immanent divinity, to the wager between affirming the transcendent God and embracing atheism, where atheism in the absence of proof reduces, as has been often said, to an act of faith in reverse. *Therefore, the axiological concept of modernity understood as "it is no longer possible" must be replaced by a problematic concept: the centuries of the modern age are those in which the phenomenon of atheism manifested itself.*

27 However, it might seem that those who associate atheism and the idea of modernity have one last card to play. Historicism was conservative, whereas atheism is revolutionary. For this reason, it seems that precisely what was said about the existence of two irreducible lines within modern philosophy can be turned to its advantage. What I mean is that one could argue that precisely the fact that there were two lines, neither of which was judged capable of prevailing over the other, constitutes the process of consumption of metaphysical and theologizing philosophy. Supposedly, this process of consumption prepares the advent of atheism, for which the historical circumstances are now ripe. With respect to the philosophies of the past, atheistic modernity positions itself

as a break and not as a continuation. Supposedly, what is modern is such not by continuity but by a radical break with the past, whose exhaustion should be emphasized. This is the idea of atheism as a result, which is well known because it was professed by theoretical Marxism. But I will not discuss this aspect at any length now because the revolution that was supposed to produce this result turned into the most extraordinary process of heterogenesis of ends[19] that ever took place in history. It promised the transition from the reign of necessity to the reign of freedom, and it created, with totalitarianism, the most oppressive regime possible. It promised to abolish social classes, and it created a new class. It promised freedom from imperialism, and it brought about a new type of imperialism, such that the leading country can support itself only by fostering instability in other parts of the world.[20]

19 [TN] Sometimes translated into English as "heterogony of ends." See the references in the *Wikipedia* entry *Heterogony of Ends*, retrieved on 23 September 2012 from http://en.wikipedia.org/wiki/Heterogony_of_ends.

20 [TN] Del Noce was speaking in 1981, at a time when the Soviet Union had recently invaded Afghanistan and was actively trying to expand its diplomatic and political influence in the Middle East and in Africa.

2

Violence and Modern Gnosticism

1 THE PHILOSOPHICAL PROBLEM OF VIOLENCE

1 In his 1970 book *L'oscuramento dell'intelligenza,* Michele Federico Sciacca described our age as the time when Nietzsche and Rosmini are relevant in a complementary fashion.[1] He explained that the thought of the first "great and merciless denouncer of the West's 'death by nihilism'"[2] manifests the inner truth of the side of modern philosophy that calls itself post-Christian; in his works this philosophy reveals its aspect of "loss of being" and thus, precisely, of "nihilism." Conversely, Rosmini is the philosopher of the "recovery of being." In him the metaphysics of being truly shines, having been purified – precisely because of the new adversaries it had to face – of the aspects that had made possible the subjectivist error.

The thesis that Nietzsche introduces us to Rosmini may sound peculiar. Well, in my judgment it will no longer seem paradoxical *precisely if we raise the question of contemporary violence.* In this respect, a remark by

The two parts of this essay were originally published separately in the book of proceedings of the 34th Symposium of the Gallarate Center for Philosophical Studies, *Violenza: Una ricerca per comprendere* [Violence: An investigation to understand] (Brescia: Morcelliana, 1980). Part 1 was Del Noce's introductory presentation to the symposium, Part 2 his conclusions.

1 [TN] Michele Federico Sciacca, *L'oscuramento dell'intelligenza* [The dimming of intelligence] (Palermo: L'Epos, 2000), 72ff. Sciacca (1908–75) was an Italian philosopher who started as a follower of Gentile. He became a distinguished advocate of classical metaphysical thought, which he viewed as a consistent line of development starting with Plato and Aristotle, continuing through the Middle Ages, and finding its greatest modern interpreter in Antonio Rosmini.

2 [TN] Ibid., 71, referring to Nietzsche.

Maritain is significant. In the preface to his work *La philosophie moral*,[3] which was left interrupted at the first volume (*Examen historique et critique des grandes systèmes*), he laments that Christian thought lacks a work of moral philosophy as a truly philosophical discipline, distinct from moral theology, and affirms its necessity. He is perfectly correct, but Maritain shows that he does not know Rosmini's *Principi di scienza morale*,[4] which is an exemplary work in this regard, and the continuation and correction of the *Critique of Practical Reason*, taken as the expression of the most positive moment of modern philosophy.

2 I spoke of "contemporary violence." The philosophical problem of violence is, indeed, typical of our century because only in it has an explicit *ennoblement of violence* taken place, as has been pointed out in several books, from Benda's *Trahison des clercs*[5] (1927) to Sergio Cotta's recent and excellent *Perchè la violenza?*[6] Traditionally, as Cotta observes, violence was considered the radical evil (*hubris*, excess), even if it was justified as necessary under certain circumstances, reflecting a pessimistic assessment of the immutable nature of human beings.

3 The ennoblement of violence is tied to the philosophical idea of *total* revolution, that is, of revolution as a transition from the kingdom of necessity to the kingdom of freedom, to a reality that is qualitatively "totally other." This transition implies a radical, necessarily violent break with history up to now. Therefore, the revolution cannot take place in the name of the traditional ethical principles because they are either empty words (justice, freedom), or legitimizations-mystifications of the existing order. The idea of total revolution implies the elimination of ethics. Thought *in terms of violence* follows this elimination.

That such an idea of revolution was already present in the young Marx is too well known. However, we must grant that the period from 1871 to 1914 was dominated by the attempt to reconcile the revolutionary idea with ethics (we could say that people tried, in various ways, to absorb the concept of revolution into the concept of progress: positivist socialism, Kantian socialism, Jaurès's personality which, within socialism, is the

3 [TN] Jacques Maritain, *Moral Philosophy: An Historical and Critical Survey of the Great Systems*, trans. Marshall Suther et al. (New York: Charles Scribner's Sons, 1964).

4 [TN] Antonio Rosmini, *Principles of Ethics*, trans. Terence Watson and Denis Cleary (Durham, UK: Rosmini House, 1989).

5 [TN] Julien Benda, *The Treason of the Intellectuals*, trans. Richard Aldington (Piscataway, NJ: Transaction Publishers, 2007).

6 [TN] Sergio Cotta, *Why Violence? A Philosophical Interpretation*, trans. Giovanni Gullace (Gainsville: University of Florida Press, 1985).

radical antithesis of Lenin's, etc.). The two world wars and their transformation into revolutions marked the failure of such attempts and are "the antecedent form of the removal of the difference between peace and war."[7]

This sentence by Heidegger raises a very important question. War, or at least any war that can be conceived as "just," aims at restoring a balance; its outcome is peace, as reconciliation between winners and losers. Of course, history has given us countless examples of wars of extermination, but, in fact, they were considered "barbaric" and they were condemned by ethics. Instead, the revolution's goal is to obliterate the adversary; nothing of the old "eon" must remain in the new: "The Western world has hitherto, even in its darkest periods, granted the slain enemy the right to be remembered, as a self-evident acknowledgment of the fact that we are all men (and *only* men) ... [The concentration camps] took away the individual's own death, proving that henceforth nothing belonged to him and he belonged to no one. His death merely set a seal on the fact that he had never really existed."[8] This passage mentions the concentration camps, where violence coincided with cruelty. Observe that although revolutionary violence and cruelty are normally associated in practice, this association is not necessary from the standpoint of essences. From the viewpoint of revolutionary violence, what matters is that even the memory of the old man must vanish; there must be change without conversion; the past must be erased, and thus even repentance. In short, the annihilation of memory, according to a popular phrase.

4 The thesis that revolutionary violence follows the disappearance of ethics has several important consequences. First, revolutionary violence cannot be discussed in terms of morality or immorality. The ethical dimension and revolutionary thought are absolutely incompatible. Conversely, it is precisely starting from revolutionary thought that one can fully understand, by contrast, the ethical principle as Rosmini defined it: respect for the order of being.[9] The terms "respect" and "violation" define the opposition of ethics and violence.

7 [TN] See Martin Heidegger, "Overcoming Metaphysics" in *The End of Philosophy*, trans. Joan Stambaugh (New York: Harper & Row, 1973), 104–5.

8 [TN] Hannah Arendt, *The Origins of Totalitarianism* (New York: Harcourt, 1985), 452.

9 [TN] "Desire or love being, wherever you know it, in the order or degree in which it presents itself to your intelligence," in Rosmini, *Principles of Ethics*, 56.

This does not mean that in revolutionary thought the distinction between good and evil is absent. But it is identified with the distinction between two forms of violence, a liberating form and a conservative or reactionary form – or *repressive* form, as it is often called today. The idea of the transition from the reign of necessity to the reign of freedom makes it obligatory to interpret all of past history in terms of oppression and violence. This does not mean that revolutionary thought does not construct its own tradition as well. Revolutions occurred in the past, but they were partial. Therefore, they resulted in the supremacy of *classes*, whose representatives set out to eliminate the true revolutionaries (e.g., think of the exaltation of Thomas Münzer in recent revolutionary literature). These beneficiaries of partial revolutions institutionalize their privileges, that is, their "thefts." Such institutionalization needs an ideal validation: hence, the origin of metaphysics ("eternal" and "immutable" truths are viewed as masks for conservatism). In this regard, Marcuse's chapter on the repressive nature of *Logos* (in *Eros and Civilization*) is exemplary.[10]

From this perspective, it is not surprising that Plato ends up being viewed as the first theorist of repressive violence because of his distinction between parts of the soul.[11] This is simply the reverse of the traditional statement that ethical theory starts with Socrates's victory over Callicles in *Gorgias*, the dialogue that outlines and prefigures the *Republic*.

5 We should point out that the eclipse of ethics is completely insurmountable within the perspective of immanentism. Hence, Nietzsche's truth is reconfirmed. From the immanentist perspective, humanitarianism and violence are two inseparable aspects of the same phenomenon. Therefore, it is no wonder that in today's world the greatest humanitarian achievements coexist with the greatest violence, Western libertinism with Eastern totalitarianism. Humanitarians say that to understand is to justify; whoever carried out certain actions could not do otherwise. Hence, the idea of responsibility is abolished. But on the other hand, from the standpoint of action, of a new reality that must be built, one must assign responsibility. Therefore, we reach the following paradox: we are not responsible but we are made responsible by others in relation to a project, to the "novelty" to be created. We reach the idea that

10 [TN] Herbert Marcuse, *Eros and Civilization: A Philosophical Inquiry into Freud* (New York: Vintage Books, 1955), chapter 5.

11 [TN] Del Noce is referring to Plato's distinction between three parts of the soul (logical, spirited, and appetitive) in Book 4 of the *Republic*. According to Plato, justice requires that the appetitive part obey the other two.

responsibility is assigned, which means that violence is justified as necessary in order to create a new reality. We reach the mortification of ethics expressed by Nietzsche's definition: it is the science whose task is to justify successful crimes.[12] This is confirmed by the failure of the attempts – which were common in the two decades between the two wars – to join revolution and non-violence in an immanentist context. Today non-violence is still discussed, but as a strategy to create a conflict when the oppressed are in a weaker position with respect to the oppressors.

6 Thus, today's ennoblement of violence follows the "non-immoralistic" eclipse of ethics and its consequent reduction to a formulation of repressive violence. The following questions arise: does this crisis have any distant precedents in the history of Western thought? If we take them into account, do we have to renew the standard schemes of the history of philosophy?

I propose the following thesis: the idea of creative violence has its roots in a reaffirmation of the Gnostic structure of thought.

The relationship with Gnosticism of the new spiritual atmosphere that arose in Germany after the First World War – largely as a repercussion of the Communist revolution, and it does not matter whether as an apology or in opposition – was already noticed by Hans Leisegang in his 1923 book *Die Gnosis*.[13] Later on, it was chiefly Voegelin who pointed to the Gnostic form of thought as the root of the revolutionary spirit.[14]

Here we should go back to Plotinus's extraordinarily relevant critique of the Gnostics in the second Ennead:

> Their doctrine, even bolder than the one of Epicurus (who only denied Providence), by *blaming* the Lord of providence and providence itself, despises all earthly laws and the virtue that arose among men from the beginning of time, and ridicules temperance, *so that nothing good can be found in this world*. So, their doctrine annuls temperance and justice, innate to the human character and perfected by reason and practice, and in general all that can make man worthy and noble ... Because for them *nothing* is noble among earthly things, except for something "different" that they will reach "in the future life." But, should not those who have gained "knowledge" [gnosis] look for the Good already in this

12 [TN] Friedrich Nietzsche, *Daybreak: Thoughts on the Prejudices of Morality*, trans. R.J. Hollingdale (Cambridge: Cambridge University Press, 1995), 59.

13 [TN] Hans Leisegang, *Die Gnosis* [The Gnosis] (Leipzig: A. Kröner, 1924).

14 [TN] On Del Noce's interest in the work of Voegelin, see the essay "Eric Voegelin and the Critique of the Idea of Modernity" in Appendix C and the references therein.

world and, searching for it first, set things in order here, precisely since they [the Gnostics] claim to derive from the divine essence? It is, in fact, proper to the nature of that essence to consider what is noble … But those who do not participate in virtue have nothing to carry them from this world to the one beyond.[15]

Plotinus's critique represented the last stand of classical thought, in which man's theoretical and practical tasks were, respectively, to contemplate and to imitate the universe, reflecting in himself the order of being. In short, the idea of virtue was inseparably linked with the idea of the order of being.

The scholars of Gnosticism have identified the rebellion against the idea of cosmic order as its essential characteristic. The Gnostics do not deny to the world the attribute of order, but they interpret it as an abomination rather than a good. They do not say that the cosmos is disordered, but that it is governed by a rigid and hostile order, by a tyrannical and cruel law. Their God is not just outside and beyond the world, but against the world, and this is where they break away from Christianity. Moral rebellion reflects a metaphysical rebellion. Therefore, the Gnostic position leads to the obliteration of ethics, as refusal to respect being and to be faithful to objective norms. This refusal was the common root of two opposite attitudes, libertinism as desecration of reality and asceticism as its radical rejection.

However, the Gnostic vision remained ahistorical, in the sense that history was absorbed into nature (theory of cosmic cycles, of the eternal return, etc.); hence, the Gnostics believed that man is powerless to transform the world, and they sought the liberation from the world of each individual soul. The new gnosis (and here we should focus again on the rise of Gnostic themes during the entire nineteenth century, and especially in classical German philosophy) can be seen as a reaffirmation of gnosis after Christianity, and thus after the Christian discovery of history.

This is why the Gnostic structure of thought as rejection of ethics is still with us, and why there are similarities, but also differences, between the attitudes of rejection. To tell the truth, the desecrating libertine attitude is basically identical: we should just notice that today's decadent libertinism is much more closely related to the Gnostic version than to the pre-Enlightenment form that originated from the Renaissance.

15 [TN] *Second Ennead*, 9th Tractate, Sec. 15. I translated into English Del Noce's Italian version in order to try to preserve some of his choices of words (especially those he emphasized by using italics).

The revolutionary attitude of creative violence has replaced the ascetic attitude of seeking liberation from the world. From a historicist perspective, what must be rejected is a specific historical reality, and the pessimistic disposition is replaced by an activist-voluntaristic one. To conclude, we have to say that we live at the time when the new gnosis is decomposing, and that the new attitude toward violence is the most visible expression of the reaffirmation of gnosis against both classical thought and Christian thought.

7 Should we now conclude that the demise of ethics is irreversible? That it started with Plato and is now ending? That Christianity can hope to survive only on the condition of separating itself completely from "cosmocentric" Greek thought?

My theses are the exact opposite of these too-common opinions. In a recent book, I tried to show that suicide is the philosophical destiny of the revolution, in the sense that it cannot go beyond the *violent* and nihilist stage of devaluing the values that previously were regarded as supreme.[16] The political counterpart of this devaluation is totalitarianism, i.e., institutionalized revolutionary violence.

Precisely the revolution's failure to fulfill its claim of bringing liberation leads us to examine the revival of Gnosticism after Christianity. We are not talking about the survival of archaic forms of thought. Gnosticism resurfaced in the context of the attempt by German classical philosophy to resolve Christianity into philosophy. Such an attempt is inseparable from the interpretation of the history of philosophy that was developed in that period and is still common, and from the axiological meaning conferred on the term "modernity."

Here we meet again, in precise opposition, the thought of Antonio Rosmini, whose work probably should be interpreted as the liberation of the metaphysics of being from all residues of Gnostic thought.

2 VIOLENCE AND SECULARIZED GNOSTICISM

1 I will now go back to the thesis that I already outlined in my introductory remarks, in order to clarify it better after the various interventions. In its most general form, it states the following: today a deeper exploration of the idea of violence allows us to rediscover, by contrast, the idea of *ethics*. What can "rediscover" mean in this context? It simply means "understand." To demand more of a talk – for instance, a proposal for a

16 Augusto Del Noce, *Il suicidio della rivoluzione* [The suicide of the revolution] (Milan: Rusconi, 1978).

restoration of values – would mean not taking seriously the gravity of the greatest crisis that the West has ever faced. Such is the crisis that the rediscovery of the West's etymological root as "land of sunset" has become a cliché so common that I even hesitate to bring it up, out of fear of banality. And also regarding "understanding" I must warn you that I will just summarize a number of issues which so far have been only partially studied, and urgently need to be studied.

From this problematic standpoint, we must use the word "eclipse" to denote the primary feature of the present crisis, for a purely methodological reason. I mean that at this initial stage of our investigation nothing allows us to rule out the possibility that the value that now is being obscured *might* come back to light. Needless to say, this is my personal conviction, but a philosophical analysis is a different thing from an expression of personal convictions.

Now, the eclipse that marks the present crisis is, first of all, an "eclipse of ethics." It is not an eclipse of the "sacred," as people often say. Regarding the sacred, we must rather speak of a "shift," of which the eclipse of ethics is a manifestation. Almost paradoxically, I dare say that the "prehistory" which for us is hardest to understand dates back only a few decades, to the time when a professor of philosophy was, above all, a professor of Kantian morality. Not far from here we had the factory – allow me this playful expression, which does not mean to convey any lack of respect – of professors of Kantian morality that Carlo Cantoni[17] had established at the University of Pavia. Some of the eldest among us were still students, at the beginning of the thirties, of some of its authoritative exponents, of whom we have very fond memories. Speaking more generally, what was the chief characteristic of spiritualism, in its various forms, if not the association of morality and religion? Well, we can definitely say that as recently as half a century ago the established "authority" was that of the "categorical imperative."

In fact, a very simple but generally overlooked observation about terminology shows that the broader connection I have proposed is legitimate. What is the exact linguistic opposite of the word "violence" if not "respect"? And everybody knows what a large role "respect" plays in the two most important works of moral philosophy of the modern age, Kant's *Critique of Practical Reason* and Rosmini's *Principles of Ethics.* Do we need to recall that according to Kant respect is a very special sentiment, because on the one hand it is awareness of our subordination to the absolute authority of the law, and on the other it is awareness of our participation

17 [TN] Carlo Cantoni (1840–1906) was a professor of philosophy and then rector at the University of Pavia.

in the absolute value of the law, and therefore it is what makes us recognize our own dignity? Thus, we can say that respect for the law prevents my will from becoming an absolute, and respect for the other person prevents my action from becoming violent. Likewise, do we need to recall the first principle of Rosmini's ethics, which is respect for the order of being?

Today's spiritual situation, therefore, can be described as follows: *we can recognize the idea of ethics only negatively by investigating the idea of violence.* However, this enables us to recognize its implications, perhaps as never before. I will add, throwing out a thought that I cannot develop, that this also enables us to understand why Kant marks a watershed in the history of philosophy. On one hand there is a side of Kant that tends toward a further development that takes place in Rosmini (and I think that this further development is especially clear in Rosmini's ethics). There is also another side of Kant that is vulnerable to the process that took place afterwards and concluded in the break with Platonism and Christianity.

2 I will now relate the thesis I outlined in the abstract to two books that have been published in Italy a few months apart from each other, *Perchè la violenza? Un'interpretazione filosofica* by Sergio Cotta[18] and *Téchne: Le radici della violenza* by Emanuele Severino.[19] They agree on one point: the acceptance of violence as normal is one of the most characteristic features of our time, and the novelty of this phenomenon requires a philosophical approach, going beyond the huge literature based on psychological and sociological considerations. I think they also agree, even if the emphasis is different, on another essential point: the novelty we face can be explained philosophically in terms of the metaphysics of subjectivity, which by now has reached a state of vertigo in its rejection of all objective standards.

At this point, their arguments start to diverge and become incompatible. According to Cotta, what needs to be done is to go back to the metaphysics of being, in the classical sense of the word, but refined by the dialectical confrontation with its adversary. According to Severino, instead, the civilization of technology is destroying irreversibly all traditional forms of civilization – Christian, bourgeois, Marxist – and this destruction of tradition constitutes a philosophical revelation because "the history of the West is the history of technology. In Greek-Christian culture God is the supreme technician. In modern culture Man is the

18 [TN] Cotta, *Why Violence?*

19 [TN] Emanuele Severino, *Téchne: Le radici della violenza* [Téchne: The roots of violence] (Milan: Rusconi, 1979).

supreme technician – who by now plans the production and destruction of the totality of things … In spite of the backwardness of the ancient world's technological capabilities, Western theology possessed from its beginning all the essential features of the civilization of technology; and in spite of the fact that this civilization rejects God most radically, contemporary technology maintains the theological character of its origins"; this implies that "in its essential meaning, the critique of the civilization of technology by secular or religious humanism is nothing but the protest by losing violence against triumphing violence."[20] The philosophical template of violence is inscribed in the origins of Western thought; hence the title of the book. The word *téchne* is interpreted as denoting the complete availability of things to the will to power that finds its apex in the operative possibilities of modern science.

Supposedly, today's nihilism cannot be opposed from the standpoint of Greek and Christian humanism (here lies the irreconcilable difference from Cotta's thesis) because this humanism is what originated it. In short, today [according to Severino] we are facing the outcome, the complete manifestation, of a process of development of the Western spirit that lasted millennia. The outcome of a process that lasted millennia: by contrast, one cannot help thinking of a certain atmosphere that dominated the University of Rome around 1920. At that time the young disciples of Gentile regarded Actualism[21] as the ripe fruit of a process of thought that had started from Greek philosophy and had spanned Christianity and modern thought. Today that perspective has been inverted. People no longer describe nihilism, as they used to, as a devaluation of what previously were regarded as the highest values, understanding it as the premise for the establishment of new values. We are rather witnessing the disappearance of the very idea of value.

But this inversion is precisely what is perplexing; could it be a symptom that we have not moved forward? Except in the sense, which certainly is also important, that we have interpreted *better* what was already being proposed at that time? This improved interpretation illuminates the ultimate results of a process of thought, but it is important to trace our way back to its premises. And it may well be the case that these two narratives share the same premises.

20 Ibid., 296–7 and 14–15.

21 [TN] The Italian word *Attualismo* denotes the specific branch of Idealistic philosophy that was developed in the early twentieth century by Giovanni Gentile and his disciples. In English it is sometimes called *actual Idealism* in order to avoid confusion with the usage of the word in analytic philosophy.

3 Now, the thesis I am proposing is the following: what I will approximately call, at first, the legitimization of violence (with the intent of making this notion more precise later on) is the final outcome *of one* of the fundamental directions of Western thought, namely Gnosticism. Why am I emphasizing *of one*? To speak of the vertigo of modern subjectivism is correct, in my opinion, but it is not enough. Conversely, to speak of an outcome of Western thought as a whole is too much. I will add three comments to this proposal. The first is that I really do not make any claim of originality, but that nevertheless this thesis has not enjoyed wide circulation even among the most attentive scholars of philosophy, as if it were an example of "bad Spenglerism." By that, I mean an abuse of the historical principle of analogy, when it is used to explain recent phenomena through formal resemblances with phenomena that are very far away in the past and can be explained only in reference to completely different historical situations. The second comment, which helps explain its limited fortune, is that this proposition is vulnerable to the worst misfortune that can befall a philosophical-historical thesis, namely *sociological trivialization*. Strangely, it has enjoyed some success precisely in such a trivialized form. The third comment is that the only way to save it from this unhappy fate is by associating it with another thesis that has both theoretical and historical significance.

Regarding the first point, the family resemblance between Gnostic speculation and the religious philosophy of German Idealism is so strong that, already shortly after Hegel's death, Ferdinand Christian Baur wrote *Die Christliche Gnosis oder die Geschichte der christlichen Religions-Philosophie in ihrer geschichtlichen Entwickelung*, which was published in Tubingen in 1835 and was recently reprinted, in 1967, in Darmstadt.[22] In works rich in erudition and insight, Eric Voegelin has developed a Gnostic interpretation of recent revolutionary and totalitarian phenomena, in symmetry with that distant age. Probably, his research can be interpreted as the final result of the historiographic work started by Karl Löwith. Without this conclusion, Löwith's work risks resembling a stroll among ruins, or even (because of this resemblance) a sort of negative introduction to a form of scientistic neo-Enlightenment (in fact, in Italy it was interpreted *also* along those lines).

However, I must add that Voegelin's work ran the risk of looking like a mere variation on many other interpretations that used terms like

22 [TN] Ferdinand Christian Baur, *Die Christliche Gnosis oder die Geschichte der christlichen Religions-Philosophie in ihrer geschichtlichen Entwickelung* [The Christian gnosis or the history of Christian religious philosophy in its historical development] (Tübingen: C.F. Osiander, 1835; Darmstatdt: Wissenschaftliche Buchgesellschaft, 1967).

prophetism, messianism, millennialism, eschatologism in order to draw a comparison between Marxism and various heretical movements, thus missing its specific character – and Voegelin himself did not always protect himself sufficiently from this danger, in my opinion. The sociologistic mindset, which today is very widespread, has adopted the scientistic viewpoint that Gnosticism is an archaic, imaginary form of thought, extraneous to the modern scientific spirit. This approach reinforced the standard opinion that Marxism, as a philosophy, includes some archaic elements that may resemble Gnostic thought, and that in this form it can be successful, or remain successful, in countries at a pre-modern cultural stage. In developed countries, however, the idea of revolution must be replaced by the idea of *modernization*. Those who think in this way – and this is the way of thinking of the intellectual *élite* of an important Italian political party[23] – do not realize that the attribution of an axiological value to the idea of modernity has a Gnostic origin, as I will discuss later. Those who claim they can fight totalitarian, violent, and revolutionary gnosis in the name of the idea of modernization are literally imitating the Baron of Münchhausen. The critique of the revolutionary justification of violence cannot be developed from a sociological or scientistic viewpoint (where scientism is characterized precisely by the judgment that the Gnostic form of thought has been surpassed for good). Scientistic arrogance is the result of an infusion of the same Gnostic spirit it wants to criticize, and the current success of scientism is itself a stage in the failure of the Gnostic fantasy, instead of a better answer to the questions perceived and raised by gnosis.

In my judgment, therefore, this thesis cannot be rescued from sociological trivialization unless it is accompanied, both from the theoretical and the historical point of view, by the thesis that we should give up the idea of a unitary process of development of Western thought. This is true regardless of whether we think that this process moves toward a final outcome of fullness and liberation, or we view it as an open-ended development (but after certain achievements which must be considered irreversible), or we think that it is headed for catastrophe. The reason is that the very idea of a unitary process, no matter how it is understood, optimistically or pessimistically, is internal to the rebirth of gnosis that originated the philosophies of history. Even if they are no longer presented in their original form, these philosophies still shape the standard interpretations of history (think, for example, of the common opinion,

23 [TN] Del Noce is probably referring to the Italian Socialist Party.

widespread also among theologians, that "modernity" indicates an irreversible process of secularization).

This is why at the beginning of the outline of this talk I recalled Sciacca's idea, which has not received the attention it deserves, that today Rosmini and Nietzsche are relevant in a complementary way. In this idea I find a confirmation of the historical thesis that I had already proposed in my book on *The Problem of Atheism.* In it I identified two irreducible lines of development in the philosophy of the modern age, one from Descartes to Nietzsche (and, of course, to post-Nietzschean thinkers) and the other from Descartes to Rosmini (and, of course, to later Christian thinkers). The second line rediscovered and deepened the tradition, Augustinian as well as Thomist. This view differs from the interpretation adopted by the majority of the most prominent historians; once again I will mention Löwith and the process he describes "from Descartes to Nietzsche," because he is the historian whom I principally had in mind when I was writing that book, as the author who most criticized the philosophy of history, while still subscribing to the standard view of the development of modern philosophy toward total immanence and the negation of the supernatural.[24] As a consequence, today's historical situation should be described as *the full revelation of the opposition between Christianity and Gnosticism,* after the meaning of the latter became fully manifested in the wake of classical German philosophy and of its continuations.

Here, allow me a digression. I believe that although the two interlocutors I mentioned at the beginning, Cotta and Severino, do not bring up Gnosticism in their books, they both agree with me on an essential point: about the primacy of the philosophical aspect in contemporary history, so much so that this history cannot be understood if such primacy is not recognized. This becomes apparent when we look at some of the countless volumes that have been devoted to contemporary history, based on international or economic rivalries. Many are very well done, and display an amazing wealth of documentation. Still, it is hard to escape the impression that they strive for such extreme philological detail in order to make up for some kind of void, which the authors themselves perceive but do not know how to fill. Undeniably, in many of these very diligent studies the facts remain opaque, and the past cannot be brought back to life, even when it is recent. Thus, when we read them we have the feeling, which is itself significant, of visiting a morgue. How to explain this? I think there is no other way except by focusing our attention on the

24 [TN] Karl Löwith, *Meaning in History: The Theological Implications of the Philosophy of History* (Chicago: University of Chicago Press, 1957).

aspect of contemporary history that makes it the manifestation of an ideal essence. And this is where we encounter the problem of violence. The impression I described is due to the fact that these authors neglect to consider the new significance that violence assumes in contemporary history, which is different from the numerous and no less atrocious manifestations of violence that took place in the past. Therefore, the so-called "transpolitical" interpretation of contemporary history – thus named because it brings to the fore the ideal aspect (and thus opposes, above all, the interpretation based on historical materialism) – is characterized by the fact that it regards as essential the *philosophical* question of violence.

Thus, let us start by considering the problems raised by the question of violence. On this topic, we are now in the position to make a decisive observation. Not many years ago it was still possible to think that people of very different metaphysical and religious convictions could easily come to an agreement about the question of violence. Think, for instance, of Benedetto Croce, and of his famous essay "Why We Cannot not Call Ourselves Christians."[25] Strangely, it is considered an example of exoteric literature for short-term political purposes, whereas it is, on the contrary, a uniquely important document in order to understand Croce's true thought. At the same time, it is a document from a distant world, in which violence was presented as an expression of irrationalism and of unhealthy Romanticism. In other words: when Marx and Nietzsche were excluded from philosophy – as Croce did, and as was very prevalent at the time of my youth – the problem of violence reduced to a matter of moral dis-value. People thought that believers in a broad variety of religions could agree on how to judge it, including believers in purely rational religions and also people who did not believe in any religion. Indeed, consider the sharp break between pre-war and postwar philosophy here in Italy. Italian Idealism was heavily influenced by the results of the Italian dispute about theoretical Marxism.[26] It had started from this dispute, and as a result it excluded the whole development "from Hegel to Nietzsche" from the history of philosophy, as an expression of philosophical decadence. Consequently, both Croce's and Gentile's "reforms of Hegelianism" still developed within the horizon of Christian

25 [TN] Benedetto Croce, "Perchè non possiamo non dirci cristiani," *La critica* 55 (1942): 289–97.

26 [TN] In the years around 1900 a group of Italian intellectuals (including Antonio Labriola, Benedetto Croce, Giovanni Gentile, Rodolfo Mondolfo) engaged in a lively debate about the philosophical significance of Marx's historical materialism. For a summary of their positions, see Costanzo Preve, *Ideologia Italiana* (Milan: Vangelista, 1993), 26–33.

philosophy, although outside all forms of religious orthodoxy. Now, the inclusion of the philosophy of the period "from Hegel to Nietzsche" was precisely what characterized the new direction in Italian philosophy, affecting practically every investigation (and it is symbolic that this development was influenced, in the years immediately after the war, by the book by Löwith bearing that same title[27]).

However, if the problem of violence is formulated as I did, in connection with the inclusion of Marx and Nietzsche in the history of philosophy, the important question is whether Christianity can withstand Gnosticism; whether it is a thing of the past, a reality on the verge of extinction. And even after having recognized – here, for methodological reasons I should say "possibly recognized" – that precisely the dead end reached by its adversaries confirms the enduring validity of Christian thought, we must wonder why today certain historical expressions of Christian philosophy and theology are inadequate. Indeed, it is natural to think that Gnosticism was able to resurface in new forms and to achieve historical dominance because it was opposed by inadequate forms of thought, which already contained the possibility of or the occasion for getting off the right track. It is certainly not the case, in absolute terms, that a philosophical system's success reflects its truth value. Philosophical popularity is also determined by other factors of a political, social, and economic nature (of an ideological nature, in the broad sense: this is where we encounter the concept of ideology "in action"). Nevertheless, we must admit that when the true conception of life is defeated by opposite conceptions, there must be a flaw in the form in which it is being proposed.

4 Clearly, when I speak of Gnosticism I am not talking about the ancient gnosis, as if that were the only expression of the Gnostic phenomenon, but about a spiritual essence that can manifest itself in different forms in different epochs. I am thinking of a mindset which in the first centuries presented itself as an alternative to Christianity (and *not* as a Christian heresy, as people keep thinking), and then resurfaced in the last two centuries, after leading a subterranean life, reaching its complete form *after* Christianity. I am interested, in short, in the philosophical concept of Gnosticism as it was elaborated in the period after the First World War. At that time the Gnostic spiritual disposition was rediscovered because people focused their attention on the analogies between the end of the

27 [TN] Karl Löwith, *From Hegel to Nietzsche*, trans. David E. Green (New York: Holt, Rinehart and Winston, 1964).

ancient world and the sunset of the West. For example, the works of Leisegang and Jonas can be understood in light of this rediscovery.[28]

Let us now limit our discussion to the most generic aspects of Gnostic thought, which are its opposition to both classical and Christian philosophy and also, and above all, the unity of such opposition. The new feature that appears in Gnostic thought is rebellion against being. With respect to the Greek world, it takes the form of anti-cosmism, with respect to the Christian world, of opposition to the creator God of the Book of Genesis. Redemption means redemption from creation, liberation from the world. But if creation is the work of an evil principle, speaking of "image and likeness of God" cannot make sense. Here we come across a fundamental point, which I will discuss later: *it is impossible to develop a critique of violence starting from any form of ethics that claims to be autonomous from metaphysics and theology.* At this point, it is superfluous to mention the sharp opposition that arises between the Gnostic idea of *fall* and the biblical idea of *sin* (even if it is essential), and the consequent appearance in Gnostic thought of intermediary entities, the *eons,* between decadence ("to be cast down") and the subsequent reintegration.

The unity in the opposition to Greek thought and Christian thought suggests an important consideration about the program of "de-Hellenization" of Christianity that many theologians have outlined, and actually pushed very far, over the last few decades. May I raise the question whether such de-Hellenization does not end up coinciding with a Gnostic regression of Christianity, *and it cannot happen otherwise because of an essential necessity*? Several factors suggest that this is the case. When Altizer, the theologian of the "death of God," replaces the traditional formula *Jesus is God* with *God is Jesus,*[29] he seems to say that God becomes truly God by becoming the Redeemer, and by negating himself as the creative and transcendent principle. After all, it is not coincidental that every criticism of the old theology by the new theologians repeats objections that had already been formulated by the philosophers whom these theologians regard as members of what I would call (interpreting their own way of thinking) the "German patrology": Feuerbach, Marx, Freud, plus Nietzsche and Heidegger as the "guardians of not-going-back."

28 As a basic reference about ancient gnosis I follow the works by Jonas, whose first volume appeared in 1934 and the second in 1954. The Italian translation was published by SEI, Turin 1973. [TN: Del Noce is probably referring to Hans Jonas, *The Gnostic Religion* (Boston: Beacon Press, 1958)].

29 [TN] Thomas J.J. Altizer, *The Gospel of Christian Atheism* (Philadelphia: Westminster Press, 1966), 44.

5 But, how can the Gnostic rebellion – even understood in the stronger sense of rejecting ethics, which can be observed in the passage by Plotinus that I quoted in the outline – be related to the idea of violence that permeates today's atmosphere?

It is an elementary observation that the idea of violence is usually associated with the idea of revolution or the idea of nihilism. In the first case, ethics is ignored in the name of a form of ultra-morality; in the second, it is simply denied. Now, it seems hard to find in the ancient Gnostics any germs of either the revolutionary idea or of nihilism. On the contrary, if we quickly review the essential features of these two positions that we face today, the difference seems huge.

The revolutionary exaltation of violence is well known. The Revolution, capitalized and always in the singular, is presented as the unique event that mediates the transition from the reign of necessity to the reign of freedom, leading to a future that has nothing in common with the old history. Then, the distinction between mythical violence and divine violence that we read in the somewhat grandiloquent pages written by Walter Benjamin immediately after the First World War becomes clear: "If mythical violence is lawmaking, divine violence is law-destroying; if the former sets boundaries, the latter boundlessly destroys them; if mythical violence brings at once guilt and retribution, divine power only expiates."[30] The former, which creates and enforces the law, is reprehensible, but not the latter, which is sacred. Apart from the literary style, it is the same distinction between reactionary/repressive violence and progressive/revolutionary violence that we find repeated *ad nauseam* in today's literature.

In other words: until now history has always been a history of disguised violence, under the cover of rights sanctioned by an extra-historical source, of the value that constitutes the individual as a *person* (Kant's sentence[31] about the feeling of respect as the only non-pathological feeling comes to mind). We can escape this situation only through a type of violence capable of breaking the *continuum* of history. When Benjamin was developing his thought, the revolution seemed to be the restoration of sacred history against a profane history that had to be freed from an inappropriate image of the sacred.

30 [TN] Walter Benjamin, "Critique of Violence" in *Reflections* (New York: Schocken Books, 1986), 297.

31 [TN] Del Noce is referring either to the well-known footnote to Section 4:401 of Kant's *Groundwork of the Metaphysics of Morals* (Cambridge: Cambridge University Press, 1998) or to sections 5:75–6 of the *Critique of Practical Reason* (Cambridge: Cambridge University Press, 1997), both translated by Mary J. Gregor.

The relationship between the revolution and nihilism then becomes all too clear. Indeed, it is apparent that the revolutionary idea implies the combination of two stages: a negative one in which the traditional order of values is devalued, and a positive one in which a "totally other" new order is established. The transition from the revolution to nihilism is mediated by what I have called elsewhere "the suicide of the revolution," whose necessity I tried to demonstrate.[32] What happens is that nihilism, instead of being the preliminary stage of the revolution (the tearing away of the masks, the night of values, and so on), becomes its result. At that point, violence is no longer accepted as necessary, or revolutionary violence exalted as divine. Rather, it is accepted as normal because ethics comes to an end. Ethics is replaced by rules of coexistence imposed by the strongest side, and violence truly is "wrong" because it is lawmaking, as Benjamin says. Such violence must be critiqued because it marks the re-entry of sacred history into profane history. The fact that it is lawmaking is the sign that the transition from the reign of necessity to the reign of freedom has failed.

There is an undeniable abyss between this process of thought and the one of ancient gnosis. Nevertheless, there is also an undeniable kinship: they both deny the order of being, of creation, of God. First, let us gauge how wide the abyss is.

6 Does it not seem that we should look at Gnostic thought in order to find the root of the opposite idea, of non-violence? Indeed, what motivates a Gnostic to reject the idea of creation, if not the imperative of separating value from strength, power, and success? And the concern not to call divine what is not divine, that is, worldly realities? Does he not deny God the attribute of being the Creator out of an extreme sense of His perfection? African Spir, a dualist philosopher of the nineteenth century and Martinetti's[33] true teacher, wrote that the belief that the conditional came from the unconditional is the most disastrous mistake and has most terrible consequences because it leads to confusion between good and evil (due to their common descent from the unconditional) and thus falsifies moral and religious conscience. Spir (a Kantian) embraced Gnostic dualism precisely because for him morality and religion were so tightly linked.

I fully recognize the value of these objections. In fact, I actually think that, as a preliminary step, they must be given great emphasis, illustrating the process that in the period between the two world wars led to the rediscovery of ancient gnosis in the name of non-violence.

32 [TN] Del Noce, *Il suicidio della rivoluzione.*

33 [TN] Piero Martinetti (1872–1943), Italian philosopher and religious thinker.

In the preface to his book, Cotta writes: "Writing about violence, therefore, means bringing together the threads of memories and reflections, both recent and remote, of an entire lifetime."[34] I agree completely, and I am inclined to add (possibly exaggerating?) that sensitivity to the problem of violence (a sensitivity that always shines through, regardless of what topics are directly discussed, and even when the word violence is never spoken explicitly) is precisely what distinguishes authentic philosophers from academic philosophers (Schopenauer's "philosophy professors"). The philosophical question of violence is tied so tightly to the question of contemporary history that it is impossible to discuss one without bringing up the other. And since we all participate in contemporary history, it is also impossible to discuss violence without introducing an autobiographical element.

Hence, I will start by describing how, because of my age, I encountered the question of violence earlier than Cotta. In December 1928, at the end of my first month as a university student, I attended a discussion led by Umberto Segre of Julien Benda's *Trahison des clercs*,[35] for Annibale Pastore's course in theoretical philosophy. Benda certainly is not one of the guiding lights of today's philosophy, but nevertheless that book is remarkable. It was one of the first warnings that the outcomes of the First World War contradicted its ideology. That war had been depicted, especially in radical-masonic culture, as the last war, as the end of violence, and thus as the fulfillment of the historical period from 1870 to 1914, which would bring to completion the humanitarian and democratic aspects already present during that period. On the contrary, already in the years immediately after the war this same depiction proved to be an ideology, a tool used by some specific groups in order to prevail and to oppress. The only possible conclusion was that "novelty" is a synonym of regression rather than progress. Essentially, Benda said: until recently humankind did evil but never approved of it. And the task of condemning evil gave rise to a special corporation of people, the "clerics," whether they wore a priestly garb or not.

The major new development was that this corporation had committed betrayal; the clerics had become apologists of violence. The *Trahison* was the first volume of a trilogy that ended with *Essai d'un discours cohérent sur les rapports de Dieu et du monde*[36] in which the philosophy that a cleric must

34 [TN] Cotta, *Why Violence?*, xi.

35 [TN] Benda, *The Treason of the Intellectuals.*

36 [TN] Julien Benda, *Essai d'un discours cohérent sur les rapports de Dieu et du monde* [Attempt at a consistent discussion of the relationship between God and the world] (Paris: Gallimard, 1931).

profess was formulated. It spoke of "being's two eternal wills." One is the worldly will to be or to feel or to make oneself *distinct*, as will of *existence and selfness* (i.e., violence, whose phenomenology is developed in a way that is still interesting); the other is the will of the cleric, which negates the first. As far as I recall, the book did not refer directly to gnosis but it did speak about the Cathars, who are usually regarded as descendants of the Gnostics. But the important thing to note is that at that time the atmosphere of the new epoch, which has not yet ended, had already led to a Gnostic type of dualism. I have mentioned Benda because the *Trahison* is well known, but in that period there was truly an abundance of rediscoveries of Gnostic dualism prompted by the atmosphere of violence. Think of Martinetti's *Gesù Cristo e il Cristianesimo*[37] and its final words: "(according to religion) the only true reality is the quiet activity of the spirit that frees itself from the world." Martinetti exalts Marcion as "the first one who continued and restored the teachings of Jesus."[38] Or think of *Le dualism chez Platon, les gnostiques et les manichéens*[39] by Simone Pétrement, Alain's pupil.[40] According to both Martinetti and Pétrement, Gnosticism is the true Christianity. I think one could say that in Pétrement we see Alain's morality ending in Martinetti's religion.

During the 1930s I experienced such opposition between ethics and violence as excruciating. As was normal for intellectuals in that time, both old and young, my perspective was Eurocentric. Deeply rooted and (what is more important) well-founded intellectual habits made us recognize Europe as the final fruit of centuries of civilization. But now this very continent was devastated by unprecedented violence. In those years I suffered this contradiction to an extreme degree, dramatically because the various fashionable philosophies of that period seemed to me attempts to accommodate violence. The only certainty was the moral certainty that one should give a witness for ethics against violence (hence my friendship with Aldo Capitini[41]). And I will not hide the fact that at that time I was fascinated by forms of religion oriented toward Gnostic dualism.

37 [TN] Piero Martinetti, *Gesù Cristo e il Cristianesimo* [Jesus Christ and Christianity] (Milan: Edizioni della Rivista di Filosofia, 1934).

38 [TN] Ibid., 358.

39 [TN] Simone Pétrement, *Le dualism chez Platon, les gnostiques et les manichéens* [Dualism in Plato, in the Gnostics and in the Manicheans] (Paris: Presses Universitaires de France, 1947).

40 [TN] Émile-Auguste Chartier (1868–1951), known as Alain, French philosopher.

41 [TN] Aldo Capitini (1899–1968), Italian philosopher, politician, anti-Fascist, and poet, was one of the first proponents in Italy of Gandhi's philosophy of non-violence.

This also explains how traumatized I was by the outcome of the Second World War and by the advance of revolutionary violence, no longer described as barbaric. In fact, this was a major break, because in the 1930s the perception of the opposition between ethics and violence had grown extremely strong, at least among small groups of lay people (here I am not speaking, obviously, about the Church and its constant protest against violence, coming from its highest teaching authority, even though many people ignore, or pretend to ignore, this protest, to the point that some have spoken of a Catholic blessing of violence). Afterwards, a form of thought spread that replaced the type of the philosopher with the one of the revolutionary. It absorbed ethics into politics, or denied – in the name of a "renewed creation" that would lead to a super-human "totally other" – that any values are absolute, since all of them are covers for class interests and the will to power. This is so well known that I do not need to dwell on it. Later on, this attitude turned into today's widespread nihilistic mindset and the resulting cynical materialism. It turned into careless acceptance of violence because many people have forgotten even the norm that makes it possible to recognize violence.

But, how is it possible to say that both revolutionary thought and the nihilistic denial of values have a Gnostic origin? How can the strongest devaluation of worldly reality have been the preparation for the strongest affirmation that there is nothing beyond the empirical world?

When we say that revolutionary thought has Gnostic roots we must refer, therefore, to a post-Christian reaffirmation of gnosis. Already by itself, the fashionable expression "post-Christianity" echoes the Gnostic interpretation. Already by themselves, certain symmetries are striking, especially in reference to that text by Plotinus, whose crucial importance cannot be overstated. The two branches of ancient gnosis are well known: one was ascetic (Marcion) and the other libertine (Carpocrates, the Cainites), but both are tied to the idea of rebellion. Thus, ascetic Gnosticism wants to oppose the Creator's plan instead of promoting it, and fight against the God of the world in the name of the unknown and foreign God. If the beyond is transposed to the future, does this not look like an exact anticipation of today's two attitudes, about which the question of violence arises? Is not the spirit of total revolution a secularized version of Gnostic asceticism? And is not the spirit of moral nihilism a secularized version of libertine Gnosticism? In this case, the correspondence is even more visible: liberation will result from the disintegration of every form of order (the "great refusal" of 1968).

After considering violence, and having then encountered the concept of gnosis, we now come to the concept of secularization, and perhaps we are getting to the point where we can give it a precise meaning. I propose that this notion, which is so common today, *applies to gnosis, not to Christianity*. This statement has four extremely important corollaries, which I cannot develop adequately but can only outline here. The first is that all attempts to distinguish "secularization" from "secularism" (as some people have done) do not make sense. Therefore, the so-called "theology of secularization" can only be described as the Gnostic prison of Christianity. The second is that secularism is merely the reaffirmation of gnosis after Christianity and coincides with immanentism. The third is that the idea of developing a critique of violence in the context of immanentism is contradictory. The fourth is that contemporary nihilism must be described as the catastrophic collapse of the Gnostic dream.

Secularization means that the "totally other" reality (and it is hard not to give this formula, dear to so many contemporary theologians, a Gnostic interpretation), which for a Gnostic lay beyond the empirical world, for a modern revolutionary lies instead in the future. Such a future will be realized because of an intrinsic necessity of history, according to an immanentistic view in which necessity and freedom coincide. In this way, Gnostic dualism is dissolved into an immanent historical process, as a sequence of consecutive temporal eons.

But, what process led to this reaffirmation of gnosis? The answer would be very simple if we interpreted gnosis as a Christian heresy, as people too often do. Things look quite different if heresies are viewed as weaker lines of defence, whose degree of error is measured precisely by their inability to resist the new gnosis, or which are destined to merge with the new gnosis because of this inability. The answer can only be the following: the "unexpected" encounter with gnosis, and its transfiguration into new forms, takes place at the end of a process that intends to interpret Christianity as a philosophy, or to reach the idea of a "Christian philosophy" understood as absorption of Christianity into philosophy; therefore, a philosophy that bans the supernatural, even though it justifies its affirmation historically at the time when people thought that Greek philosophy was the only possible philosophy.[42] Thus, at this point we find ourselves facing Hegel.

7 A text that singularly illuminates this transition – or, at least, the text that struck me most strongly – is found in Alexandre Kojève's lectures at

42 This scheme is essentially the one that also appears in Gentile's "Christian philosophy." Perhaps, it is above all in this respect that Gentile can be said to be a Hegelian. But it would take a lengthy argument to make that case, and this is not the right place.

the École des Hautes Études from 1933 to 1939.[43] As is well known, they marked a rebirth of Hegelian and Marxist studies in France, and thus contributed most decisively to the turning point in French philosophy after the war, when the Cartesian-Pascalian-Malebranchian-Biranian line, which had been expressed by the *Philosophie de l'Esprit*,[44] went into a crisis. Kojève does not actually talk about gnosis; nevertheless, I think his commentary is very important in order to clarify the transition from the old gnosis to the new and post-Christian one, also because he emphasizes the "atheistic" character that Hegel's "Christian philosophy" must assume precisely in the course of its effort to achieve the status of "Christian philosophy." His commentary centres on the idea of negativity. Hegel's originality lies in the fact that

> Freedom does not consist in a *choice* between two *givens*,[45] it is the *negation* of the given, both of the given which one is oneself (as animals or as an "incarnate tradition") and of the given which one is not (the natural and social *World*) ... The freedom which is realized and manifested as dialectical or *negating* Action, is thereby essentially a *creation* [and here lies the difference from ancient gnosis]. For to negate the given without ending in nothingness is to produce something that did not yet exist; now, this is precisely what is called "creating." [Gnosticism, which had been characterized since its beginning by negativity and by an anti-worldly God, therefore incorporates the idea of negativity] ... Man does not change himself and transform the World for himself in order to realize a conformity to an "ideal" given to him (imposed by God, or simply "innate"). He creates and creates himself because he negates and negates himself "without a preconceived idea": he becomes other solely because he no longer wants to be the same.[46]

In this passage we find (a) the idea of a new creation which is entirely human, (b) the complete rejection of the order of being, and (c) the

43 Alexandre Kojève, *Introduction à la lecture de Hegel* (Paris: Gallimard, 1947). The introduction and the two most important essays have been translated into Italian (*La dialettica e l'idea di morte in Hegel*, trans. Paolo Serini (Turin: Einaudi, 1948)). My citations refer to this translation. [TN: I refer to *Introduction to the Reading of Hegel*, trans. James H. Nichols Jr (New York: Basic Books, 1969), which, however, includes only about half of the original French volume.]

44 See footnote 12 on page 14.

45 Think, as the exact opposite, of the choice discussed by Rosmini between subjective goods and objective goods, in which man's divine likeness shines because the faculty of free will is manifested. In nineteenth-century philosophy there is no more poignant expression of the opposition between Christian thought and new gnosis than this antithesis between Hegel and Rosmini.

46 [TN] Kojève, *Introduction*, 222–3. The comments in the square brackets are by Del Noce, the quotation marks and the italics by Kojève.

consequent rejection of every trace of absolute values, since what will be or can be represents an ideal – which justifies man's negating or creating action (that is, his change), giving it a "meaning" – only because man no longer wants to be *what he is*. Now, Kojève affirms that this position comes after the Judeo-Christian conception, and is made possible by it alone: "dialectical Anthropology is the philosophic science of Man as he appears in the (pre-philosophic) Judeo-Christian conception – that is, of Man who is supposed to be able to *convert himself*, in the full sense of the word, or to become essentially and radically *other* ... the steps of the Dialectic described in the *Phenomenology* are nothing but a series of successive 'conversions' that Man carries out in the course of history."[47]

In other words, Hegel abandoned the Greek cosmological conception and embraced the Judeo-Christian anthropological one, but he parted way with the latter as well by understanding it not as a religion but as a philosophy. Therefore, it is in reference to the preservation of ancient philosophy that Christian transcendence could be presented "as 'faith' in a transcendent reality beyond the natural world. Hence, transcendence is identified with an infinite and eternal Being, God, and man is spiritual and immortal because he is made in the image of God and participates in a transcendent world."[48]

The transition to a no-longer religious but philosophical conception of Christianity, to Christian philosophy, means interpreting transcendence as transcendence within the world, exalting man as activity that negates the given, but at the same time limiting his life to a transcendental historical world, immanent in nature.

I think we can say without any doubt that Hegel, believing that he had achieved "Christian philosophy" in the sense I described, encountered Gnosticism and created the conditions in which the opposition between Gnosticism and Christianity could reach the highest degree. There was a sort of victory of Gnosticism over Christianity, in the sense that Christianity was absorbed into a context defined a priori by the Gnostic negations. Let us now recall a sentence by Meinecke[49] who said that classical German philosophy, and especially Hegel, represents the legitimization through history of "evil's great bastard" (Meinecke was referring to the assessment of

47 [TN] Ibid., 223–4.

48 [TN] As far as I can tell, this passage comes from one of the parts of Kojève's book that was not translated into English. I translated it from Del Noce's quotation, which can be found on p. 153 in the Einaudi Italian edition.

49 [TN] Del Noce is apparently referring to Friedrich Meinecke, *Machiavellism: The Doctrine of Raison d'État and Its Place in Modern History*, trans. Douglass Scott (New Haven: Yale University Press, 1957), 350.

Machiavelli and to what later was called "the demonic aspect of politics"[50]). But the truly crucial point that must be emphasized is that Hegel's process of gnosticization and immanentization implies the elimination of the divine image. In this respect, two complementary quotations from Kojève's book are decisive: "therefore, there is no Spirit outside of Man living in the world. And 'God' is objectively real only within this natural World, where He exists only in the form of human theological discourse." "In the final analysis, the God of Christian theology (whose inspiration is ancient and pagan) is given-Being eternally identical to itself, which realizes and manifests itself in and through a natural World, which only manifests the essence and the power of Being that *is*. On the contrary, Hegel's Man is Nothingness which annihilates the given-Being that exists as world, and annihilates himself (as real historical time or History) in and through such annihilation of the given."[51]

It is all too easy to point out that Hegel's doctrine is not an apology for violence, to the extent that it is a speculative gnosis (even if it is an apology for violence in the past), but it becomes one when it is developed into a revolutionary gnosis. And, certainly, I will not discuss here once again the form of political amoralism that can already be found in Marx, and must not be attributed to Leninist or Stalinist deviations; except that there is a strangely persistent optical illusion that makes many people believe that genuine moral ideals guide revolutionary thought, against "mystified morality." What should be a subject of critique today is rather the persistence of this delusion, which affects especially certain Catholic scholars. Is it not completely obvious that a revolution which is supposed to lead to a "totally other" humanity – freed from the slavery and dependency to which it has been subjected until now – cannot be carried out on the foundation of values that belonged to the stage of "human slavery"? In this respect, the sentence that Engels wrote at the beginning of his pamphlet on Feuerbach is worth our consideration: "the thesis that reality is rational leads, according to the rules of Hegelian dialectics, to this other one: everything that exists deserves to die."[52]

Thus, the concept that reality is rational means recognizing that every finite reality is mortal, and extending such an idea of mortality very broadly, to the point of including the very values that are regarded as

50 [TN] See Gerhard Ritter, *The Corrupting Influence of Power*, trans. F.W. Pick (Westport, CT: Hyperion Press, 1979), whose original German title was precisely *Die Dämonie der Macht*.

51 [TN] These quotes also appear to be unpublished in English but can be found in Kojève, *La dialettica e l'idea di morte in Hegel*, 157 and 202.

52 [TN] Friedrich Engels, *Ludwig Feuerbach and the Outcome of Classical German Philosophy* (New York: International Publishers, 1941), 11. In fact, Engels himself is quoting the words of Mephistopheles in Goethe's *Faust*: "Alles was entsteht, ist wert, dass es zugrunde geht."

extra-historical. Mortality in this sense is also tied to the negation of "God's image," and thus to the recognition that empirical reality is normal, and therefore to the rejection of any notion of *natura lapsa*, of a decadence from an original situation as a consequence of some kind of sin.

In Engels this sentence probably had to be read in a Kautskyian sense, which later would be the typical interpretation of the "orthodox Marxist" wing of German Social Democracy. In the sense of trusting that the evolutionary process of history will lead by itself to the collapse of the bourgeois capitalistic system, through the greater and greater efficacy of the very organs that the bourgeoisie has created: parliaments, social-economic centres, parties, trade unions. However, if we read him in terms of philosophy of praxis, we have the most complete justification of violence: *the revolutionary is the executioner of a death sentence that history has pronounced.* Actually, if I remember correctly, there is a sentence of Marx (worded just a little differently[53]) exactly along these lines. What matters is that in the most rigorous formulation of revolutionary thought, which is precisely the Marxian one, all the themes of Hegelian gnosis are preserved, and the renewal of gnosis is accompanied by the ennoblement of violence.

However, if we look at today's situation, it is interesting to consider – more than revolutionary violence, which has been the subject of so many studies – the violence associated with the type of nihilism that is the result of the revolution. This violence is symmetric to the libertine form of gnosis. On this topic, I must say that my ideas match those of Fromm, an author whose background is completely different from mine; even if, of course, I am speaking only of his diagnosis, not of the form of religiosity he proposes – a form of syncretism centred around Zen Buddhism – and even if probably *To Have or to Be?*[54] owes its great success precisely to the vague nature of this religiosity (as for the diagnosis, a traditionalist Catholic could have said the same things, but who would have noticed?). Let us recall how Fromm envisions the relationship between nihilism of values and violence. The earthly city of progress – that is, the *civitas hominis* opposed to the *civitas Dei*, whose development marked the centuries of the modern age, has reached its climax today and is based on an a-religious technocratic spirit – has made dominant the having mode, as burning desire to possess and, consequently, as depersonalization and

53 [TN] "History is the judge – its executioner, the proletarian," in Karl Marx, "Speech at Anniversary of the *People's Paper*," *Marx/Engels Selected Works* (Moscow: Progress Publishers, 1969), 1: 500.

54 [TN] Erich Fromm, *To Have or to Be?* (New York: Bantam, 1981).

reification of oneself and of others. This dominance is in danger of leading not only to partial catastrophes but to a final worldwide catastrophe. Therefore, we must realize that today "for the first time in history *the physical survival of the human race depends on a radical change of the human heart.*"[55] In other words, for the first time in history worldly survival is entrusted to religious conversion.[56]

Leaving aside the particular religiosity that Fromm proposes, let us stop at the first point, the recognition of the primacy of the ethical-religious aspect. It is important to note that *precisely starting from and thanks to this recognition,* and thanks to the consequent use of categories like "to be" and "to have," Fromm has been able to develop a description of alienation in today's world which is undoubtedly much more rigorous than what we are generally used to. Let us focus especially on the Western turn toward nihilism, in order to clarify how the relationship between "nihilism as result" and violence reflects the symmetry with ancient libertine gnosis. According to Fromm, in the second half of our century the authoritarian-obsessive-hoarding character, which appeared for the first time in the sixteenth century, was replaced by what he calls *marketing character.* Thereby, a true revolution took place but *within the bourgeoisie* (it was a transposition of the revolution into the bourgeoisie, so to speak. We can say, in words he does not use, that this transposition defines what today is called "radical society"). By "marketing character" he intends to indicate a phenomenon based on the experience of oneself as a commodity, and of one's value not as "value of use" but as "value of exchange." A living being becomes a commodity on display in the "personality market." Value is established in the same way in the personality market and in the commodity market. What is on sale in the first market are personalities, in the second commodities.

Thus, we reach the highest degree of reification; the reduction of people to objects becomes universal. Indeed, if the concerns of an individual centre on being as desirable as possible, he will give up his I. In fact, we cannot even speak of the I as an unchangeable reality, because it must be constantly changed according to the principle of desirability. Making reification universal is clearly the same as denying ethics altogether and elevating the economic dimension to an absolute. From this perspective, efficiency becomes the only value. But this is not enough: total reification due to the marketing character coincides with the most extreme

55 [TN] Ibid., xxxi (italics in the original).

56 [TN] In the original this sentence is inside the quotation marks, but actually it is not found in Fromm's book.

greed for things (and for other people reduced to things). Therefore, violence is absolutely dominant.

Now, Fromm's description of the having mode can also be interpreted in Augustinian terms, and actually we can say that it reveals all its truth when it is read in this way. Indeed, if we look carefully, the instrumentalist idea of well-being is just a transposition from the vertical dimension to the horizontal dimension of the Augustinian idea that human love is infinite and cannot be satisfied by any finite good. The ascent to God is replaced by the idea that one can conquer the world, that each individual is entitled to do so. This entitlement has no bounds because the subject, having been called into the world without his assent, feels entitled, almost as a compensation for this call, to infinite satisfaction within the world itself. But, of course, an individual man cannot fully realize this conquest. He can reduce other people to his own instruments, but makes himself their instrument in turn, in that cycle of mutual instrumentalization that I mentioned before. In his intervention, Prini rightly recalled that there are three types of violence: against nature, against others, and against oneself.[57] Well, the fully developed having mode coincides with the complete unity of these three types.

Thus, the recent transition of the bourgeoisie to the marketing character (the fact that, in short, the bourgeois spirit has rejected all compromises with traditional values) makes violence universal. It is a sort of *bellum omnium contra omnes*, a situation that will make people look for a Leviathan in sociological techniques, which will work until they stop working (but this would be the beginning of a different and complex discussion, which now I cannot even begin). How to explain this development? The most common explanations are sociological: supposedly, it is a side effect of technocratic progress, of the affluent society. To me, these explanations are wholly insufficient. This metamorphosis of the bourgeoisie implies a philosophy. In a way, the bourgeoisie has defeated the revolutionary spirit through the greatest extension of historical materialism, as materialism that claims to explain historical and human realities. In this respect, this transformation can be said to be the response of the bourgeoisie, in the most secular sense of this word, to the revolution. Alternatively, it can be described as the suicide of the revolution – which indeed originally presented itself as the defender of being

57 [TN] Pietro Prini (1915–2008), Italian existentialist philosopher. Del Noce is referring to Prini's lecture "Analisi filosofica della violenza" [Philosophical analysis of violence] in the same proceedings as the present text, *Violenza: Una ricerca per comprendere*, 15–24.

against having (in Marx's famous *Manuscripts of 1844*[58]) – or as pure secularism.

But the essential point that emerges from Fromm's diagnosis is the following: Marxist and sociological categories are inadequate to carry out a rigorous analysis of the contemporary moral situation. One must resort to the fundamental categories of religious existentialism, "to have" and "to be." One is forced to do so even when one starts from a completely opposite philosophical background, and it is important to note that Fromm admits that he borrowed the title of his work (*To Have or to Be?*) from a book by Gabriel Marcel (*Être et avoir*[59]), which previously he did not know. This is hugely significant. What has been said for the last thirty years? That existentialism was a philosophy of crisis, unaware of its deep social and political roots, and so it belonged to the historical period between 1930 and 1940. That, furthermore, one must distinguish between a leftist form and a religious form of existentialism. The first could play a progressive role against spiritualistic and idealistic rhetoric and in preparing a renewed and improved Enlightenment, or a form of Marxism more adequate to a higher civilization (and we know that these themes were the subject of countless philosophical exercises). The second was said to be a new, nicely packaged version of traditional thought, prompted by the confused circumstances of the crisis, or at best (think of Kierkegaard) an expression of the agony of Christianity. But recent followers of Kierkegaard were considered "beautiful souls" (this expression was very popular in the years immediately after the war) whose concern was to live on good terms with a crisis which they recognized verbally.

Today we discover that religious existentialism – with its specific characteristic of being a philosophy that is "modern" and in no way "modernistic" or amenable to a modernist development because it does not intend to adapt faith to the modern word, but rather to retrieve truths and values that modern thought and civilization have sacrificed – instead of being an exhausted form of thought, is the type of philosophy that can explain the alienation and violence (which, if one looks closely, are the same thing) that characterize today's world.

Clearly, this is only the beginning of a discussion. I think that its future lines of development are relatively well delineated. As a temporary conclusion, I will recall a very beautiful sentence by Kierkegaard: "it is the

58 [TN] Karl Marx, *Economic and Philosophic Manuscripts of 1844*, trans. Martin Milligan (New York: Prometheus Books, 1988).

59 Gabriel Marcel, *Être et avoir* (Paris: Aubier, 1935) [TN: *Being and Having: An Existentialist Diary*, trans. Katherine Farrer (New York: Harper & Row, 1965)].

peculiarity of the human race that just because the individual is created *in the image of God* 'the individual' is above the race."[60]

During the last few years, Kierkegaard has been an unfashionable thinker. He was considered the expression of a tragic awareness that has now been left behind in favour of revolutionary thought or of a renewed Enlightenment or, more recently, of the permanent insurrection of the man of desire. On the contrary, it seems to me that today the conditions are ripe to fully understand him. A moment ago I briefly outlined the process of development from Hegel to the ennoblement of violence, emphasizing that in Hegelian negativity the image of God is lost. Kierkegaard's sentence contains the only possible critique of violence. It also says that the first truth of Genesis ("man created in the image and likeness of God") must be understood literally and not metaphorically, that is, not according to the typical interpretation of humanitarianism, in which others are regarded as God's children because we love them, so that the brotherhood of God's children is just a metaphor to indicate a merely human love.

But we now have a recent document that illustrates this truth in the highest possible way, by demonstrating that only if we recognize it can we settle the *pari* that man faces on the eve of the second millennium, which can mark a new advent or an unprecedented catastrophe. I am speaking, obviously, of John Paul II's first encyclical, *Redemptor Hominis,* which is a fundamental text for anybody interested in studying the question of violence. The emotion I felt when I read it has permeated all the thoughts I have shared, and I think and hope that I did not betray its spirit.

60 [TN] Søren A. Kierkegaard, *The Journals of Kierkegaard,* trans. Alexander Dru (New York: Harper and Row, 1959), 187; italics by Del Noce.

3

Revolution, Risorgimento, *Tradition*

THE WORD "REVOLUTION" has multiple meanings that, at first sight, do not seem unifiable. So much so that it is always accompanied by some adjective and seems to be circumscribed to the area indicated by that adjective. To bring up an example that may seem frivolous to the point of absurdity, sometimes one hears, and reads in magazines, that miniskirts mark a "revolution" in women's fashion. But how is this "revolution" related to socio-economic or religious revolution? (Although, looking carefully, there is a relationship because there is no minute detail of human life that does not reflect or, to be exact, does not "symbolize" a general conception of life.)

But a deeper examination shows that the different meanings can be set in order, until one arrives at a definition of the concept of "total revolution." The study of this process leads us also to define the lines of thought that are antithetical to the revolution and that cannot be reduced, as we shall see, to the generic notion of "reaction." This goes against the popular habit, which is also shared by many scholars, of generically setting in opposition the words "revolution" and "reaction." I will also try to identify the philosophical premises that inform this habit.

Let us ask, first, why the word has multiple meanings. Revolution denotes a "break" of continuity: an order is replaced by another that is not a mere "development" of the previous one (at the end of the last century people used to contrast the concepts of "revolution" and "evolution").

This chapter is from the first three parts of "Rivoluzione, Risorgimento, Tradizione," *L'Europa* 6, no. 17 (1972): 129–41. Republished in *Rivoluzione Risorgimento Tradizione* (Milan: Giuffrè, 1993), 427–43. The complete original piece also includes a fourth section on the concept of alienation in Marxian philosophy.

Such a break implies a stage in which the previous order is destroyed and a stage in which the new order is built. Keeping in mind these two stages, we understand and we can easily organize the various meanings. We only have to list the different ways in which the word revolution is used in common speech:

a. The first and oldest meaning, which is also the only one to have been used before the end of the 1700s, associates this word primarily with the idea of "disorder." Thus, a revolution is the same as a popular, leaderless rebellion, or one steered from outside by demagogues and adventurers, by sectarian and doctrinaire figures. In short, the leadership includes simpletons, fanatics, and profiteers, and the latter always prevail. From this perspective, the revolution has a purely political and social significance, as a change of government carried out by force and violence, either as a popular uprising or as a popular usurpation. Therefore, in this case the emphasis is placed mostly on the destructive aspect, without making any clear distinction between "rebellion" and "revolution." This was the common meaning until the French Revolution.

However, it remained in use also within the conservative branch of positivism and among the sociologists who criticized democracy, who usually drew their inspiration from Taine's works. Thus, the revolution becomes "an aspect of the psychology of crowds," according to a formula that was used at the turn of last century by a French sociologist, Gustave Le Bon, who authored a very important book about crowd psychology.[1] It is a "disease of the social body whose causes we have to find," and so on. In this case, the antidote to the revolutionary position is usually sought in a form of liberal conservatism, aimed at finding orderly ways for progress to take place, without any crises that may lead to a plebeian dictatorship. A clear example is found in the works of Gaetano Mosca, whose thought is directly connected to Taine's.[2]

b. A second meaning is juridical: revolution denotes any change of the political system of the political societies known as states when that transformation takes place in violation of the principles of constitutional law that give concrete form to the order itself, i.e., without following the procedures that regulate its legitimate partial transformations. This meaning differs from the first because violence, in the destructive sense, is essential to the first and not to the second. In the first sense the

1 [TN] Gustave Le Bon, *The Crowd: A Study of the Popular Mind*, trans. D.S. Snedden (New York: Macmillan, 1896).

2 [TN] Gaetano Mosca (1858–1941), Italian political scientist and journalist.

revolution is an irrational event; in the second it may be allowed or required by meta-positive juridical principles.

c. A third meaning is ethico-political: the "sorgimento" [rising] of a new order, as an inseparably moral and political reality which cannot be explained as a simple evolution of what existed before. For instance, we speak in this sense of the Italian Risorgimento as a revolutionary process, inasmuch as it was a "sorgimento" [a rising]. This is what motivates its description as a model of a "liberal" revolution, and not a "Jacobin" one. (Along these lines *L'Europa* often speaks of European unification as a true revolution[3]).

d. In a fourth sense, "revolutionary" is an ideal category that is reached through a philosophical process. It means man's liberation, through politics, from the "alienation" that has been forced on him by the hitherto existing social orders and that derives only from the structure of such orders. Therefore, this fourth meaning implies the replacement of religion by politics as the source of man's liberation, since evil is a consequence of society, which has become the subject of blame, and not of an original sin. As varied as revolutionary forms can be, their common feature is, in this sense, the correlation between the elevation of politics to religion and the negation of the supernatural. This category or structure was analysed for the first time, in negative terms, by Joseph de Maistre, who was the first to recognize it not as an accident but as an "epoch." He pointed out that the revolution uses men, instead of being guided by them, and is not aware of its own teleology, which is destructive since it is directed toward total disintegration, regardless of the delusions that may be entertained by those who prepared the revolution or by those who guide it. For them, instead, the "Revolution" – capitalized and singular – is the unique event, as painful as the travail of childbirth, that mediates the transition from the reign of necessity to the reign of freedom, where the latter is described (and it could not be otherwise) merely by negating the institutions and the ideas of the past. This event generates a "future" in which nothing will resemble the old history. It thus brings to completion the work of history.[4] Needless to say, this last sense is the only one that truly concerns philosophy, and the process of incubation of this idea has been relatively brief: from Rousseau to Marx, in whom we find the complete and insuperable formulation of the idea of total revolution. Certainly we can also speak of

3 [TN] The present essay was originally published in the journal *L'Europa*.

4 Clearly, whoever is a revolutionary in this sense can never talk about "revolutions" in the plural. What he participates in is "the" revolution.

another direction of revolutionary thought, irreducible to the Marxist one, which goes from de Sade's atheism to Surrealism and which found its expression in the Marx-Freudian mixture and in the revolutionary attempt of the student rebellion. But to me this second direction seems rather a stage in the process by which the revolution turns into disintegration. Of course, one can speak of forerunners, and there are infinitely many: strictly speaking, it is possible to find within Marxism, in a peculiar *coincidentia oppositorum*, all forms of heterodox thought separated from the aspects that made possible a reconciliation with transcendent thought. For instance, utopian and, especially, heretical thought. The encounter, in Marxism, between gnostic and revolutionary thought is especially important. But these forerunners are not to be interpreted in the sense of being part of a development. On the contrary, we must insist on the "novelty" of revolutionary thought, in which some aspects of earlier philosophies are transfigured and brought to completion. This also applies to the relationship between Hegel and Marx.

REVOLUTION AND *RISORGIMENTO*

There is yet one more meaning, which is clearly distinct from that of "total revolution." It is the idea of a restoration of an eternal ideal order which supposedly has been violated. Hence the idea of a "moral" revolution, moral because it is required by traditional moral principles. It is about promoting an action which is morally necessary and which is revolutionary in the sense that it aims at toppling a global system which can no longer be reformed because any reform would only make it worse and more inhuman. Therefore, this type of revolution coincides with a restoration of values and with a deepening and a purification of tradition. In this sense, Mazzini is a revolutionary (hence the opposition between him and Marx, which is absolutely radical) and also Gioberti,[5] whose philosophical exploration was deeper. But we cannot stop at these names, or just at Italy or just at the 1800s. Strictly speaking, not even at religious thinkers (in the sense of those who affirm the existence of a transcendent God). For instance, Auguste Comte fits in this line of revolution-restoration because his concern is to restore the spiritual power that in the Middle Ages had been exercised by the Church and today can be exercised only by science.

Strictly speaking, this is the same *renovatio*, in the sense of "going back to the principles," which can already be found in Machiavelli,

5 [TN] Vincenzo Gioberti (1801–52), Italian philosopher and politician of the age of *Risorgimento*.

although in a different sense, which was also discussed by Leo XIII, and which was the source of inspiration for every reawakening of the religious spirit during the Middle Ages (think, for instance, of the Franciscan movement).

In our century a writer who greatly emphasized this theme, in fascinatingly beautiful pages, was Charles Péguy (who died in 1914 in the First World War), followed in various ways by several French writers (let us recall, even if they are different, the works by Jacques Maritain and those by Simone Weil; among more recent works those by Jacques Ellul, who has given us one of the best books about the idea of revolution, *Autopsie de la révolution*[6]). Generally, the French prefer to use the word revolution to describe this position as well, qualifying it with various adjectives: "moral," "personalist," "necessary," etc. This usage, however, lends itself to misunderstandings and sometimes to confusion with the very different concept of revolution that I just discussed.

In Italy, instead, we have available a word which is perfectly adequate to express this notion, if it is used (as Gioberti did) to indicate not just a historical event but a real philosophical-political category: the word *risorgimento.* It conveys the idea that nations can rise again only by exploring more deeply their tradition, and by criticizing the historical order from the standpoint of an ideal order. If the first principle of the "total revolution" is the "future," the ideal principle of the *risorgimento* (understood in this way) is the "Eternal."

With this discussion, we have also briefly defined the ideal positions that are antithetical to the revolutionary one. Conservatism in the best sense, as "conservation of freedom," corresponds, by antithesis, to disorder or to the plebeian or Jacobin dictatorship into which an inadequate revolution disintegrates (in this regard it would be important to study how Gaetano Mosca and Benedetto Croce, starting from different philosophical premises, found common ground on this point). The other position that I just briefly described, and that has not yet found a sufficiently rigorous definition (it has not found its Marx, we might say), corresponds by antithesis to the total revolution.

It is very important to formulate this interpretation because it differs sharply from a judgment that today is common: the idea that, at least after the Russian revolution, counter-revolutionary thought can only take the form of Fascism and go down a line of increasing irrationalization until in Nazism it becomes radically evil. This is the position that is argued, for instance, in Lukács's well-known book *The Destruction of*

6 [TN] Jacques Ellul, *Autopsy of Revolution,* trans. Patricia Wolf (New York: Alfred A. Knopf, 1968).

Reason, which is essentially a commentary on Lenin's statement that today the only choice is between Communism and radical barbarism, based on the study of the process of irrationalization, in the sense of constant decadence, that supposedly took place in German philosophy from the late Schelling all the way to Hitler.[7] In my judgment, Fascism is actually a heresy of Communism based on the thesis that Marxist revolutionary thought must be sublated, a sublation that supposedly can be achieved by accepting the Idealistic critique of Marxist philosophy. As for Nazism, it is a "revolution going in the opposite direction" rather than a reactionary form, and seems to confirm the condemnation of this type of politics that had already been expressed by de Maistre in a famous statement ("A counter-revolution is not a revolution in the opposite direction, but the opposite of a revolution"[8]).

CONSERVATION, REACTION, TRADITION

However, it is important that we try to clarify a little better the concepts of conservation and tradition and the irreducible distinction between them.

Doctrinally, conservatism is reached through the critique of utopia, of the idea that it is possible to achieve a worldly situation in which all contradictions have been solved, and to create conditions in which there is a perfect harmony between virtue and happiness, so that happiness can be realized without effort and without sacrifice. Going to the limit, we can say that the essence of utopia is the idea of "universal worldly happiness." Ultimately, this principle leads to the denial of the very idea of virtue in the traditional sense (which is replaced by material happiness) or to the provisional justification (but the meaning of "provisional" would deserve a lengthy discussion) of every cruelty and every violation of the moral order for the sake of future universal happiness.

The critique of utopia and of its practical consequences is carried out in the name of experience. One then arrives at the general principle that the duration of a given country's institutions proves that they exist for a reason, and that modifications and improvements are possible but always within the context of such institutions. This genetic process shows that,

7 [TN] Georg Lukács, *The Destruction of Reason*, trans. Peter Palmer (London: The Merlin Press, 1980).

8 [TN] Joseph de Maistre, *Considerations on France*, trans. Richard A. Lebrun (Montreal & Kingston: McGill-Queen's University Press, 1974), 169.

in general, conservatism is associated with a skeptical type of empiricism. Sometimes, however, it is also associated with an Idealistic type of historicism, and thus reflects an identification of God with history.

This identification makes the negation of the past that is typical of revolutionary thought repugnant. This is the case of the mature Hegel, and also of Croce (it is not coincidental that Croce found common ground precisely with that Hegel, as opposed to the Hegel of the *Phenomenology*, who is still "tragic" and filled with revolutionary ferments). It sometimes leads to a form of religious pessimism that, during the modern centuries, was widespread especially in the 1600s (Pascal, Malebranche. It is the religious pessimism that the progressivism of the Enlightenment reacted against).

The structure of reactionary thought is completely different, and again we have to fight a widespread opinion that says that thought becomes reactionary to the extent that progressive or revolutionary movements advance and pose a real threat of seizing power. Then, before giving up, conservatives supposedly stop being tolerant and become authoritarian. They finally end up accepting or running a police state, and thus become reactionary in the strict sense of the word.

This thesis is superficial. Obviously one can find in the world both noble and ignoble souls, and among conservatives one can find people who "own" (you cannot be conservative unless you defend something you already own, either in an ideal or in a factual sense) and who regard as the best regime the one that best defends their interests and their selfishness, possibly sending to jail whoever dares to criticize it. However, identifying "conservative" with "selfish" is just as arbitrary as identifying "revolutionary" with "troublemaker." From a pessimistic standpoint, we can say that every "selfish owner" is "conservative" and every "troublemaker" is "revolutionary," as long as we add that the opposite implication is not true, in both cases.

Let us now consider the structure of reactionary thought. Whereas a conservative is reconciled with present reality, even if only in the sense of regarding it as the least bad possible, a reactionary is completely dissatisfied and regards the present as a state of decadence with respect to some past historical situation. Hence, he wants to go back in time, to an age when the seeds of such decadence and disintegration did not exist, or rather when they were hardly perceivable. Thus, the forms of utopia that take an archaeological form belong to reactionary thought. This form is destined to be "always" defeated by some revolutionary form of utopia. For instance, in Marxism we find all the themes of reactionary and counter-revolutionary thought of the first half of the nineteenth century, but transfigured by tension toward the future.[9] The mistake of reactionary thought is that it confuses the affirmation of supra-historical principles with the image of a realized historical situation, so that it ends up thinking that in order to affirm eternal principles one cannot admit "new problems," problems that must be solved in relation to those principles but after having been recognized as "novel." Otherwise, one is in mortal danger of thinking that the principles themselves are historical. Because of this mistake, it has been said that the formula *sic vos non vobis*[10] applies to reactionary thought, meaning that it is destined to be a stage in the development of something else, i.e., in the transition from one phase of progressive thought to the next.

In this regard, it is interesting to observe that precisely when Catholics forgot de Maistre – who, however, is not "only" reactionary in the sense I just described – Omodeo[11] instead rediscovered him, in one of his best books, as the transitional stage from the unmediated and uncritical spirit of Jacobinism to the maturity of nineteenth-century liberalism.

A similar theme, in fact, has become habitual and clichéd in Communist historiography. I have in front of me a book by a Soviet scholar, L.M. Batkin, *Dante and the Italian Society of the 1300s.*[12] At face value, who is looking back at the past more than Dante, the defender of the imperial idea and of universal monarchy at the time when it was fading away and the nations were rising, a nostalgic of Cacciaguida's[13] patriarchal world, and a ferocious critic of the mores of his time? But actually, according to this scholar, by despising "the cruel and petty merchant mentality of nascent capitalism,"[14] Dante supposedly spoke for the great popular

9 Restricting ourselves just to Germany, we find truly remarkable analyses of the proletarian condition precisely in the most reactionary writers, such as Adam Müller and Franz von Baader. The latter, in an essay of 1835, uses explicitly the word "proletariat," starting with the title [TN: "Über das dermalige Mißverhältnis der Vermögenslosen oder Proletairs zu den Vermögen besitzenden Klassen der Sozietät" (On the existing disproportion between the have-nots or proletarians and the propertied classes of society) in Franz von Baader, *Schriften zur Gesellschaftsphilosophie* (Munich: 1835), 319–38]. Of course, in these authors such analysis goes together with the idea of a decadence that supposedly took place with the transition from the Middle Ages to the modern age.

10 [TN] "Thus you [do but] not for yourselves" (traditionally attributed to Virgil).

11 [TN] Adolfo Omodeo (1889–1946) was an Italian historian. The book Del Noce refers to is *Un reazionario: il Conte Joseph De Maistre* [A reactionary: Count Joseph de Maistre] (Bari: Laterza, 1939).

12 [TN] Leonid M. Batkin, *Dante e la società italiana del '300*, Italian trans. Sergio Leone (Bari: De Donato, 1970).

13 [TN] Cacciaguida degli Elisei was an ancestor of Dante who appears in *canti* XV–XVII of the *Paradise.*

14 [TN] Batkin, *Dante*, 202.

masses and thus for the "Communes, which were the healthiest and most progressive part of Italian society."[15] Not only this: although there seems to be an abyss between Dante and Marsilius of Padua, according to this scholar they actually were spiritual brothers. I suppose that the recent Soviet rediscovery of Dostoevsky must move along similar lines.

So, from the truth that "purely" reactionary thought must yield to revolutionary thought we move to abusive cooptation, to the claim that the great critics of revolutionary thought are progressive, or germinally so.

But in fact "purely" reactionary thought does not exist. It is a mixture of the supra-historical interpretation of the permanence of principles with utopianism shifted to the past. It seems to yield to revolutionary thought only if it is considered according to the second aspect, absorbing into it entirely and arbitrarily the first aspect. However, if we take both aspects into account and we view the second as a defect of the first, we realize that it is instead a transitional stage both between the principle of conservation and that of tradition and also, from another point of view, between different stages of progressive thought.

Now let us consider the concept of "tradition." By itself the word may seem rather ambiguous. Indeed, what does tradition mean according to its etymology? What is transmitted, what is handed down. However, the ambiguity is more apparent than real. In fact, it is clear that we cannot attribute "value" based on tradition. It is clear that nothing "has value" only because it has been handed down, since, for instance, the rituals of black masses or the most evil arts are also handed down and taught. Thus, it is completely evident that "value" is the foundation of tradition and not the other way around. However, the formula "traditional values" has the following meaning: there exist absolute and supra-historical values which "therefore" must be "handed down." There exists an "order" which is unchangeable, even for God Himself. His "authority" is not at all a "repressive" imposition because it is an uncreated order, the object of non-sensitive intuition. Only with this meaning does the word "authority" recover its etymological significance (from "augere," to make grow) and we can speak of liberating authority.

If we understand the concept of tradition in this way, we realize that today the ultimate categories that define the struggle between opposing political positions are not "progress" and "reaction," but rather "revolution" and "tradition." At the theoretical level Marxism draws its significance from being the most radical negation, simultaneously and inseparably, of original sin and of the principle of non-contradiction, the

15 [TN] Ibid., 203.

affirmation of the primacy of being over becoming, which is the foundation of classical metaphysics and of the idea of tradition. Every revolutionary negation of traditional values depends on this initial negation. Perhaps nobody has illuminated this point better than Marcuse in his best work, *Reason and Revolution* from 1941.[16] Therefore, the possible theoretical and practical defeat of Marxism brings us back, on the one hand, to the question of original sin and to an awareness of all the themes related to it, which we have forgotten because of a long-standing Pelagian mindset. I mean the themes of libido, which have now been rediscovered by science but from a rationalistic perspective, which warps them. And, at the same time, it allows us to understand anew and more deeply the principle of non-contradiction on which, according to St Thomas, the whole system of truth is founded and which can be proved only in a negative fashion, through the self-refutation of its adversaries as is happening just now. And, finally, it makes possible a renewed understanding of the unity of classical philosophy and Catholic religious faith, whose negation is the origin of religious-political Modernism in all its manifestations. Let me emphasize that this is crucial. The ultimate endpoint of Marxism is the endpoint of the whole cycle of political thought that started with Marsilius of Padua. And it leads us to solve the new problems in light of the principles elaborated by the cycle of political thought that goes from Plato to Dante.

16 Herbert Marcuse, *Ragione e Rivoluzione*, Italian trans. Alberto Izzo (Bologna: Il Mulino, 1966), 159ff. [TN: Herbert Marcuse, *Reason and Revolution* (New York: Humanities Press, 1968), 136ff.]

4

The Latent Metaphysics within Contemporary Politics

TODAY WE ARE DISCUSSING THE QUESTION of the role of philosophy in the history of our century. What is the relation between the developments of philosophy and political history? How significant are the causal effects of ideas? One realizes immediately that these questions can be answered in two opposite ways. In fact, one may think that in our century philosophy and history went their separate ways, like never before in previous ages. Certainly, every political movement sought legitimization from some philosophical tradition in order to receive its cultural sanction, especially during the last few decades. This gave rise to the profession of the ideologue, which is not too different, essentially, from what used to be the job of courtiers in the age of humanism; the difference being that back then courtiers compared political leaders to the heroes of Plutarch, whereas the new teachers depict them as forward looking people and pioneers of new ages. But, according to the current opinion, the first task of those who really shape history is to set aside ideologies and look at things realistically. And the reverse is also said to be true: the only authentic philosophies are those that do not lend themselves to becoming political ideologies. It is easy to support this thesis with examples. Indeed, think of which philosophers never went out of fashion during the last few decades: so far, Heidegger and Wittgenstein, who seem to be the least political among philosophers, whose philosophy cannot be extended into politics, have never experienced any decline in their fortunes. Conversely, interest has unquestionably waned – and I am not formulating any judgment of value – in all the philosophers who engaged in politics, regardless of what side they took. For example,

This chapter was originally published as "La metafisica latente nella realtà politica contemporanea" in the volume *Cultura del fare e cultura dell'essere* [Culture of doing vs culture of being] (Rome: Japadre, 1988), 61–76.

speaking of Italy, in Gentile and also in Croce. On the Catholic side, in Maritain himself. On the opposite side, in Sartre and Lukács.

However, accepting this thesis requires a critique of the thesis that prevailed for many years, which says that never before in modern history was the relationship between philosophy and history so close. It is a fact that the nearly half century from the end of the war until now has been marked, from a philosophical standpoint, by the rediscovery of the philosophers of the nineteenth century who had previously been regarded as marginal (at least as philosophers), Marx and Nietzsche. They were rediscovered precisely as interpreters of our time, in the sense of Hegel's famous statement that philosophy is its own time apprehended in thought.[1] What I want to add now is that today we must move on from the relevance of Marx and Nietzsche to the relevance of de Maistre, precisely in the sense that we cannot give Marx and Nietzsche the place they deserve in the history of philosophy without recognizing what de Maistre represents. Thus, from Marx and Nietzsche to de Maistre: this statement may seem paradoxical and it is not.

Some clarifications are in order: I am not thinking of de Maistre as the theoretician of a hierocratic restoration, but as the phenomenologist of the revolution, and at the same time as the initiator of the rebirth of Catholic philosophy after the French Revolution. Nineteenth-century Catholic thought, which is the precondition for our century's Catholic thought, cannot be understood apart from the Savoyard writer. This thesis would deserve to be discussed at length, since it goes against the standard opinions. Here, I will just mention that there has been work in this direction, even if the prevalent interpretation still regards de Maistre's thought as a form of Gnosticism that, deep down, is extraneous to Catholicism.

Thus, I will elaborate only one thought: what does it mean that de Maistre is relevant today after the recognition of Marx's philosophical power *and* of the catastrophe of Marxism? The recognition of this catastrophe coincides with the present relevance of Nietzsche, understood in its proper sense (meaning that today we view Nietzsche differently from the way people viewed him at the beginning of the century, and so on).

It is a commonplace that the philosophies of history, from Lessing onwards, are secularized forms of the theologies of history that preceded them, and that this gradual secularization of theology sets the tempo for the process of secularization of the modern world. This was the topic of a book by Karl Löwith, widely read forty years ago, about the theological

1 [TN] Georg W.F. Hegel, *Elements of the Philosophy of Right*, ed. Allan W. Wood, trans. Hugh B. Nisbet (Cambridge: Cambridge University Press, 1991), 21.

premises of the philosophy of history, which, however, has the limitation of pushing to the side the entire Catholic philosophy of history, from de Maistre and Bonald to the Thomist revival.[2] It thus supports the usual opinion that such a philosophy of history is just the mirror image of the other, in opposition. If we follow this line – and if we actually consider another thinker who is more directly interested in the political dimension, Voegelin – then the assertion that the philosophies of history conceived in the nineteenth century became realized – or produced their catastrophic outcomes – in our century does not look paradoxical at all.

Let us recall the most important among Marx's famous *Theses on Feuerbach*, the second one: "The question whether objective truth can be attributed to human thinking is not a question of theory but is a practical question. In practice man must prove the truth, i.e., the reality and power, the 'this-sidedness' of his thinking. The dispute over the reality or non-reality of thinking which is isolated from practice is a purely scholastic question."[3] In other words, the truth of a philosophy is verified by the historical reality it is able to produce. Modern philosophy breaks away from scholasticism, and from whatever scholastic elements it still includes, only inasmuch as it becomes philosophy of praxis. Since the characteristic of Marxism that distinguishes it from Hegelianism is that of being a philosophy *ante factum rather than a philosophy post factum* – i.e., aimed at realizing a totality instead of understanding an already-realized totality – we could go as far as to regard the history of the twentieth century as a *philosophical experiment,* and ask ourselves whether that experiment failed or not.

Today, talking about Marx feels like discussing a distant thinker. Undoubtedly, the 1980s marked the decline of the great fortune of Marxism that characterized the decades immediately after the Second World War. It was a sudden decline and was followed by the rediscovery of the philosopher who used to be viewed as Marx's greatest adversary, Nietzsche. Accordingly, the word revolution was replaced in popularity by the word nihilism. However, upon reflection, the fortunes of these two words are not as unrelated as they may seem. Indeed, Nietzsche's current relevance is not associated with the theme of the superman, but rather with the theme of nihilism, and this nihilism is accepted rather than experienced as tragic (think of "weak thought," its spread and its popularity). We could say that the transition from the fortune of the

2 [TN] Karl Löwith, *Meaning in History: The Theological Implications of the Philosophy of History* (Chicago: University of Chicago Press, 1949).

3 [TN] In Frederick Engels, *Ludwig Feuerbach and the Outcome of Classical German Philosophy* (New York: International Publishers, 1941), 82.

revolutionary myth to the fortune of nihilistic thought has coincided with the transition from strong thought to weak thought. In other words, the current nihilistic fashion is simply the acceptance of the outcome of the total revolution, inasmuch as it failed. However, this acceptance is still shaped by the revolutionary perspective, as is demonstrated by the fact that, generally speaking, the people who have embraced today's forms of nihilism are those who earlier practised revolutionary thought. Equivalently: considered according to its ultimate meaning, which it achieves precisely in Marx, the idea of revolution implies the idea of a meta-humanity; this means a reality that is totally other; hence, it implies a previous denial of the values that earlier had been regarded as supreme; stopping at such a denial is the definition of nihilism. Therefore, there is really nothing remarkable about the fact that nihilism follows revolutionary thought. It is the result of the revolution: of its success in demolishing the old values and of its failure to build new values. Not by chance, the same young intellectuals who earlier preached the revolution in the name of Marx have become reconciled with neo-capitalist society in the name of Nietzsche, making a perfectly smooth transition from their old position to the new. It is a reconciliation via a negative route, but still a reconciliation.

I spoke of the particular meaning that the idea of revolution takes in Marx. Here, it is worth making a digression about the fact that Marxism is different from all other philosophical positions, and incompatible with every one of them. As a result, in Marx every single term of political philosophy takes a different meaning from the one that was used, and is still used, in common speech. Consequently, Marxism cannot be understood within the categories of the "sociology of revolutions," possibly viewing it as the extreme manifestation. Indeed, according to the common use of the word, revolution means that a new ruling class replaces, with a sharp break, the one that was in power before. According to Marx, instead, it means abolishing classes and the struggle between them. Therefore, the core of Marx's philosophy – which is already found in the writings of his youth and to which he remained always faithful – must be identified as *the rejection of every form of dependence* and thus the extinction of religion, since God is the archetype of a worldly lord. Hence, the revolution represents a transition not just from one social situation to another, but from one stage of mankind to another. That is, *there is no analogy between the reign of necessity and dependence and the reign of freedom; i.e., the transition from one to the other requires a revolution capable of transforming human nature itself.*

The two meanings of the word revolution must be rigorously distinguished. Even according to the most traditional forms of thought, there may be legitimate revolutions, when human rights are violated. But a revolution that denies all rights to present humanity in order to transfer the fullness of rights to a future humanity is a different object. It is in this sense that de Maistre described the French Revolution as an unprecedented historical event, referring to its Jacobin aspect. Later, that same revolutionary idea, whose novelty had been understood by the Savoyard thinker, reached its final point of development in Marxism. When I said that the Marxian revolution is aimed at building a new humanity or a totally other reality, I was referring to this strong sense of the word. This formula "a totally other reality," which has been often used in contemporary theology, can also be used, understood in a secular sense, to define Marx's position. It is at this point that revolutionary thought meets a Gnostic type of religiosity. In the Gnostic texts we find the idea of two worlds, each one with its own God, and the idea that the true God is the God of the "new" world, of a world still to come which is the very opposite of the present world in which man lives as a "stranger" (what Marxists call alienation). The future or "world-to-come" of the revolutionaries seems the modern translation of the "true" God of the Gnostics. Thus, it seems that, with respect to revolutionary thought, we can legitimately speak of a post-Christian gnosis, meaning a form of gnosis that has been renewed after the Christian affirmation of man's transcendence over nature and has shifted from a cosmological to an anthropological perspective. Undoubtedly this shift includes one huge difference, that between the liberation of the soul from the world, the goal of ancient Gnosticism, and the revolutionary transformation of the world itself. Nevertheless, the parallel with Gnostic thought is meaningful because it lets us dispose of the interpretations that were so common just a few years ago and viewed Marxism as a Christian heresy or as a form of anonymous Christianity, and thus as a schism to be healed. I do not need to discuss now how much such an idea burdened post-conciliar theology and also some political movements. Let us just say that it was extremely influential. The repeated attempts at reconciling Christianity and Marxism, that sort of broader ecumenism to which so many theologians devoted themselves, were based, essentially, on this completely incorrect idea.

Ending the digression, now we can say that the true antithesis of the idea of revolution, understood in the strong sense, is not the idea of nihilism but that of Providence. The idea of Providence, as affirmation of the divine governance of the world, is the opposite of the idea of Revolution, aimed at achieving its complete human governance. For such an idea of Providence, let us use Vico's classic definition: "but this world without doubt has issued from a mind often diverse, at times quite contrary, and always superior to the particular ends that men had proposed to themselves."[4] However, we must understand it in a sense closer to de Maistre's than to Vico's original sense, which was essentially optimistic. Indeed, if the revolution completely succeeded and completely failed at the same time, since it realized not something different from what it intended, but the very opposite, if in its regard we must speak of a complete heterogenesis of ends,[5] then the outcome of the revolution brings us back to counter-revolutionary thought. In particular, it reveals to us the deep meaning of remarks by de Maistre that previously were ignored. Because, which account of the history of philosophy (including Catholic accounts) has so far paid adequate attention to the thinker from Savoy?

Precisely the historical outcome of the revolution, viewed as man's greatest attempt to deny his own limitations, creates the conditions to reopen theological discourse. Essentially, this line of thought comes close to that of Dostoevsky, who regarded atheism pushed to the highest degree as the condition for the discovery of God. Recognizing the philosophical power of the two great atheists Marx and Nietzsche is the condition for a renewal of religious thought.

Attributing philosophical significance to the historical experience of Communism in our century, as proof of the simultaneous success and failure of the revolutionary idea, is not possible unless we can demonstrate: (1) that Marxism could only become realized historically precisely in the way it did; (2) that it must be viewed as the primary subject of contemporary history, because the movements that sought to dominate the world after Marxism (and that cannot be explained as developments of previous traditions) either are subordinate to Marxism in opposition because they just turn it upside down – because, in the words of de Maistre,[6] they are just revolutions in the opposite direction – or are consequential aspects of Marxism's necessary philosophical decomposition.

But what do I mean by philosophical decomposition? We must realize that Marxism constitutes the greatest synthesis of opposites that ever appeared in the history of thought. Let us consider the two essential dyads, the unity of materialism and dialectics and the unity of utopianism and political realism, both of which are pushed to their extreme consequences.

4 [TN] Giambattista Vico, *The New Science of Giambattista Vico*, trans. Thomas G. Bergin and Max H. Fisch (Ithaca: Cornell University Press, 1984), 425.

5 [TN] See footnote 19 on p. 18.

6 [TN] Joseph de Maistre, *Considerations on France*, ed. and trans. Richard A. Lebrun (Montreal & Kingston: McGill-Queen's University press, 1974), 169.

In fact, materialism is an essential aspect of the revolution understood in the sense I stated before. The revolution cannot be carried out by man as a participant in absolute and meta-historical values, or as an expression of an immanent God. Instead, it will have to be carried out by sensible reality, understood in the broadest sense that also includes history; by such material reality inasmuch as man participates in it with his sensible activity, in an organic exchange with nature. The dialectical aspect is just as necessary.

Utopianism reaches the highest degree. This is why Marx, unlike ordinary utopians, does not linger on describing the future society, and only says generically what it will not be like. He does so because he conceives his future society as so completely other with respect to the existing one that trying to describe it would be slipping into reverie. Another reason is that earlier forms of utopic communism had been able to indulge in such descriptions because what they proposed as the ideal reality was present reality freed from its contradictions, whereas for Marxism the reality to be created by the revolution was the result of those very contradictions and of their explosion. But this utopianism coexists with an extreme form of political realism. Indeed, the fact that all values are merged into one, the Revolution, must end up dissolving ethics into politics altogether. We can then understand the deep meaning of a sentence by Lenin during the October Revolution, which at first may sound like hyperbole, a propaganda slogan uttered at a particularly tense time: "Morality is whatever serves the success of the proletarian revolution."[7] This statement is presented as obvious, and it would be easy to find its antecedents both in the statements about ethics by Marx and Engels and in later theoreticians of Marxism-Leninism, Gramsci included. People like to see in Gramsci the most humane expression of Communism, but he did write that every act can be regarded as virtuous or wicked only in reference to its effect in helping or hindering the success of the revolutionary cause.[8] We can say that the novelty of completely including ethics within politics also constitutes the novelty, with respect to all other previous political orders, of what is usually called totalitarianism. In fact, it is

7 [TN] I believe Del Noce is either paraphrasing or using a different translation of one among various statements to this effect found in V.I. Lenin, "The Tasks of the Youth Leagues" in *Collected Works*, trans. Julius Katzer (Moscow: Progress Publishers, 1966), 3: 283–99.

8 [TN] "Any given act is seen as useful or harmful, as virtuous or as wicked, only in so far as it has as its point of reference the modern Prince itself, and helps to strengthen or to oppose it." from "Brief Notes on Machiavelli's Politics," in Antonio Gramsci, *Selections from the Prison Notebooks*, ed. and trans. Quentin Hoare and Geoffrey Nowell Smith (London: Lawrence & Wishart, 1971), 133.

totalitarianism's only precise definition, and we can find its necessary theoretical premises in Marx's thought and nowhere else.

Let go through the links in the chain that leads to the heterogenesis of ends. The fulfillment of the revolution can only be entrusted to a force born from a concrete historical situation; only historical reality itself, the result of man's alienation, can turn dialectically into the suppression of such alienation. In order to be total, the revolution requires a social class that can realize itself only by negating entirely the existing society. Thus, Marx arrives at the theory of the proletariat as the only mediator of the transition to the society of equals.

But to fulfill such a historical task the proletariat needs self-awareness. Who can provide it? In 1903, setting the premises on which later the Communist Party would be built, Lenin answered that "class political consciousness can be brought to the workers *only from without*"[9] since "the working class, exclusively by its own effort, is able to develop only trade-union consciousness."[10] He added that, regarding social status, the founders of contemporary scientific socialism, Marx and Engels, were bourgeois intellectuals. Thus, according to Lenin – who in fact can rely on precise statements by Marx, and to whom the thesis already advanced by Lukács in a small book[11] from 1924 applies, namely that he must be regarded as the greatest thinker of the revolutionary movement since Marx, and as the man who re-established Marx's teachings in their pure form – true philosophy is immanent in the proletariat only virtually, as obscure and confused knowledge, if for no other reason than because the proletariat cannot help being contaminated by the bourgeois thinking that dominates the culture. Hence, in order to be put into practice, this true philosophy needs the action of intellectuals who, however, cannot be regular intellectuals who are unable to escape the bourgeois mindset and whom, therefore, the bourgeoisie chooses as its watch dogs, according to a popular slogan. Thus, what is needed are intellectuals who possess a superior knowledge, which enables them to grasp the development of history in its entirety. Here, the aspect of new gnosis that I mentioned earlier appears in full light. These intellectuals who possess a superior knowledge are effectively the new Gnostics, who in modern times have taken on the appearance of "professional revolutionaries."

9 [TN] V.I. Lenin, "What Is to Be Done?" in *Collected Works*, trans. Joe Fineberg and George Hanna (Moscow: Progress Publishers, 1960), 5: 422.

10 [TN] Ibid., 5: 375.

11 [TN] Georg Lukács, *History and Class Consciousness*, trans. Rodney Livingstone (Boston: MIT Press, 1972).

But their role is necessary, and the alternative described by Lenin is correct: either a revolution made possible only by bringing class consciousness to the proletariat from the outside, or a reformist approach that gives up for good on the idea of the Revolution.

From this follows the replacement of the proletariat by the party, then the dictatorship of the party, and then the new techno-bureaucratic class whose characteristics have received so much attention and are universally known. But what matters is not diagnosing each one of these phenomena in isolation, but rather understanding that they are necessary links in a chain that starts from Marxism considered in its philosophical aspect. This aspect must be recognized as primary in comparison with the revolutionary and the economic aspects.

Understanding this necessity means also understanding the necessary link between Marxism and Leninism, against an opinion that has still some supporters and some important and dangerous reverberations in the political arena, namely the idea that the roots of Lenin's culture and practical action should be sought in Russian revolutionary populism, and that Marxism was completely transfigured when it came in contact with it. On the contrary, we must acknowledge that Lenin was the most consistent interpreter of Marx and, at the same time, that the Communist revolution could succeed only by encountering the Russian populist tradition.

Since time is short, let me make just a brief comment about an extremely important point, which came up at a conference sponsored by some socialist intellectuals a few days ago. We often hear people speak of a Stalinist degeneration of Leninism, of a "Stalinist interlude," and so on. In fact, it is absolutely impossible to separate Leninism from its Stalinist outcome. The justification for Stalin's horrors was the absorption of ethics into politics that I mentioned earlier, and in any case it is hard to imagine that Communism could have established itself in Russia without the Stalinist terror. Indeed, Stalin was able to radicate Communism in the Russian popular tradition by exploiting the idea that Russia has a special task for the liberation of the world, which until then had been of a religious nature. Tsarism had dropped this idea when it entered a war that could not be given any religious interpretation, at least from the side that at that time was called the Entente. Communism took it over, as a reversed religion. In this way, Stalin saved Communism, but at the price of linking it back to the Tsarist tradition. Here the heterogenesis of ends, the sign of the Providence I talked about, comes full circle. Marxism realizes itself historically by continuing and increasing Tsarist imperialism, by fully empowering precisely the danger Marx had most feared. The process leading from Marx to Soviet Communism is a complete and exemplary process of heterogenesis of ends, if ever there was one in history.

I spoke of three new forms of secularism that arose after the Soviet revolution and did not originate from any previous tradition, but that can be explained *only in reference to Communism, albeit in terms of radical opposition.* By now two of them are extinguished, Fascism and Nazism. The third is in full strength,[12] so much so that some people can think with some truth that it will be able to bring Soviet Communism itself to its knees. One of these forms is characterized by being subordinate to Communism as its inversion. The other two track closely the forms into which theoretical Marxism is destined to decompose.

Let us begin from the subordinate form, Nazism. In its regard I think that we should emphasize not so much the relationship with Fascism – of which it is said to be an extreme form, which is a rather vague analysis – as much as the relationship that ties it to Communism as its *exact opposite.* I mean that we should focus on the fact that Nazism reproduces, in reverse but with perfect symmetry, the characteristics of Communism at the stage when it reaches the heterogenesis of ends. It reflects the defeat of Marxism in its aspect of promising a revolution that could only take place worldwide (Stalinism, socialism in one country). I have already said that it seems the perfect realization of what de Maistre considered the mortal disease to which the counter-revolution is susceptible: ending up as a revolution in reverse. After all, this is also Ernst Jünger's description, when he defines Nazism as a "revolution against the revolution."

I will briefly linger on the symmetries. In Nazism everything develops as if the criterion of truth were to replace each Communist category with its exact opposite, *but still within the same materialistic perspective of Marxism.* Thus, class is replaced by race, the bourgeois by the Jew. Hence, history is interpreted as a death struggle between the Aryan and the Jew, which has now reached the decisive stage when evil will be defeated or will triumph. It is not by chance that the anti-Semitic passages of *Mein Kampf* take a universalistic missionary tone – the same idea as the universal mission of the proletarian revolution – and that Hitler could feel that he was the world's saviour. In opposition to Marxism's emphasis on the future, Nazism emphasizes the past. In opposition to the secularized Marxist eschatology that places the perfect society at the end of times, Nazi mythology places it before history. The Nazi revolution, albeit in the form

12 [TN] Del Noce is referring to the ideology of the technocratic society, which he discusses briefly here below and at greater length in numerous other essays, also in this volume.

of revolution against the revolution, aimed at realizing a new man that would fulfill the Aryan type, which had never been realized before in pure form. This is why Nazism wished to call itself a revolution. Hatred for Bolshevism, which may seem reactionary, was accompanied by revolutionary hatred for the old world, as shown by the fact that no previous period of history was taken as a model. The antithesis between nature and anti-nature is essential to Nazism, on the basis that man is the only living being that tries to transgress the laws of nature. Thus, to Marxist historicism Nazism opposes the most radical naturalism. And this may be its most adequate description, capable of explaining the full meaning also of the opposition between class and race.

Different considerations apply to Fascism and to the technocratic society. Here we must go back to the topic of Marxism as a philosophy, to the fact that it cannot be the object of any "sublation," and that instead it must undergo an unavoidable process of decomposition.

What do I mean by using this word? I talked earlier about the fact that revolutionary thought must necessarily join together the terms materialism and dialectics. Now, the following happened and had to happen: when they were developed in full, the dialectic and the materialistic aspects split apart. Pushed to its ultimate consequences, the dialectic aspect abolished the materialistic aspect, and vice versa; extreme materialism and scientism eliminate dialectics.

The extreme extension of the dialectic aspect is found in Italian neo-Hegelianism, and more precisely in its final outcome, Gentile's Actualism. The extreme extension of the materialistic aspect is found in the various forms of contemporary scientism. They are indebted to Marxism because in the past materialism was generally associated with pessimism, whereas today it is associated with the progress of the technical spirit. In the past, since the time of Democritus, materialism sought to be on good terms with ethics and always failed. The new materialism is marked, instead, by the abandonment of ethics and by the primacy of economics. We could say that precisely in this respect it accepts Marxism, except for the apocalyptic aspect of the revolution. This thesis can be rephrased in various ways: that the new materialism is the bourgeois version of Marxism, or that it represents the victory of the bourgeois spirit over Marxism, even though this spirit must change deeply and reach its highest degree in order to achieve it.

Now we face two philosophico-historical questions that are very important and far from exhausted. What is the relationship *de jure* between Actualism and Fascism, independently of the relationship *de facto* which we know, and between the new scientism and technocratic society?

Answering the first question is the ultimate goal of the so-called revisionist[13] interpretation of Fascism, meaning the interpretation that aims (polemics aside[14]) at bringing Fascism back into history (i.e., at leaving no gaps in the interpretation of history, knowing that every gap ends up voiding the whole narrative; I believe that if such a question is not discussed, this entire interpretation, which has already reached such remarkable results, is left truncated). I will discuss only one fundamental text, which actually I have never seen cited by recent historians. It is the essay "Politica e filosofia" of August 1918, which started Gentile's collaboration with the journal *Politica*, edited by Alfredo Rocco and Francesco Coppola.[15] In this essay, which later reappeared in a volume of political writings published in 1920 and titled *Dopo la vittoria*, Gentile distinguishes two types of philosophy.[16] The first is the traditional type from Plato to Hegel, symbolized by the owl of Minerva, which rises at sunset after the day has ended. Gentile calls this type intellectualistic or naturalistic or speculative, in the sense that it separates contemplation from action. According to it, in his precise words, "we can say that philosophy is born *post festum*: when all knowable reality has been exhausted, be it history or nature."[17] The other type, instead, unifies theory and praxis and today would be called philosophy of praxis, as has become habitual over the last few decades. Now, the peculiar thing is that according to Gentile, this new philosophy – a philosophy that is also politics – can be expressed in only two forms: Marx's and his own, i.e., the materialistic and the spiritualistic forms of the philosophy of praxis. "Indeed," Gentile writes, "we could fight materialism as an inadequate philosophy, and by defeating it we could defeat class struggle and establish other methods of political action. But we cannot eliminate the fact that historical materialism was a historically very important philosophy *precisely because it was also politics*, nor the fact that historical materialism

13 [TN] The Italian term "revisionista" used here by Del Noce conveys the general meaning of "scholarly re-examination of the Fascist period" and refers to the work of historians like Renzo De Felice, George Mosse, Ernst Nolte, A. James Gregor, etc. It has none of the negative connotations that the English word "revisionist" has taken over the years.

14 [TN] Del Noce was writing during the *Historikerstreit* [historians' dispute] of 1986–89 in West Germany about comparing Nazi and Soviet crimes.

15 [TN] Giovanni Gentile, "Politica e filosofia" [Politics and philosophy] in *Politica* 1 (1918): 39–54. As Del Noce mentions, the essay was dated August 1918, even though it appeared in the 15 December issue of *Politica*.

16 [TN] Giovanni Gentile, *Dopo la Vittoria* [After victory] (Rome: La Voce, 1920). "Politica e filosofia" is the last essay, 188–215.

17 [TN] Gentile, "Politica e filosofia" in *Dopo la Vittoria*, 203.

can be beaten only with a philosophy that is just as realistic, and actually even more realistic ... And philosophy is realistic, with respect to politics, when it becomes one with actual politics, by being its critical conscience, like Marxism can be regarded as the critical conscience of the Communist movement that started from Marx."[18] This shows that in August 1918 Gentile already aspired to be the critical conscience of a new political movement, new like his philosophy. Next, he recognized Mazzini and Gioberti as the initiators of this spiritualistic form of philosophy of praxis that unifies philosophy and politics. Next, he saw it at work in Fascism, as the movement of which he wanted to be the philosophical guide, and he became the author of the doctrine of Fascism. Here it is important to highlight that Gentile invokes Mazzini as the other great (to him, the greatest) revolutionary of the nineteenth century. Perhaps (I say "perhaps" simply because this is not the place to prove it, and I cannot cite any other proofs, which are lacking) it would not be paradoxical to see in Fascism the simultaneous fulfillment and defeat of Mazzinianism, just as in Communism we see the simultaneous fulfillment and defeat of Marxism.

As for the technocratic society (by using this word I do not intend to diminish in any way the value of technology, but to denote a society that replaces, as its own foundation, the philosophy of being with the philosophy of doing), its link with neo-positivist philosophy is so obvious and explicit that I do not need to emphasize it again here. I would have to repeat what I wrote already a quarter of a century ago, in 1963, when the nature of the new society was not yet completely clear.[19] At that time, I described it as "the society that succeeds in eliminating the dialectic tension that sustains the revolution by pushing alienation to the highest degree,"[20] and at the same time by disassociating alienation from poverty. By alienation I meant "the mutual de-humanization of the relationship with the other. Each subject perceives the other as alienus, extraneous, separated, i.e., not joined to me by devotion to a shared value ... and therefore as an ob-jectum, regardless whether I deem this 'thing placed in front of me' to be a useful instrument or an obstacle."[21] Marxism cannot do anything against this new type of alienation, and yet this is the disease that is consuming Western civilization.

18 Ibid., 213–14, my italics.

19 [TN] In the essay "Appunti sull'irreligione occidentale" [Notes on Western irreligion] included in Augusto Del Noce, *Il problema dell'ateismo* [The problem of atheism] (Bologna: Il Mulino, 1990), 293–333.

20 [TN] Del Noce, *Il problema dell'ateismo*, 314.

21 [TN] Ibid., 314–15.

I am aware that some people will object to my interpretation of the role of Marxism in the history of philosophy, and above all to my way of connecting the stages of contemporary history. But a one-hour lecture cannot conclude a discussion, only start it.

5

Secularization and the Crisis of Modernity

MY THESES ON THE PHILOSOPHICAL INTERPRETATION of contemporary history set me apart from the majority of scholars, from those on both the right and the left, from both the Marxists and the secularists, and also from the prevalent Catholic culture and from the forms of progressivism, at times moderate and at times radical, that this culture generally professes. I recall what the Berlin historian Ernst Nolte wrote to me: that regarding this line of interpretation – which in fact is developed quite differently by each of us – we find ourselves nearly isolated in the world.[1] An explanation of the reasons that set my interpretations apart from those I mentioned would take an inordinate amount of time. Since this is impossible, I will present some preliminary propositions, basically three, that are the premises to my following statements.

The first is that the history of our century represents the complete success of Marxism, in the sense that it really changed the world – and not only the part of the world where Communism succeeded – as stated in the famous eleventh thesis on Feuerbach.[2] However, this complete

This chapter was first published in *Secolarizzazione e crisi della modernità* (Naples: Edizioni Scientifiche Italiane, 1989), reprinted in *Verità e ragione nella storia*, ed. A. Mina (Milan: Rizzoli, 2007), 139–52.

1 [TN] Del Noce and Ernst Nolte became correspondents in 1966, when Nolte asked Del Noce for permission to translate and publish in German the essay *Idee per l'interpretazione del Fascismo* [Ideas on the interpretation of Fascism]. The whole set of letters, from 1966 to a few weeks before Del Noce's death in 1989, are found in the article by Francesco Perfetti "La concezione transpolitica della storia nel carteggio Nolte-Del Noce" [The transpolitical view of history in the letters between Nolte and Del Noce], *Storia Contemporanea* 24, no. 5 (1993): 725–84. The sentence quoted by Del Noce is from Nolte's letter of 8 January 1985.

2 [TN] "The philosophers have *interpreted* the world in various ways; the point however is to *change* it," in Friedrich Engels, *Ludwig Feuerbach and the Outcome of Classical German Philosophy* (New York: International Publishers, 1941), 84.

success coincides with its complete defeat because the positions, both theoretical and concrete, that have been taken afterwards by rationalistic-secular thought are aspects of Marxism's decomposition. Furthermore, the process from Marx's original philosophy to what is usually called real socialism delivers exactly the opposite of what that philosophy promised, even if it follows a path that at a close look turns out to be strictly rational and necessary. I found confirmation of this thesis in Vittorio Strada,[3] an author many of you probably know, who starts from an examination of the current situation of the Soviet Union in order to reach its theoretical premises, travelling in the direction opposite to mine. Of course, this thesis is confirmed also by Aleksandr Solzhenitsyn, who sees Communism as a reality that cannot be explained by the Russian soul, as many claim, but was somehow superimposed on it. Obviously, this judgment cannot be expressed or shared by Marxists, and not even by those who exclude Marxism from the history of philosophy. The latest version of this exclusion, by Karl Popper, can be related in some ways, if you wish, to Nietzsche, if we view his works as the beginning and the foundation of the literature of crisis;[4] but the link with Nietzsche would take us so far that I must stop at this hint.

The second premise is the idea that what today is called real socialism is at the same time the full realization of what was already implicit in Marxist philosophy since its beginnings, and the complete reversal of its promoters' hopes and predictions. Precisely because of this *exact* opposition, of this lack of fidelity, this idea is a special case of another idea, which in my opinion holds more generally, about the heterogenesis of ends that befalls all the revolutionary forms of the nineteenth century; and I am glad to be stating this – I would say – "degnità"[5] in the city[6] of the philosopher of Divine Providence, Gianbattista Vico. In my opinion, the same heterogenesis of ends affects the thought of Mazzini, the other great revolutionary of the nineteenth century. It may seem strange to affirm that Fascism was the totally unforeseen conclusion of Mazzini's revolution, a thesis that would obviously require very lengthy

3 [TN] Vittorio Strada (1929), Italian scholar of Russian history and literature.

4 [TN] In Italy the expression "letteratura della crisi" [literature of crisis] is often used to indicate the various literary and philosophical movements that pointed to a crisis of European civilization in the early twentieth century.

5 [TN] In the *Scienza Nuova*, G.B. Vico uses the term "degnità" to indicate certain propositions that can be regarded as intuitively certain and are "worth knowing." It is a Latinized analogue of the Greek word "axiom."

6 [TN] The present essay was originally a lecture that Del Noce gave in Naples a few months before his death.

explanations.[7] Yet, it is not so strange if we think of how it was through Mazzini that the encounter between Gentile and Mussolini took place in the years after the First World War, and that Fascism was able to take roots in Italian culture through the tradition of the Risorgimento.

The third premise is that if a philosophical event, namely Marx's philosophy, marks the beginning of our historical period, then contemporary history offers the heuristic advantage of being fully rational. I have read a sentence by Norberto Bobbio to the effect that the contemporary world disproves the claim "that the history of ideas and the history of facts run on the same track,"[8] and thus shows that there is nothing less rational than belief in the rationality of history. This is not a casual remark, because this judgment represents the end point, which is found precisely in Bobbio, of one of the prevailing directions of Italian philosophical-political culture, the one that originated from Gobetti[9] and is inspired by Cattaneo,[10] in brief what is called liberal-socialism. In short, according to Bobbio, the contemporary world is marked by the struggle of modernity, equality, and democracy – three ideas that he sees as a unity – against irrationalism. For Bobbio, the contrast between Rousseau and Nietzsche illustrates this conflict: Rousseau being the father of egalitarian ideas and thus of contemporary democracy and socialism, and Nietzsche the father of irrationalism.[11] On the contrary, I think that in order to understand history from the First World War and the October Revolution to the present, we should give priority to what I would like to call ideal causality, that is, to the philosophical-religious aspect. I think that from this point of view, this history displays a full rationality in its essential features, as the expression (we will see in a moment what I mean by this statement) of the unfolding of a philosophical system.

I now discuss the word secularization. Looking closely, it seems to have suffered a fate similar to the word humanism, which by being

7 [TN] See Augusto Del Noce, *Giovanni Gentile* (Bologna: Il Mulino, 1990), especially chapter 4, section 7.

8 [TN] Norberto Bobbio, "Bilancio di un convegno" [Conference conclusions] in *La cultura filosofica italiana dal 1945 al 1980 nelle sue relazioni con altri campi del sapere* [Italian philosophical culture from 1945 to 1980 in its relationships with other fields of knowledge] (Naples: Guida, 1982), 303.

9 [TN] Pietro Gobetti (1901–26), Italian journalist and intellectual. Gobetti was an early and uncompromising anti-Fascist, and advocated a radical form of liberalism.

10 [TN] Carlo Cattaneo (1801–69), Italian philosopher and patriot. During the *Risorgimento* he distinguished himself for his uncompromising republican and federalist positions.

11 [TN] See, for instance, Norberto Bobbio, *Left and Right: The Significance of a Political Distinction* (Chicago: University of Chicago Press, 1996), 68–9.

interpreted in many different ways ended up having no precise meaning. Nevertheless, the correlation between the idea of secularization and that of modernity remains undeniable; in secular thought the term modernity is tied to the idea of an irreversible process toward radical immanence. The theologians who spoke of secularization also linked the idea to that of modernity; for example, let us recall the famous phrase by Dietrich Bonhoeffer, the father of such theology of secularization, who said that today humanity has come of age, so that it is necessary to present religious truths to modern man in a new form.[12]

In my opinion, the term secularization attains its full meaning if we think of it in connection with what we can call the Marxist counter-religion; namely, Marx wants to achieve the complete rejection of any dependence of man on God, and so, in the first place, of dependence on God the Creator. The relevant passages from his early writings are very well known; however, we cannot say that the Marxist counter-religion is just a simple rejection of religion: the two aspects of radical atheism and of the religion destined to kill Christianity – to use a famous phrase by Gramsci[13] – alternate in Marxist literature. One can also think of Bloch, of his union of Christianity and atheism,[14] and somehow also of Lukács, whose ideas are not so distant from Bloch's. In fact, the rejection of the dependence on God the Creator goes hand in hand with an extreme interpretation of the aspect of religion as liberation and redemption. The Marxist revolution keeps the appearance of a religion because it requires a conversion, since it marks a transition to a higher reality and to a reality that is totally "other," even if absolutely not transcendent or supernatural. I think that in this sense the term secularization is more appropriate than many discussions about the messianic, prophetic, and millennialist aspects of Marxism, or about the subconscious presence of Jewish religious archetypes in Marx's soul, which by now have ended up far away from a correct understanding. These messianic and prophetic aspects are present in Marx, but, it seems to me that they are just part of the context of the novelty of what we could call a secularization of religion.

The idea that the term secularization should be applied first of all to Marxism includes also what is valid in the interpretation of Marxism as a

12 [TN] Dietrich Bonhoeffer, *Letters and Papers from Prison*, trans. Reginald Fuller, Frank Clark, et al. (New York: Touchstone, 1997), 325ff.

13 [TN] Antonio Gramsci, "Audacia e fede" [Audacity and faith] in *Avanti!*, 22 May 1916.

14 [TN] See Ernst Bloch, *Atheism in Christianity*, trans. J.T. Swann (New York: Herder and Herder, 1972).

new Gnosticism. The neo-Gnostic interpretation of Marxism is well known; it was introduced by the political philosopher Voegelin[15] and then re-proposed by Pellicani,[16] who discussed it in this lecture series. The appearance of a new Gnosticism at the end of classical German philosophy marks the reopening in the nineteenth century – and from the nineteenth century to the present – of the conflict between Christian and Gnostic religiosity. One has to be cautious in this Gnostic interpretation of Marxism, because it is a new Gnosticism, irreducible to the old one.[17] Nevertheless, it is a fact that in the Gnostic texts we find the idea of two worlds, each with its own God, and the idea that the true God is the God of the new world, of a world to come, totally opposite to the present world in which man lives as a stranger. The future of the revolutionaries sounds like a modern translation of the Gnostics' true God. Here we have to stress the adjective "modern" in order to explain why one can correctly speak of a post-Christian gnosis in reference to revolutionary thought. It is a gnosis that has been refashioned after the Christian affirmation of humanity's transcendence over nature, and therefore transformed from a cosmological view, proper to the old gnosis, to an anthropological one.

Naturally, here the discussion should be broadened and more arguments should be provided; we could show how Hegel, in his attempt to resolve Christianity into philosophy, encountered gnosis,[18] and how, actually, this was already highlighted in the first decades of the nineteenth century. However, looking at today's religious world, it is pretty clear that the historical context for the appearance of theologies that use the term "secularization" in a positive sense is always provided by a judgment on contemporary history which is generally favourable either to the Marxist revolution or to the idea of an irreversible process through which the worldliness of the world has established itself during the modern centuries. This was stated for example by the theologian Johannes Metz, one of the main theologians of this current of thought.[19] Regarding this quest for a compromise with modernity understood as an

15 [TN] Eric Voegelin, *The New Science of History* (Chicago: University of Chicago Press, 1952); *Science, Politics and Gnosticism* (Chicago: Regnery, 1968). See also Del Noce's essay "Eric Voegelin and the Critique of the Idea of Modernity" in the present volume.

16 [TN] Luciano Pellicani, *Revolutionary Apocalypse: Ideological Roots of Terrorism* (Westport, CT: Praeger, 2003).

17 [TN] On the relationship between old and new gnosis, see the essay "Violence and Modern Gnosticism" in this volume.

18 [TN] See again "Violence and Modern Gnosticism."

19 [TN] See Johannes Baptist Metz, *Theology of the World*, trans. William Glen-Doepel (New York: Herder and Herder, 1969).

irreversible process, it would be sufficient to look at some of his theses that have become universally accepted.

The various forms of the theology of secularization, all based on a claimed, yet false, distinction between secularization and secularism, oscillate between two positions:[20] one is the more or less veiled dissolution of religion into revolutionary thought, the other a distinction, which actually is a separation, between the temporal and the religious. The second position reduces grace to something juxtaposed, so that it is hard to understand how it could then become part of our life. In fact, by now these theologies of secularization have had their day, and are – I would say – in a terminal crisis. Now, on the one hand we can say that Marxism – and here I agree with Lukács, Bloch, and Gramsci – represents the climax of modernity, inasmuch as modernity is intended as complete rejection of dependence, and that we should understand in this sense also the replacement of immanentism – which in some ways is still theological (*Deus manet in nobis*) – with materialism. But, on the other hand, Marxism also represents the crisis of modernity, a crisis that cannot be overcome because Marxism is subject to decomposition, and not to sublation. In fact, it represents the greatest synthesis of opposites ever proposed in the history of thought: of the greatest utopia with the greatest political realism: of extreme materialism with dialectical thought, freed from the hindrances that led to the closed system. This two-fold synthesis of opposites is necessary for the total revolution it wants to foster. In fact, Marx, not by chance and unlike all other utopians, does not dwell on the description of the future society; generally, he describes its features only in a negative fashion, because his future society is conceived as so "other" with respect to the existing one that any attempt to describe its attributes would be an arbitrary fantasy. Therefore, in his case we must speak of an absolute utopianism at odds with common utopianism, which in fact he criticizes on the ground that common utopianism is a false form of utopianism because it thinks of present reality freed of its contradictions. On the contrary, his utopianism is carried to the extreme, to the point that the new reality must arise as the result of the explosion of the contradictions (here the inseparable relationship with Hegel is very clear). At the same time, however, the aspect of political realism is pushed to the extreme, because the total revolution, precisely because it is total, cannot happen in the name of universal values already present in the very reality that needs to be destroyed (i.e., the ideals of freedom and justice), but because of the very movement of reality. Marx's materialism is

20 [TN] See "Notes on Secularization and Religious Thought" in this volume.

precisely the negation of universal ethical values in the name of this total revolution. Therefore, all values need be incorporated in the one and only value of the Revolution, a process that cannot result in anything but the total disintegration of ethics into politics.

Now we can understand the deep meaning of Lenin's statement during the October Revolution – which at first may sound like a propaganda slogan, uttered in a very tense situation. Lenin said, "Morality is whatever brings about the success of the proletarian revolution."[21] Actually this phrase is a perfect description of the inclusion of ethics into politics. In fact, it is easy to find its antecedents in Marx's and also in Hegel's judgments about ethics, and its developments in the statements of the theoreticians of Marxism-Leninism. The history of the practical realization of Marxism shows how the two aspects, the utopian and the realistic-political, get separated in favour of the second, which is carried to the extreme of a total inclusion of ethics into politics. For example, when we speak of totalitarianism, we want to indicate precisely this phenomenon, this split between the utopian and the realistic-political aspects, and the victory of the latter.

Since in Marxist theories philosophy is surpassed and subsumed into politics – because Marxism, in its opposition to Hegel, is an *ante factum* philosophy, aimed at the development of a totality, instead of a *post factum* philosophy, as awareness of an already attained reality – the consequence is that the new Marxist idea of man can prove itself only through its historical realization, and can be realized only through the total revolution as transition from one state of the world to an opposite state. In this regard the second thesis on Feuerbach is particularly interesting, precisely about the fact that *ante factum* philosophy can be verified only empirically, based on its realization.[22]

Then, from this point of view we can ask the following question: can Marx's philosophy and economy be discussed as if the Russian Revolution never happened? Many seem to think so and therefore they envision a Euro-communism, a not-yet-realized Marxism, being convinced that the model is not the same as its concrete implementation in reality. However,

21 [TN] I believe Del Noce is either paraphrasing or using a different translation of one among various statements to this effect found in V.I. Lenin, "The Tasks of the Youth Leagues" in *Collected Works*, trans. Julius Katzer (Moscow: Progress Publishers 1966), 31: 283–99.

22 [TN] "The question whether objective truth can be attributed to human thinking is not a question of theory but is a practical question. In practice man must prove the truth, i.e., the reality and power, the 'this-sidedness' of his thinking. The dispute over the reality or non-reality of thinking which is isolated from practice is a purely scholastic question," in Engels, *Ludwig Feuerbach*, 82.

this understanding does not apply to Marxism at all. Actually, because of his negation of absolute truths, Marx must place the criterion of truth of his philosophy in empirical verification, in the historical result it has produced. One may ask whether this verification ever happened; indeed, there is a Trotskyist interpretation that claims that the revolution, after starting well with Lenin in 1917 and in the following years, was later betrayed by Stalin. There is also another interpretation that resurfaces periodically which wants to dissociate Marxism from Leninism; according to this interpretation, the roots of Lenin's culture and practical work should be found in Russian revolutionary populism, which supposedly transformed Marxism completely when the two met each other. In Italy this thesis has been developed in a valuable book by Enzo Bettiza, in which Lenin is described as non-Marxist because what should be ascribed to him is precisely a transfiguration of Marxism due to the contact with Soviet populism.[23] According to others, for example, Franz Borkenau,[24] Lenin introduced into Marxism, from the time of the pamphlet *What Is to Be Done?* in 1903, the theory of elites, which contradicts it. Supposedly, his voluntarism and subjectivism are at odds with the respect for the laws of history that is necessary for a properly Marxist revolution. In all these interpretations Marxism becomes either a sort of ghost which, for all we know, may never have the opportunity to prove itself in history, or even a mere nineteenth-century utopia which the most mature Western thought has surpassed once and for all. I must say that I totally disagree with these interpretations. In my opinion Marxism could become reality only in the exact way it did; therefore, it was verified in terms of its power, and at the same time refuted in terms of its outcome. Lukács's old thesis that saw Lenin as the second major thinker of the revolutionary movement after Marx himself, or as the one who restored Marx's doctrine to its fullness, seems to me still completely convincing even if, obviously, my assessment of said doctrine is completely different from Lukács's.[25]

Let us look at the famous thesis of the pamphlet *What Is to Be Done?*, which is at the origin of the Communist Party and at that time provoked a great scandal in socialist circles: class political consciousness can be brought to the worker only from without, because on its own the working class is able to develop only a trade-unionist consciousness.[26]

23 [TN] Enzo Bettiza, *Il mistero di Lenin* [The mystery of Lenin] (Milan: Rizzoli, 1982).

24 [TN] Franz Borkenau, *Pareto* (London: Chapman and Hall, 1936), 178–9.

25 [TN] Georg Lukács, *History and Class Consciousness*, trans. Rodney Livingstone (Boston: MIT Press, 1972).

26 [TN] V.I. Lenin, "What Is to Be Done?" in *Collected Works*, trans. Joe Fineberg and George Hanna (Moscow: Progress Publishers, 1960), 5: 422.

Conversely, in terms of their social status, the founders of contemporary scientific socialism were bourgeois intellectuals. In short, in Lenin's opinion the consciousness of the members of the working class has been contaminated by the culture of the intellectuals, who have become the watchdogs of the bourgeoisie, and can regain its purity only after the intervention of intellectuals of a different kind. It is easy to show that this judgment simply repeats a passage already found in Marx's *Manifesto.*[27] Undoubtedly, it may seem peculiar that the class that in history has been given the task of bringing about universal redemption is unable to fulfill this mission unless directed by a culture coming from outside and, moreover, from intellectuals belonging to the very class it was supposed to overthrow. In truth, it seems to me that in the history of Marxism an exhaustive answer was never given to the problem of the "exceptions," of why some bourgeois are able to evade the false consciousness that enslaves them because of their class. Nevertheless, Lenin's claim is undeniable: true philosophy is present in the working class only in a virtual and confused way, if only because it cannot be immune to contamination by the bourgeois thought that dominates the culture. What is needed in order to turn this philosophy into action is the action of intellectuals who, however, cannot be ordinary intellectuals, because ordinary intellectuals cannot see beyond the horizon of the bourgeoisie. What is needed, instead, are intellectuals with a superior knowledge that enables them to grasp the historical movement in its entirety.[28] Here the figure of the New Gnostics comes in: the New Gnostics who, in modern time, have taken on the appearance of professional revolutionaries, reflecting the transition from a cosmological to an anthropological vision. In this case, Lenin simply develops Marx's thought, and the alternative he proposes is correct: either a revolution made possible only by bringing class consciousness to the proletariat from the outside, or a reformist approach that gives up for good on the idea of revolution. Although, at this point, ideal causality takes priority over material causality. In my opinion, this is precisely what fully legitimizes the interpretation of contemporary history that has been called, for example by De Felice,[29] transpolitical,

27 [TN] Del Noce is probably referring to "the bourgeois ideologists, who have raised themselves to the level of comprehending theoretically the historical movement in its entirety," mentioned in chapter 1 of the *Manifesto.*

28 [TN] A direct reference to the passage in the *Communist Manifesto* I quoted in the previous note.

29 [TN] Renzo De Felice, *The Interpretations of Fascism,* trans. Brenda Huff Everett (Cambridge: Harvard University Press, 1977).

meaning the interpretation that attributes an essential role to the philosophical aspect.

Lenin's thesis opens the way toward so-called real socialism through a sequence of links so strongly connected that breaking the chain is impossible; these links appear frequently in the analyses of the mainstream press, but they are seldom connected to the original philosophical aspect. Thus, without this connection, the statement that the dictatorship of the working class has been replaced by the dictatorship of the party over the working class sounds banal. Another banal truth repeated a thousand times by the mainstream press is the formation of a techno-bureaucratic class, based on the party, with specific connotations: the famous new class.[30] This thesis assumes its full significance only in reference to the process described previously. Similarly, the thesis of the encounter between Marxism and Russian populism is also true and does not contradict the fact that Lenin was Marx's most consistent interpreter and that the revolution could not have been successful without encountering the Russian populist tradition. The intervention into the First World War, which in no way could be given a religious significance, at least from the perspective of what at that time was called the Entente, was a self-imposed death sentence for Tsarism. Indeed, with this action it destroyed the essential foundation of the political regime which rested on the people's belief in Russian supremacy for the sake of world redemption. Afterwards, the originally religious thesis of Russian supremacy for the sake of world redemption, forsaken by Tsarism, was taken over by revolutionary Communism. The theme of Russian supremacy in the revolutionary cause then shows the connection between Stalin and Lenin; in fact, Stalin's fundamental achievement was to join together Russian tradition and Marxism, which is what allowed Marxism itself to survive over time.

I will address very briefly another crucial point: the break between two philosophical aspects, materialism and dialectics, which are both necessary for the total revolution. This break shows that we have not gotten past Marxism's decomposition and that it coincides with the crisis of modernity. In fact, let us reflect on the inconsistency of dialectical materialism, which basically had already been intuited in the book that Gentile dedicated to Marx's philosophy in 1899 – if we translate it in slightly more modern language and leave aside some philological inadequacies, it still is probably one of the most profound books on Marx's

30 [TN] Milovan Djilas, *The New Class* (New York: Praeger, 1957)

philosophical thought.[31] If we push to the extreme the dialectic aspect, having acknowledged Marx's criticism of Hegel and moving on beyond it, we need to dismiss the materialistic aspect. If, conversely, we push to the extreme the materialistic aspect, we must dismiss the dialectic aspect. Now, a large part of contemporary philosophy, or at least the part that has had the greatest effect on morals and politics, takes place within this context; think, for example, of Gentile's philosophy, which can also be interpreted as the rigorous development of Marxism's dialectic moment, according to the tendency shown by Marxism to go beyond Hegel and express itself as a philosophy of praxis. I said "also" because, obviously, Gentile's philosophy may be defined in other ways, which, however, do not contradict this interpretation. On the other hand, think of the materialism found in the human sciences, and of the many Western forms of contemporary materialism. Definitely, I would not say that all contemporary philosophies fall into this scheme, or in this crisis without solution, but I think that in order to really move on they need to carry out a critique of the ideas of modernity and secularization, whose connection I briefly described.

Last, I want to discuss my claim that the Marxist revolution, albeit contradicting itself, in some ways was a worldwide event, and not only because it conquered more than a third of the world. Because it is true that Western countries are not Communist, but it is not true that Marxism has not affected the culture and customs of their peoples. Today Marxism no longer fuels a revolutionary faith in the Communists themselves, but its philosophical negations have penetrated mainstream opinion. Let us even ignore the ubiquity of words like alienation, for example, which does indicate a real phenomenon but different, in its present form, from what Marxism described; or of other expressions such as demythologization, the school of suspicion, technique of distrust, which, even if they were not created by Marxism, follow in its wake and became popular when Marxism became successful in the years after the Second World War. Think, instead, of the term nihilism as it is used today to indicate the collapse in the Western world of the values that until now had been regarded as supreme. We have to say that Marx did not foresee at all the rise of this attitude; in fact, according to him, religion's disappearance should have coincided with a reappropriation of the powers from which man had become alienated during the course of history in order to project them onto God. On the contrary, in the Western world Marxist culture, during its revival after the Second World War, produced nihilism; the

31 [TN] Giovanni Gentile, *La filosofia di Marx* [The philosophy of Marx] (Florence: Sansoni, 1974).

nihilism of Western society cannot be explained without referring to this repercussion of Marxism. Perhaps Marxist culture was not alone in promoting it, but it had a primary and decisive role in this phenomenon.

To sum up, when secularization turns into nihilism it coincides, therefore, with the crisis of the idea of modernity, due to the fact that reality no longer corresponds to the axiological meaning implicit in this idea. This crisis is expressed by the decomposition of Marxism, which takes place without the possibility of sublation into a superior form. This impossibility is attested both by the secular forms of philosophy and by the Modernist forms of theology which, precisely while they are under the-delusion of attaining a higher viewpoint, nevertheless remain within the horizon of such decomposition.

PART TWO

The Advent of the Technocratic Society

6

Toward a New Totalitarianism

IN AN ARTICLE THAT APPEARED in the previous issue, I argued that the most important phenomenon and the gravest danger of these last few years is the emergence of a new form of totalitarianism.[1] This danger is even greater because so far it has not been diagnosed precisely.

Unlike Stalinism or Hitlerism, its main characteristic is not that of being a political movement that aims at world domination. It is marked, instead, by a quest to bring about the disintegration[2] of one part of the world (in the case at hand, Europe). Nevertheless, the word totalitarianism is still appropriate because the essential features remain the same: the individual is extinguished and the idea of politics is subsumed within the idea of war, even in peacetime. This means that all forms of criticism must be "prevented" – whenever they are addressed at "real power" – because, instead of advancing rational arguments, supposedly they reflect or conceal the conservatism or reactionary spirit that are typical of a "repressed" psychology, "regardless of the self-awareness of those who criticize." It is easy to see that this argument belongs to the same category as the old thesis about concealed interests of class or race, which was the foundation of the totalitarian systems, inasmuch as they denied the universality of reason. However, just as totalitarianism based on the idea of race was completely different from totalitarianism

This chapter is from the introduction and first three sections of "Verso un nuovo totalitarismo," *L'Europa* 4, no. 7/8 (1970): 10–15. Republished in *Rivoluzione Risorgimento Tradizione* (Milan: Giuffrè, 1993), 131–45.

1 [TN] "Che cos'é la 'lotta contro la repressione'" [What is the 'fight against repression'], *L'Europa* 4, no. 6 (1970): 10–15. A more detailed exposition of the same ideas can be found in the essay "The Roots of the Crisis" in the present volume.

2 [TN] Here and elsewhere I translate as "disintegration" the Italian "dissoluzione," which could be translated more literally as "dissolution."

based on the idea of class, this new totalitarianism is profoundly different from the previous two.

For the sake of exposition, and in order to be more synthetic, I will outline my viewpoint through the following theses.

1 FROM VERTICALISM TO HORIZONTALISM

Scientism, eroticism, and theology of secularization (where I am referring to all neo-Modernist trends, both Catholic and Protestant) are just "aspects of one and the same reality."

This affirmation may sound strange because it is so different from the common reassuring opinions. "Still today" the exaltation of science is usually associated with what used to be called humanitarianism. Eroticism is viewed as a form of decadent primitivism. As far as the theology of secularization is concerned, we are told that it was born out of a primacy of charity over an individualistic, and almost selfish, concern about salvation.

Actually, I think I have already clarified the connection between scientism and eroticism in the article in the last issue. I also demonstrated the perfect logical consistency of Reich's ideas, according to the principle *salus ex inimicis*. Certainly, one could reply that this connection applies to the new scientism rather than to the old – because nineteenth-century scientism did try to reconcile sexological studies, or more generally all studies of the human world, with traditional morality. This was a consequence of the idea of a reconciliation with tradition that ran through nineteenth-century culture. But we must add that today de Sade's point of view has been reconfirmed. His heroine, Juliette, rejected all idols except science.[3] The new Enlightenment is linked to the old one precisely at its endpoint.

But, you will ask, what does the new theology have to do with scientism and eroticism? I will take the liberty to formulate here an idea that, to my knowledge, has never before been proposed but sheds light on this phenomenon. Modern science, whose great contributions to its own field obviously nobody can deny, started in the 1600s when the search for "vertical causality" (from physics to metaphysics) was replaced by the one for "horizontal causality," in the sense of searching for laws that express constant relationships between phenomena. It is hard to miss the analogy between the scientific revolution of that time (which, however, was limited to science in the strict sense) and today's religious revolution,

3 [TN] Marquis de Sade, *Juliette*, trans. Austryn Wainhouse (New York: Grove Press, 1968).

which openly declares its own horizontalism as well, in the sense of shifting attention to "worldly realities." In short, horizontalism is thought to be the distinctive characteristic of the "Copernican revolution" of the modern age, which today has reached its climax by taking over the domain of religion itself, in which the "verticalism" of the past had survived longer than in other fields. Thus, secularization theology intends to conform to the "modern spirit" which, in its view, is characterized by science. Ultimately, it is a surrender of religion to science, regarded as the only truly valid form of knowledge. As for its connection with eroticism, I think there is no possibility of mistake: one of the most visible aspects of the world view of the "new Christians" is their refusal to criticize any form of sexual liberation. In fact, it is the only really clear aspect, since all others can be suspected, to say the least, of using a double standard.

2 THE "TOTALITARIAN" CONCEPTION OF SCIENCE

These three characteristics (including the renewed Church, which is indispensable, at least for now) define the so-called technological society, also known as the consumerist or affluent society. I certainly do not need to repeat again that I do not confuse at all the critique of this society with some absurd denial of the progress of science and technology, and of the benefits they bring. Indeed, the transition from "technical progress" to the "technological society" is not at all immediate. It is mediated by another factor, which is the "totalitarian" conception of science, in which science is regarded as the "only" true form of knowledge. According to this view, every other type of knowledge – metaphysical or religious – expresses only "subjective reactions," which we are able, or will be able, to explain by extending science to the human sphere through psychological and sociological research.

3 CONTRADICTION WITH TRADITIONAL ETHICS

A scientistic thinker (and a society inspired by his thought) cannot help being totalitarian inasmuch as "he cannot possibly prove"[4] his claim that

4 Therefore, we understand why I spoke earlier of totalitarianism as the permanent absorption of the idea of politics within the one of war. Remember von Clausewitz's definition of war as "an act of power aimed at forcing the enemy to submit to our will." Inasmuch as the new scientism is a radical *unproven* denial of traditional values, it can only subordinate the *will* of its adversaries by using psychological weapons. And because the negation is *radical*, it must in practice relegate them to "moral ghettoes" (see the way in which the progressive press speaks about traditionalists).

science rules out all other forms of knowledge, and thus certain dimensions of reality, which are declared to be either unknowable or nonexistent ("nonsensical questions" according to the most barbaric form of thought that ever appeared, so-called analytical philosophy). Indeed, scientism neither "sublates" other forms of thought nor tries to elevate them to a higher level, but simply "negates them." At the same time, just like the supporters of every other form of totalitarianism, an advocate of scientism "must" think that the society he proposes will be legitimized by some future "unverifiable" outcome. His reasoning is strictly analogous to that of a Communist. Just as a Communist thinks that after the revolution, after the dictatorship of the proletariat, etc., mankind will enter an age of super-human happiness, so does a believer in scientism. The only difference from a Communist is that he contradicts himself and, what is worse, he does so hypocritically, inasmuch as he thinks that, because his philosophy asserts that only what can be verified by everybody is real, he is the true ideal champion of democracy. Thus, by accepting the guidance of science we will march toward a full reconciliation of nature and civilization through a peaceful evolution.

As a matter of fact, many people do not realize that scientism and the technological society are totalitarian in nature. They say: let science organize the social sphere. There is still the other sphere, interior life, in which science has no jurisdiction. This would be true if there was a "moral" consensus between the proponents of scientism and other people. In fact, however, scientism includes as essential a form of morality (what is often called the "pleasure principle" or, as I wrote elsewhere, the pure increase of vitality) which is "absolutely contradictory" to traditional ethics.

I have already said that scientism is more opposed to tradition than Communism because in Communism we can still find messianic and biblical archetypes (e.g., in the idea of the proletariat as the universal mediator) which give it the appearance of what was often described as a "secular religion." Nikolai Berdyaev, now forgotten, wrote that the Marxist revolution carries within itself "the reflected light of the apocalypse" and that it was able to succeed because of the strong inclination toward an apocalyptic mindset found in the Russian soul and in the large majority of Russian intellectuals at the end of the nineteenth and the beginning of the twentieth centuries.[5] This was the reason why Marxism could appear, from this Russian perspective, as "a doctrine of deliverance, of the messianic vocation of the proletariat, of the future perfect

5 [TN] Nikolai Berdyaev, *The Origin of Russian Communism*, trans. R.M. French (Ann Arbor: University of Michigan Press, 1960), 132.

society in which man will not be dependent on economics."[6] Now, this messianic aspect, which allowed Marxism to put down roots in the Russian tradition, is precisely what is being rejected by scientism and by the technological society.

But, in light of this, we understand why scientistic anti-traditionalism can express itself only by dissolving the "fatherlands" where it was born. Because of the very nature of science, which provides means but does not determine any ends, scientism lends itself to be used as a tool by some group. Which group? The answer is completely obvious: once the fatherlands are gone, all that is left are the great economic organisms, which look more and more like fiefdoms. States become their executive instruments, confirming the old Marxist-Leninist thesis, but through a different route from that predicted by Marxism-Leninism.

6 [TN] Ibid., 98.

7

The Shadow of Tomorrow

"In the Shadow of Tomorrow" (In de schaduwen van morgen) was the original title of a very beautiful book by Johan Huizinga.[1] *It appeared in 1935 and was translated into Italian in 1937 under the bland title "The Crisis of Civilization" because, for obvious reasons, Huizinga's own title risked sounding too provocative at that time when "Italy was a beacon of light." Thirty-five years went by, and we can again say that threatening shadows are looming in the near future.*

A NEW FORM OF TOTALITARIANISM

Let us look back at the thirties: Croce was the leading light of secular anti-Fascism and Maritain of Catholic anti-Fascism, at a time when it seemed extremely likely, if not completely unavoidable, that Fascism would triumph worldwide, or at least endure for several generations. And when many of the most admirable spirits (in Italy, I am thinking of Martinetti) seemed to incline toward Gnostic-Manichean forms of dualism and pessimism.

Then let us look at the present, twenty-five years after victory: the forms of thought most exactly opposed to the forms advocated by those distinguished thinkers are prevalent, or actually almost absolutely dominant. In the 7 March issue I talked about an unbreakable unity of scientism, eroticism, and secularization theology.[2] This is an unusual

This chapter was first published as "Le ombre del domani," *L'Europa* 4, no. 15 (1970): 11–35. Republished in *Rivoluzione Risorgimento Tradizione* (Milan: Giuffrè, 1993), 187–215.

1 [TN] J. Huizinga, *In the Shadow of Tomorrow*, trans. J.H. Huizinga (New York: W.W. Norton & Company, 1936).

2 [TN] *L'Europa* 4, no. 7/8 (1970): 10–15; partially included in the present volume as "Toward a New Totalitarianism."

thesis – in fact, so far I have never heard it stated by anybody – which I think must be taken very seriously. It gives us a glimpse of a new, more dangerous, and more radical form of totalitarianism, even though these new positions claim to represent the highest degree of democracy and anti-Fascism. This claim is a falsification of language that I will discuss later on.

To see that the reversal has been complete – because it was a reversal, and not a dialectical reversal but pure antithesis: the opposition is such that any sublation of the two opposites into a further synthesis is inconceivable – consider, in Croce's case, the following crucial passage: "Absolute historicism does not deny the divine, because it does not deny philosophical thought. It only denies the transcendence of the divine and the corresponding metaphysics, unlike positivism, empiricism and pragmatism which, in order to get rid of transcendence and of metaphysics, suppress philosophy itself ... Therefore, how can there be any affinity, let alone identity, between them? If anything, historicism feels a greater affinity for religions and for the old metaphysics it fought against – which in its own way welcomed and thought the divine – than for dry positivism, empiricism and pragmatism." This quote comes from one of his most secular philosophical works and shows that the final stage of his secularism is also a prelude to the last, religious, period of his philosophy.[3] In that final period he aimed explicitly at restoring the divine, even if outside of any positive profession of faith. As far as eroticism is concerned, remember that in his *History of Europe* Croce looked for the origin of the current crisis in morbid Romanticism, which invaded first the arts as decadentism, and then practice as irrationalism, activism, and vitalism.[4] Its first representative was de Sade, the founder of eroticism (even though Croce does not mention his name, I believe out of a sentiment of both horror and contempt, as if his works expressed an impersonal force; but Croce clearly alludes to him). As for the new theology, remember Croce's negative assessment of the Modernist movement of the early twentieth century.

Regarding Maritain, in *Le paysan de la Garonne*[5] not only did he clarify in an exemplary and definitive fashion, I think, the true sense of

3 Benedetto Croce, *Il carattere della filosofia moderna* [The character of modern philosophy] (Bari: Laterza, 1941), 195–6.

4 [TN] Benedetto Croce, *History of Europe in the Nineteenth Century*, trans. Henry Furst (New York: Harcourt Brace & Co., 1933).

5 [TN] Jacques Maritain, *The Peasant of the Garonne*, trans. Michael Cuddihy and Elizabeth Hughes (New York: Holt, Rinehart and Winston, 1968).

Humanisme intégral[6] – demolishing the facile interpretation that depicted him as the beginner of a trend that later continued in Mounier and Teilhard – but he also clearly illuminated (e.g., see 16, 86, etc.[7]) that when the new Modernism knelt before the world, it also knelt before scientism and sex. Such a purely negative reversal is especially visible in Croce's and Maritain's cases, but in fact something quite similar happened regarding the thought of Karl Barth, the leading thinker of anti-Nazi Protestant theology, who until recently was adulated by all the fashionable schools of thought. Well, the work that can be considered his spiritual testament denounces the neo-Modernist error, and between the lines it seems to propose, against the Modernist type of ecumenism, the idea of an opposite type of ecumenism that could take shape around the opposition, within all churches, to the threats posed by the theology of secularization, of the death of God, and of the revolution.[8] As a matter of fact, one could demonstrate that the position of the theologians of the "death of God," whom he calls "today's fools," is the rigorous antithesis of his. This statement goes against a widespread but very mistaken opinion that Barth's theology started this trend. In fact, this opinion is the mirror image of the one about the relation between Maritain and the new Modernism.

A SUMMARY OF THE CHARACTERISTICS OF THE NEW TOTALITARIANISM

a. The new totalitarianism is founded on the unity that I mentioned and that, in a sense, makes it complete, inasmuch as it absolutely denies traditional morality and religion without preserving or sublating any aspect. This absolute opposition, based on scientistic dogmatism – science is viewed as exclusive of all other forms of knowledge, so that all the problems that cannot be analysed by modern science in terms of measure and verification are declared to be pure "nonsense" – necessarily

6 [TN] Jacques Maritain, *Integral Humanism: Temporal and Spiritual Problems of a New Christendom*, trans. Joseph W. Evans (New York: Charles Scribner's Sons, 1968).

7 [TN] Del Noce does not specify the edition of *Le paysan de la Garonne* he is citing. Based on a comparison of various French and Italian editions, I believe that the corresponding page numbers in the Holt, Rinehart and Winston edition of *The Peasant of the Garonne* are 7 and 55.

8 Karl Barth, *La Chiesa sulla via del rinnovamento* [The Church on the road to renewal] (Rome: Silva Editore, 1969), 9–29 [TN: Italian translation of a public lecture that Barth gave a few months before his death (in February 1968) to a gathering of Swiss Catholic and Protestant clergy. I have not been able to find the original German title, or an English translation].

means that no dialogue whatsoever is possible with those who do not accept its conclusions. Supposedly, such people do not express any rational argument but only some kind of psychological condition. Their expressions must be repressed when they have any impact on reality, cured when they are too weak to pose any danger, or more generally ignored.

b. Therefore, this new totalitarianism represents the most complete negation of the spiritual forces that sustained the resistance during the 1930s: the Christian tradition, liberalism, and humanitarian socialism. This latter because, as a result of an ever greater convergence with the other two positions, it aims not at generic collectivism but at a regime in which the whole social order is at the service of each individual – in short, at the complete abolition of every remaining trace of slavery.

c. Unlike Communist totalitarianism as a "secular religion," which is able to establish some continuity with tradition for the reasons I briefly mentioned in the previous article, the new totalitarianism is a totalitarianism of "disintegration," because the complete negation of tradition coincides with the negation of all "fatherlands." As a result, large corporations and political parties take the semblance of fiefdoms,[9] and only foreign powers can play the role of mediators between them.

This could be how the "sunset of the West" will take place. It has been a growing possibility, constantly progressing and accelerating, as we know, over the last few years (it has also been partially recognized by some people, and has met some resistance). For now, a future extension to the whole world of this destructive form of totalitarianism is a remote

9 I think that these ideas about the current "feudal disintegration" are confirmed by the ideas proposed by Gianfranco Miglio, starting from a different set of questions: "State authority could meet a fate not very different from the one that befell 'feudal monarchy' in an analogue constitutional situation. Indeed, at that time the power of kings – having lost the prerogatives and functions of actual sovereignty that somehow had survived the transition from the late-classic 'dominatum' and from the Germanic kingship to the Roman-barbaric monarchy, and that had made a final comeback in the Carolingian princedom – was reduced to survive, in an atrophied and so-to-speak mummified form, within the context of a pluralistic-seigneural order which followed a completely different 'type.'" ("Il ruolo del partito nella trasformazione del tipo di ordinamento politico vigente" [The role of parties in the transformation of the current political order], in the collective volume *La funzionalità dei partiti nello stato democratico* [The functionality of parties in a democratic state] (Milan: La Nuova Europa, 1967), 51–2; see also his remarks about the establishment everywhere of "political orders based on the legitimacy of the interests of special groups," ibid., 50). Let me add that today's collapse of the idea of fatherland "within Europe," by taking place during a period of extreme nationalism and imperialism, is equivalent to a form of moral disarmament.

possibility, given the forms of nationalism and imperialism that are strong in other countries. If that extension were to happen, the historical process of the modern age would conclude with the reappearance of slavery, with the enslavement of those who are defeated in the political and cultural wars. Incidentally, this leads to a very unconventional judgment about "Russian imperialism," which is actually "obligatory" in order not to give in to the process of disintegration.

d. In the context of these propositions, it becomes clear that the current political formulas are completely inadequate.

For example, people keep talking in terms of left and right. All that people on the right do, essentially, is identify totalitarianism with Stalinism and deny that Communism might undergo a democratic evolution (and in this they are certainly correct, but they stop at one limited aspect of the problem). People on the left evoke the ghost of a Fascist threat, tracing it back from the Greek colonels to the CIA and to some kind of ill-defined "American imperialism"; and all they can do is repeat the slogan "no enemies to the left," which is quite comical if it is sincere. There are also centrists who want to oppose all forms of totalitarianism, both Communist and Fascist. What utterly escapes all three positions is the new totalitarian reality that is taking shape. Sufficient evidence of this is the fact that all three political positions failed to predict the student protests – which can be criticized in every possible way except for not having recognized the ongoing process, although this recognition may have been, and still be, quite confused.

THE GENESIS OF THE PROCESS OF REVERSAL

Thus, today's politicians are completely unaware of the "present ethical reality." Therefore, they are not politicians in the sense of the perennially valid Platonic definition as "correctors of an imperfect world," because the source of the imperfections escapes them completely. This is the meaning of the statement, which has been emphasized so often by this journal, that the main reason why politics is so ineffectual is a "lack of meta-politics."[10] Of course, this is not happening by chance. The new ethical reality is bound to remain completely unintelligible to those who

10 [TN] *L'Europa* was a political and cultural journal that had been founded in 1967 by Angelo Magliano. Its explicit goal was to facilitate the process of European unification by exploring Europe's shared cultural roots and by fostering a sense of belonging to a common European civilization (what Del Noce here calls "meta-politics.")

rely only on old words like Communist or Fascist totalitarianism, liberalism, democracy, and so on; and even on relatively new words like technocratic, consumerist, or affluent society, etc. Sociological analyses, no matter how accurate, at best are able to describe certain outcomes, but cannot adequately explain how they came about.

Here I can only sketch some initial remarks. Certainly, nobody can explain the current Western situation as an evolution, or a disguise, or a posthumous revenge of Fascism due to the fact that the resistance's revolutionary work was left unfinished. People may even say that, but what is said does not always express thought, and sometimes it just manifests its absence. Since some people said that large-scale capitalism "invented" Nazism, we could also say that today it invented the current situation, which supposedly is another conservative phenomenon disguised as a revolution, like Fascism and Nazism before. Such explanations ought to generate boundless admiration for the powers of creative imagination of large-scale capitalism – but it has no such powers. Using an expressive French word, this would be a *primaire* explanation. The same could be said, however, of the opposite explanation in terms of Russian Communism's diabolical ability to open its way by inventing attitudes that undermine Western resistance. It is true that Russian Communism seems to have well understood the advantages it can draw from the new Western situation, and to have promptly adjusted its policies. What else is the theory of "limited sovereignty" if not the negation that there can be different national ways to Communism? The ongoing process aims at making the European Communist parties completely dependent on the Russian party. But it is conceivable that, in order to reach this primary objective, Russian politicians may not want these parties to become too powerful, and may prefer that their strength be balanced by the power of other fiefdoms, and that such fiefdoms interact in ways that accelerate the process of disintegration. It was said – by Hannah Arendt, who, however, considered totalitarianism only in Hitler's and Stalin's versions – that the goal of every form of totalitarianism must necessarily be world domination.[11] This statement is perfectly correct, as long as we add that domination can be achieved in different ways: revolution, conquest, disintegration, including indirect support for a process of self-disintegration. Now, this latter seems to be the only way open to Soviet Communism today. Thus, having ruled out all fanciful explanations, we must recognize that the current ethical-political situation originated from an "internal crisis of anti-Fascism." We must have the courage to say it: today we

11 [TN] Hannah Arendt, *The Origins of Totalitarianism* (New York: World Publishing, 1958), 392.

need to criticize a certain version of anti-Fascism for the sake of "faithfulness to anti-Fascism."

ABOUT THE "CULTURAL MISTAKE"

This leads us to rediscover the arguments of a little-known Italian political writer: Giacomo Noventa. I would tentatively describe him as a heretic with respect to the anti-Fascist orthodoxy in Turin in the 1920s,[12] and at the same time as the true representative of a Catholic alternative to Gramsci. Having been myself a heretic with respect to the anti-Fascist orthodoxy in Turin in the next decade (the 1930s), I would like to link my argument back to his.

Immediately after the Second World War, between 1945 and 1947, Noventa had already raised the following question: Were the Fascisms a mistake "against" culture (i.e., a reaction that ended by logical necessity into radical barbarism) or did they result from a mistake "by" culture?[13] Here, conforming to the common opinion, I use "Fascisms" in the plural, as if the forces that at that time fought against the Treaty of Versailles and the Russian Revolution, and against liberalism and socialism, could all be included in the same category. I hold a different view,[14] which I will have occasion to mention below.

However, the opposition between these two views should not be understood too schematically. Those who talk about a "mistake against culture" do not intend to deny that certain cultural attitudes did actually help prepare Fascism, and that certain intellectuals were its accomplices – either out of delusions or to pursue their own selfish advantage (the *trahison des clercs!*) – and helped it become entrenched. Nor do they deny that certain forms of thought have been completely wiped away as a result of its collapse. This is true even of the author who described Fascism as a "parenthesis," Croce. Just read his *History of Europe*.[15] On the opposite side, Lukács outlined a history of irrationalism from Schelling to Hitler in which all forms of non-Marxist German philosophy supposedly took shape in opposition to the transition from Hegel to Marx, and all

12 He meant to be the one who would continue Gobetti's work (see *Nulla di nuovo* [Nothing new] [Milan: Il Saggiatore 1960], 293, his 1946 brief comment on a work from 1937). But his continuation was actually a heresy.

13 This was already Lenin's thesis, "either Communism or radical barbarism," which later was developed historically, above all by Lukács.

14 See my work "Appunti per una definizione storica del fascismo" [Notes toward a historical definition of Fascism] in the volume *L'epoca della secolarizzazione* [The age of secularization] (Milan: Giuffrè, 1970), starting on 116.

15 [TN] Croce, *History of Europe*.

constituted an irreversible process of decadence that finally concluded in barbarism.[16] We must also remember, going back to the distant origins of contemporary Italian culture, that immediately after the war Elio Vittorini[17] started the new journal *Politecnico* with an editorial about non-Marxist anti-Fascist intellectuals. His judgment was milder: he saw them as representatives of a culture that could not go beyond moral condemnations and was unable to promote any effective political action. But since Fascism seemed to have lost all its greatness, what happened was that all the intellectuals whose value could not be denied, including even Nietzsche and Heidegger, ended up being acquitted on appeal. Only a few secondary figures remained in a ghetto; although it was hard to understand what real influence they could have had, their misfortune was that they could not rely on any anti-Fascist disciples.

So, what idea of culture led people to generalize the idea of Fascism to the point of including any movement that was either authoritarian or generically inclined to defend the past – even the "Action française," about which everyone is free to think whatever he wants, but which certainly had very little to do with Fascism and Nazism? How did people come to interpret Nazism as the necessary conclusion of this idea, and to judge Fascism, understood in this global sense, as the "barbaric epilogue of the reactionary spirit"?

You must think of the standard education of a secular intellectual. It was based – and it is still based, although recently there has been more critical awareness[18] – on an act of faith which is analogous to the faith in religious revelation of medieval philosophers. By now, everybody agrees that the great interpretations of history and its general periodization schemes – by Hegel, by Marx, by Comte – developed in the context of the reflection about the French Revolution, viewed as the decisive event that marked the transition to a post-Christian civilization. Out of this

16 [TN] Georg Lukács, *The Destruction of Reason*, trans. Peter Palmer (London: Merlin Press, 1980).

17 [TN] Elio Vittorini (1908–66) was a distinguished Italian writer and journalist. During the Second World War he joined the Communist Party, and after the war became one of the most influential Italian intellectuals. Del Noce is bringing him up as an example of somebody who held the old Italian Idealistic culture partially responsible for the rise of Fascism, not because this culture was Fascist but because it was politically sterile and ineffective.

18 In the wake of well-known works by Löwith (*Meaning in History* [Chicago: University of Chicago Press, 1957]) on the genesis of the philosophies of history and by Voegelin (*The New Science of Politics* [Chicago: University of Chicago Press, 1952], translated into Italian in 1968) on the critique of the idea of modernity; see also my book *Il problema dell'ateismo* (Bologna: Il Mulino, 1964).

reflection came the idea of "modernity" as a "value," i.e., the vision of history as an irreversible process toward the disappearance of religious transcendence, regarded as a "mythical" picture of transcendence. This was the origin of the cliché "today it is no longer possible to speak of ..." Supposedly, a certain order of truths and values passed away, and it is no longer possible to return to them. Those who want to do so at the intellectual level make themselves unable to understand the modern world. Those who want to act at the political level must rely on myths, and this is where the road to practical irrationalism and barbarism begins.

Very simple examples show that this is the starting point of the intellectuals who call themselves secular, in the sense of excluding the supernatural. We only need to look at recent Italian philosophy. Croce starts from the presupposition that the question of transcendence, in the traditional religious sense, has vanished. Gentile starts from the certainty, prior to any proof, that the historical development of philosophy can be explained only as a process toward radical immanence. It is then easy to explain why today's culture in all its forms, including academia and the mass media, has tried to interpret contemporary history within this framework. It is also clear why the bourgeoisie agreed, since Sorel already illuminated in a definitive fashion the connection between the idea of progress and the bourgeois spirit.[19]

However, there is a superabundance of evidence showing that the new situation does not fit into this framework, and we have to wonder how little the pressure of reality has been felt and recognized. People have often spoken of a delay of culture with respect to reality. My (admittedly unusual) answer is that it is a delay in criticizing the progressive framework.

According to this view, which I will call the "progressive" or "modernist" view, history unfolds as a process of transcendence, with respect to which people split into two camps. Some fear it, need an order to protect them, and venerate the very concept of order (they "sacralize" a historical situation, according to an expression that used to be dear to Marxist scholars and has now been adopted by people on the Catholic left, who are late as usual). These can be called the people who "fear transcendence," where by transcendence I mean the intra-worldly process of historical transformation. Other people accept and promote the progressive value of this transformation. Besides reactionaries and progressives, there are also reassurers, those who live during relatively calm periods. Even if they go along with the progress of modernity, they wish that

19 [TN] Del Noce is probably referring to Sorel's *The Illusions of Progress*. See footnote 31 below.

history had stopped at some point (for example, it has been said countless times that Croce would have liked history to end with the liberal age or even, in Italy, with Giolitti[20]). Or else they want to establish some continuity with the philosophies of the past, so that they can be preserved and merely developed to a higher degree of awareness.

Now, what happened after the Revolution of 1917? Supposedly, faced with Communism, the fear of transcendence exploded. All the social groups that had been left behind and condemned by history, in which fear had turned into hatred because of the threat of losing their social status, formed a *fascio* and put themselves in the hands of some "providential man."[21] Sometimes it was a military man, sometimes a man who had experienced poverty and was able to address the masses with a language that sounded revolutionary. The reassurers, the mediators between tradition and novelty, played the role of involuntary accomplices, even if later on they generally broke off to follow their moral conscience. In short, according to this interpretation, Fascism is a sin against the progressive movement of history. As a consequence, in the final analysis, every sin boils down to a sin against the direction of history.

Undoubtedly, this modernist interpretation of contemporary history has prevailed and has shaped most contemporary spiritual attitudes. In fact, this is one instance of a larger truth: all value judgments of our time are incomprehensible apart from contemporary political history. This is due to a reason that we should never forget: Marxism is a world view that sublates itself into practice and becomes history, having been born as a reflection about a revolution that supposedly was left unfinished. The greatest error is to think of Marxism as a superstructure or as an ideology of a political movement, and to separate the philosophical and the political aspects of contemporary history. However, this modernist interpretation reached its greatest strength when it invaded the religious world, Catholic as well as Protestant. Shortly, we shall see how this happened.

The degree of popular appeal, however, is not important. What is certain is that we cannot in any way "identify the modernist view and anti-Fascism," and that the equation traditionalism-equals-Fascism (at least potentially) and progressivism-equals-anti-Fascism is nonsense. "Actually

20 [TN] Giovanni Giolitti (1842–1928), Italian politician and five times prime minister between 1892 and 1921.

21 [TN] The description "uomo della Provvidenza" was first applied to Mussolini after the Lateran Treaty of 1929 between the Italian state and the Roman Catholic Church. It was mistakenly attributed to Pope Pius XI, who had made a rather more nuanced comment to the effect that divine providence had used a man like Mussolini to accomplish what so many respectable pre-Fascist governments could not achieve.

the break between traditionalists and progressives takes place within anti-Fascism itself." Now I have to postpone a deeper discussion of the following point: the nature of the opposition is moral and not economic. So much so that the up-and-coming bourgeoisie, the one that can look forward to a constant expansion of its oligarchic role, sides with the progressive interpretation. The ethical-political aspect and the economic aspect have never seemed as distinct as they do today.

Indeed, there is certainly another approach, which regards the critique of modernism and of the idea of progress as the only possible route to leave behind the horrors of the contemporary world. The first name that should be mentioned is Simone Weil, even if today her contribution is completely ignored in its deepest aspect. She is often dismissed, somewhat condescendingly, as a "Platonist," which for the supporters of the new theology is a derogatory term. Or else she is remembered merely because of her example as an intellectual who accepted to share in "the condition of the working man," or as an anti-clerical Christian (and thus a rebel, who belonged to the same context from which Catholic progressivism would later emerge). Not by chance, progressives of all stripes, both secular and Catholic, always say that they knew her work back in 1948 or so. By that they imply that she belonged to that era, not to the present. Nevertheless, it is still true that nobody predicted both the advent of scientism and the surrender of religious circles to neo-Modernism as exactly as Weil did.

Restricting ourselves to Italian culture, Giacomo Noventa was the author who pursued most thoroughly a critique of the modernist idea. I summarize some of his fundamental ideas:

1 He argued that serious post-Fascist politics could only be founded on a critique of the vision of Italian history that had been formulated by De Sanctis[22] and has been the foundation of all secularist interpretations ever since (even Gramsci regarded it as the ideal model, and could not do otherwise, even if he democratized it in comparison with the Idealistic versions).
2 Noventa criticized De Sanctis because the history of Italian thought does not lend itself, given its ideal character, to progressive-secular interpretations. But on this basis he argued that there is a primacy of the Italian tradition, as the only one that could provide, if its

22 [TN] Francesco De Sanctis (1817–83) was the most distinguished Italian literary critic and historian of literature of the nineteenth century. His name is associated with a liberal-progressive interpretation of Italian history, and in particular of the *Risorgimento*, viewed as the time when Italy finally caught up with modern Europe after being held back by the effects of the Counter-Reformation.

essential themes were developed, a meta-political foundation to European unity and European civilization.

3 He maintained that modernity can be reconciled with Catholic thought, which evidently meant that the problems that arose during the modern age could and should be solved by extending and developing traditional Catholic wisdom. This was the reason why he embraced Maritain, whom he regarded as the greatest historian of thought since the Reformation and the Counter-Reformation.

4 However, Maritain could not bring his history to a clear and precise conclusion because he had not explored in depth the Italian tradition. Maritain's history "could only find its conclusion in Italy."

I think some remarks are in order:

The idea of "modernity" in the secularist sense of "making transcendence horizontal" is not at all intrinsically evident. Moreover, in my opinion, and as I tried to show in my book on the *Problem of Atheism,* the inclusion of atheism in the history of philosophy leads us to demolish the notion that the history of modern thought is a unitary process toward immanence. It also leads us to distinguish two fundamental and irreducible lines of development, one from Descartes to Nietzsche and the other from Descartes to Rosmini (in this way I rediscovered at that time, without knowing it, Noventa's idea about the Italian tradition).

Affirming this idea of modernity as unquestionable already implies a "conservative" mindset. It is the only idea that is never contested by progressive anti-Fascism, which supposedly critiques every opinion. Against the common thesis that the revolutionary dynamics of the Resistance was stopped by conservatism, I claim instead that the renewal or re-form that are intrinsic to tradition (Karl Barth: "renewal does not mean revolution, nor does it mean restoration, but rather 're-formation'"[23]) have been blocked by the progressive mentality's choice for conservatism (first of all as cultural conservatism), and by the consequent failure to criticize the idea of revolution. In fact, the idea of a "mistake against culture" clearly reveals a conservative disposition. It is a refusal to give up on a heritage, even if only of the philosophical kind. This disposition contains the germ of a sequence of contradictions that, in the final analysis, led to the reversal I described at the beginning. To be clear, I am not saying that this reversal was intentional. I am talking about a necessary process which certainly very few people coming from anti-Fascism, and also very few members of the latest generation, would willingly choose, but which they are powerless to resist due to an intrinsic mistake in their position.

23 [TN] Barth, *La Chiesa,* 19.

The contradiction between conservatism and revolution within the progressive position leads to a process of falsification of language, which is the foundation of every aspect of today's situation, both of the crisis of democracy and of moral disintegration.

Progressivism is incompatible with the transition of Fascism and Nazism from objects of polemics to objects of history (in fact, it does not favour this transition at all). Thus, it is incompatible with the need to "see clearly" which, supposedly, should be the first consequence of its kinship with the Enlightenment. Indeed, all serious researchers agree that the interpretation of Fascism and Nazism as reactionary movements should be abandoned. Deep down, that interpretation relies on a single a priori idea: that since the revolution has been turned into a "value," or even recognized as the only value, there cannot be a "bad revolution." In fact, Mussolini always had in mind the figure of Lenin, and regarded him as a competitor. He claimed to be the true revolutionary, the expression of a deeper culture. I think he should be described as a revolutionary who had accepted the Idealistic critique of Marxism. And this acceptance was the origin of his revolutionary failure.[24] Furthermore, traditionalism and Fascism cannot be confused, because traditionalism must necessarily go back to Plato (it is impossible to speak of "tradition" without making reference to the thesis that "truth in itself" and "good in itself" are absolute, eternal, etc.), whereas Mussolini and Hitler come "after" Nietzsche and his destruction of the idea of truth. I am not saying that they were his disciples, because Nietzsche is not a practical guide but rather a diagnostic, the greatest diagnostic of what would happen in the twentieth century. And Mussolini and Hitler are just confirmations of his diagnosis. Still, because they came "after" Nietzsche and accepted his negations, even when they affirmed traditional ideas, they could present them only as "myths," and thus falsify them completely.

However, the decisive factor that accelerated the process of disintegration was the conversion (although, in religious terms, it would be more appropriate to say anti-conversion!) of a large part of the religious world, both Protestant and Catholic, to the idea of modernity.

THE STAGES OF THE PROCESS

In the January 1946 issue of *Costume* I had already criticized the replacement of the real Resistance with the myth of the Resistance.[25] That arti-

24 See my work, previously cited, "Appunti per una definizione storica del fascismo."

25 [TN] Augusto Del Noce, "Politicità del cristianesimo oggi" [The political dimension of Christianity today] in *Costume* 2, no. 1 (1946): 59–68.

cle intended to examine the events immediately after the liberation and their philosophical implications from the standpoint of the theses of Maritain's *Humanisme intégral.* What had the resistance been, if not the refusal to collaborate, to accept being enslaved, after Nazi Germany had implicitly declared a war of colonization against the whole world, having proclaimed itself a different and superior race (racism as the extreme form of colonialism)? But such a refusal could be shared by people who held completely different political ideas, religions, and even moral principles. It could reflect completely different ideal motives, and even no ideal motives at all, since it was a vital refusal before being a moral one, even though in this case vitality agreed with the requirements of moral conscience. Therefore, the practical collaboration that took place between very different groups did not imply at all that they shared the same ideals.

At that time this analysis was destined to fall on deaf ears – and I was under no illusion that it could be otherwise. Because on the one side there were those who were already mature when Fascism came to power; to them it seemed obvious that, after the Fascist parenthesis and its tragic ending, the only option was to go back to the old parties. On the other side there were the young and very young people who had participated in the Resistance and had generally experienced it as a revolutionary war, if for no other reason than because they had chosen to join it voluntarily, without being forced by any external authority. Therefore, they were inclined to believe that there was an ideal unity within the Resistance, which would generate a new world. Actually, this idea of an ideal unity, such that "the Resistance was transformed into a Revolution," was precisely the starting point of the process we are discussing.

How did this idea arise, and what developments did it implicitly contain?

Actually, the myth of the ideal unity of the Resistance was correlated with the interpretation of Fascism as reactionary, which, as we have seen, was an "obligatory" consequence of the progressive interpretation of history.

In the 1930s, European anti-Fascist intellectuals could still afford to ignore Marxism-Leninism, regarding it as a Russian phenomenon (the Stalinist involution was used as proof), as some sort of Eastern-style version of Marxism. But Communism played an undeniably significant role in the Resistance, and so it seemed that anti-Fascism required giving up anti-Communism, in light of the interpretation I just mentioned, because the Communist threat had been the argument used by the Fascist movements in order to appeal to groups that did not share their background and their mindset. They had been able to do so in spite of the fact that the Fascists had fought against all the positive aspects of the modern world, while using the technical instruments provided by that same world – supposedly this was their new feature in comparison with previous reactionary movements. Moreover, people were rediscovering the philosophical power of Marxism, which Idealistic culture had ignored, along paths like those of Lukács (from the pre-existentialist position of *Soul and Form*[26] to the Marxist position of *History and Class Consciousness*[27]) and Gramsci. However, only a few intellectuals could embrace Marxism completely. This was due to its two philosophical aspects, historical materialism and dialectic materialism. Each one of them seemed susceptible to leading to positions that would break with the system. The former would lead to sociologism, the latter was in danger of turning into absolute Idealism, an evolution that, after all, had already taken place with Actualism.[28] Hence, the tendency to distinguish between a critical or "open" form of Marxism, or Marxism as a science, and a metaphysical or reverse-theological Marxism, whose practical expression supposedly was totalitarianism. It was expected that the co-existence of both aspects and the dialogue with Western thought would enable the first aspect to prevail and, as a result, lead to the famous "democratic evolution" of Communism.

Therefore, for the majority of secular intellectuals, and for a then-small group of Catholic intellectuals, understanding the Resistance as a revolution did not mean simply embracing the Communist view, which was that the Resistance would extend to Western Europe the transformation of a war into a revolution that Lenin had carried out in 1917. They wanted to achieve a higher unity in which liberalism (viewed as essential to the modern spirit as process of critique of authorities – a formula inspired by the Enlightenment, which was coming back in fashion at that time) and socialism would be reconciled, and the revolution Westernized.

At this point the road was chosen: the route was easy, and it matched so well the common habits of the cultural world that, in the mid-1950s, widespread approval was all but certain. Reconciliation was possible on the condition that liberalism be cut off from any tie with transcendent or immanent religion (hence the criticisms of Croce's "religion of freedom," a thesis that, having already been stated in 1932, was the premise

26 [TN] Georg Lukács, *Soul and Form*, trans. Anna Bostock (New York: Columbia University Press, 2010).

27 [TN] Georg Lukács, *History and Class Consciousness*, trans. Rodney Livingstone (Boston: MIT Press, 1972).

28 [TN] Or "actual Idealism," the philosophical school founded by Italian philosopher Giovanni Gentile.

of the essay "Why We Cannot not Call Ourselves Christian"[29] ten years later, which at that time was completely dismissed). Marxism, in turn, had to be cut off from the above-mentioned forms of metaphysicism and theologism, whose practical expression had been, supposedly, totalitarianism.

This position marked a reversal with respect to the orthodox position of Marxist philosophers, because according to them the Enlightenment was a preparatory stage, still tied to the bourgeois revolution, which Marxism had surpassed in a decisive fashion. On the contrary, progressive intellectuals considered Marxism – combined with elements of left-wing existentialism, of Dewey's version of pragmatism, and of rationalism in a methodological, no longer metaphysical, sense – to be part of the spirit of the Enlightenment, as its second stage. However, this disagreement did not lead to sharp cultural conflicts because the progressive position replaced a romantic and conservative type of historicism with an Enlightenment-based form of historicism that criticized tradition and all practical habits associated with it, and this criticism was what Communists really cared about. Thus, what used to be called "cultural politics" headed in a positivist and anti-metaphysical direction. Indeed, the double negation I described implied the embrace of a form of scientism tied to the expansion of the human sciences (psychoanalysis, sociology, linguistics, structuralism). Once again, this embrace was "obligatory" (progressivism is not creative, but this characteristic would deserve a separate discussion). This form of scientism also included themes from Nietzsche (and thus from atheistic existentialism) since it criticized as dogmatic the notions of objective truth and objective goodness, and reduced truth to a set of tools that help direct life (Deweyan instrumentalism; Russellian anti-metaphysical rationalism). Thus, it was a form of left-wing eclecticism (this sentence should be discussed at length, too), in which positivist and pragmatist elements were combined with Marxist themes separated from messianism, and with Nietzschean themes separated from the tragic aspect. But above all, I must emphasize that this combination constituted one of the greatest, or possibly *the* greatest, contradictions that ever appeared in history. The reason is that scientism, in this extremely expanded form that claims jurisdiction over all human realities, represents the climax of conservatism because it professes a complete relativism about values, which are explained as expressions of psychological and social situations. In this respect it is radically different from Marxism, which proclaims its faith in

29 [TN] Benedetto Croce, "Perchè non possiamo non dirci cristiani" [Why we cannot not call ourselves Christians], *La critica* 55 (1942): 289–97.

an absolute, which is history, the supreme judge whose verdict was to be executed by the proletariat – later replaced by the Communist Party.

But, on the other hand, this scientism was being called to play a revolutionary role, and an essential aspect of the revolution is the idea of starting a new history in which it is guaranteed that the mistakes of the past will not be repeated. Thus, how could scientism fulfill its revolutionary task except as mere negation, by dissolving all the values that tradition had affirmed? In this respect, the transition from Freud, who was still a representative of a conservative form of scientism, to Wilhelm Reich is extremely significant. Reich is not especially famous as a psychoanalyst in the strict sense. Nevertheless, there is no question that today psychoanalysis is given a moral significance that, in general terms, coincides, openly or not, with the revolutionary significance that Reich attributed to it.

If we go back to what I said earlier about Mussolini's and Hitler's "modernism," we understand the paradoxical position into which progressivism is forced. The tradition it destroys is exactly the same one to which Simone Weil appealed, having rediscovered it through anti-Fascism. It is the Platonic tradition.

I mentioned before that progressivism rethinks Marxism within the mindset of the Enlightenment, and that this marks a reversal. In the course of this reversal, progressivism is forced to retrace backward the process of development of the Enlightenment and to go back to its origins. Thus, it must rediscover libertinism and express it in a pure form, taking away the aspect that made it a prelude to the Enlightenment in the strict sense (or isolating the libertine current within the Enlightenment, which was a more complex phenomenon), and also eliminating the aspect that made it incline toward pessimism. It rediscovers freedom "from" (in practice, freedom from the burden of all moral obligations), separating it completely from freedom "for." This freedom "from" is, after all, precisely the libertine freedom. What is the "hippie" movement if not the consistent final outcome? These apparent rebels are only protesting against the stage at which progressivism would like to stop. I know well the one and only possible objection: today we face a new revolution, after we have recognized that the true character of modernity cannot be found in the metaphysics of immanence but rather in the scientific spirit. This revolution does not manifest itself in the usual forms but as technical progress. As a reply I only need to quote Ellul's words in his recent, very beautiful book *Autopsie de la révolution*: "we must recognize that technology produces a society that is essentially conservative (though rapidly developing, of course), integrated, and totalizing, at the same time that it introduces far-reaching changes: but these are changes of an identity, of a constant relationship to itself. Technology is anti-revolutionary yet suggests *total* change because of the 'developments' it brings, whereas in reality only forms and methods are altered. It destroys the revolutionary impulse by increasing conformity to its own integrated structure. It brings on a fundamental 'implosion' by creating the impression of a liberating explosion, which is purely superficial."[30]

The ideas I have presented so far about the fundamental contradiction that allows conservatism to absorb and neutralize completely the idea of revolution through progressivism, match perfectly Ellul's ideas about the "banalization" of the revolution, about its current reduction to a "consumer good." Finding examples is all too easy: nowadays, how can an artist, a writer, a musician, or even a philosopher be successful in the eyes of the bourgeoisie if not by appearing to be revolutionary? But perhaps the most decisive example is the incredible success of the new theology among the most dynamic *élites*. It is true that an interest in theology that lay dormant for centuries has reawakened, but in what circles?

Also, in this case, we must observe that success among the privileged classes is achieved by reducing the revolution to desecration, i.e., to the aspect it shares in common with libertine thought.

Here, we are brought back once again to Sorel's best works and to his masterpiece, *The Illusions of Progress*,[31] which is so much better than *Reflections on Violence*.[32] We are reminded of his theses about the connection between the idea of progress and the bourgeois spirit, about the fact that the rise of this idea at the end of the seventeenth century coincided with a regress of the traditional spirit and a decadence of behaviour and of the moral life, and about the antithetical relationship between the idea of progress and the idea of revolution. Certainly, we should not underestimate how much Sorel at his best could serve as a guide to illuminate today's situation.

THE PROCESS OF SELF-DISINTEGRATION

The characteristics of the new type of totalitarianism that I mentioned at the beginning can be easily explained in terms of the fundamental contradiction created by "progressivism after Marxism." I will compare my

30 [TN] Jacques Ellul, *Autopsy of Revolution*, trans. Patricia Wolf (New York: Alfred A. Knopf, 1968), 178.

31 [TN] Georges Sorel, *The Illusions of Progress*, trans. John and Charlotte Stanley (Berkeley: University of California Press, 1969).

32 [TN] Georges Sorel, *Reflections on Violence*, ed. Jeremy Jennings (Cambridge: Cambridge University Press, 1999).

ideas with those of an author who is neither a reactionary nor a traditionalist in the sense I described before, and least of all a Fascist: Jean Cau.[33] He is simply a pessimist because he claims for himself the democratic right to keep his eyes open. In the future it may be possible or even necessary to move beyond the views he formulated in *L'agonie de la vielle*,[34] but only after having accepted them, as mere observations of facts.

In the Western world we have reached a "democracy devoid of the sacred." Some will reply, resorting to a standard rhetorical device, that this is precisely the progress. This kind of democracy marks the transition to an "open society," which accepts and respects all forms of thought and enables religion to become purer by separating politics from religion, and so on. In actuality, this democracy "devoid of the sacred" coincides with absolute atheism. But is this new atheism a new foundation of values, or does it mark the impossibility of speaking in terms of values? If religious foundations are replaced by social foundations (rules of coexistence accepted by everyone), it is too easy to point out that society can be opposed. But, on the other hand, also a protest in the name of a new order based on human brotherhood (in the only possible sense left: that men are not brothers but will become such) is actually a meaningless enterprise.

Observe that some of the student protesters, thinking precisely along these lines, would like to go back to original Marx-Leninism (it is strange how little they talk about Trotsky, who seems even more isolated after his death. The fact is that today people are afraid of being on the side of those who lost!), against the betrayal by official Communism, which by now has become bourgeoisified (for them, Togliatti[35] is the greatest example of a traitor!). In order to show that their hope is delusional, we must recall something that many people have pointed out, but that Ellul discussed better than anybody else, in my opinion.[36] The revolution has been "truly betrayed" and Trotsky is correct in this regard. But, on the other hand, a revolution of the Marxist type can succeed historically only if it is betrayed. Indeed, in Marxism the revolutionary principle and absolute historicism join forces (actually, historicism becomes absolute precisely because it becomes integrated with the revolution). From this perspective, the revolution becomes the only value, neither limited by

33 [TN] Jean Cau (1925–93) was a French journalist and writer, after having been Jean-Paul Sartre's secretary.

34 Jean Cau, *L'agonie de la vielle* (Paris: La Table Ronde, 1970).

35 [TN] Palmiro Togliatti (1893–1964) was the leader of the Italian Communist Party from 1927 until his death.

36 [TN] Ellul, *Autopsy of Revolution*, 157–72.

nor ordered toward other values (for rigorous Marxism, freedom and socialism are the result of the revolution and not its goal. Marxist doctrine should not be confused with the linguistic compromises it must strike for propaganda purposes). Accordingly, the truth of Marxism is measured by its success. But how can success be ensured, if not by strengthening to the maximum the structures of the state? The state is given limitless power, unconstrained by any principles (this is precisely totalitarianism). The development from revolution for the liberation of humanity to revolution for the conquest of power is, at the same time, the betrayal of the Marxist revolution and its fulfillment.

In the course of this strengthening, because of the betrayal, some traditional values are rediscovered. However, they are cut off from the meaning they had within tradition. For instance, the nation is rediscovered but becomes inseparable from imperialism; or the family, and so on. In principle, it is even possible to imagine a reconciliation with religion. But this would happen according to the principle that religion is a type of opium. Today Communism relies on the opium of the earthly happiness that will come after the sacrifices required by the qualitative leap. But this opium may run out eventually, and then why not resort to the religious opium?

Jules Monnerot,[37] who is undoubtedly one of the most intelligent among Communism's intransigent critics, writes: "The essence of Communism is defined here in terms of the mutual immanence and functional inter-dependence of three factors: an 'empire' (which pretends to be something else than an empire), a 'secular religion' (which pretends to be something else than a secular religion) and a 'subversive organization of world-conquerors' (which pretends to be something else than a subversive organization of world-conquerors)."[38] I must only add that this false self-presentation is not intentional but obligatory due to the essence of Communism, and this is its strength.

Essentially, Cau agrees:

> So, recently two systems had the will to be totalitarian: Stalinism and Nazism. I will take them as points of reference in order to predict which one is most likely to bear children. The Stalinist system was based on absolute mendacity. The Nazi system was based on absolute sincerity. At the time when the Soviet Union was

37 [TN] Jules Monnerot (1908–95) was a French sociologist, best known for his studies of the totalitarian movements of the twentieth century, and in particular of Communism as a "secular religion."

38 Opening words of the preface to the new edition of Jules Monnerot, *Sociologie du communisme* (Paris: Gallimard, 1963).

moaning under a monstrous tyranny ... Stalinism declared that the USSR was the freest and happiest country on earth, the land where "true" democracy flourished and beautiful justice was finally realized ... millions of men died believing its lies ... martyrs of a system and a tyrant who had devoted himself to one of the most prodigious "inversions of ideals" in history. Nazism, another monster, presented itself naked. It affirmed its cruelty, its hatred and its uncompromising and murderous racism. It proclaimed its lust for genocide ... it shouted out its will to enslave. Two terrifying faces. One masked, the other naked.[39]

The question whether Nazism won philosophically, or even whether its defeat on the battlefield was necessary for its philosophical victory, is not at all absurd. "Let us wonder, with icy lucidity, whether the future will not be Nazi, whether the prophet of the times to come will be neither the Jew who was born in Galilee nor the one who was buried in London almost two thousand years later, but a man with a large mustache who died crazy and devastated by his own vision: Friedrich Nietzsche, the philology professor. Let us wonder, with the cold eye of a clinician, whether Nazism was not the only consistent answer to the proud proclamation of the death of God. The final consequence of humanism, which thought naively that it could set man free (by emptying him of the sacred)."[40]

Today it is fashionable to mellow down Nietzsche in all kinds of ways. He is turned into a man of the Enlightenment, or into a Christian, and every side claims him to itself ... Here, let us just abstract one aspect of his personality and let us look at him as a phenomenologist who studied one particular essence, the "death of God," and highlighted what it includes, the end of the idea of truth. Subordination to truth is still an "all too human" characteristic. The transition to the superman is the transition to a man who dominates ideas and reduces them to instruments that can help direct life and favour the success of the will to power. The "death of God" implies a decisive break with Platonism, and therefore with Christianity. In fact, he said so in the opening pages of *Beyond Good and Evil*: "the most dangerous of all errors ... namely Plato's invention of pure spirit and the Good in itself ... since Christianity is Platonism for the 'people.'"[41]

In this sense, we could also say that the reason for Hitler's defeat was, in the final analysis, his sincerity. Instead of giving up on thinking

39 Cau, *L'agonie de la vielle*, 140–1.

40 Ibid., 116.

41 [TN] Friedrich Nietzsche, *Beyond Good and Evil*, trans. Judith Norman (Cambridge: Cambridge University Press, 2001), 4.

according to the idea of truth, he treated Nietzsche's statement as if it were the truth.

Now, if we consider what is still conventionally called the free world, we must observe that the new phenomena follow necessarily from one another. They have come to the fore through a daily (not by chance) process of growth over the last ten years, but they had already been prepared by the culture that became established in the 1950s, after the opposition between Christianity and Communism – about which believers and non-believers (like Croce) had agreed a few years earlier – started to sound like almost empty rhetoric, or material for politicians' campaign speeches.

If this world had betrayed the ideal of freedom, the problem would not be too serious. The trouble is that it remained rigorously faithful to that ideal, but interpreted it in a particular way. Renewal was understood as liberation from the constraints and ideals of tradition, which were regarded as invalid precisely because they belonged to the past; they expressed a different historical situation (this is why people at that time ridiculed the "good old times," emphasized a so-called "manly" rejection of all forms of nostalgia, and formulated a program of "complete liberation from Romanticism"). Anti-Communism itself was turned into an aspect of this process, because supposedly in Russia the new world had been temporarily overpowered by ancient traditions, both bureaucratic and theocratic. Nevertheless, (people said) the "new" was necessarily going to emerge through a democratic evolution inscribed in the reality of things, and would lead Marxists themselves to understand that the revolutionary-messianic aspect was just a necessary ideology in order to accelerate the process of renewal in under-developed countries. Therefore, man was cut off from the past and at the same time deprived of any tension toward the future (in order to be "new" he had to conform to a world that kept changing at a faster and faster rate, but without any interior change; in short, the technological world). He was reduced to pure present – and was peculiarly celebrated as "creative freedom" because of this liberation. Nothing was handed down to him (tradition derives from *tradere*), he had nothing to hand down, and he was only supposed to take his place in a process that was irreversible but without any qualitative leaps. At this point, man's freedom thus understood reduces to man's fragmentation. He can derive his vitality only from "novelty." Novelty derives its value only from the fact that it "denies," and inebriates man, thus giving him a refreshing feeling of being alive. Needless to say, this opens the way to drug addiction, and it would be absurd to deny its significance, because what in ages past could be a vocation or a vice becomes today an essential, even indispensable, component. I remember reading in an article by a sociologist that there is no difference between eating and using drugs. In the context of this fragmentation, drugs become a necessary food indeed.

But this is not the essential point, yet. Where can man find the novelty that makes him feel alive if not "in something other"? Here, we must mention the strict connection between this notion of liberation and devirilization. Today one of the topics most deserving of investigation is the transition to the "reign of the woman." Noventa, who was a traditionalist, wrote: "When a society starts pursuing an effeminate ideal, through its books and its laws, 'women' themselves and 'men' gradually abandon the leading elites, the social classes that produce those books and those laws, and take refuge among the common people. The field is taken over by 'males' and 'females,' by pederasts and lesbians. Where woman is submitted to man, intelligence and strength triumph; where man to woman, imagination and violence. Reign of the woman: tyranny. Reign of the women: anarchy."[42] Also, how could we forget that André Breton,[43] in a work that I believe was his last, hailed the advent of the "reign of the woman" as the preparation for a radical transformation (Breton seems to regard this reign as the equivalent, for the Surrealist revolution, of Communism's "transitory" dictatorship of the proletariat).

For democracy, anti-traditionalism has meant a purge of all faiths and ideals. This is the origin of the sequence that Cau pointed out. First, order-for-the-sake-of-order. Order was reduced to the pure exercise of power and separated from any authority of values; hence, a tyranny that pretends not to be one because it conceals itself as group tyranny, in which the people in charge remain hidden. Second, disorder-for-the-sake-of-disorder. The student protesters accurately perceived that the current order is oppressive; but since they did not trace back their criticism to its original principle, their protest became the "failed revolution," because it was pure disorder. This happened not because of the obstacles they faced, but by essence, so to speak. The protest ended up being complicit with the oppressive order because its action targeted for destruction the old structures that still protected individual freedoms: pure painting, pure sculpture, pure literature, pure sexuality.

A quarter of a century ago there was a widespread notion that individualistic democracy should be replaced by a "personalist and communitarian revolution." We have already discussed the revolution. Let us now consider the "personalist" and "communitarian" parts. Since the group that controls production and power does not aim at realizing an

42 Giacomo Noventa, *Caffè Greco* (Florence: Vallecchi, 1969), 62.

43 [TN] Actually, Breton's disciple Jean-Louis Bédouin. See footnote 24 on p. 172.

ideal order, however understood, but only at affirming itself, the individual is reduced to his instrumentally useful "function" within this group. At the same time, the system tends to make less and less room for the individual, until he cannot live without being part of a group. This is the greatest possible negation of liberalism, and also the highest degree of homogenization. The attempt to surpass liberalism and socialism ends up negating both.

By definition, democracy is the recognition of the equal dignity of every human person. Conversely, today's democracy establishes an absolute and irreconcilable opposition between traditionalists and progressives. For instance, the whole world stood by passively during the genocide of the traditionalist people of Biafra,[44] while that same world protests loudly every time a progressive intellectual is wronged (not that I approve of that, on the contrary!). It is a complete negation both of justice and charity.

Since contradiction and falsification – and thus unproductive immorality, which is different from justifying for the sake of a universal goal means that would not be licit for private profit – mark all aspects of contemporary Western society, this discussion could go on forever.

However, there is one group in which the contradiction has truly become extreme: the large fraction of Catholic theologians who have accepted the progressive myth. The language they use is always the same: they appeal to the ideals of the Gospel against the Roman order. On the contrary, what left-wing Catholics are able to generate is the purest form of clericalism, such as has never been achieved. Indeed, there is clericalism when the Church becomes a necessary organ in order to establish or maintain some historical order, and when this becomes its exclusive task. Now, a scientistic society does need priests, and they really must be "new priests" because the task they have to fulfill is completely different from the task in the societies of the past. In fact, scientism must necessarily leave some room for agnosticism, because the non-existence of God and of another world cannot be an object of proof. And here the "demythologizing" theologians come into the picture, in order to reassure people not against atheistic doubt but rather against religious doubt. Not by chance, the doctrines of original sin and hell are the kind of reactionary dogmas from which religion should be purified according to psychologists (because they are "projections" of a bad consciousness), according to some biblical exegetes (because they do not belong in scripture), and according to some historians (because they are Gnostic

44 [TN] Del Noce was writing during the Nigerian civil war of 1967–70.

residues). Moral theologians come in next and declare that morality is autonomous and shared by Christians and atheists alike, since morality reflects the direction of history and its progress. We call sin what corresponds to a lower stage of evolution, virtue what corresponds to a higher one. I cannot further develop this analysis here, and show that the thesis of the "death of God" is truly the necessary end point of this theological development. Note this: a long time ago people talked already about "atheistic Catholicism" or "clericalism without Catholicism" in reference to a certain right-wing movement. Its mistake consisted in being on the right. Conversely, the fullness of clericalism is possible only "on the left."

The new Catholicism of the "adult age" represents the most complete inversion of the position of Maritain, the most important theoretician of Christian Democracy. According to him, recognizing the positive value of the modern discovery of the subjective dimension, as a development and not as a negation of traditional thought, opened the way to reconciliation between Catholicism and liberalism. And Christianity was able to facilitate the transition from liberalism to democracy (in the sense of an effective recognition of the dignity of every person), as opposed to liberalism's inadequate foundations.

• • •

Because too many things had to be crammed into the limited length of this essay, I was forced to make an inevitably rambling argument. But it was not possible to do otherwise because today we face a situation in which all the various aspects are necessarily interconnected.

Nevertheless, I think I established two crucial theses:

1 The process of self-destruction of Western society was not per se an unavoidable process. Rather, it is the necessary result of having confused the transition to democracy with the progressive myth. Once again, it derives from an error by culture. It is a true sunset because the old ideals are thought to be exhausted, and new ones not only did not rise but cannot rise. What sometimes are presented as new ideals are just contradictory disguises.

2 Conversely, the contradictions that this process engendered show its own mythical character. Its collapse is also the collapse of the visions of history that legitimated it and whose origins I have briefly discussed.

We could speak, with Ellul, of a "necessary revolution" after the collapse of the Marxist "revolution according to the direction of history," first in the "betrayed revolution" and then in the "banalized revolution" (our contemporary Western situation).[45] But we must be aware that we are only at the beginning of the huge process of philosophical revision that this task requires. Whether the crisis will turn into a catastrophe is also a matter of time.

45 [TN] Ellul, *Autopsy of Revolution*, 233.

8

The Death of the Sacred

EUROPE AND THE OCCIDENTALIST HERESY

I read in a splendid book by Manuel García Pelayo that, for many years now, Soviet historians have honoured the monk Philotheus of Pskov – who, at the end of the fifteenth century, invented the myth of "Moscow the third Rome" after Catholic Rome and Byzantine Rome – with the title of "progressive."[1]

What is strange about that, you will ask. Every young man knows by heart all possible disquisitions about "Russian imperialism." Every intellectual keeps saying that by now we have entered the age of *homo progressivus,* and that demythologization is a sign of our maturity. Supposedly, Russia's historical delay is due to the fact of being, in part, still under the spell of myths.

On the contrary, it would be appropriate for adults to learn, possibly from the book I just cited, that "mythical consciousness is not just a residue of the original consciousness which survived the advent of rational thought, but rather something necessary to human beings, in order to meet each other and find their way"[2] in the sphere of rational thought itself. When religious consciousness descends into political reality, it necessarily comes across as myth, as union of the natural and the supernatural due to the intervention of a heavenly power. Therefore, the idea of the holy city as an ordering centre is essential in order to affirm the

This chapter was first published as "La morte del sacro," *L'Europa* 4, no. 22/23 (1970): 29–45. Republished in *Rivoluzione Risorgimento Tradizione* (Milan: Giuffrè, 1993), 233–53.

1 [TN] Manuel Garcia Pelayo, *Mitos y simbolos politicos* [Political myths and symbols] (Madrid: Taurus Ediciones, 1964). Del Noce cites from the Italian edition, *Miti e simboli politici,* trans. Lucio D'Arcangelo (Turin: Borla, 1970), 81.

2 [TN] Ibid., 169, my translation.

reality of the sacred. This was the origin of the myth of Rome. It arose in pagan consciousness, which regarded Rome "as a theophany, as the revelation in history of divine power, a power that manifests itself neither in a natural order nor in a primordial moral order, but in a political order."[3] Later on it was Christianized because "from the beginning its destiny had been marked by a kind of hierophany. [Rome] is the mediatrix between the cosmic order and the human order. It is an instrument of salvation because, even if it is not a divinity, Rome is a vehicle or an instrument of the divine. It is the only political form that coincides with the divine structure of the world. It establishes political peace. It turns plurality into unity."[4] The origin of the myth of Moscow as the "Third Rome" was the same because, after "the fall of Constantinople in 1453, and the permanent liberation from Mongol domination in 1480, Moscow could regard itself as the heir of Byzantium," and thus claim to be "an ecumenical empire" in "opposition to the West."[5]

Thus, we face the greatest paradox of contemporary history: whereas Russia's official atheism "guards" an explicitly sacral myth – which must necessarily bear the mark of its origins and act accordingly, regardless of the intention of the rulers – the non-atheist West (at least officially) can stand against it only as a democracy "devoid of the sacred."

Who, in the West, still thinks about the unity of the religious and political spheres? Actually, a few people do. For instance, I have in front of me an excellent work that provides a definitive argument against those who see a similarity between Savonarola's cause and the cause of today's progressive-demythologizing protesters. It highlights that at the core of Savonarola's thought, and of his fight against Alexander VI, lay precisely this idea of the assimilation of the Roman spirit to the divinity of the Church of Christ, not in the sense of affirming the temporal power of the Church but in the exactly opposite sense.[6] But this is a very rare example.

Anyway, it is unquestionably true that Russia constitutes the last bastion of the sacral mindset in the field of politics. Can this defence be limited to the political field? Or, instead, is this the reason why in Russia religiosity has made a comeback, as attested by many observers? Is this why the Orthodox Church has been affected the least (or not at all) by the new Modernism, the theology of secularization and of the death of

3 Ibid., 110–11.

4 Ibid., 113.

5 [TN] Ibid., 80–1.

6 Fr. Giacinto Scaltriti o.p., *Savonarola, il vero contestatore* [Savonarola, the true protester] (Turin: Borla, 1970); see especially 67 and 75.

God has impacted it very little, and Russian theology schools are the most traditional and also (I have heard) the most rigorous in their teaching? On the contrary, Europe thought that it could renew itself by adopting the ways of the civilization of well-being,[7] in which well-being is the only political-social goal – and then whoever wishes to believe that this well-being will continue or increase in another life is free to do so (but, in fact, who thinks about that any longer?). It would be easy to show that if this kind of civilization triumphed completely – which, however, is impossible – every form of faith or hope in another world would disappear. To tell the truth, Europe went down this road following in America's footsteps, but after America itself, during the last quarter of a century, was strongly influenced by European intellectuals, so that its traditional Puritan mindset has been decisively undermined, even in mainstream culture.

Do these considerations shed any light on the current political situation? Contrary to the common opinion, still today "the sacral principle is triumphant." This is the reason why, so far, Russia has been left essentially unscathed by the process of self-destruction that is affecting, without exception, the European countries and even the United States, although in a different form.

A DANGEROUS SIMPLIFICATION

A quick excursus about the history of the last quarter of a century is indispensable.

It is important that we free ourselves from the conventional picture, which says that between the West and Russia there was first the Cold War, then co-existence, then détente, and now the possibility of a dialogue ... This picture is not exactly accurate. Or, at least, these words hide a dangerous simplification.

In fact, there was a period when the main concern was the defence of the West, based on the idea of its humanistic and Christian tradition. One could distinguish, certainly, between a Christian humanism, a liberal humanism, and a socialist humanism, but all of them belonged in the context of a common Christian civilization. People thought that the time had come to become aware of this. It has become customary to

7 [TN] Here and elsewhere I translate literally the Italian "benessere" as "well-being." This translation is not completely satisfactory because in English "well-being" is used in the general sense of "being well," whereas "benessere" means more specifically "material well-being" or "confortable life" or "affluence." In fact, Del Noce's concept of "civilization of well-being" is very similar to what has been called the "affluent society."

dismiss the importance of Croce's essay "Perchè non possiamo non dirci cristiani"; we are told that it was an expression of senility.[8] I reply that, among the stages of Croce's philosophy, the final period is actually the most important – in fact, many people think so – and that this particular essay represents its manifesto. In Italy, the recognition of this common context – instead of a conflict that had turned out to be both sterile and damaging – was the soul of De Gasperi's political action.[9] By saying this I do not intend to deny that in that period, which roughly spanned the first ten years after the war, tension and fear of Russia were greater than today. But this was a secondary feature with respect to the essential features: the defensive posture and the religious character of the conflict.

Subsequently, people began to say that we should be careful never to engage in crusades, religious wars, or theological hatred (but is "defence" a crusade? If anybody spoke of a crusade, it was only very small groups that exercised little or no influence on actual policy. Because it is hard to detect any crusading intention even in Foster Dulles's "rollback" policy, regardless of what some people said). That was the prevalent public discourse – or chatter – during the years from 1955 to 1960.

Afterwards, another attitude took over, which was the exact opposite of the first and had already been prepared at the cultural level over many years: the West would be able to prevail against Communism only on one condition: by outdoing it "in irreligion."[10]

"SPIRIT OF MODERNITY" AND "CAROLINGIAN" EUROPE

The idea of a competition taking place on the ground of a greater secularity seemed attractive in several respects. It seemed that several trends could find in it common ground: the rethinking of Marxism in the spirit of the Enlightenment; technological progress which, by eliminating poverty, made possible the replacement of violent revolution with a democratic and orderly process; the American spirit that had found in

8 [TN] Benedetto Croce, "Perchè non possiamo non dirci cristiani" [Why we cannot not call ourselves Christians], *La critica* 55 (1942): 289–97.

9 [TN] Alcide De Gasperi (1881–1954), Italian politician and statesman. He led the Christian Democratic party and served as prime minister eight times from 1945 to 1953, leading the reconstruction efforts after the Second World War. He is also remembered as one of the founding fathers of the European Union.

10 I take the liberty to cite my own essay "Appunti sull'irreligione occidentale" [Remarks on Western irreligion] in the volume *Il problema dell'ateismo* [The problem of atheism] (Bologna: Il Mulino, 1964). I think that in that piece, written in the spring of 1963, I identified the most important features of the crisis of the Western world that was then just starting and has become fully visible in the following years.

Pragmatism its philosophical expression; the development of the human sciences and especially of psychoanalysis (which orthodox Marxism was trying in vain to deny or to ignore); pacifism (because the so-called "Manichean" opposition between the two worlds was abolished); and the spirit of the Resistance that had brought together Russians, free Europeans, and Americans. It was the triumph of the "spirit of modernity" over the temptation to be reactionary and go back to a "Carolingian" Europe. This temptation was trying to make a comeback by taking advantage of the occasion created by Communist "atheism" and "totalitarianism," and was sponsored by the last old-fashioned pope, Pius XII, the "Vicar."

A pre-established harmony of sorts brought together all the ideas that in modern times had been called "generous." It reconciled them with the interests of a new form of capitalism, and with intellectual habits that had sedimented since the time of the Enlightenment.

European secular intellectuals were happy because they were used to thinking in terms of "sublation" and progress. Indeed, the new trend kept all the negations that Marxism had formulated, and added a new, modern-sounding one: the negation of the reverse-theocratic spirit of Marxism itself. This spirit was the reason why the Communist revolution had been able to succeed only in under-developed and semi-oriental countries like Russia, or in fully oriental countries in which it had become allied with a reawakening of national awareness (indeed, did the Chinese revolution rediscover the Marxist categories because of a class struggle, or rather because of the constant humiliation of China's national sentiment?).

American intellectuals were happy because, as Michele Federico Sciacca pointed out with remarkable foresight in 1954,[11] "even if society in the United States calls itself Christian, American philosophy is essentially all atheistic. Not only that: it is marked by the idolatry of science, the tool that will radically change humanity by producing technical development, and will bring to mankind all the happiness that man by his 'nature' can desire."[12] In this way, the gap in America between a progressive culture and a reactionary political world was filled.

11 Michele Federico Sciacca, *La filosofia oggi* [Philosophy today] (Milan: Bocca, 1954), 2: 168–9.

12 At almost the same time as my article in *L'Europa*, the book *L'oscuramento dell'intelligenza* [The dimming of intelligence] by Michele Federico Sciacca was published (Milan: Marzorati, 1970). I cannot recommend it enough to the few people (but today are we really so few?) who think against the mainstream.

The perfect agreement between the ideas I outlined in that article and those of Sciacca goes to show how much observing history leads people to rediscover similar ideas, without any mutual influence. What Sciacca calls "Occidentalism," as opposed to the true West,

Scholars in the human sciences were, by and large, enthusiastic. Sociologists thought that their dream of completely replacing "archaic" philosophy with sociology was about to be fulfilled. Nobody would talk any more about being and about the spirit, but only about situations and relations. As usual, there was no lack (on the contrary!) of Catholic sociologists who agreed. In their view, the ultimate achievement would be a world ruled only by science and by calculation. A place for God could always be found, perhaps by placing Him in the subconscious. God is so humble and also so good that He certainly does not want to upset public relations!

To say nothing of psychoanalysts like Fromm or Reich, who in the 1930s had already proposed combining Marx and Freud, anticipating the arguments of the new form of revision of Marxism. I mention Fromm and Reich primarily because of their interpretation of Fascism as the explosion of an aggressive and authoritarian mindset, resulting from traditional repressive education. From their perspective, the new trend achieved the highest degree of anti-Fascism, since it aimed at purifying Communism from the "Red Fascism" (Reich's expression[13]) that had been incarnated by Stalin. Thus, this distinction offered Communism the criteria to rid itself of any lingering commonalities with the Fascist movements.

Businessmen could not be unhappy either, because what claimed to be a step forward was actually just the regression of Marxism to Saint-Simonism (admittedly, to an updated form, but with all the essential features. Saint-Simonism is the origin of sociology, of the secular version of Americanism, of the rehabilitation of the flesh, and of the progressive "new Christianity"). Thus, the great transformation of 1917 and the two world wars ended up fulfilling Saint-Simon's program of an aristocracy of industrialists, bankers, scientists, and technicians.

---

agrees perfectly with what I call the "Occidentalist heresy," a choice of words that was suggested to me by reading his book. By that, I mean the involution of modern immanentistic culture that has taken place "after" and "against" Marxism, even if in the form of a pacifying dialogue. I call it self-dissolution and he calls it nihilism, using a Nietzschean term, and his analysis of Nietzsche's relevance today is very rigorous.

Because of its general outlook, this book could be defined as a return to Plato, called to be almost a philosophical judge of contemporary reality, which is marked by the domination of what Plato called the appetitive principle over the intellective and irascible principles. All the characteristics of a society centred on production and consumption can be deduced from this domination.

13 [TN] See Wilhelm Reich, *Reich Speaks of Freud* (New York: Macmillan 1967), 274–6.

With Saint-Simonism, the new trend also embraced utopia, but not in the sense of the word that goes back, besides Plato, to Saint Thomas More. From More's perspective, the blueprint of the ideal city represented not what could be realized in practice (in fact, its complete realization was impossible because of original sin), but rather a model obtained by abstracting away from the consequence of sin, namely "superbia" in the Augustinian sense. Therefore, utopia served the purpose of showing to what extent existing reality is inadequate and far from the ideal. The goal was certainly to correct this reality, but without hoping to turn it into a perfect city. On the contrary, today we face utopianism in the modern sense, which first appeared when Bacon equated science with power. It is the idea that science is capable of transforming the moral world itself. Since the time of Bacon, the discovery of every new science has been accompanied by the proposal of a utopia. Incidentally, this is why I regard Condorcet as the essential author in order to understand this essence, because in his philosophy he established a rigorous connection between calculus of probability, criticism of metaphysics, definition of the idea of progress, and utopia. The latest utopia arose in the context of psychoanalysis and was given its clearest formulation as "sexual revolution" by Dr Reich, whom some people have raised to the Olympus of the liberators of the human spirit.

Now, one can reach utopianism starting from practice as well as from science, as, for example, in the case of the proponents of absolute non-violence. Thus, it has been something new to see the advocates of production and consumption stand side by side with the theoreticians of a completely irreligious form of pragmatism, with those of the sexual revolution, and lastly with the apostles of non-violence. Or even to see these latter in the same movement as the liberators from all sexual inhibitions (poor Capitini![14]).

Finally, Saint-Simonism was also the endpoint of the form of modernism – as euthanasia of religion – that has infested all denominations but especially the Catholic and Protestant churches. Because, what is the single theme of the various new theologies of demythologization, secularization, the death of God, and so on, in the simplest possible terms? It is the following: that the modern age is marked by the transition from the vertical to the horizontal dimension. Supposedly, this process started with the new science, the true and irreversible expression of the modern spirit, which changed the focus of research from vertical to horizontal causality, by searching for laws in the sense of constant relationships

14 [TN] Aldo Capitini (1899–1968), Italian philosopher, politician, anti-Fascist, and poet, was one of the first proponents in Italy of Gandhi's philosophy of nonviolence.

between phenomena. Today we have reached the stage when finally the same attitude must be applied to religion. Therefore, we need to move from vertical to horizontal transcendence. Religion must make a difference in the world: we no longer need private and repressive ascetic virtues, but active love of others and the promotion of change. No more metaphysics, which was linked with the vertical conception. Religion must undergo scientific, sociological, and psychoanalytical tests and evaluations. The final and unavoidable result is the thesis of the death of God, which is often concealed, not so much out of prudence as out of concern about being left without anything else to say.

TWO UNDENIABLE ADVANTAGES

Our epoch enjoys two undeniable advantages. The first is that processes develop very quickly. It took two centuries to clarify the dialectics of the old Enlightenment, which was destined to turn upside down into the most oppressive possible system.

The dialectics of the new Enlightenment has become explicit in just a few years. Certainly, nobody can tell how long its repercussions will last, and how large, perhaps even catastrophic, its impact will be. Once a mechanism is set in motion, recognizing it rationally is not sufficient, at least by itself, in order to stop it. Nevertheless, without such recognition no other power is sufficient either. Any purely political ability (shrewdness, prudence, decisiveness, astuteness, etc.), even of the highest degree, is not capable of stopping this type of process. The reason why today politics need most urgently "metapolitics" is, in the very first place, because of the dialectics of the new Enlightenment, which may lead to Europe's eclipse for an undetermined, but certainly very long, period of time (perhaps, it may even lead to a permanent sunset: who knows?). By now, the margin of error is already extremely small.

The second advantage is that theoretical ideas, moral positions, and lifestyles are perfectly consistent. Clearly, these two aspects are really one and the same, and cannot be discussed separately. Only by starting from the dialectics of the new Enlightenment or new progressivism or whatever-you-want-to-call-it, as the first step, is it possible to understand the apparently less significant aspect of the change in lifestyles. There has never been a tighter *chaîne des raisons.*

So, how can one think of surpassing/sublating/etc. Marxism? The ideology of total revolution includes two inseparable aspects – and this is the point that Lenin understood perfectly well. One aspect is historical materialism, the other a reform of dialectics that transforms Hegelianism from a speculative philosophy into a philosophy of action.

Now, from the standpoint of philosophical rigour, if either one of these two aspects is pushed to its final consequences it will exclude the other. Indeed, Gentile's Actualism could hardly be described in any other way except as the most rigorous development of the reform of dialectics, which to be fully consistent must expunge the materialistic aspect. Elsewhere, I have clarified that Gentile's embrace of Mussolini was necessary, although not in the sense of being a guide but in the sense that his philosophy required him to adhere to Fascism and stick with it until his death.[15] Gentile was the first who tried to "sublate" the philosophy of Marx – a completely different attitude from standard revisionism, which tried instead to combine eclectically Marxism and philosophical ideas coming from other sources – and the practical outcome was certainly not positive. After the war people picked up again the idea of sublation in the exactly opposite direction, by extending historical materialism all the way to absolute relativism and to the idea that what is lowest is also what is deepest.

Let us now discuss how, as a result, the synthesis of generous ideas that I mentioned earlier turned out to be a mask covering the most complete process of disintegration.

Let us observe, first, that absolute relativism (which is no longer skepticism, which declares that truth is unattainable, nor pessimism, which presupposes a contradiction between what exists and the idea of the good) affirms that there are no permanent values. Values are always relative to a particular situation. Actually, they cannot even be discussed, because they are mere tools of self-affirmation. But of whom? Not of all mankind. Because it was old Marxism that talked about the proletariat, which – unified by poverty and pushed into despair by increasingly inhuman conditions – would carry out the revolution all by itself, and by freeing itself would free mankind as well by abolishing social classes. On the contrary, in the new vision affluence melts the proletariat away. There is no longer any unifying principle, neither material nor ideal, and what resurfaces is the *libido dominandi*, the individual will to succeed. There are no good or bad means: success justifies. What is required, at most, and only to some extent, is that we abide by certain sociological norms that ensure coexistence.

The True in itself and the Good in itself (permanent values) are denied, and thus religion, metaphysics, and morality in the traditional

15 [TN] Augusto Del Noce, "Appunti per una definizione storica del Fascismo" [Notes for a historical definition of Fascism] in *L'epoca della secolarizzazione* [The age of secularization] (Milan: Giuffré, 1970).

sense are destroyed. Since there is no longer any tradition, and in fact every expression (novel, show, etc.) is made meaningful only by the intensity or novelty with which it denies some traditional value, there is nothing that can be handed down (tradition from *tradere*, to hand down). Thus, no more fatherland, or family. And not just in the sense that devotion to a particular fatherland declined for some historical reason, or that family bonds grew weaker. At the time of my youth, there were still people (who already then were said to belong to a different era) who talked about the unbreakable triple nexus of religion, fatherland, and family. To us it seemed empty rhetoric. By contrast, today's situation makes us rediscover that such a nexus was, and still is, deeply meaningful. But there is no future either, in the sense of a qualitative change toward a different and better reality. Strictly speaking, there is not even the possibility of progress toward greater justice, but only of an expansion of reality as it is now. It has been said that the last twenty-five years marked the beginning of the age of *homo progressivus*, a decisive turning point with respect to a civilization that until now was concerned, essentially, about continuity between novelty and tradition. But what does that mean? This claimed primacy of the future over the past, as recognition that the future is entitled not to be limited by the past, cannot obviously mean a primacy of the ideal over the real. It just means that today's man, cut off from the past and from the future, lives through a sequence of discontinuous instants. And in order to feel alive he needs not to feel imprisoned by the past, which is merely "dead" (even the past as recent as yesterday). Therefore, perfect novelty is his oxygen, not in the sense that he creates it, but that he receives it passively. Once again, negation prevails. They talk about a "right of the future," but this assertion is just a byproduct of the negation of the past.

After all this destruction, what is left? A social atom, man completely reduced to his task within an organism in whose purpose he cannot share anyway, because it boils down to sheer production. Reification has reached the highest degree. To put it better, it has become a universal principle.

Here we truly reach a crucial point: this process moves, ultimately, toward complete falsification of language, toward the rule of systematically organized mendacity. For instance, people never talked so much about altruism, universal love, and so on. However, can one really love a "thing"? Is not love always directed toward another subject with his personal individuality? Does it not aim at grasping his irreducible reality? But what if such personal individuality is dissolved?

PROGRESS OF THE WELFARE STATE

Let us consider first the highest virtues: charity, mercy, compassion. There has certainly been progress in the social welfare systems, and in some countries poverty has disappeared. It would be absurd to deny that this is objectively good, and I have no intention of doing so. But let us ask ourselves: from the subjective standpoint, how is this improvement "experienced"? Does it mean greater charity? Not at all. The common sentiment is that poverty is disgusting and therefore must be pushed out of sight. Welfare systems also serve the purpose of shielding people from depressing feelings of charity and compassion. The atomized individual is more and more imprisoned in radical egocentrism.

I will discuss only in passing and very briefly some aspects on which I do not like to linger, if for no other reason than that people already talk about them too much – almost always spouting nonsense, on both sides of the debate.

For instance, consider the ostentation of nudity. Besides certain secular people who hail the liberation from taboos, certain priests also say that this is the end of a hypocritical and pharisaic form of morality. These are clichés, in which the poverty of language itself reveals a lack of thought. A few days ago I read in a major newspaper an article about "the explosion of freedom, the lust for life, the passion for freedom and brotherhood of the young people of the seventies, their rebellion against the violence, the hypocrisy, the race for money and the war that society prepares for them. Therefore, they exalt everything that society condemns: drugs, sex without constraints, nature, absolute freedom."[16] The article was signed, but the ideas it proposed are so coarse that it might as well be considered anonymous. At least, one should have the courage to say that this cult of nudity is linked, as a consequence is linked to its premise, to the sublation of Marxism that I mentioned earlier, which can only be expressed as a mixture of the worst aspects of Marx and Freud. It has become widespread, and practically cannot be criticized, because it is supported explicitly by that culture. Then, if what is lowest is also deepest, it becomes clear that shows like *Hair, Oh Calcutta*, and so on are just triumphant celebrations of the new course. Indeed, if that principle is accepted, how could anybody argue that some parts of the body must be covered? However, if the premises were formulated explicitly, very likely they would be criticized. It is much more effective to push the

16 [TN] Liliana Madeo, "Corsa alla prima di Hair ci saranno repliche?" [Big attendance for *Hair's* premiere, will there be any repeat performances?], *La Stampa* 102, no. 175 (31 August 1970), 3.

consequences, which feel attractive, without mentioning explicitly the premises. Therefore, this education to the "spirit of the times" produces split individuals, people who are intellectually schizophrenic. Not only is the individual reduced to a social atom, but this atom is also fragmented. The same applies, of course, to the ubiquity of foul language, which today is regarded as the "right to use bad words" and a form of criticism of the semantic hypocrisy of euphemisms. And since it is a moral right, or even a quality, it is very widespread among the members of what, once upon a time, used to be called the "gentle" sex.

THE REPLACEMENT OF LOVE BY SEX

By reflecting about the principle of universal reification, we easily understand the replacement of love by sex. And since in free sexual unions duration has no value, making moral distinctions between homosexual and heterosexual unions no longer makes sense. If anything, the latter are "for common people" whereas the former are more sophisticated.

At this point a question arises naturally about all of this, and about so many other aspects of contemporary eroticism which I would rather not discuss: *cui prodest?*

The answer is easy: the humanitarian neo-Saint-Simonian society can recognize as meaningful only production and consumption. Thus, it can only stimulate to the highest degree what Plato called the appetitive soul – the organ of sensitive desires – making it escape completely the control of what Plato called the "Guardians."

It may seem that criticizing the self-proclaimed progressive alternative to Marxism from the standpoint of Platonism – which was until very recently, in its many forms, sometimes in disguise, sometimes implicitly, the ideal foundation of European civilization – means imposing an extrinsic criterion of judgment. The answer seems easy: what we want is precisely to establish the opposite of Platonism, i.e., to free ourselves completely from the mythical mindset and the primacy of the invisible. Every idiotic intellectual knows how to parrot the party line that "today's man" has "the courage of knowledge," meaning that he knows that only what can be empirically verified (and thus is measurable, computable, usable, etc.) exists (or at least is the only reality we can talk about).

Well, since such culture claims to represent a step "beyond" Marxism that eliminates its alienating and mystifying aspects, let us adopt a Marxist perspective. Then we will have to say that such a replacement of the revolution by progress represents the highest degree of bourgeois mystification. We saw that already: absolute reification, complete falsification of both inter-personal relationships and language, complete falsification of education and culture, at the service of a ruling elite which looks exactly like the one Saint-Simon theorized (although, to be fair, I must add that his thought had different philosophical goals), and which was never so powerful. The bourgeoisie has indeed changed during the last quarter of a century, but in the sense that it has taken ownership of Saint-Simonism.

THE CONDITION FOR WORLD UNIFICATION

The transition to this new perspective was presented as the necessary condition for world unification, for full détente, and for peace.

In fact, it was something else entirely. The real intention behind the transition from defending tradition to making its negation the primary value was to go on the offensive against Russia.

Since 1917 radicalism has been consistent. It hailed the February revolution as a great event because it was scandalous that Russia, the most despotic power, had joined as an ally a war that had been conceived as democracy's final battle against authoritarianism. Now, Russia was taking its place among the democracies, even if as a newcomer still in need of education. Things changed when Lenin rose to power, and it would be quite useful and interesting to go through the history of the radicals' responses. Eventually, they reached the judgment I will describe. After some time, the eggheads came up with the following theory: Communism is merely a technique in order to greatly accelerate the process of industrialization of under-developed countries. Therefore, the achievement of a substantial degree of industrial development satisfied the condition for Russia to evolve to the modern and democratic stage. The goal was to establish an enormous technocratic empire, of which Russia would be one province. It would keep making progress, certainly, but it would remain in a condition of inferiority with respect to truly democratic countries. It would be a dialogue, yes, and not a crusade, but with Russia brought back to its role as a pupil.

Sciacca[17] defines "stupidity" as the presupposition "that only what is subject to empirical observation and can be empirically 'represented' … and as such can be known and verified through the experience of the senses and through reason, 'is' … and what is not visible and not touchable, and therefore is not computable and usable, 'is not.' Hence, the identification of knowledge with what can be experienced and rationalized."

17 Sciacca, *L'oscuramento dell'intelligenza*, 62.

If this definition is correct, the offensive certainly started under the banner of "stupidity." That it is correct is proven by the fact that in order to succeed, it had to assume that Russians are stupid, and that turned out not to be the case.

Anyway, during the last ten years, the great army started moving, and it was perhaps the strangest that ever appeared. When it stated its opposition to the crusading spirit, it was indeed correct, because its members were anti-crusaders by essence. Nietzsche said of the Socialists that "they wink because they invented happiness."[18] But we must say that he was talking about the wrong people. The theorizers of the society of well-being are those inventors.

We can conjecture that the plan was to send the new pupils marching at the front, as poster children for the delights of the new world. According to the principle of stupidity, anything that breaks with tradition, in any way, is revolutionary, and Communist "Puritanism" was an archaic residue. If Communism means happiness, and if happiness is material well-being, Russia should have become indistinguishable from the West. This would have been a capitulation under a different name: from being a teacher Russia would go back to being a pupil, drop the iron curtain, and agree to Westernize. Behind the pupils would march the teachers, i.e., the scholars in the various human sciences, to the extent that they claim that their disciplines replace philosophy: cultural anthropologists, sociologists, psychoanalysts, pedagogists, statisticians, and so on, all intent on dissolving metaphysical thought into social and psychological situations. Next would come the philosophers who theorize a new Enlightenment, of which Marxism would be a component, having shed its dogmatic aspect. Each one in his own way, they would offer Russian Communism the philosophy that would ensure its further development. Last would come the new theologians, with the task of reassuring people, of freeing them from scruples – because, due to scientism's intrinsic agnosticism, someone may still think that God might exist, even though we cannot talk about Him and He does not interfere at all in autonomous human relations. For example, they would assure us that we need not fear hell, which is just a projection of our bad thoughts; that the Church's traditional teaching on sexual relations must be completely rediscussed; that ascetic morality was appropriate for epochs in which man had not yet achieved domination over the world, and therefore consumer goods were scarce; that the transition to affluence allowed us also to discover the beauty of the sexual act; that we

18 [TN] Friedrich Nietzsche, *Thus Spoke Zarathustra*, trans. Walter Kaufmann (New York: Modern Library, 1995), 17.

should no longer speak of original sin; that some dogmas are first class, others second class, and others I do not know what class; and many similar things. Perverting language as usual, they pretend to be anticlerical while their originality, so to speak, is that they realize the highest degree of clericalism.

ATHEISTIC DOUBT AND RELIGIOUS DOUBT

I already wrote it in *L'Europa*, but I take the liberty repeat it, because it has not been pointed out very often. "There is clericalism when the Church becomes a necessary organ in order to establish or maintain some historical order, and when this becomes its exclusive task. Now, a scientistic society does need priests, and they really must be 'new priests' because the task they have to fulfill is completely different from the one in the societies of the past ... And here the 'de-mythologizing' theologians intervene, in order to reassure people not against atheistic doubt but rather against religious doubt."[19]

Excuse me for bringing them up last. I do so because – with all due respect – they are not as attractive as the new sirens. And also because they display a peculiar tendency to come late and discover novelties at the exact moment when they have solidified into slogans which are what, in fact, should be demythologized; thus, today they discover "modern man," "worldliness," "secularization," "resistance," and "revolution." And lastly, because they are prepared to switch sides in order to join the winner, as is the nature of clericalism: from the theology of secularization to the one of revolution, from evolution to the "God who will be."[20]

"AMERICANIZATION" OF EUROPE

Thus, this offensive fulfilled what Simone Weil had prophetically anticipated in 1943:

We are all aware that there is a grave danger of Europe's becoming Americanized after the War, and we know what we should lose if that were to happen. What we

19 [TN] Augusto Del Noce, "Le ombre del domani" in *L'Europa* 4, no. 15 (1970): 11–35, published in the present volume as "The Shadow of Tomorrow," pages 92–117.

20 [TN] I translated literally the Italian "Dio che sarà." I imagine that Del Noce is referring to the eschatological trends that became popular in theology at the end of the 1960s. See, for instance, Jürgen Moltmann's *Theology of Hope* (London: SCM, 1967), which was influenced by the works of Ernst Bloch, who had stated, in *The Principle of Hope* (Oxford: Blackwell, 1986), 210, that God has "future as the essence of his being."

should lose would be that part of ourselves which is akin to the East … it seems that Europe periodically requires genuine contacts with the East, in order to remain spiritually alive. It is also true that there is something in Europe which opposes the Oriental spirit, something specifically Western. But that something is to be found in America in its pure state and to the second power, and we are in danger of being devoured by it … the Americanization of Europe would lead to the Americanization of the whole world.[21]

I would rather not use the expression "American imperialism." I would speak, instead, of a universalistic awareness of their mission that Europeans lent to Americans as they waged the Enlightenment's war against their own past. It is a fact that today America is the wellspring of the principle of disintegration, but the poisoning of America has largely been the work of Europeans. Not by chance, Wilhelm Reich regarded the United States as the only country where the sexual revolution could take off, in spite of many obstacles and of Puritan resistance. This psychoanalyst has exerted a huge posthumous influence during the last decade, and in his books we find the blueprint of the principle of disintegration (admittedly, they are somewhat banal, but does not such principle coincide with the dimming of intelligence?). In fact, the sublation of Marxism that typifies the offensive I described is a faithful reflection of the formula he had already stated in 1944: "It is not a matter of a class struggle between the proletariat and the bourgeoisie, as a mechanistic theoretical sociology would like us to believe … The social struggles of today, to reduce it to the simplest formula, are between the interests *safeguarding and affirming life* on the one hand, and the *interests destroying and repressing life* on the other."[22]

A CHANGE OF STRATEGY

Then what happened? Russia, facing this threat disguised as dialogue, changed strategy[23] on the basis of a very correct observation, which

21 Simone Weil, *Écrits historiques et politiques* (Paris: Gallimard, 1960), 371, 373, and 375 [TN: In the essay "A propos de la question coloniale," which was published in English as "East and West – Thoughts on the Colonial Problem" in *Selected Essays 1934–43*, trans. Richard Rees (London: Oxford University Press, 1962) 195–210. The passages quoted by Del Noce are on pages 203, 205, 206].

22 [TN] Wilhelm Reich, *The Sexual Revolution* (New York: Noonday, 1963), xvii–xviii.

23 [TN] In other articles from 1970 Del Noce argued that in the late 1960s the Soviet Union changed its strategy toward the West. On the one hand, the Communist regime took a neo-Stalinist turn, increasing military expenses and enforcing the doctrine of "limited sovereignty" in Eastern Europe, e.g., with the invasion of Czechoslovakia in 1968. On the

certainly did not need to rely on cutting-edge sociology. Colonization can be achieved by only one method: by uprooting a people from its traditions. Europeans have a long history of extensively practising this method (and this was Europe's greatest historical fault). Now – oh, wonder! – in order to feign regret they are applying the same method to themselves. Since this process of self-uprooting was conjoined with well-being, what could remain standing in the end, except for economic organizations, which could be easily turned into vassals and whose fidelity would be ensured by the leftist parties?

The West planned to work by attraction: it would bring about a decisive evolution in Russia just by showing itself. Now Russia is merely collecting the spoils of an offensive that fizzled out on its own. But stupidity as the principle of false Occidentalism is still active and blinds its advocates. Thus, today they scream against Russian imperialism, against neo-Tsarist policies, against alliances with capitalist forces, and so on. They pretend to teach Russian Communism what it should be, or what policies it should have followed in order to facilitate the success of the Occidentalist offensive.

But how can they speak of imperialism if, this time, Russia was on the defensive? They should just acknowledge a defeat that "should" be beneficial. It is the last chance for Europe's rebirth.

EXTREMELY SERIOUS DANGERS

In fact, the dangers could become extremely serious if we keep moving in the same ethical-political direction that has reached a climax over the last ten years. In the West, in the years since the "new frontier" (this is not the place to discuss Kennedy's legacy; I am talking about the culture that accompanied his politics and determined their tone), democracy was completely emptied of the sacred, and a true pedagogy of atheism was

other hand, the Soviets encouraged the Western European Communist parties to embrace the new progressive movements and the "fight against repression." Rather than trying to establish a Communist regime, Western Communists should ally themselves with the "enlightened" fraction of the bourgeoisie that interpreted "anti-Fascism" in a Reichian sense, as a fight against traditional moral and religious authorities. See, for instance, "Che cos'è 'la lotta contro la repressione'" [What is the 'fight against repression'], *L'Europa* 4, no. 6 (1970): 6–10. Del Noce's analysis echoes an observation in Étienne Gilson's book *Les Tribulations de Sophie* [The Tribulations of Sophia] (Paris: Vrin, 1967), 104–5, which in turn refers to an article by French journalist David Rousset. *Les Tribulations de Sophie* was the result of a suggestion by Del Noce, who had proposed that Gilson assemble in a volume four lectures he had given in Italy in April 1965. Del Noce was also instrumental in having the book published in Italian as *Problemi d'oggi* [Problems of today] (Turin: Borla, 1967).

established. Initially, this produced great satisfaction among the clergy because of the dumb idea that there is some sort of antagonism, such that the Church will triumph if the state is weakened and deprived of all ethical aspects. New phenomena appeared, which I think are unprecedented, like the fact that there is definitely more female than male irreligiosity among the young.

As if that was not enough, here in Italy we had the question of divorce.[24] Here, I do not intend to discuss the problem in the abstract, but just to say one thing about "this" divorce in the current situation. It is proposed precisely at the time of greatest crisis of the family, as an aspect of the crisis of tradition (there is no family if there is no ideal heritage to hand down).

Having been started, by now the machinery of Western irreligion moves forward by inertia. The work of popularization can advance even without new supporting arguments (which, actually, are not needed).

Then what? Could it happen that the Vatican – and I am speaking of the component most faithful to traditional orthodoxy – will start looking at Russia, having lost all hope in the West? The fight against disintegration might bring together powers that until now have been philosophical enemies. This would happen not out of Machiavellian convenience but because of a changed historical situation. It might even mark the beginning of a revision at the level of ideas. *Relata refero*: I have been told that among young Russian intellectuals there is again great interest in Berdyaev – an émigré philosopher whose work nowadays is completely forgotten in the West, after having been somewhat successful in the 1930s – and also in Solovev, who can be considered his ideal teacher. What can that mean? Observe that Berdyaev's work was born in the context of the Russian controversies about Marxism at the beginning of the twentieth century. If we think of the complete transformation that has taken place in the West, it becomes clear that Russia must face a new adversary. Will Marxism be sufficient for the task, or will Russia need its own revision process, but of the opposite kind with respect to the Western process I have described? And where will such process lead it?[25]

24 [TN] A few months after this article was published, on 1 December 1970, the Italian parliament legalized divorce after a contentious debate.

25 In my essay "Appunti sull'irreligione occidentale," which I referred to earlier, I stated that this type of irreligion and the technocratic society it produces represent a theoretical form that Marxism cannot beat, because it carries to its ultimate consequences one of the aspects of Marxism itself. If this is true, and if the political opposition between the two societies is complete, "the revision process and its interpretation become necessary," even though, of course, nobody can say how long it will take or set any deadlines.

On the other hand, who could blame the Vatican, from a religious perspective, for this possible change of course? Is it a power at the service of one particular continent? It remains true, however, that Europe cannot escape decadence except by radically rejecting what could be called the "Occidentalist heresy."

At the beginning I distinguished between two opposite approaches that the West has adopted with respect to Russia. Both failed, although the second failed much more ingloriously. Criticizing it does not imply going back to the first. Indeed, both suffer from the same mistake, so that the first approach already contained the seeds of the second. The mistake is the idea of the primacy of the West, which supposedly reached its climax in America as complete opposition to the characteristics of the East. This is where the idea came from, in the second approach, to seek détente by Westernizing Russia. Culturally, this program was expressed in the idea of a continuity between liberalism and Communism in the name of the Enlightenment. From this perspective, the Enlightenment was the theoretical expression of the initial break between East and West. Whereas, on the contrary, the periods in which European civilization truly blossomed were those marked by a fruitful relationship with the East.

9

The Roots of the Crisis

THE YEAR 1971 WAS MARKED BY the rediscovery of Fourier as the precursor or first theorizer of the permissive society.[1] There was a proliferation of new editions, introductions, and essays. Everybody forgot, however, that the best introduction to the works of this French utopian had already been written in 1849 by Antonio Rosmini, and was easily available because it was reprinted in 1968.[2] Rosmini highlighted the contradiction of Fourierism as follows: the promise of the greatest freedom and greatest unity among men, achieved by giving complete freedom to the passions, or, as Fourier used to say, to passionate attraction, would be followed in practice by the greatest slavery, by the

Originally published as "Le radici della crisi" in A. Bengsch et al., *La crisi della società permissiva* (Milan: Ares, 1972), 110–42. Republished in *Rivoluzione Risorgimento Tradizione* (Milan: Giuffrè, 1993), 147–70.

1 [TN] Clearly Del Noce is referring to French philosopher and utopian Charles Fourier (1772–1837).

2 Antonio Rosmini, *Frammenti di una storia dell'empietà* [Fragments of a history of impiousness] (Turin: Borla, 1968), with an introductory essay by Alfredo Cattabiani on "Il Saint-Simonismo, sistema culturale della società tecnologica" [Saint-Simonism, the cultural system of the technological society] in the series *Documenti di cultura moderna* [Documents of modern culture] edited by A. Del Noce and E. Zolla. The *Frammenti* include two essays on Benjamin Constant (1829) and on the Saint-Simonians, which were collected and published under this title in the volume *Apologetica* [Apologetics] (Milan: Boniardi-Pogliani, 1840). The editors of the new volume had the idea to include the short essay on Fourier that had been part of the *Saggio sul comunismo e il socialismo* [Essay on communism and socialism] (Florence: Società Tipografica, 1849), anticipating the rediscovery of Fourier that would take off two years later. Nothing shows Rosmini's relevance to today's situation better than these essays, and it is hard to find contemporary writings that detect more perceptively what at that time were germs, and today have turned out to be possibly deadly diseases. We expected widespread interest, at least among Catholics. Instead, there was almost complete silence [TN: None of these works by Rosmini is available in English.]

complete destruction of freedom and of human society, "condemned" he said "to be drowned in the sugary bath of the passions."[3]

Today I would like to illustrate precisely this contradiction by proposing the following thesis: "there was never before such a well-organized system of political mendacity, and it matters very little whether its supporters know it or not. And it is malignant mendacity because it is purely destructive." I mean that it cannot be described as a mixture of truth and falsehood, and not even as a myth in Sorel's sense of the word.[4] We can regard it as the protective shell of a process of universal disintegration, and in Europe's case of its suicide. Indeed, from its perspective, the idea of Europe is replaced by that of the West, and by the reality of a West marching toward the fulfillment of its etymology (the land of sunset).

THE PERMISSIVE THESIS

Boiled down to its simplest formulation, the justification of the claim of the permissive society is based on the idea that inhibition changes man at the structural level, in such a way that he acts, feels, and thinks against his own natural interest, the enjoyment of life, the inclination toward happiness. Inhibition produces a personality that is repressive, authoritarian, reactionary, and, as a result, aggressive. This definition is found in Reich's book *Mass Psychology of Fascism* (1933),[5] which applies to contemporary history some theses that had already been stated in *The Sexual Revolution* (1930).[6] The psychological-utopian analysis goes hand in hand with the ethical-political one, and owes to it most of its success. Supposedly, the "Fascist" is the complete incarnation of the "repressive" type. As we shall discuss later, the great propaganda tool of permissivism is the claim to represent the fullness of anti-Fascism. Hence, a critique of permissivism requires a critique of *the conditions that make this identification plausible.* Supposedly, if we eliminated repression, if we cleared the way toward the full satisfaction of the passions, aggression would disappear. Thus, permissiveness would lead to non-violence.

3 [TN] Ibid., 189 (my translation).

4 Indeed, according to Sorel, a myth is an organic framework of motivating images, through which the moral will acts on present reality. The permissive society operates in the context of a "demythologization" that undermines not only questionable mythical theories but also the moral will that sustained Sorel like few other people.

5 [TN] Wilhelm Reich, *Mass Psychology of Fascism,* trans. Vincent R. Carfagno (New York: Farrar, Strauss & Giroux, 1970).

6 [TN] Wilhelm Reich, *The Sexual Revolution,* trans. Theodore P. Wolfe (New York: Noonday, 1963).

Let us understand this idea more precisely: it is not the idea of non-violence as a superior moral ideal but its utopic counterpart, which supposedly will be achieved without any sacrifice. The notion of a social mechanism that will ensure virtue without sacrifice, and make it simply coincide with well-being,[7] does belong to the realm of utopia. Indeed, the separation of the idea of morality from that of sacrifice follows immediately from the abandonment of the idea of the initial fall, which is the condition for the idea of utopia. This observation is a special case of a general proposition, which I have not yet seen fully developed and which must be explored more deeply: at our time in history heresies and utopias have all come together *giving science the task of legitimizing them.* In fact, there is a link between utopia and science that has not received enough attention, in the sense that, historically, to the rise of every new science has corresponded the rise of a new form of utopia. Well, the idea of the permissive society is the utopia that has accompanied the spreading of psychoanalysis, even though the most serious psychoanalysts have not subscribed to it.

CULTURAL MISDIRECTION

However, the opposition between repression and permissiveness cannot be adequately understood without taking into account a philosophical context which is usually left unmentioned. The opposition must be linked to two opposite conceptions of the nature of values. The first is the traditional view that values are immutable, that they possess an objective reality which, even if it is different from the objective reality of empirical objects, is just as independent from the situation of the human subject. At least generally, this objective reality is tied to a metaphysical-theological conception of an objective order of being, such that morality consists in respecting it. According to this view, there is, in brief, a universal and eternal reason, higher than man, which provides the foundation for the hierarchy and the absoluteness of values. Therefore, values cannot be reduced to any psychological and sociological explanation (and thus to affective states or social situations). Participating in this order is regarded as the foundation of man's autonomy and dignity.

This conception can be called traditional in a twofold sense. First, because it is the most ancient; it was already essential to Greek thought and continued in various forms, so that it defined what is called "common moral sense," which remained essentially unchanged until the

7 [TN] "Benessere" in Italian. See footnote 7 on page 120.

Second World War. Second, because this immutability is what makes possible the idea of tradition (tradition from *tradere*, to hand down). It can also be called the "Platonic" conception, from the first philosopher who proposed it in rigorous terms, where of course we are using the word Platonism in the broadest possible sense.

The opposite conception – which goes back to thinkers who could not have been in greater disagreement but who shared the common feature of anti-Platonism, or in fact atheism,[8] Marx and Nietzsche – regards values as reflections of given historical situations, so that they cannot be abstracted from their context. Values subsist only within the movement of history, and they too are subjected to the laws of birth and death. Hence, any transformation of the social conditions, of the technical means of production and communication, etc., must produce a transformation of values. In recent years this idea has become very widespread in the culture, and even more in what would be better described as semi-culture. What do I mean by this word? I mean the outlook of those who receive from outside, from the *mass media* and thus from the groups who direct and control the flow of information, certain "new" opinions and accept them without any serious consideration of the premises that shape them: those who incarnate perfectly, to use a fashionable expression, the other-directed type.[9] The semi-educated man "does not know that he does not know." Semi-culture is defined as the radical antithesis of the idea of *docta ignorantia*, in the broadest sense of this magnificent traditional concept.[10] One suspects that many of the

8 Regarding Marx's anti-Platonism, the sixth thesis on Feuerbach (1845) is decisive: "Feuerbach resolves the religious essence into the human. But the human essence is no abstraction inherent in each single individual. In its reality it is the *ensemble* of the social relations" [TN: as found in Friedrich Engels, *Ludwig Feuerbach and the Outcome of Classical German Philosophy* (New York: International Publishers, 1941), 83–4]. This means that the transition to revolutionary thought is possible only by eliminating whatever aspect of Platonism is still left in Feuerbach because he preserves the ideas of human "essence" and "nature"; therefore, by reaching a radical critique of metaphysics. This is also the meaning of the famous transition from "speculative philosophy" to "philosophy of praxis." This latter is characterized precisely by a complete rejection of Platonism, and this is the common feature shared by Marx and Nietzsche, even if otherwise they are completely opposed; and for both of them anti-Platonism and anti-Christianity coincide. Starting from here one can find the formula that describes the error of the new Catholic Modernism: it wants to replace the agreement between Christianity and classical metaphysics with an agreement between Christianity and the philosophy of the primacy of action, which is intrinsically atheistic.

9 [TN] An expression originally coined by sociologist David Riesman in *The Lonely Crowd* (New Haven, CT: Yale University Press).

10 [TN] See St Augustine, *Epist. Ad Probam* 130, c. 15 §28; Pseudo-Dionysius, *De Mystica Theologia*, c. 1, §1; and also St Bonaventure and Cusanus, as discussed in Johannes Übinger, "Der Begriffder docta ignorantia in seiner geschichtlicher Entwicklung" [The concept of

new pedagogical techniques are designed precisely to destroy whatever is left of *docta ignorantia.*

Let us quickly end this digression, which would lead us to many bitter thoughts, and make a crucially important observation: *the terms repressive and permissive are meaningful only within the second conception.* Hence, the idea of the permissive society requires *that atheism be presupposed.*

An extremely simple example will clarify this question. It is completely clear that according to Plato the rational part of the soul must have a dominant role, both in the life of the individual and in the life of the state, and that we must be vigilant lest the non-rational part should prevail (because the goal of spiritual life is the soul's participation – in the sense of contemplating and drawing strength – in the world of Ideas which takes hold of us and calls us to serve its realization). However, let us suppose that the world of Ideas (which is a world of values, since it is ruled by the idea of the Good) be eliminated, and that every trace of the divine be erased. Then the Logos will appear to be "the origin of the logic of domination": "Nature (its own as well as the external world) was given to the ego as something that had to be fought, conquered and even violated … The struggle begins with the perpetual internal conquest of the 'lower' faculties of the individual: his sensuous and appetitive faculties. Their subjugation is, at least since Plato, regarded as a constitutive element of human reason, which is thus in its very function repressive. The struggle culminates in the conquest of external nature, which must be perpetually attacked, curbed and exploited in order to yield to human needs."[11] These words of Marcuse clarify perfectly the origin of the terms repression and permissiveness, precisely in the sense I explained before. At the same time, they reveal the typical confusion of the Frankfurt School, which views Platonic purification and the modern idea of scientific-technical domination of nature as stages of the same process. And they show the roots of the huge misunderstanding on the part of the student protests, which took place as a rebellion against both the technocratic society and the traditional spirit (i.e., against two opposites, which were conflated without mediation), ending in the renewed libertinism of permissive licentiousness as the unavoidable outcome.[12]

docta ignorantia in its historical development], *Archiv für Geschichte der Philosophie* 8 (1895): 206–40.

11 Herbert Marcuse, *Eros and Civilization* (New York: Vintage Books, 1962), 99–100.

12 The analogies between the libertine lifestyle of the young aristocrats of a long time ago and that of the children of the new elites are quite visible. The only difference is that the new culture gives foolish young people a broader field of action: they are allowed to insult professors, police officers, and so on. After some time the new libertines fall back in line. Actually, the way good families look upon them is not different from the attitude they used to have toward the young fools of the past.

Thus, if we put together the claim that the permissive society is necessarily mendacious with the claim that it is founded on a presupposition of atheism, we arrive at the following statement: *the permissive society manifests the mystifying character of atheism.* The idea that religion has a mystifying character has been repeated infinitely many times, and the words mystification and repression have been linked (e.g., by Marcuse: "Eternity, long since the ultimate consolation of an alienated existence, had been made into an instrument of repression by its relegation to a transcendental world – unreal reward for real suffering").[13] On the contrary it must be said that religion can certainly be used for the sake of mystification, just like everything else, but that such use is accidental with respect to the essence of religion, whereas the mystifying character of atheism is essential and necessary, so that it ensnares whoever wants to realize the "city of atheists." He is ensnared by the heterogenesis of ends – this point is a major opportunity to recall the Christian theory of Providence – even when he starts with the most disinterested intentions. Can this be demonstrated?

THE PERMISSIVE SOCIETY PRESENTS ITSELF

The permissive society presents itself as the fulfillment of the ideals of freedom and democracy, which nips in the bud whatever leads to totalitarianism and makes possible a democratic and non-communist combination of personal freedom and socialism. The reasons are as follows.

1 Supposedly, it eliminates for good all remnants of the idea of an "ethical state," the idea that produced totalitarianism as its ultimate outcome, according to an opinion as widespread as it is mistaken.
2 Because of this elimination, the laws of the state are viewed as mere sociological rules of coexistence, which can be evaluated not on the basis of abstract models but according to their ability to facilitate the free development and the free expression of each individual's personality. Conversely, the opposite theory and practice, supported by all possible forms of moralism, are accused of endorsing conformism, a spirit of inertia, misoneism, and – when they reach their pathological conclusion – a commitment to keep the world in the exact situation in which it was found. Hence, they result in the "regressive tendency" to lose oneself and become a "common man," and ultimately to embrace "mediocrity" in the strong and precise sense of the word.

13 Marcuse, *Eros and Civilization*, 111.

3 The permissive society promises to eliminate forever the possibility of wars of religion. This possibility arises from the claim that values are objective and super-personal, which in turn supposedly implies the right, or creates the duty, of imposing values by force. At the same time, we are told that the permissive society will not lead to religious persecution. Science leaves some space open to the unverifiable, even though religion is useless from a worldly perspective. Whoever wants to believe should be free to believe whatever he wants. Therefore, the right to have a religion will be recognized, to the extent that it does not hamper the worldly advancement of mankind. The aspects that hamper such development are due to a form of religion that is still captive to taboos, to ancestral superstitious elements from which more enlightened believers now intend to free it.

4 Finally, I have already mentioned the idea that the full satisfaction of the passions will make aggressiveness disappear.

THE PERVERSION OF LIBERALISM

Let us now discuss these claims one by one. Let us begin by pointing out that permissivism represents the most complete negation of liberalism, even though it must call itself liberal. *It must:* because this is not, so to speak, an accidental lie on the part of its proponents, but rather an *obligatory* lie, which follows from their philosophical presuppositions. They do not choose to lie: they are forced to lie for the sake of consistency. In order to show this, it is useful to recall a remark by Croce, which remains valid and perfectly true even when considered outside the broader context of Croce's thought. In the epilogue to *History of Europe in the Nineteenth Century* (1932), Croce writes that if freedom is "deprived of its moral soul, if it is detached from the past and from its venerable tradition, if the continuous creation of new forms that it demands is deprived of the objective value of such creation" then liberalism is replaced by "activist libertarianism." He also writes that this replacement is equivalent to replacing the worship of God with that of the Devil, which draws us like the *malignitas* to which, in Tacitus's words, *falsa species libertatis inest.* He then speaks of "Devil worship … and yet still a religion, the celebration of a black mass, but still a mass" and of the Devil who is *simia Dei.*[14]

Croce was talking about the irrationalist movements of the first decades of our century. Now we have to wonder: is not today's permissivism precisely the final stage of that "activist libertarianism," which is the

14 [TN] Benedetto Croce, *History of Europe in the Nineteenth Century*, trans. Henry Furst (New York: Harcourt Brace & Co., 1933), 342–3, 352.

diabolic falsification and perversion of freedom? I would like to ask the reader to pay special attention to this point because of its truly extreme importance for the understanding of contemporary history. When he speaks about activist libertarianism, Croce is thinking of Fascism as one of its possible forms; however, there is no reason to believe that he thought that this phenomenon would be limited to Fascism. Based on what he wrote, cannot we say that permissivism is the endpoint of a process of which Fascism was a stage? What makes us think so is the fact that according to Croce this perversion of liberalism follows from the separation of freedom from tradition. Shortly we shall see how the permissivist proposal of freedom is tied to anti-traditionalism pushed to its most radical consequences,[15] and that this is precisely why it presents itself as revolutionary. Perhaps we could describe it as the spirit of libertinism taking over the revolutionary spirit.[16]

Moving now to totalitarianism, we must say that it is explicitly endorsed and proposed in the last chapter of the book by Wilhelm Reich, the theoretician of the struggle against repression, which I am tempted to call the *Mein Kampf* of permissivism: *The Sexual Revolution*. The two books were chronologically close (*Mein Kampf* is from 1924, *The Sexual Revolution* from 1930) and they share the common feature of promising what they really intend to deliver.

15 The appropriate name for this radical break with the past, or even with yesterday, is *Futurism*. In fact, what we have today is a generalization of the theses of the Italian literary movement that bore that name, which fulfills today what was its original aspiration, by shaping practical life. Observe that the emancipation of women as understood by the various feminist movements conforms exactly to the model of the "futurist woman," which had already been proposed before the First World War. Keeping in mind the relationship between Futurism and Fascism, we can speak of a "futurist continuity" in our history, which achieves its final stage in today's permissivism. It is very peculiar that this fulfillment of Futurism is the outcome of a cultural attitude that until today has advanced under the banner of the most intransigent form of anti-Fascism.

16 The rise of a form of true philosophical atheism can be observed starting with the *libertinage érudit* of the early seventeenth century. It was a negative and corrosive form of atheism, which must be distinguished from the later positive and revolutionary form, aimed at creating a new reality. Two opposite moral attitudes are associated with these two types of atheism: with the former, what used to be called libertine licentiousness, and is now called permissiveness; with the latter, austerity and the severity of the revolutionary, which is literally a secularization of Puritanism. It seems that the historical development of atheism goes through a cycle, going through the revolutionary stage and coming back today to a radically expanded libertine form. And that the revolutionary stage plays the role of mediating the transition from what used to be aristocratic libertine atheism to what is today libertine atheism for the masses.

Reich writes that the only ideas that should be tolerated are those that do not undermine "sexual happiness"[17] and the process of disintegration of the traditional form of family. Here we touch an important point about liberation from tradition as a crucial aspect of this type of revolution. If one reads carefully this book by Reich, one realizes that sexual liberation is not desired *per se* but rather as a tool to break down the family. In turn, the family is fought against as the organ through which certain values – regarded as meta-historical – are communicated.

But there is more. Consider what he says about Christianity (these movements never fail to offer an outstretched hand): "Primitive Christianity was basically a communist movement. Its life-affirmative power became converted, by simultaneous sex-negation, into the ascetic and supernatural. By taking the form of the church, Christianity, which was striving for the delivery of humanity, denied its own origin. The church owes its power to the life-negating human structure which results from a metaphysical interpretation of life: it thrives on the life which it kills."[18] Without much effort, Reich can be definitely viewed as a precursor of the fight against post-Constantinian Christianity. I do not know if any new theologian has already pointed this out.

Thus, we see how fraudulent is the idea, which is often proposed, that the permissive society is religiously neutral. Let us observe, first, in what way the agnosticism it professes is very different from the agnosticism of the old type of secularism.

Old-style secularism wished to preserve the traditional tablet of moral values, being convinced that they do not require any metaphysical and/ or religious foundation. Therefore, it confined religion to the private sphere. The new secularism affirms a radical inversion of values.

One of the necessary features of totalitarianism is the persecution of all transcendent religions, because they propose an ideal of life that cannot be reconciled with ethical immanentism. And totalitarians know that it is difficult for a global persecution to be fully successful, especially if it is violent, and that the best type of support for their policies is a persecution of the traditional faithful organized and carried out by religious reformers. Therefore, the best line of action is to be intransigent about lifestyles, and to support progressive and modernist trends whenever possible. Who can fail to recognize that all these elements are present in Reich's statements?

17 [TN] Reich, *The Sexual Revolution*, 265.

18 Ibid., 266.

AGGRESSIVENESS UNFOLDS

Common sense, as long as it is not corrupted by the culture industry, tends to recognize that the promise of the eventual disappearance of aggressiveness is just a mirage, used in order to give free rein today to the full expression of aggressive instincts. This is supported by the most elementary act of observation; because, based on what we see, we are led to recognize a typical attitude that cyclically resurfaces, namely anti-traditionalism, which has gone crazy, after having reached its final stage of development and its most radical form. Indeed, the "novelty" that people talk about no longer means "going beyond." It is mere negation, the replacement of what existed with its opposite, novelty as negativity, which serves as criterion of "validity," as people say today, so that duration is replaced by the instant. But, what does such negativism mean, if not aggressiveness? By what miracle should this aggressiveness turn into its opposite? Uncritical trust in paradoxes is one of the symptoms of irrationalist decadentism. And stopping at a paradox, without reconciling it with common sense, means stopping half way.

Paradox can be a justifiable reaction against the vulgarization that sometimes befalls ideas as they go through the experience of history. This is an unavoidable phenomenon because an idea needs to be distinguished from the formula in which it is expressed, which can be used manipulatively like everything else. For instance, in the past the formula "sacred human person" has been used to justify abuses. However, let us try to deprive the human person of any "sacredness." We would end up in de Sade's world, a writer who nowadays is regarded by the permissivists, not coincidentally, as one of the "liberators." His thought is, instead, the exact refutation of the link between de-sacralization and disappearance of aggressiveness, a link that had already been affirmed by the Enlightenment's "republic of letters" in the decades before the French Revolution. It is also hard to imagine a society where every desire of every person will be satisfied, or where everybody will be spared the sorrow of being sometimes rejected (in a permissive society rejection must be allowed, too), a sorrow that would be made unbearably painful by the principle upon which this community would be founded. It is true, however, that the real principle of utopian thought is not equality but rather "everything to all," which implies the unstated but real presupposition that individual consciousness should be absorbed into a collective consciousness.

In this case, common sense does not stand alone, because Rosmini's criticism of Fourier ("you seriously claim that all human passions must be given completely free rein, like you say, and then how would you fulfill your promise to achieve by such device a peaceful and happy society?"[19]) was given a most unexpected confirmation by the mature Freud, as found in *Civilization and Its Discontents* (1930).[20] It is Freud at the time when he encountered philosophy through Schopenhauerian themes, and I was about to say through the truthful themes in Schopenhauer. I think this work constitutes the greatest possible critique of permissiveness and pure eroticism. It is not true that the vital instinct, *Eros*, is destined to prevail. It is not true that, after the removal of inhibitions and repression, *Eros* unites people. On the contrary, the opposite force, *Thanatos*, the principle of aggressiveness and destruction, is just as primordial, and the two cannot be separated. Neither *Eros* nor *Thanatos* can be found in a pure state, but only mixed together in various proportions, so that the struggle between these two forces is unending. Whereas this construction is certainly somewhat mythological, as is always the case for metaphysical conceptions developed by scientists, nevertheless an unbiased reader can get out of it either a confession of the pessimistic implications of a naturalistic view, or a confirmation of Rosmini's thesis that there is an original distinction between good and bad passions. This distinction implies a reaffirmation of human dignity, which lies in the exercise of freedom through which it reins in the passions and submits them to the moral order.

However, it is better to move on, without stopping just at common sense or at philosophical authorities, and point out the root of the necessary link between permissiveness and aggressiveness. This will be made clear presently.

FROM MARXISM TO PERMISSIVISM

We have already talked about Reich, and we have described him as the utopianist of psychoanalysis. Not really a philosopher and not really a scientist. It is a fact, however, that the ideas of the permissive society date back to him and cannot even be said to be novel, since they were presented in their entirety in 1933. It is hard to hide the fact that no new steps have been taken since then, and that the idea of the permissive society has spread through a process that has progressively worsened. There is a big drop from Marcuse to Reich, although we must recognize that there is continuity between Marcuse's contribution to the student protests and the dissemination of Reich's ideas. Marcuse opened the way

19 Rosmini, *Frammenti*, 192 [TN: my translation].

20 [TN] Sigmund Freud, *Civilization and Its Discontents*, ed. and trans. James Strachey (New York: Norton, 1962).

to Reich's fame, and this may help explain the crisis or defeat of the Frankfurt School.

It is interesting to understand how Reich's ideas were rediscovered. The primary motivation is ethico-political, because it involves the interpretation of contemporary history and of Fascism in particular. Here I can only touch in passing on an exceptionally important point. By exceptional I mean that it is the most challenging question, the one where culture and politics meet, and today's primary theme in political philosophy. It is not a paradox to use here the word "philosophy" in conjunction with "contemporary history." Does anybody doubt that the development of nineteenth-century philosophy can be understood by reflecting about the situation after the French Revolution, i.e., about that time's contemporary history? Going back to our topic, the question is whether Marx-Freudism – meaning the revolutionary interpretation of Freudism, from which follows the idea of sexual revolution, of which the permissive society is just an extension – is the necessary endpoint of the positions that want to "sublate" Marxism. I mean, in short, the positions that accept all the negations uttered by theoretical Marxism, but claim to be able to surpass them and to embrace older ways of thinking and living, but completely renewed and purified. Thus, a religious progressive speaks of a new Christianity and a new theology, and a secular progressive of a new Enlightenment.

I have already expressed many times my ideas about the results of this approach.[21] I think they are completely confirmed by the current religious, moral, and political situation of the West.

The two attempts to sublate Marxism, the secular and the religious, achieve perfectly symmetric results. The former leads to the simultaneous disintegration of Marxism and of the Enlightenment. The latter leads to the simultaneous disintegration of Marxism and of the various religious traditions.

Why does this happen? Scholars of Marxism agree that it is a form of religious thought, even if secularized or perverted. Those who want to sublate it seek a point of contact with their previous culture (liberalism/socialism for secular people, various forms of progressivism for religious thinkers). Thus, they try to isolate one aspect of Marxism, either by rejecting the messianic and eschatological aspect or by trying to reconcile it with a different kind of eschatology. After a quarter of a century and several attempts, the following conclusion is unavoidable: Marxism is a

21 [TN] See, for instance, "Civiltà tecnologica e cristianesimo" [Technological civilization and Christianity] in Augusto Del Noce, *L'epoca della secolarizzazione* (Milan: Giuffrè, 1970).

unitary construction, and the attempt to sublate it can only end up dissociating the destructive and negative aspect of revolutionary thought from the constructive aspect – which is related to the sacred, although secularized; or end up making Christianity atheistic instead of making Marxism Christian (as is expressed precisely by the "theology of the death of God").

The permissive society on one side and the theology of the death of God on the other – explicit or in disguise – are expressions of the same phenomenon, the failure to sublate Marxism.

The thought of Reich must be understood within this context. It is interesting because it shows that the attempt to surpass Marxism results in the dissolution of secular moralism.

His reasoning is extremely simple and, in its own way, consistent. Let us eliminate from Marxism all messianic aspects, every trace of metaphysical thinking. All that is left is pure historical materialism. Now, does historical materialism provide an adequate explanation of contemporary history? Reich maintains that Marx's great discovery was to understand that so-called absolute values can be explained completely in terms of historical and social circumstances. So, everything has to be examined from below, because what is deepest is found in what is lowest. However, has Marxism really fulfilled this task or, instead, must it be extended and reformed along Freudian lines? According to Reich, the need for such reform is manifested by the success of the Fascist movements. They refute the usual understanding of historical materialism, because the impoverished masses supported their rise to power, creating the impression that the decisive factor at the practical-political level is not economic stratification but rather ideology. Therefore, historical materialism must be completed by analysing history's subjective factor, which Marx could not do because scientific psychology did not exist in his time. This completion is now possible thanks to sexual economics.

From this claim it follows that "*There are no 'class distinctions' when it comes to character.* For that reason the purely economic concepts 'bourgeoisie' and 'proletariat' were replaced by the concepts '*reactionary*' and '*revolutionary*' or 'free-minded,' which relate to man's character and not to his social class. These changes were forced upon us by the Fascist plague."[22] If we examine the history of the secularist attempt to sublate Marxism, we see that already from the start the words "reactionary" and "revolutionary" or "progressive" replaced "bourgeois" or "proletarian." Later, by a process that could be easily pieced together, these two opposites took such a broad significance that they replaced the terms true and

22 From the 1942 preface to Reich, *The Mass Psychology of Fascism*, xxiv [TN: the italics are in the original].

false. It would be interesting to analyse step by step the process through which, after trying to synthesize various lines of thought, the movement that here in Italy had called itself liberal-socialism (to indicate the quest to surpass liberalism and Communism) was forced to yield to Freudo-Marxism,[23] especially after the student protests. Reich claimed to be anti-totalitarian, and actually argued that the ethical-political proposal based on his scientific thesis is the only one that can avoid the danger of totalitarianism, from which Marx-Leninism itself cannot escape. Indeed, we read: "The removal of individual capitalists and the establishment of state capitalism in Russia in place of private capitalism *did not effect the slightest change in the typical, helpless, subservient character-structure of masses of people.*"[24]

On the other hand, I have already discussed the typical totalitarian character of the permissive society. How is it different, then, from other forms of totalitarianism, since we surely have to agree with Reich that the type of society he proposes is different from Fascism, Nazism, Stalinism, or, in fact, from Communism in general?

FROM THE ENLIGHTENMENT TO SCIENTISM

We have previously cited the passages that show this totalitarian character. What matters is to understand why Reich *cannot* say anything different. Indeed, let us observe the following.

23 It is well known that a historical definition of liberal-socialism – as the attempt to find a theoretical foundation for the cultural and political attitude that is generally denoted by the word *Azionismo* – must highlight the fact that it was formed through a *sequence of negations.* It wants to be the most accomplished form of anti-Fascism, and since the most visible feature of Fascism is the negation, at the same time, of liberalism and socialism, it wants to achieve a synthesis of both, by radically erasing from each of them the characteristics that they seemed to share in common with Fascism. It wants to erase conservatism from liberalism and totalitarianism from Communism. This was the reason for the break with Croce. Liberal-socialism must erase the religious aspect from Croce's liberalism (the "religion of freedom") in order to try to reach a synthesis. Likewise, it had to break with Marxism, whose religious aspect it must also erase. Moreover, because it depends on Fascism in the sense that it wants to be its radical antithesis, liberal-socialism must downplay the fact that Fascism was a historical phenomenon, and turn it into some sort of meta-historical category (the principle of radical barbarism), which it must understand in a naturalistic sense, based on what I just said. At this point, it must inevitably embrace the naturalistic-psychological interpretation [of Fascism], which in the most consistent version is precisely the one developed by Reich, even though the original liberal-socialist culture was quite different. This is why the newest generation has lost interest in liberal-socialist culture, and has turned its attention to Marx-Freudian culture. This is a perfectly understandable phenomenon, since the latter is the former's legitimate descendant.

24 Reich, *The Mass Psychology of Fascism*, xxvi. The italics are in the original.

1 Scientism cannot present itself to the awareness of its own advocates as a rational truth, i.e., as susceptible of an irrefutable proof. It is, literally, *a resolution of the will*: the resolution to accept as real only what can be verified empirically by everyone. On the other hand, it can only *be presented* to others as the expression of the adult age of reason, of the age when myths have vanished (even the wording of this presentation is necessary: scientism was born with the Enlightenment, in the wake of the analogy between the history of mankind and the stages in the life of an individual, which is the foundation of the idea of progress. Hence, the metaphor of the adult man). Due to this contradiction, it must be recognized as the endpoint of the rationalistic falsification of reason. It is rationalism revealing itself as a *falsifying ideology*.

This point is worth emphasizing, because some people still consider scientism as a mere extension of the scientific spirit; it may be unwarranted, but still shares its characteristics and is led by it to ask curious questions. I will offer a personal example: during a conversation, in reply to my claim that there is a connection between scientism and totalitarianism, a very educated and intelligent man argued that the scientific spirit, being characterized by constant self-criticism, cannot give rise to a practical attitude of a dogmatic nature, and in particular to totalitarianism. The answer can be found in a remark by one of the most acute young French philosophers of the 1930s, who died prematurely in a concentration camp, Benjamin Fondane. Speaking of the pseudo-elevation of psychoanalysis to a philosophy, he pointed out already in 1936 that it makes manifest in the most transparent way possible that the essence of scientism is *hatred for religious transcendence*.[25] The illegitimate extension by which science is regarded as the only valid form of knowledge is actually mediated by an *irrational factor*.[26]

2 This hatred of religious transcendence, from which derives the idea of a sharp break – a revolutionary break, indeed – between two stages of human history, and absolute anti-traditionalism, defines

25 Benjamin Fondane, *La conscience malheureuse* (Paris: Denöel et Steele 1936), 154 [TN: my translation from Del Noce's Italian].

26 This point deserves special attention, because I think that nobody has surpassed, in later years, the point reached by Fondane, who was a disciple of the greatest philosopher of the Russian emigration, Leon Chestov. The transition from science to scientism is not just an illegitimate intellectual extension but a voluntary and completely a priori rejection of religious transcendence. Such a rejection without a reason, on the part of those who want to subordinate everything to reason, seems to be a repetition of original sin and a proof of its effects.

the radical distinction between scientific immanentism and Idealistic immanentism. According to the latter, philosophical thought preserved the truth of religious thought in a different and higher form. It also preserved the fundamental core of religious morality so that, ultimately, coexistence would not be problematic.

On the contrary, scientism claims to sweep away the delusions and the ghosts of transcendence, but how can it do so if it has no *arguments* to support its negations? Let us listen again to Fondane: "(As for unbelievers), it is enough that the given argument establish formally *what they desire* in order for this argument to assume the sacred character of irrefutable proof, no matter what it is and even if it is as naive as Freud's argument about the 'primitive father.'"[27] Let us look at another beautiful book, *Organizing the Revolution* by Augustin Cochin, which has been recently translated into Italian.[28] In it we read: "Before the bloody terror of '93, in the republic of letters there was, from 1765 to 1780, a bloodless terror, for which the *Encyclopedia* was the Committee of Public Safety and d'Alembert the Robespierre. This terror swept away reputations just as the other chopped off heads. Its guillotine was slander, 'infamy' as it was then called."[29] Perhaps Cochin did not emphasize enough how the formation of this republic of letters and its methods were the necessary consequence of scientism, and only of scientism.

3 Without any proofs, one must rely on the empty promise that characterizes every form of totalitarianism, namely future happiness. When classes will be no more – when Jews will be no more – The permissive promise talks also about the transcendent idols that originated the spirit of repression, but the substance is the same. We see also the ultimate reason why the promise is a fallacy: permissivism is tied to scientism, and scientism to negation and hatred. This is the source of what was observed earlier on empirical grounds: *aggressiveness is tied to permissivism to the extent that this latter can find its ideal foundation only in scientism.* This statement is not paradoxical, or even less is it motivated by confessional spirit, as demonstrated by the fact that it can be traced back to the judgment of Croce which I quoted earlier. Writers dedicated to providing spiritual tranquilizers will make their usual counter-argument: it is true that so far the progress toward permissive liberalization has coincided with an increase in aggressiveness, or actually in real criminality. However,

27 Fondane, *La conscience malheureuse*, 160.

28 Augustin Cochin, *Meccanica della rivoluzione* (Milan: Rusconi, 1970) [TN: *Organizing the Revolution*, trans. Nancy Derr Polin (Rockford, IL: Chronicles Press, 2007)].

29 [TN] Cochin, *Organizing the Revolution*, 36.

this is an unavoidable phenomenon in times of fast transformation. In other words, aggressiveness is a result of the crisis of values associated with social transformation, and will decrease to the extent that the new mentality becomes consolidated. In order to realize how superficial this explanation is, it is enough to reflect about current phenomena like profanity and the will to desecrate. It is not a mere "crisis of growth" because what is lacking is finality, the "*for.*" In this situation, action cannot take any other form but negativity. It is in this connection that one should understand the spirit of desecration and profanity.

4 Given these premises, it is easy to understand the process through which permissivism can establish itself. The remaining believers in a transcendent authority of values will be marginalized and reduced to second-class citizens. They will be imprisoned, ultimately, in "moral" concentration camps. But nobody can seriously think that moral punishments will be less severe than physical punishments. At the end of the process lies the spiritual version of genocide. The individual will be denied the right to his environment, to his traditions, to modesty. Indeed, the total liberalization of passions, as the principle of the permissive society, coincides with the complete negation of modesty.

THE NEW TOTALITARIANISM

And it could not be otherwise, if you think of it, because totalitarian regimes silence their enemies by claiming that their arguments, regardless of how they understand them, do not express rational motives but "class" or "race." The same applies to the scientistic view that is the ideal foundation of the permissive society: "conservative" and "reactionary" arguments are said to reflect just a "repressed" psychology. Inasmuch as this "character structure" is the only obstacle to universal happiness, it seems right that those who carry it should be isolated and ostracized. This reminds me of Clausewitz's definition of war as "an act of violence intended to compel our opponent to fulfill our will."[30] Starting from it we can describe totalitarianism as a permanent absorption of the idea of politics within the idea of war. The new scientism, inasmuch as it is an *unproven* radical negation of traditional values, cannot but try to subjugate the will of its foes, rather than their reason, by means of the regime of terror created by the republic of letters that Cochin mentioned in the passage I just cited. And since this negation is radical, it must confine

30 [TN] Carl von Clausewitz, *On War,* trans. J.J. Graham (Radford, VA: Wilder Publications, 2008), 27.

them in "moral ghettoes." In this respect, one only has to look at how the progressive press speaks of traditionalists; here, an analysis of language truly would be useful.

In an article two years ago I discussed the possibility of a new totalitarianism, which is still possible and is already threatening us.[31] In today's Europe it would not be a totalitarianism of the Communist or Nazi kind, that is, a totalitarianism characterized by a "secular religion" that makes it strive to affirm a national primacy. The totalitarianism that is possible today in the countries of Western Europe is of a completely different kind. We must also recognize that the threat of a Communist totalitarianism, of the Russian or Chinese type, is extremely unlikely, both because Russia certainly would not support Communist revolutions in Western countries (out of fear of being surrounded, because the first requests, in countries where Communism comes to power from within, is always autonomy from the "firstborn nation"), and because theoretical Marxism suffers from a crisis that prevents it from sustaining any longer a revolutionary faith. In other words, our attention is always focused on paradigms of past enemies, and we pay only scant attention to the enemy who is dangerous now or in the near future.

Its general features can be described. Science studies reality as a system of forces, not of values. Thus, human sciences will study how certain values are tied to certain psychological and social situations, but they will not be able, as such, to establish if these values are real. Thus, the destruction of values, their reduction to such situations, or the tearing away of the masks (as we often hear today) that they use in order to claim to be absolute, are not the work of science, which per se has nothing to do with these questions, but of scientism.

Now, what morality will flow from scientism? If science is neutral with respect to ideals and values, the same cannot be said about scientism, which suppresses metaphysics and claims to make science the exhaustive knowledge of reality. As we have already said, science regards reality as a system of forces. Hence, to the elevation of science to philosophy will correspond the elevation of force to value. And force will no longer be regarded as an instrument for the fulfillment of ideals. In short, all values will be subsumed into the category of vitality. Here we understand Reich's perfect logical consistency when he linked scientism to eroticism. Not by chance, after all, de Sade's heroine Juliette rejected all idols

31 [TN] Augusto Del Noce, "Verso un nuovo totalitarismo," *L'Europa* 4, no. 7/8 (1970): 10–15; partially included in this volume as "Toward a New Totalitarianism."

except science.[32] Thus, the new Enlightenment links up with the old one precisely at its endpoint.

But let us pay attention to a deep truth, which was recognized by Croce at the end of his journey. Vitality, taken by itself and not turned into matter for the higher moral form, coincides with the selfish aspect, that is, with the principle of evil. I have already talked about the intrinsic totalitarian character of scientism. The novelty of this totalitarianism lies in the fact that it protects a process of disintegration, unlike the other totalitarianisms that have appeared so far.

PERMISSIVISM IS ANTI-DEMOCRACY

It is time to reach some conclusions.

1. On the one hand, the proposal of the permissive society pushes to the limit the idea of total revolution, if revolution means a radical break with tradition. But on the other, it also marks the failure of this idea in its most rigorous formulation, Marxism. Because according to Marxism the revolutionary transition would mark the passage from an individualistic and anarchic stage of mankind to another stage in which individual consciences would coalesce in a higher totality. On the contrary, the permissive society seems to push to the limit the features of bourgeois society that Marxism had already denounced, and at the same time proves that it is impossible for Marxism to overturn them. Because, wherever Marxism was able to root itself in reality, this was due precisely to the aspects coming from ancient traditions from which it should be freed according to those who want to sublate it.
2. We have examined by what connection the negations of religion, of freedom, of family, and of country are linked together, and at the same time concealed, at least from the general public, in the philosophy that is implicit in the permissive society. We may add that at the political level this implies the negation of the very idea of Europe, since this idea is founded on the tradition of the Logos. It is pointless to talk about European unity once the perception of Europe as a moral territory has been lost and we can talk only of a unified "European market."[33]

32 [TN] Marquis de Sade, *Juliette*, trans. Austryn Wainhouse (New York: Grove Press, 1968).

33 It is interesting to compare the literature about the idea of Europe from the period, roughly, from 1930 to 1955 with later works. The former is dominated by the question

It follows that the dangers of the permissive society cannot be overcome by political means alone. A religious reawakening is needed, because religion, country, and family are supreme ideals and not practical instruments. And it is certainly a valid point that the formula *corruptio optimi pessima* applies to the deterioration that befalls these ideals when they are viewed, at least primarily, as pragmatic instruments of social welfare. In order to be socially useful they must be thought within the categories of the true and the good; the opposite is impossible. Certainly, such a reawakening cannot be a merely human work. But nevertheless it requires, in order to be realized, that the hearts of men be attentive. Today, however, attention is obstructed by a multitude of idols, so that the permissive society is identified, for no reason whatsoever, with "democracy," with an "irreversible turning point of history," with "progress," with "modernity," and so on. Unfortunately, these idols have also penetrated the place where one would least expect to find them, the Catholic world itself. Hence, it is urgent to understand the process that has led, over the last few years, to the adoption of permissive spirit and repressive spirit as the fundamental ethico-political criteria, and to show that this process is based on invalid presuppositions.

of spiritual unity and of religious-ethical-political meaning. This question gradually disappears in favour of questions of an economic nature. It seems that we have chosen as the road to European unification the one that starts from the economy, rather than the ethical-political road. We must be very clear on this point, and understand that whereas economic unification can be a favourable condition for spiritual unification, nevertheless it is not possible to go from the former to the latter by a simple process of evolution; and that, so far, the "European spirit" has covered up a mere disintegration of the traditions and ideals of the various fatherlands, rather than a composition of pre-existing unities into a higher harmony.

10

The Ascendance of Eroticism

TODAY NO MORAL OPINION IS MORE WIDESPREAD, and more passively accepted, than the one that says that we should recognize, as an irreversible reality, that society's sense of modesty has changed significantly over the last few years. So that today the average man, i.e., the *normal* man (meaning neither nostalgic nor neurotic) accepts without any moral reaction displays of sexuality that a few years ago were inconceivable. Hence, laws need to conform to the new morals, since the very notion of lewdness has changed: who can deny that mores, dress styles, fashions change, even though the formal concept of morality remains unchanged?

Many Catholics also share this opinion. They are persuaded that at a time when man has succeeded in mastering and using to his own advantage the powers of nature, and when technological miracles make possible an ever greater and more widespread prosperity, the ancient ideals of ascetic behaviour and self-mortification should be regarded as irreversibly outdated. And this is simply a factual observation, even if it is unpleasant.

I often find myself envying unbelievers: does not contemporary history provide abundant evidence to prove that Catholics are a mentally inferior species? Their rush to conform to the opinion about Catholicism held by rationalist secularists is stunning. Still, no opinion deserves the grand prize of banality more than the one I just mentioned.

Indeed, a very elementary reflection is sufficient in order to understand that today we are dealing with something completely different from variations about what was considered to be offensive of the sense of modesty. When it is said – and this is the present situation – that there is

This chapter was first published as "L'erotismo alla conquista della società," in Augusto Del Noce et al., *Via libera alla pornografia?* [Free rein to pornography?] (Florence: Vallecchi, 1970), 9–48. Republished in *Rivoluzione Risorgimento Tradizione* (Milan: Giuffrè, 1993), 61–95.

no word in the dictionary that cannot be uttered and, correspondingly, there is no body part that cannot be exposed in public, as long as it does not hurt our sense of aesthetics (this is where today's nudism shows its nature, which is very different from *hygienic* naturism, which after all is rather naive), what we are facing is not just a variation in society's sense of modesty. We are facing a condemnation of modesty as *abnormal,* and this condemnation is *moral* in its own way. In fact, it is described as a *sexual revolution.* This is not at all an exaggerated or overly bold expression used to describe something more moderate and simpler, like the "full integration of sex within human life" that has been discussed – in very ill defined and imprecise terms, anyway – by many theologians, who muddy the waters and the heads with such a benign interpretation.

Today the greatest threat to intelligence is posed by the inflation of printed materials. Books are not read; at most they are browsed and then shelved. Well, Dr Wilhelm Reich said everything essential about the sexual revolution forty years ago in a book bearing that very title.[1] It can be read carefully in one day. Having done that, one is no longer surprised by the mores found in the kingdom of Denmark, because *they are the full realization of what Reich wrote.* One is not surprised by the most advanced ideas, including marriage between homosexuals. One no longer needs to look up, or to discuss, Moravia's[2] comments about pornography as a phenomenon associated with a puritanical society: without puritans there would be no pornographers; if every erotic expression is "normal," it follows that pornographers exist only because abnormal

1 [TN: *The Sexual Revolution,* trans. Theodore P. Wolfe (New York: Noonday, 1963)]. It was published in Vienna in 1930 and had three later editions – 1935, 1944, and 1949 – whose prefaces are important. It reflects well a certain Viennese climate of the twenties, in the same way, I would say, as Hitler reflects a certain Viennese climate of the years before the war. See the interesting book by Wilfried Daim, *Der Mann, der Hitler die Ideen gab* [The man who gave Hitler his ideas] (Munich: Ueberreuter, 1958), which deserves to be translated into Italian. The man in question is a former Benedictine, Jörg Lanz, who pushed the doctrine of race, and thus anti-Semitism, to levels never seen before in pamphlets published during the first decade of the twentieth century, which today are almost impossible to find. Reich was also the author of a book on Fascism [*Mass Psychology of Fascism,* trans. Vincent R. Carfagno (New York: Farrar, Straus & Giroux, 1970)] whose thesis is easy to guess: supposedly Fascism was a revolt of the sexually repressed which, however, took a deviant, sadomasochistic, and destructive form because it failed to focus its critique on the principle of repression itself. After the "puritan regression" of Stalinism, Reich described Communism as *red Fascism* [see his work of 1953 published in the volume *Reich Speaks of Freud* (New York: Macmillan 1967), 274–6]. But perhaps his thought would be better described as a form of "reverse Nazism," in which military vitalism is replaced by sexual vitalism. This interpretation is supported by statements that I will quote later on.

2 [TN] Alberto Moravia, (1907–90), Italian novelist and journalist.

puritans exist; there is no pornographer except in the eyes of a puritan. What a discovery! One no longer needs to keep up with lectures by people like Enzo Siciliano,[3] not because of psychological or moral aversion but just out of duty to use well one's own time. Reading Reich's book really *forces* one to recognize that these authors' writings – be they novels or essays – and those by many others, who can be left unnamed, are literary elaborations (that is, works of the "culture industry" genre) or literal illustrations of the works by this heterodox Austrian psychologist (with respect to the psychoanalytic mainstream). Those who provide illustrations and tangible examples for other people's writings do not discuss, and so do not deserve to be discussed. It is perfectly possible that they came up with their ideas on their own, or sniffed them in the air. But we must focus our attention on the author who first formulated them and who, above all, did it in an organic and consistent form.

Reich died in an American prison in 1957, almost completely forgotten, after having been condemned by the still *moral* United States. The various *beat* and *hippie* movements then rediscovered him. He belongs to what in the 1920s called itself the movement of European liberation, born in the shadow of the Russian revolution. But he replaced the categories of bourgeoisie and proletariat with those of the advocates of *repressive* morality (the use of the word *repression* in the general sense we give it today dates back to him) and the advocates of sexual freedom. Supposedly, only such a replacement and the achievement of *sexual happiness* would lead to the extinction of the *authoritarian* spirit and to a form of internationalism free from all compromises.

The teachings that can be drawn from his *sexual revolution* are numerous and extremely important.

First, it is worth pointing out that the ideas about absolute sexual freedom were already fully formulated in the years between 1920 and 1930. They were not popular in the next decade: on one side, they were opposed by the totalitarian regimes, by Fascism as well as Nazism and also by Stalinism, for reasons that we do not need to investigate now. On the other side, anti-Fascism, which at that time was keen on upholding spiritual values against the exaltation of the vital and earthly elements, could not accept them. They made a comeback after 1945, which initially went almost unnoticed but was continuous and progressive. They exploded after 1960, in the form and with the intensity that we know well, certainly not because of a direct influence by Reich's works, which were merely rediscovered, but for reasons that we will discuss.

3 [TN] Enzo Siciliano (1934–2006), Italian writer and literary critic.

The book's rigorous consistency shows that no compromise is possible between traditional morality, taken in its entirety and without modifications, that is, fully recognizing its first premises, and thus without emphasizing unilaterally any particular aspect, and sexual liberation. Hence, we have to say that Reich is completely correct – apart from his form of expression and his judgment of value, which of course is the opposite of mine – when he writes that the "concept of the sexual urge as being in the service of procreation is a method of repression on the part of conservative sexology. It is a finalistic, i.e., idealistic concept. It presupposes a goal which of necessity must be of a supernatural origin. It reintroduces a metaphysical principle and thus betrays a religious or mystical prejudice."[4] We can translate this into slightly different words: in history we find, as constants, two typical structures in permanent conflict: the *moral* structure, which in the final analysis presupposes a metaphysical-transcendent, or actually supernatural, foundation, and the *libertine* structure, which, having denied this foundation, must identify the full realization of life with "sexual happiness," taken as an end in itself and thus freed from the idea of reproduction. If Reich deserves any credit, it is for having pushed the practical judgment of the libertine type to its ultimate consequences.

Indeed, Reich's thought is based on the premise, which of course is taken as unquestionably true without even a hint of a proof, that there is no order of ends, no meta-empirical authority of values. Any trace not just of Christianity but of "idealism" in the broadest sense, or of a foundation of values in some objective reality, like history according to Marx, is eliminated. What is man reduced to, then, if not to a bundle of physical needs? When these needs are satisfied – when, in short, every repression is removed – he will be happy. Nietzsche's sentence about socialists comes to mind: "they wink because they have invented happiness."[5] Few writers typify the character of the "inventor of happiness" as well as Reich does.

Having taken away every order of ends and eliminated every authority of values, all that is left is vital energy, which can be identified with sexuality, as was already claimed in ancient times and is actually difficult to refute. Hence, the core element of life will be sexual happiness. And since full sexual satisfaction is possible, happiness is within reach. Man will free himself from neuroses and will become fully capable of work and initiative through absolute, unbounded sexual freedom. His psychic

4 [TN] Reich, *Sexual Revolution*, 51.

5 Friedrich Nietzsche, *Thus Spoke Zarathustra*, trans. Walter Kaufmann (New York: Modern Library, 1995), 17.

structure will be transformed and he will also be freed from militaristic and aggressive tendencies and from sadistic fantasies, which are typical of repressed people – as the example of de Sade himself supposedly demonstrates.

But, what is the repressive social institution *par excellence*? To Reich it is the traditional monogamous family; and, from his standpoint, certainly he cannot be said to be wrong. Indeed, the idea of family is inseparable from the idea of *tradition*, from a heritage of truth that we must *tradere, hand on. Thus, the abolition of every meta-empirical order of truth requires that the family be dissolved.* No *merely sociological* consideration can justify keeping it.

At the cost of repeating myself,[6] I should insist on some truths that have been almost completely forgotten. The idea of indissoluble monogamous marriage and other ideas related to it (modesty, purity, continence) are linked to the idea of *tradition*, which in turn presupposes (since *tradere* means to hand down) the idea of an objective order of unchangeable and permanent truths (the Platonic True in itself and Good in itself). On top of everything else, the affirmation of these themes is one of the glories of Italian thought, because what else is Dante's *Comedy* if not the poem of order viewed as the immanent form of the universe? And who else was the great defender of the objective Order of Being, during the modern centuries, if not Rosmini?

But if we separate the idea of tradition from that of an objective order, it must necessarily appear to be "the past," what has been "surpassed," "the dead trying to suffocate the living," what must be negated in order to find psychological balance. The idea of indissoluble marriage must be replaced by that of free union, renewable or breakable at any time. It does not make sense to speak of sexual perversions; on the contrary, homosexual expressions, either masculine or feminine, should be regarded as the purest forms of love. Therefore, at the scientistic-materialistic level, on which Freud also operated, Reich is undoubtedly correct.

However, his thesis breaks also with the idea of political-social revolution, because this latter is dominated by the idea of the future, in which there will be an order – even though it will be "new" and not eternal – that we have the task of bringing about. According to the pure revolutionary mindset, free love will be tolerated between "comrades" (in fact,

6 [TN] In the Italian original, this paragraph and the following four form an extremely long footnote, which would be incompatible with the format of this volume. Del Noce's main text resumes after point 3 on page 162.

truly committed comrades) but mutual fidelity between comrades of opposite genders will be the ideal.

Thus, the domain of free sexuality is the pure *present*, and this brings us back to the sub-human level, to animalism (think of Leibniz's *mens momentanea*). We try to get out of this situation by escaping into "another reality." This is why there is a *necessary* connection between eroticism and the "artificial paradises" of drug addiction. And it certainly does not help, after having called "retrograde" any criticism of sexual freedom, to try to fall back by arguing that drugs hurt virility, first, because eroticism and virility have very little in common, and also because unlimited sexual freedom and the quest for drug-induced bliss are developmental stages of the same essence.

This leads to three very important conclusions.

1 The question of eroticism is first of all *metaphysical*. Only a restoration of what for brevity I will call "classical metaphysics" can truly dismantle the framework of judgments that make up eroticism.
2 Politically, eroticism is linked with "democracy devoid of the sacred," which today has manifested itself as never before. The affirmation of this type of democracy has been helped (to say merely "not contrasted" would be too little) by the Christian Democratic parties, even if it is the exact opposite of democracy as Leo XIII conceived it. Of course, it was also facilitated by the new Modernists, for whom speaking to "today's man" means recognizing the "profanity" of the world.
3 Any "dialogue" with the advocates of sexual liberalization is perfectly useless, simply because they start by denying a priori the metaphysics that is the source of what they regard as "repressive" morality. For instance, what would be the point of a dialogue between me and Mr De Marchi or Enzo Siciliano?

Hence the consequences that are spelled out in Reich's book as clearly as they could be. The overturning of the "human structure [that exists] in the form of what is called tradition"[7] could not be more complete. We can perhaps find a distant analogue in the utopias of one of the most representative writers of eighteenth-century libertinism, Cyrano de Bergerac. A girl who is still a virgin at eighteen years of age must be put to shame. What an adolescent girl needs is "an undisturbed room, proper contraceptives, a friend who is capable of love, that is, not … with a

7 [TN] Reich, *Sexual Revolution*, xxvi. I slightly modified the English translation to make it closer to the Italian translation quoted by Del Noce.

sex-negative structure; she needs understanding parents and a sex-affirmative social atmosphere."[8] Total nudity must be unconditionally accepted and facilitated. Public intercourse must be allowed. Nobody can forbid his/her partner to have other lasting sexual relationships: a principle that today is called "full freedom of exchange between married couples" and "complete liberty of group sex." Nothing gives the right to criticize homosexual unions. Sexual education must be understood as the removal of all ancestral complexes that lead us to value abstinence, and so on.

Let us now ask ourselves: compared to these ideas, what is new in the so-called *Scandinavian morals*? What is new in certain expressions of the students' protests (not in all of them, not even in the most revolutionary forms, because certainly Mao is not Reich, nor is Marcuse), as when students demanded the privilege of having their girlfriends visit their private dormitory rooms (including the students of a German school of Protestant theology, according to what I read)? Or even the privilege of free intercourse in the hallways (as in Nanterre, during the famous May events). This demand could not fail to be endorsed by a very conformist professor who, for the sake of fully consistent conformism, chose to sign his statement with a pseudonym while he was waiting to conform to the winning side.

Another example: "Religion should not be fought, but any interference with the right to carry the findings of natural science to the masses and with the attempts to secure their sexual happiness should not be tolerated. Then it would soon be apparent whether the Church is right in its contention of the supernatural origin of religious feelings."[9] And what else is the founder of the *Deutsche Sex Partei* (the Hamburg journalist Driessen) proposing today if not precisely *the* "verification of the constitutional legitimacy of the Catholic Church regarding the limits it sets to sexual freedoms?"[10] Note that the Church is tolerated only to the extent that she does not take any stance on the moral assertions that supposedly derive from science, understood as the only valid form of knowledge! She must be a spectator, without even being granted the right to criticize, of a new sexual morality prescribed by science (actually, by a scientist, because Reich admits that his position was completely isolated among the scientists of his time), which shatters completely the Church's own principles through a process that goes from practice to theory. Recently,

8 [TN] Ibid., 15.

9 [TN] Ibid., 265.

10 [TN] I have been unable to identify the source of this quotation by German journalist Joachim Driessen.

Jean Brun, a formidable French philosopher who is not as well-known as he should be, has written that "the Grand Inquisitor, so beautifully portrayed by Dostoevsky, is no longer a religious fanatic, but a scientist who has exclusive possession of the truth, in front of whom men must kneel in order to be no longer slaves to error."[11]

Even leaving aside the thesis of the greatest philosopher of the Russian emigration, Leon Chestov, who said that the type of the Grand Inquisitor derives exclusively from the essence of scientism – even if historically it may have taken a religious form due to an intrusion of the scientistic mentality into the field of faith – it remains true that *this type is essential to scientism* and that today the threat of its dominance comes from scientism.

But there is more. If I am not mistaken, Reich was the first to speak of a connection between sexual repression and Fascism. This idea was successful as well. Indeed, some time ago I read on the cover of a book by a man named Albert Ellis, head of psychological services of the state of New Jersey, that "sex fascists tend to be just as prevalent among the politico-economic liberal groups as they are among the social bigots and reactionaries."[12] Even though this expression has not yet become very widespread – on this topic, the scientistic sexologists would be forced into a debate with the historians, for which they are ill equipped – nevertheless, the idea underlies many current opinions. Much commentary can be easily traced back to the persuasion that there is a correspondence between a democratic society and complete sexual freedom. It is certainly not coincidental that the most advanced proponents, among us, of "sexualized morals" state that their goal is to free Italy from that degree of obscurantism that supposedly prompts people in more civilized countries to compare it with Spain, Portugal, and Greece, and that ultimately poses a permanent danger of regression. It is also not coincidental that precisely the three best-known Italian figures in the fight for liberation from sexual taboos, Moravia, Maraini, and Pasolini,[13]

11 See his article "Dalla scienza al terrorismo intellettuale" [From science to intellectual terrorism], in *L'Europa*, 31 January 1970, 50.

12 [TN] Albert Ellis, *Sex without Guilt* (New York: Hillman, 1958), 160.

13 [TN] Italian writers Alberto Moravia (1907–90), Dacia Maraini (b. 1936), and Pier Paolo Pasolini (1922–75). On 21 December 1969, all three attended the "committee" in question, which was actually a public assembly organized by a group of radical leftist university students in order to protest against possible "repression" by the police in the wake of the Piazza Fontana bombing of 12 December 1969 in Milan. The attendance at such a meeting of three among the most famous Italian intellectuals was the subject of much discussion in the press. For instance, see the interviews with Nicola Chiaromonte and Alberto Moravia himself published in *Il Mondo*, 8 January 1970, and re-published in Michele

have recently agreed to participate in a "revolutionary committee against repression."

Based on what we have seen so far, Reich does not advocate free love and sexual hygiene as isolated propositions, not at all. On the contrary, he is a thinker who understands exactly all the implications of the advancement of sexual freedom, and defines precisely all the negations that such freedom implies in the metaphysical-religious domain. Does he not get to the point of writing, in spite of all his anti-Nazism, that "the National Socialist mysticism of the 'surging of the of blood' and of the 'closeness to blood and soil' was progress as compared with the Christian concept of original sin," even though it was "smothered in mystification and reactionary politics," and that hostility to Nazism must not make us prefer the teaching of the doctrine of original sin to the doctrine of "the purity of blood," which "will have to be guided into different, positive channels?"[14] He grasped perfectly the sequence family-tradition-objective order of values and ends. And if the words "tradition" and "revolution" are set in rigorous opposition, there is no question that nobody ever pushed this opposition as far as he did, and that he is right when he writes that not only does the revolution imply a transformation of our understanding of sexual relationships, but it is first of all a "sexual revolution."

It is strange how today the ideas of the scientistic inventor of happiness have triumphed, without any direct influence on his part, not only in people's lifestyles but also among a very large segment of Western political opinion. In fact, consider what he wrote in the preface to the third edition of *Sexual Revolution* (1944), after having been disappointed by Russian Communism:

> It is not a matter of *class struggles* between proletariat and bourgeoisie, as a mechanistic theoretical sociology would make us believe. No: working individuals with a character structure capable of freedom fight working individuals with an authoritarian structure ... members of the higher social strata with a freedom structure fight ... for the rights of *all* working individuals against the dictators who, by the way, arise from the proletariat. Soviet Russia, which owes its existence to a proletarian revolution, is today, in 1944, sex-politically reactionary, while America, with its background of a bourgeois revolution, is at least progressive, sex-politically. The social concepts of the nineteenth century, with their purely economic definition, no longer apply to the ideological stratification we see in

Dzieduszycki, *Pagine sparse: Fatti e figure di fine secolo* [Scattered pages: Facts and characters of the end of the century] (Empoli, Italy: Ibiskos Editrice Risolo, 2007), 26–32.

14 Reich, *Sexual Revolution*, 266–7.

> the cultural struggles of the twentieth century. The social struggles of today, to reduce it to the simplest formula, are between the interests *safeguarding and affirming life* on the one hand, and the *interests destroying and repressing life* on the other.[15]

It is clear that what today is called the left fights less and less in terms of class warfare, and more and more in terms of "warfare against repression," claiming that the struggle for the economic progress of the disadvantaged is included in this more general struggle, as if the two were inseparable.

A question that should be discussed is whether one can avoid Reich's proposals after having started down this post-communist road. An examination of the ideas of its secular intellectual advocates seems to suggest that the answer is negative. But even for Catholics, being on the left seems to coincide with abandoning *old-fashioned* ideas about sex, or limiting them in ways that can only be essentially contradictory.

Certainly, a rigorously orthodox form of Communism would still regard Reich's ideas and their implementations as a case of *bourgeois* decadence, as in Stalin's age. Nevertheless, the Communist parties in the West have not declared war at all on the new sexual morals and, on the contrary, have chosen to be on the front line in the fight against every form of censorship. Not only has the new left become sexualized, but in this regard the Western Communist parties have become subordinate to it. It would be extremely important to discuss the deep philosophical reason for how this happened, but it would take too much time.

• • •

We have reached the conclusion (which seems paradoxical but is not) that Dr Reich was the precursor of the worst and most dangerous aspects of today's mores as well as of today's politics. It is only an apparent paradox because what he carried out was the first consistent attempt at a *revolutionary psychoanalysis,* and Freud and Marx are still the guiding lights of the current situation; and today's left is defined precisely by its unwillingness to reject either Freud or Marx.

However, in the years around 1930, both psychoanalysts and Marxists rejected Reich's ideas. According to Freud, it was unquestionable that civilization can exist only by repressing and denying the instincts. As an old positivist, he still thought that the prevalent morals of the period

15 Ibid., xvii–xviii.

between 1870 and 1915 constituted the highest degree of evolution, and that they had to be strengthened, not destroyed. For him, psychoanalysis does not mean at all – these are his words, quoted by Reich himself – curing neurosis by giving free rein to sexuality. On the contrary, the process of becoming aware of repressed sexual desires, in order to control them, aims to "liberate the neurotic from the shackles of his sexuality."[16] In Reich's judgment this means that in Freud the bourgeois philosopher had prevailed over the scientist, and this had distorted the meaning of his discovery. Clearly, this was a judgment that Freud could not accept.

As for Marxism, Reich stood on the opposite side of a veritable philosophical abyss. According to Marxism there is an end that can be deduced from the movement of history. Being a Hegelian, Marx thought that the absolute is not found at the beginning of history, but rather is its outcome. According to Reich, on the contrary, there is a primitive dimension from which we moved away through sexophobic morality, and to which we must return by reinserting civilization into nature. His opus already contains all the elements of the recent reappearance of the myth of the noble savage.

However, Reich hoped to find common ground with Marxism in the critique of the family. During the pre-capitalist stage, the family had an economic root. Its function changed together with the development of the means of production, and its economic basis was replaced by a political function. Thus, it became the supporting pillar of the conservative structures. Supposedly, all authoritarian and reactionary interests stand together in its defence. The Marxist revolution could truly become a total revolution only by becoming a sexual revolution.

But he was completely wrong in his assessment of theoretical Marxism. As I have already said, the idea that values have an objective foundation forbids Marxism, at least in its revolutionary version, from becoming a vitalistic doctrine advocating unlimited sexual freedom. On the contrary, it is inclined to regard such freedom as the last stage of disintegration and degeneration of bourgeois society.

This character had to become gradually stronger as Marxism assumed the appearance of a Russian revolution, and the Russian character replaced the Marxist one. This process implied an aspect of reconciliation with tradition, which is what allows revolutions to succeed and not to end up being processes of disintegration. Hence the inevitable return to the ethics that Reich calls sexophobic, even more so under Stalin. He

16 [TN] Sigmund Freud, *Gesammelte Schriften* [Collected writings] (Vienna: Internationaler Psychoanalytischer Verlag, 1928), 11: 217–18, as cited in Reich, *Sexual Revolution*, 14.

interpreted this return incorrectly, as a petition to rehabilitate Communism in front of the moral world. This is why he placed his hopes in America, as he declared in the preface to the fourth edition of his book in March 1949: "I assure the reader that I am also fully conscious of the reactionary tendencies in the United States. But here, as nowhere else, *it is possible to stand up for the pursuit of happiness and the rights of the living*" (his emphasis).[17] Unfortunately, he was right, even though his American adventure ended in jail.

How could his ideas become so wildly successful in the last decade *independently of his direct influence* (which remained very limited, even after he was rediscovered: I have a sense that very few people read *The Sexual Revolution*)? In Europe the 1960s have ended with the well-known mass demonstrations: May 1968 in France, rallies last August and last December, Danish exhibits, ever greater diffusion of erotic literature in Germany, and even in Italy so-called risqué movies and pornographic magazines, which however are not just pornographic magazines in the old sense. The times when rebelling against modesty was considered pornography, and the question was the extent to which it should be tolerated, now seem very distant. Today, it is rather modesty that, at best, is tolerated in people who are inhibited or cannot give up ancestral prejudices. In much of so-called "good" society, it is something one has to apologize for. Anybody who says "I am still attached to a certain type of traditional morality" may expect to be excused because it is just an affirmation of fact. But woe to him if he claims that this fact should be recognized as a value! It would be interesting to track the recent history of such "open-mindedness" toward vice, starting from Proust's description of the Faubourg Saint-Germain. We would realize how far we have gone in this evolutionary process. By now, "being scandalized" is condemned without appeal. Of course, there are (not a few) Catholics who regard this condemnation as a progress in charity. The demonic always creeps in by creating an opposition between certain truths and virtues that, when they are separated, become errors. In the case at hand, charity vs respect for the objective order of being.

To summarize what I have said in a comprehensive formula, contemporary eroticism corresponds to an interpretation of psychoanalysis as a *moral revolution* (a transformation of the psychological structure), which sums up within itself the positive aspects of previous revolutions, including the Marxist one. But how did this interpretation, which had already been proposed and rejected after the First World War, become successful

17 [TN] Reich, *Sexual Revolution*, xv.

after the Second? A complete answer would require an analysis of the spiritual situation since 1945, focusing on aspects that at that time did not draw much attention, but that later turned out to be the most significant. Let us sketch an outline.

It is often said that the first few years after the war were marked, in Western Europe, by the *great fear* of Communism. This is very true, but one should not forget that another great, less expressed fear accompanied it: fear of a religious awakening. Certainly, at that time the persuasion that the "Islam of the twentieth century" could be stopped only with the decisive contribution of religious (in particular, Catholic) forces was very widespread. But, on the other hand, no broad movement of religious conversion accompanied this political judgment. Therefore, large segments of society faced the question of finding a force that could counterbalance within civil society the Catholics' increased political power.

There was also another phenomenon: the idea that the crisis associated with the victory of Fascism and Nazism in the European continent marked the final decay of old Europe, in its ideal tradition which had proved inadequate to face the reality of facts, since it had been unable to put up any effective resistance against the onslaught of barbarism. In other words, the attitude was born that elsewhere I have called "negativist millennialism."[18] It was a new attitude because, although all previously known forms of millennialism announced the end of a world that had become Babylon, they also contained a *promise* that could be described in sufficiently precise terms. Conversely, the recent kind was not, and is not, able to go beyond a vague affirmation of a radical change, and even when it tries to spell out positive ideals, it seems to view them more as tools of negation than as values to be affirmed.

Naturally, this disposition was bound to become more and more widespread as the new generation replaced the older one and the men from *yesterday's world* died away. Until, today, it seems the *natural* and almost unquestioned way of thinking. The idea that the crisis associated with the world wars did not involve *the tradition,* but rather the particular form taken by the tradition during the secular-liberal period from 1870 to 1914, was shut out by the prevalent progressive scheme, which says that in history nothing can have been lost, and nothing that has been regarded as *surpassed* can be brought back. And it is still shut out, even if today a few contrary voices are able to make themselves heard.

If we consider these two attitudes, taking into account both their widespread influence and the groups they mobilized, and also the way in

18 See "Tradizione e innovazione" [Tradition vs innovation] in Augusto Del Noce, *L'epoca della secolarizzazione* [The age of secularization] (Milan: Giuffrè, 1970), 43.

which they reinforced each other, we will understand the reasons for the success of the sexual revolution.

Let us consider, first, the stance that had to be taken by the intellectuals who were most hostile to Christian thought. And let us begin from the movements that are generically called the literary and artistic avant-garde, in particular from the one that, in its manifestos, constitutes the avant-garde's philosophical awareness: *Surrealism.*

It would be incorrect to regard Surrealism as a merely artistic phenomenon, instead of a comprehensive attitude toward life that aims at embodying the fullness of the revolutionary idea in its primary aspect, which is the will to mark a radical break with the past and the beginning of a new history. It is defined, therefore, by the intention to create a new reality in which mankind will supposedly reach the fullness of its powers, taking back what it had projected outside of itself by creating God (the powers from which it was alienated, to use language that by now can be found even in small-town newspapers). This is the origin of the phraseology habitually found in this type of thought: total man, surreality, superhumanity, and so on.

In this respect, Surrealism and Marxism share the same program. They differ on the following point: whereas according to Marxism the transformation of man will be a byproduct of the social and political revolution, according to Surrealism the first priority is "to remake the human intellect." The society of free men will arise, eventually, as a consequence of this transformation. From the ethico-political standpoint, the history of Surrealism is the history of this affinity and of this difference. There was a transition from an initial embrace of Communism – which led in 1939 to changing the title of the magazine *La Révolution surréaliste* to *Le surréalisme au service de la révolution* – to disagreement with Stalinism and to an attempt to find common ground with Trotsky, ending up in a break in 1947 due to the realization of the different character of the two revolutionary positions. Because of its emphasis on the sexual aspect within the revolutionary process, the declaration of this break is extremely important.

It can be found in the collective manifesto *Rupture inaugurale,*[19] a "declaration adopted on June 21 1947 by the group in France in order to define its position against any partisan policy," published on the occasion of the international Surrealist exhibit in Paris, 1947. It is useful to read it in conjunction with Henry Pastoureau's preparatory work *Pour*

19 "Rupture inaugurale" in *Le Surréalisme en 1947* (Paris: Maeght Éditeur, 1947) [TN: "Inaugural Rupture," in Michael Richardson and Krzystof Fijałkowski, eds., *Surrealism against the Current: Tracts and Declarations* (London: Pluto Press, 2001), 42–9].

une offensive de grande style contre la civilisation chrétienne[20] (the title documents nicely the "great fear" of a religious revival!), in which the same ideas are stated in a more articulate form.

The age-old enemy that today must be dispatched by the fullness of the *Copernican Revolution* is the Christian system which, supposedly, came together around the year 1000 "when the surviving elements of the Greek and Latin magisterium, of the Celtic and Frankish traditions, of the contributions by the Arabs and the Jews in the West, of the reflection of the doctors of the early Church and of the heretics of the first centuries and of an exoteric initiation that dates back to a time before the beginning of history, all fused together in an alloy so malleable that St Thomas Aquinas, working on it a few years later, was able to turn it into the most perfect expression of the doctrine that since then has become universal."[21]

Until now this old Christian-Thomist framework has been able to change shape infinitely many times in order to survive the successive disappearance of various exploiting classes. It cannot be toppled by changes in economic relations. The bourgeois revolution and capitalism ended up finding an accommodation with this pre-existing civilization, demanding only that the older institutions adapt to the new economic conditions, without disappearing. Today, Marxism faces the danger of going down the same road. Not even its most revolutionary wing, Trotskyism, is safe. Indeed, if we read one of Trotsky's last works, *Their Morals and Ours*,[22] we see that he remained faithful to Lenin's thesis that there are no moral limitations to revolutionary action. There is no separation between ends and means since these latter are organically subordinated to whatever goal has been discerned from the evolution of history. Hence, every kind of violence, every ruse, every illegal action, every dissimulation, and every deception become licit if they are deemed to be necessary to reach the goal. This is the classical thesis of Marx-Leninism, which says that politics absorbs morality within itself, and it would seem that there could not be a more radical violation of the traditional moral code. However, the Surrealists raise the question that such a-moralism may also allow "regressive practices." Is it certain that

20 [TN] Henry Pastoureau, "Pour une offensive de grande style contre la civilisation chrétienne" [For a large-scale offensive against Christian civilization"] in *Le Surréalisme en 1947*, 78–83.

21 See Jean-Louis Bédouin, *Storia del surrealismo dal 1945 ai nostri giorni* [History of Surrealism from 1945 to the present] (Milan: Schwarz, 1960). The text of "Rupture inaugurale" is found at 255–63 [TN: this particular quote is actually by Pastoureau, "Pour une offensive," 78–9].

22 [TN] Leon Trotsky, *Their Morals and Ours* (London: New Park Publications, 1968).

Communism's freedom to break the current moral law will always work "to the benefit of progress"? Could it also justify, instead, collaboration by the Communist Party in running the bourgeois state? The Surrealist group had in mind the stance of the French Communist Party in 1947; certainly, if they had written their manifesto in Italy they would have regarded Togliatti's party as the insuperable model of this type of deviation. "The ultimate outcome of historical evolution, marking the end of the misfortunes of the spirit, at last triumphant over its past, alone justifies people's actions. Only those actions that do not compromise the evolution of the moral law could be justified and it is precisely because we do not believe in its fixity (this would be absurd as the fixity of history) that we do not accept being constrained, under the pretext of preparing for the proletarian revolution, to regressive practices of which political collaboration with the class enemy is only the general aspect. In other words, we will always find it acceptable to transgress the current moral law, but only in order to progress it."[23] Certainly these are not occasional statements, since the thought of the greatest theoretician of Surrealism, André Breton, could be summarized, still on the eve of his death, in the following program: "To bring forever to ruin the abominable Christian notion of sin, of original fall, of redeeming love, to replace them without hesitation with the idea of the divine union of man and woman ... Morality based on the exaltation of pleasure will, sooner or later, wipe away the vile morality of suffering and resignation, preserved by forms of social imperialism and by the Church ... The tyranny of man ... must be replaced ... by the reign of the woman."[24]

The Marxists of that time would reply that the collaboration in question was temporary, and had the purpose of making possible the economic revolution. The Surrealists would easily counter that it was not at all certain that the economic revolution would have decisive moral effects. Nothing guaranteed that it would automatically bring about the defeat of the Christian order; actually, everything suggested the opposite conclusion. In fact, history shows that morals change with great delay in comparison with economic transformations, and that the process of moral development does not depend only on economic factors: "The moral doctrine of Christianity, sanctioned in all civilized lands by a common and constant profane right, expresses itself in the ten

23 "Rupture inaugurale" [TN: "Inaugural Rupture," 44].

24 See Jean-Louis Bédouin, *André Breton* (Paris: Seghers, 1967), 18 [TN: my translation from the first 1950 edition, 63–4. The passage quoted by Del Noce is from Bédouin's introduction to this anthology of Breton's works, and was actually written in 1949, several years before Breton's death].

commandments which remain the essence of the revelation of Moses. Marxists should conclude that since Moses was called to the top of Mount Sinai no important economic change has occurred."[25]

The manifesto consistently concludes: "Let us return to morality, the most constant object of our preoccupations: it would be absurd to count on the political revolution alone to change them ... These theoreticians [Marx's successors] have never denounced the current morality except when they saw an immediate political advantage in it. De Sade and Freud, on the other hand, opened the breach. Whatever the doctrine that must succeed Christianity, we see de Sade and Freud as the assigned precursors of its ethic."[26]

Does this now remote document mark the transition of Surrealism – and of the avant-garde in general, we could say – to anti-Communism? This is how it was interpreted at the time by most of the not many people who paid attention to it.

In fact, such an assessment is completely incorrect. In this document the avant-garde became aware of what its true attitude toward politics had to be in order to be consistent with the nature of its revolutionary idea. It did not even judge the Communist proposal to be incorrect, but just inadequate. Marxism had to be completed at the moral level with de Sade and Freud, and it was necessary to be intransigent about this morality, even at the cost of sacrificing political effectiveness. Pastoureau's piece explains why Surrealists must also refuse to participate in the opposition to the Communist Party from the left, which is necessarily destined to defeat because it does not call into question the relationship between politics and morals, as affirmed by those it wants to criticize, but merely refuses to push to the ultimate consequences the political use of deviousness and deceit that must result from it. Hence, "their efforts will tend to achieve the same goals and to hasten man's liberation, but *through other means*."[27]

We can say that in practice this separation resulted, objectively, in creating the conditions for a possible collaboration with the Communist action in the Western world, through a division of labour. The avant-garde would act on "morals" and uproot from the soul of the bourgeoisie the principles that underpinned the famous "dam" against

25 [TN] "Inaugural Rupture," 45. I modified the translation, replacing the words "need to recognize" with "should conclude," which are more faithful to the original French and also closer to Del Noce's Italian translation. An almost identical statement is found in Pastoureau, "Pour une offensive," 81.

26 See Bédouin, *Storia del Surrealismo*, 259 [TN: "Inaugural Rupture," 45].

27 [TN] Pastoureau, "Pour une offensive," 80.

Communism (a common expression at that time. Today even the word has been forgotten). Communism would follow its own route to seek power, free from the difficult problem of taking a position about traditional morality. But this is not the crucial point. What matters now is to emphasize that *having started from de Sade, Surrealism (and, in general, the avant-garde) rediscovered through an independent development Reich's idea about the necessity to complete Marxism with the new sexual morality, in order for the total revolution to succeed.* And that it chose as its task the transformation of morals through art. This task has been thoroughly carried out: whereas one could question (and it was done also in remarkable works) whether avant-garde art after the First World War was atheistic or mystical, even if unconsciously, there is certainly no longer any reason to raise this question after its development following the Second World War.

• • •

Certainly, one could remark that avant-garde art has a limited field of action and cannot have played a decisive role in the mass revolution of morals. But let us now discuss what created the impression – which is typical of the millenialist atmosphere that I mentioned – that tradition was exhausted for good.

Millennialism forced literature and cinema to be *engaged.* Negativism determined their content: to de-mythologize, to unmask, to de-mystify, to denounce alienation; and we do not even need to add *et cetera* because the program stopped at those four words. Nothing could churn out this kind of product better than the materials provided by psychoanalysis, taken in their desecrating aspect.

Thus, eroticism was smuggled under the moral cover of de-mystification and "dis-alienation." The newborn "culture industry" regarded literary works as "products" meant for "consumption." As such, they had to conform to the taste that was already being predetermined by a certain widespread historico-political judgment, which had been received passively rather that thought through. But since Europe had been formed by the tradition of an objective order of ends and a meta-empirical authority of values, this progressive and de-mystifying literature led precisely, due to its attitude toward traditional values, to the new sexual morality, through the process that I have already described.

Let us now move to the higher forms of secular culture. Vis-à-vis the political republic, a new *republic of letters* (to use the terminology of the Enlightenment) was constituted, under the banner of *cultural politics,* which pronounced much sterner and harsher interdicts. The plan was *to find common ground in the name of the Enlightenment* between liberalism and

Communism, which required a mutual reformation. Now, such a reformation required that liberalism, in order to stop being bourgeois in the usual sense, rediscover the anti-traditional side of the Enlightenment, radicalizing it in order to avoid the aspects that had caused the defeat of the Enlightenment by Romanticism. But such radicalization included necessarily, even when its proponents did not mean it, the abolition of sexual prohibitions or – as people say today, using an expression so abused that I would rather avoid it – taboos. If Gramsci was thinking of moving on from Croce to Marx, the new enlightened bourgeoisie wanted instead to go from Marx to Diderot. But, once this route has been taken, can one stop at Diderot or does one instead have to move on toward de Sade?

Thus, in the field of secular intellectual life, avant-garde art, the culture industry, and the cultural politics of philosophers and historians came together – intentionally or unintentionally, aware or unaware – in spreading the themes of the new sexual morality. Regarding intention and degree of awareness, philosophers and historians certainly had the least of both, although some certainly perceived the danger and tried to stop, and even made intelligent remarks. But, how could they stop?

Let us consider the facts. Having accepted the collapse of the metaphysical-religious tradition, only *science* remained standing, as mankind's only salvation, symbol of *modernity*, and pillar of the new civilization. But science, at least in its modern sense, studies reality as a system of forces, not of *values*. It provides instruments but it does not determine any goals. From the perspective of those who regard science as the only valid form of knowledge, one can speak of only one goal: *incrementing vitality*. I am sorry to quote again Dr Reich, whose thesis was rediscovered once again. Certainly he is not a great thinker, but he deserves the praise due to consequential reasoners, those who accept an aberrant but unavoidable conclusion that other scholars who are richer in humanity vainly try to avoid. The sexual revolution is indeed the point of arrival of "scientism."

Certainly history is not just the history of the intellectuals. However, the new bourgeoisie was susceptible to the great fear of a religious renaissance because of its recent origins, because of the business activities through which it had established itself – which generally did not depend on the traditional values or went against them – and because of the radical-masonic mindset with which it had been associated since the beginning of its dominance. Seldom had it felt such consonance with the proposals advanced by the intellectuals. It easily recognized sex as the weapon that could be used to push back the Catholic hegemony. Indeed, sex provided cover against the accusation which, at that time, seemed to be the sum total of all accusations: back then, morality tended to be identified with anti-Fascism, as if all evils had condensed in Fascism, and especially in Nazism. And with respect to sexual ethics the Fascist movements had generally presented themselves as defenders of the traditional views.

Neo-capitalism was even more inclined to accept the new ethics. It could find in widespread sexual happiness a very effective barrier against revolutionary dangers, or in fact against every kind of subversion, from the right as well as from the left. Let us remember again that Reich wanted to replace class struggle with "struggle against repression." In November 1944, in order to explain his thinking on this topic, he wrote: "The basic social question is no longer, 'Are you rich or poor?' It is: 'Do you favor, and do you fight for, the safeguarding of and the greatest possible freedom of human life? Do you do, in a practical way, everything in your power to make the masses of working individuals so independent in their thinking, acting and living that the complete self-regulation of human life will become a matter of course in a not too distant future?'"[28] In practice, this means that in the society coming after the sexual revolution, economic inequality can persist, even in the midst of universal well-being. On this point the sexual revolution can agree very easily with the ideas of the theorists of the affluent society. It is well known that the old radicalism, the political expression of the old bourgeoisie, used anti-clericalism as a diversion against the Socialist advance. In perfect analogy, the new radicalism, the expression of the new bourgeoisie, tends to use the sexual diversion against the Communist advance. If one looks carefully, there is continuity in the history of radicalism, from anti-clericalism to anti-Christianity.

It remains to be discussed why the progress of the sexual revolution has coincided with the success of Social Democracy. Scandinavia is the region where Social Democracy has been in power for the longest time. In England the disappearance of the last remnants of the Victorian mentality has coincided with the affirmation of the Labour Party. In Germany the advance of eroticism has been directly related to Social Democratic progress. In order to explain this phenomenon, we must remember that two souls live together within Social Democracy, one moralistic-Kantian and the other scientistic-positivistic. When Kantian morality went out of fashion, especially in its form as autonomous morality, which was dear to many Social Democratic intellectuals, it was unavoidable that scientism would prevail. In fact, the countries I mentioned are also those where today the new scientism is most widespread. By this I do not mean to say

28 Reich, *Sexual Revolution*, xviii.

that there is a necessary link between Social Democracy and sexual liberalization, but rather that Social Democracy has not yet carried out the revision of its ideas that seems necessary, and in fact does not seem very inclined to do so.

As for the attitude that Communists would take, the answer is easy: they favoured the sexualization of mores in the West to the exact same extent that they opposed it in their own countries. Another one of today's clichés says that Victorian moralism and imperialism have ended. It would be more correct to say that they have moved. The Communist position toward Europe or the West replicates that of nineteenth-century England toward Asia (an easy example would be the Opium War). Here, to grant Communists the partial truth that they may possess, we must think of the difference between the still expanding industrialization in Communist countries and the one of late capitalism. Therefore, also, the writers who are the scourge of "hypocritical moralism" and claim that free sexual activity is "normal" are in fact pawns in the Communist game. They are vulnerable to the accusation, which actually is very true and unquestionable from the sociological standpoint, of being mouthpieces of the decadent bourgeoisie. On the other hand, their security and prosperity are ensured by the services they render both to the new bourgeoisie – which we have already discussed – and to Communism. They have been often called "useful idiots"; based on how they show themselves capable of taking care of their own interests, I would rather call them "non-foolish servants," while stressing that they are still servants. It is well known that Russia hardly likes Communist parties in other countries to seize power by their own revolutionary strength. The precedents for their relations with the first-born nation are not encouraging. It is much better to have a situation in which all ethical and religious principles that could support an effective resistance disintegrate to such an extent that the only possibility at the political level is a puppet government, which in fact would be in a subordinate position. The fellow travellers, charged with the task of disintegration, have also been good at ensuring their own future.

• • •

In the course of this necessarily brief – but, I think, fairly accurate – examination of the intellectual and political motivations that favoured the success of the erotic offensive that had already been theorized after the First World War but had failed, I have thought it appropriate to give special relevance to an almost-ignored Surrealist document. The reason is that Surrealists were almost the only ones to *realize a fundamental truth:*

the decisive battle against Christianity could be fought only at the level of the sexual revolution. And therefore the problem of sexuality and eroticism is today the fundamental problem from the moral point of view.

Now we can explain a few monstrous errors of judgment, which lead people to think that the current erotic explosion is an irreversible fact.

The first error is to think that eroticism is an essential and unavoidable feature of a technological, or affluent, society, because such a society is characterized by an increase in vitality due to greater and greater domination over nature. This then leads to the opinion, which unfortunately is widespread even among religious observers, that Christianity must reform itself in order to fit into the new type of society. Or even that the ascetic element was foreign to primitive Christianity, but entered into it because of a contagion from Gnosticism. From here it is easy to take another step, playing with words, and say that "negation of sex" was extraneous to it (which may even be true, but only if understood in a certain sense), so that Christianity is perfectly reconcilable with today's vindication of sexuality. And that the dogma of original sin must be set aside, again as a gnostic addition, and so on.

Now, it is absolutely true that eroticism is essential for the affluent society because *scientism is its philosophical paradigm; however, the features of the so-called technological society have not been determined by technical progress per se.* They derive instead from the interpretation of contemporary history that I have outlined, according to which all traditional values have passed away for good. This interpretation is based on an entirely a priori affirmation and is becoming less and less able to withstand criticism.

From this opinion, which can be said to be "educated," let us move on to another one that belongs to the category of banal clichés, which unfortunately are broadcast and presented as unquestionably evident truths. I will state it in the same words in which I read it in a news story about a protest against eroticism that took place in Paris: supposedly, the anti-erotic reaction is "a movement as impetuous as it is naive which accepts the consumerist society but, in the name of morality, wants to outlaw a common object of consumption like sex, sold in movies, theatrical productions, magazines, books and records."[29] The claim here is that the erotic wave is just a quantitatively larger diffusion of pornography. There is a greater consumption of all types of products, and therefore … Not true: what has changed is the judgment of value. With eroticism, what until yesterday was regarded as a dis-value is now affirmed as a value.

29 Lietta Tornabuoni, "I commandos della virtù" [The commandos of virtue], *La Stampa* 104, no. 20 (28 January 1970): 3.

There is also an opinion voiced by some intellectuals that sounds like an echo (but very distorted!) of Croce's thought. Supposedly, today's mores constitute progress because sexuality has been permanently pushed back to the morally neutral sphere of economic and vital realities, so that we should talk about morality only for higher purposes.

Is this not the greatest possible factual error? Not recognizing that "morality" has its own place beyond "vitality," or absorbing completely what is "moral" into what is "vital," is part of the essence of eroticism.

But, what was the attitude of the "keepers" of tradition? By tradition I mean not the preservation of a past, but the recognition of an order of eternal and metaphysical values, which therefore must be handed down and transmitted from one generation to the next. So, what was the attitude of the representatives of religious thought, and in particular of the Catholic Church? We must acknowledge that the importance and the novelty of the phenomenon were recognized quite late, and that still today there is much confusion.

You are free to think whatever you want about Joseph de Maistre. My view is that his theses always contain an element of truth as long as they are interpreted *secundum quid.* This *secundum quid* is what is constantly lacking in his statements and makes them look like reactionary paradoxes. For instance, consider this passage: "It is enough to quench or, at least, to weaken to some extent, the influence of divine law in a Christian country, while keeping the freedom it gave women, and soon enough you will see that same freedom, which in itself is noble and moving, degenerate into shameless license. Women would then become fatal tools of widespread decadence, which soon would eat away the vital organs of the state. This latter would suffer gangrene and spread ignominy and terror as it disintegrates."[30] This is certainly offensive in the way it seems to sanction the inferiority of women. But it is full of truth if the liberation of women is identified with absolute sexual freedom, as is the case today. Thus, the campaign of de-Christianization through eroticism is the more powerful the more it relies on feminine irreligion, and is the best way to produce it.

It is probably accurate to say that even the highest religious authorities did not adequately recognize that they were facing a large-scale offensive against Catholic morality. Perhaps because in the years between 1945 and 1960 they were focused above all on the resistance against Communism, they did not grasp the importance of the literary avant-garde and of the whole philosophy driving the process from de Sade to

30 Joseph de Maistre, *Éclaircissement sur les sacrifices* [Clarification on sacrifices] in Oeuvres, tome V (Lyons: Vitte et Perrussel, 1892), 322–3 [TN: my translation].

Surrealism (it is also true that at that time there was no chapter about it in the histories of philosophy). They regarded its manifestations in fiction and in the performing arts mostly as a matter of bad taste or commerce: they saw pornography in what, instead, was eroticism.

I would rather not talk about those Catholics whose eyes light up in ecstasy when they hear the sound of the word "world," since they are ready to justify any aberration as a protest against a form of Catholicism centred on asceticism and mortification, so that, according to these people, any aberration is fine as long as it is consecrated and blessed.

A few comments are necessary. A certain neglect of issues of sexual ethics by some segments of the clergy began at the time of the Resistance. Political virtues were assigned the utmost priority over private ones, and the new Catholics often included chastity and purity among the lesser private virtues that had been excessively emphasized since the Counter-Reformation – the usual culprit. In a sense, it was natural and unavoidable that this would happen. However, it was the first step in a very dangerous direction, that of *dividing the virtues,* which I have already mentioned.

At that time this remained a limited phenomenon, but we know how widespread it became later on. We must make some distinctions among those who share in this way of thinking. Some have in mind a new unification of virtues that supposedly became separated in the course of history. Such a reconciliation must be achieved through a reconciliation of Catholicism and Communism, which they view as the only way to heal the diseases of our century. This is not the place to explain again how dangerous and delusional this program is, in my opinion. What is important to say here is that this view leads to an incorrect assessment also of today's eroticism. According to it, the non-Communist world (i.e., from this perspective, the bourgeois Western world, which supposedly holds Christianity captive) today does not offer and cannot offer anything but the experience of emptiness. Therefore, sex and drugs present themselves to young people as the only ways to renew their vitality. This is a dangerous proposition because one could deduce from it that all protests against the erotic wave are in vain and useless in the current situation. It also leads to an attitude of benevolent indulgence toward the protagonists of such a wave, because supposedly they express a degree of vitality that later on could sustain religious and political engagement, whereas their opponents are, in general, passive or vainly nostalgic souls, or people who hide their inhibitions under the banner of morality: cannon fodder for a military regime. But, above all, we must realize that this thesis is *false*: I showed that the sexual revolution is taking place not because today's young people are "empty," but on the contrary because they are "full" of the ideological themes that I have described.

However, there is a much worse position, which unfortunately is more widespread, with which no dialogue is possible: the position of the Catholics who do not aim at reconciling virtues that until now were considered essential, but at replacing some virtues with others. In their view, ascetic Christianity, which was typical of bygone eras, today must be replaced by "secularized" Christianity, in which the fullness of the virtues destined to advance the human condition will wipe away the passive and mortifying virtues (which they consider "repressive," even if they do not dare say that explicitly). Also in *La Stampa* of 28 February I read that at the anti-pornographic rally in Paris, the left-wing Catholics of *Témoignage Chrétien* handed out flyers against the speakers: "Why are you not protesting against the humiliation of the dignity of the Vietnamese, of the American black, of the victims of torture in Greece, of the strikers who have been arrested? Why are you concerned only with useless battles?"[31] This is a very significant text. Indeed, (1) to state that the battle against pornography and eroticism is useless means to concede that they cannot be censored on moral grounds. Which implies that today's Catholicism must embrace a "new attitude toward sexuality." But this new attitude can only coincide, as we have seen, with complete liberalization, and thus with a complete reversal of the traditional Catholic position. (2) The battle to help the poor and the persecuted and the battle against eroticism are viewed as alternative, so that the second seems to be just a conservative diversion. This is perfectly consistent, and confirms the discrimination among virtues. (3) Then, a peculiar thing happens, almost a self-refutation and a punishment for such a discrimination among virtues: it leads to discrimination among the poor and the persecuted themselves. Indeed, why is there no mention of the Czechoslovak, of the South Vietnamese, who are certainly in danger of being slaughtered, of the Tibetans, of the Biafrans themselves, of the persecuted Church in Eastern Europe? Clearly, according to these Catholics, poor and persecuted people of a traditionalist bent, or in general those who are not dear to the left, cease automatically to be poor and persecuted. There has been so much talk of the "false consciousness" of the right. Now this argument has run its course, and we should speak of the "false consciousness" of certain parts of the left.

31 [TN] Tornabuoni, "I commandos della virtù," 3.

One more word about the Catholic laymen who take care of secular matters and who are expected to protect, within democracy, religious values and also our fatherland – we must say that, since this word is so much out of fashion. The fact that eroticism advances without facing almost any obstacles shows how much the so-called realism of the politicians (which is especially common in the Catholic party, due to the habit that politicians should be concerned only about temporal welfare and be experts almost exclusively in the arts of prudence) has proved itself abstract and false as never before, because never before has history been shaped by ideal, not economic, factors as it is today.

• • •

Thus, the sexual offensive is explained by the simultaneous occurrence of three factors: the most radical political anti-Christianity, the conservatism of the progressive schemes within secular culture, and an inadequate understanding of contemporary history by Catholics.

Is it destined to advance even further, or has it reached its climax? Is it possible that in the 1970s it will start receding?

One of the most insidious delusions is that there is a correlation between the sexual revolution and peacefulness. It is a very tempting delusion: those who feel good do not move, says an old proverb. Therefore, the achievement of sexual happiness should free people from all kinds of resentments, and thus from aggressiveness. It is a utopian idea, which can easily be traced back to Reich, who in this was the heir of a common leitmotif in the history of utopian literature. Today, it is also expressed in the popular clichés that man has acquired the feeling of normalcy and has become reconciled with nature, a reconciliation facilitated by technical progress, which allows us not to see nature as an enemy but to insert it into civilization.

A detailed study of the French May movement would be the best document to show that this idea is completely false, because in it we can observe the explosion of the Marx-Freud mixture in an almost perfectly pure state. If we compare its features with the Surrealist program of 1947 of a full-scale offensive against Christian civilization, it cannot be denied that everything happened *exactly as if that program had become reality*. Let us recall again for a moment the revolutionary nature of Surrealism, and its critique of Marxism on the ground that it could lead to "repressive practices." It was easy for Marxists (and for Sartre, who at that time expressed the point of view of the "fellow travellers") to reply that by declaring such a break, Surrealism was showing its bourgeois nature. The extremely radical formulation of its rebellion masked the fact that the rebellion was so imbued with aestheticism that it led to complete acceptance of the existing social order, which was simply "put in parentheses." Pseudo-annihilation took the place of transformation. However, this assertion is not correct. A more extended discussion would lead to the conclusion that the Surrealist critique of Communism and the Communist critique of Surrealism are equally true. This symmetry reflects a contradiction that probably is intrinsic to the very idea of a total revolution. By attempting to reaffirm it in intransigent form, the Surrealist could not go beyond the stance of pure negativity, and attributed to the idea of negativity a sort of magical power, as if it was capable of creating a new humanity. In fact, they ended up in pure nihilism.

I think that future historians will have to use the expression "Surrealist revolution" as an overall description of the May events, since they were the epilogue of the sadistic-decadent revolution that claims to subsume within itself the positive aspects of Marxism. The connections between those events and the Surrealist program are obvious, even though that program did not act directly but was rediscovered with its proposals through that complex process which I have tried to outline.

One common feature is psycho-erotic-Freudian-Marxist de-Christianization. Another is stopping at negativity and believing in the magic power of the idea of negativity. It must be followed by the quest for sensuous and emotional novelties through drugs, precisely in order to go beyond ordinary reality (hence, of course, the inevitable appearance of friars and theologians who interpret drug use as the beginning of a form of mysticism, in perfect correspondence to what some literature and art critics had already imagined about Surrealism). Notice also how the criticism of Communism formulated by the Surrealists in their time (that the Communist revolution, inasmuch as it rejects de Sade and Freud, is also in danger of fitting into the system) corresponds to the criticism by the various *groupuscules.* In light of what could be called its "philosophical formula" – to push to the limit Marxism's revolutionary aspect by linking it to psychoanalysis understood in a revolutionary sense – we understand by what process eroticism must lead to the quest for a surreal world through drugs, and because of this rejection of reality it must encounter anarchism, keeping only its nihilistic aspect and leaving out the moral one. Surpassing Marxism on the ground of the sexual revolution leads, therefore, to total negativism, not only against civilization and values but also against the very principle of reality, and is accompanied by the most sacrilegious and blasphemous expressions. We should speak not of peace but rather of "permanent violence" as a replacement for the ideal of "permanent revolution," which was still oriented toward a future peace.

However, looking at the facts is not enough. We have at our disposal a book that is very important from the phenomenological point of view, independently of the opinions of its author, which are certainly very far from Christianity. It is *Erotism* by Georges Bataille (1957).[32]

I will simply quote some passages.

> The transition from the normal state to that of erotic desire presupposes a partial dissolution of the person as he exists in the realm of discontinuity … for the male partner the dissolution of the passive partner means one thing only: it is paving the way for a fusion where both are mingled, attaining at length the same degree of dissolution. The whole business of eroticism is to destroy the self-contained character of the participators, as they are in their normal lives. Stripping naked is the decisive action. Nakedness offers a contrast to self-possession, to discontinuous existence, in other words. It is a state of communication revealing a quest for a possible continuance of being beyond the confines of the self. Bodies open up to a state of continuity through secret channels that give us a feeling of obscenity. Obscenity is our name for the uneasiness which upsets the physical state associated with self-possession, with the possession of recognized and stable individuality.[33]

If we think about the idea of the devil as *simia Dei,* it seems – and a careful analysis would be appropriate – that these passages, which define perfectly the essence of eroticism, provide some kind of indirect confirmation and interpretive key for the description of creation and of original sin presented in the first few chapters of the book of Genesis. Indeed, eroticism is the precise opposite: its principle is, so to speak, de-creation, as opposed to creation. Having denied every trace of the divine image within human individuality, the process moves toward dissolution, fusion with totality through the negation of individuality (hence also the separation, within eroticism, of love from generation, and the aversion against giving birth. On this last point de Sade is decisive once again).

This is the reason also for the sacred character, as sacred turned upside down, that is intrinsic to eroticism: "the development of eroticism is in no respect foreign to the domain of religion, but in fact Christianity sets its face against eroticism and thereby condemns most religions."[34] Or, to put it better, it was Christianity that separated religion from eroticism, which, not by chance, comes back punctually in all forms of heresy. Today is the time when all heresies seem to have gathered together.

32 [TN] Georges Bataille, *Erotism: Death and Sensuality,* trans. Mary Dalwood (San Francisco: City Lights Publishers, 1986)

33 Ibid., 17–18.

34 Ibid., 32.

"The orgy is not associated with the dignity of religion, extracting from the underlying violence something calm and majestic compatible with profane order; its potency is seen in its ill-omened aspects, bringing frenzy in its wake and a vertiginous loss of consciousness. The total personality is engaged, reeling blindly toward annihilation, and this is the decisive moment of religious feeling."[35] In other words, the religious aspect (in its own way) of eroticism is shown by the fact that it takes a ritual form in the orgy. This is why sacrilege, black masses, the "Sabbaths, vowed in the lonely night to the secret cult of the god who was the other face of God,"[36] are essential.

This explains also the necessary link with devil worship (and also on this point, do we need contemporary examples? Just think of the current interest in books about satanic rituals).

Moreover, the history of the decadence of the Roman Empire shows in the clearest and most familiar way that the decomposition of civilizations is accompanied by the spreading of orgiastic cults. And please excuse me for bringing up for a moment the analogy, which has been discussed so many times, between Europe's present situation and the situation during the disintegration of the classical world. A statement does not become false for being repeated, and in this case it fits well all the people who, in the official media of the enlightened bourgeoisie, go as far as to attribute to pornography, even in its lowest forms, a liberating role from the taboos that supposedly still affect the Italian mentality and prevent it from conforming to a more mature level of civilization. The typical radical-*azionista*[37] refrain about Italian "immaturity" is often intermingled with the recognition of the liberating role of pornography.

• • •

An enormous cultural revision will be necessary in order to really leave behind the philosophical processes that have found expression in today's sexual revolution.

But, in the meanwhile, how can society defend itself? Should pornographic publications and shows be unconditionally allowed, including

35 Ibid., 113.

36 Ibid., 125–6. [TN: The published English translation "the other face of God" of the French "l'envers de Dieu" removes some of the theological ambiguity of Bataille's original, which could also be understood to mean "the opposite of God." The Italian translation quoted by Del Noce says "il rovescio di Dio," the "reverse of God"].

37 [TN] The word *azionista* refers to the ideas of the *Partito d'azione*, an Italian political party of the period immediately after the Second World War. It advocated a form of radical liberalism which had an enduring influence on many sectors of Italian culture, even though the party itself disbanded in 1947.

the most extreme cases, based on the principle that the sense of modesty has evolved and changed? There is a widespread idea that any form of "repression" in this field would be a violation and a diminishment of democracy. Now, it must be observed that mainstream pornographic publications share the characteristic of *presenting themselves as independent of the deepest processes of thought which constitute their philosophical foundation.* One has to ask if presenting "consequences separated from premises," far from implying respect for freedom of thought, may not actually violate it, because it replaces rational argumentation with an appeal to irrational powers. Can democracy allow this replacement without becoming a suicidal democracy? Because totalitarianism, considered in the aspect that makes it a new phenomenon irreducible to past forms of tyranny, is born precisely from the corruption of democracy, i.e., from the concessions that democracies make, because of a false idea of freedom, to those who manipulate the irrational.

PART THREE
The Predicament of the West

11

Authority versus Power

1 The eclipse of the idea of authority is one of the essential characteristics of today's world; in fact, it is the most immediately observable characteristic. Therefore, it can be said that the relevant literature is found not so much in the specific studies on this topic – which are mostly inadequate – but rather in the reflection about the contemporary world itself in its various aspects, taken as objects of study. This observation should be accompanied by the disposition to look at these aspects with a mind free from the dogmatic presupposition that the present state of affairs is superior or irreversible, or that it should be regarded as the starting point for a process of liberation that will take place in the future.

There is no point in lingering on the various possible metaphors that express the eclipse of authority – which ultimately can be summed up in just one: "the disappearance of the idea of the Father" – or on the description of its manifestations (crisis of the family, of education, of the Church). In order to understand the depth of this reversal and to gauge its amplitude, it will be enough to reflect on the opposition between the etymological root of the word "authority" and the meaning that this same word has generally assumed today. Indeed, *auctoritas* derives from *augere,* "to make grow." A shared etymological origin ties it to the words *Augustus* (he who makes grow), *auxilium* (help provided by a higher power), *augurium* (also a word of religious origin: a vow made to obtain divine cooperation in growth). If other languages are considered, one finds a common ideal structure. Thus, the German *auch* (also) is the imperative of the Gothic *aukan* (to make grow). Therefore, the etymology of authority includes the idea that *humanitas* is fulfilled in man when

"Autorità" [Authority], posthumously published in Augusto Del Noce, *Rivoluzione Risorgimento Tradizione* [Revolution, *Risorgimento,* Tradition] (Milan: Giuffré, 1993), 513–78. An abridged version was published as the entry "Autorità" in *Enciclopedia del Novecento* [Encyclopedia of the twentieth century] (Roma: Istituto della Enciclopedia Italiana, 1975), 1: 416–26.

a principle of non-empirical nature frees him from a state of subjection and leads him to his proper end, as a rational and moral being. Man's freedom, as power of *attention* and not of *creation*, consists in his capacity to subordinate himself to this higher principle of liberation and be freed from the pressures from below. Conversely, today the common mentality by and large associates the idea of authority with that of "repression," and identifies it with what stops "growth," what opposes it, reversing what the etymology implies.

Hence, it is important to realize that the present eclipse of authority represents *the* greatest among the reversals that have come to pass in history. It can be regarded as the stage that has been reached so far by the "total revolution," which is close to being fully realized in its *pars destruens*. The natural questions that arise are whether this eclipse marks the defeat of the revolution (its turning into disintegration, or into preservation of a disintegrated world) or whether it represents something irreversible. And whether such irreversibility, even when it is recognized in its philosophical significance, represents a process toward nihilism or whether the negative aspects of the present situation may rather be explained in terms of a crisis of growth.

2 The traditional substance of authority can be understood most clearly by focusing in particular on the family, because in it physical and moral generation are present together: father and mother are truly authors in the physical sense, through bodily generation, and "*auttori*" – in the sense that Vico gives to this word – through education, understood as a process of elevation from the immediate experiences of the spirit to the recognition of the order of values.[1]

By reflecting on the traditional family as a paradigm, we learn that we have authority to the extent that we are *auttori*; but, clearly, parents can be that only to the extent that they "hand down" and help. Now, in the modern world the unity of generation and education has been shattered. What parents can "hand down" in moral terms has no longer, at least in very large areas, any real substance or is regarded – according to what is commonly described as the "transformation" of the moral common sense – as a "value" (but actually as a "dis-value") and therefore as an obstacle to what is usually called "self-realization." (Forgive me for using these worn-out expressions. Progressivism is not accompanied by

1 [TN] In his *Autobiography* (Ithaca: Cornell University Press, 1944), 154–5, Giambattista Vico says that during the development of his philosophy he "set before himself" four *auttori* (authors) "whom he admired above all others" and who became his guides: Plato, Tacitus, Francis Bacon, and Hugo Grotius.

enrichment of language but by its banalization and, when it tries to be original, by its decomposition.) Here, we come to a crucial point: the crisis of the idea of authority is linked with the crisis of the idea of "tradition." Therefore, this crisis cannot be regarded primarily as a sociological phenomenon; it involves all the philosophical categories. If we start from its philosophical dimension we will then be able to move on and consider the social phenomena that facilitate it. Conversely, an investigation moving in the opposite direction cannot achieve meaningful results, and, because of the very abundance of materials that it can offer, runs the risk of losing sight of what is essential. Even worse, it would mean tacitly accepting the presupposition that all metaphysical systems arise only because they reflect certain given historical situations.

The link between the crisis of the family and that of education is obvious. Schools no longer present themselves as institutions where teachers guide "newcomers" to an awareness of the civilization that they must join and that they must continue (so that the appropriate adjective to describe the authority of the teacher is no longer "authoritarian" but rather "authoritative"). That means discovering those truths/values that are eternal, that directed the formation of the positive aspects of civilization, and that serve as a norm to judge any given circumstance: the idea of the Word, as inner Teacher and uncreated wisdom. Participation in the Word makes possible the communion of the spirits in one same truth. On the contrary, we have a kind of self-government of the young, who emancipate themselves from the burden of the past and use the teacher as an instructor in the methods of liberation. The reduction of tradition to "the past" (to what "is no longer") explains the widespread criticism of traditional teaching as "rote learning" (as the transmission of "dead" notions). This complaint, too, and the corresponding rebellion in the schools, can be explained only in connection with the eclipse of the idea of authority. Reflecting about the schools is important because by now everybody can see (which, of course, does not mean that everybody acknowledges) that "self-government" means coercion of the individual student by the group, and the possibility of isolating him if he dissents, and that the function of the teacher's authority is precisely to free the student from this kind of pressure.

Another obvious aspect of the eclipse of authority is the current crisis of the Church. As will become clearer later on, the critique of the authoritarian structures of the Church, as developed, for instance, by H. Küng,[2] is completely rooted in the quest to reformulate Christianity

2 See Hans Küng, *Infallible? An Inquiry* (New York: Doubleday, 1971) for a synthesis of his thought.

within the context of a philosophical position that has no place for the idea of authority. This philosophical background is clearly visible, for instance, in the polemical exchange between Küng and Rahner,[3] from which it is hard not to get the impression that Küng is more consistent with respect to propositions that Rahner had already formulated: one cannot stop half-way on the road to such a reformulation.

Another confirmation of the central role of the theme of authority is provided by the most baffling outcomes of the new religious Modernism, in the so-called theology of the "death of God," the endpoint of the "theological revolution." It is certainly not a coincidence that Altizer, the most consistent among these theologians, speaks of the death of God the Father in Jesus Christ.[4] The elimination of the idea of the Father had to reach theology as well.

What has been said so far makes evident the *ideal* and ultimate adversary of the revolution that wants to erase authority. It is the Greek-Roman-Christian unity that found its expression in the traditional Catholic Church. It was already said of old Modernism that it represented a surrender of Catholicism to Protestantism. This formula may help us understand the continuity between the two Modernisms and, at the same time, show that the second one constitutes an invasion of the Catholic sphere by a type of Protestantism that in the course of its historical development has progressively cut every residual tie with Catholicism. It is the *ideal* adversary, I said, because in the current situation, if the Catholic Church faded away, it would be a *consequence* of the disappearance of the idea of authority rather than the result of a direct attack: in other words, it would be one aspect of a more general transformation of values in which intentional anti-clericalism has vanished.

3 Thus, the study of the idea of authority leads us to the heart of today's crisis. While, on the one hand, we must acknowledge its eclipse, on the other hand, studying how it was born can at least lead us to grasp its pure essence, freeing it from all the encrustations and deformations that it suffered in the course of history.

First of all, we must distinguish authority from power: "the word 'power' almost inevitably evokes the idea of strength or force, and above

3 [TN] For the story of the Rahner-Küng dispute (including detailed bibliographic references) see L. Bruce van Voorst, "Küng and Rahner: Dueling over Infallibility," *The Christian Century* 88 (1971): 617–22, and John Jay Hughes, "Infallible? An Inquiry Considered," *Theological Studies* 38 (1971): 183–207.

4 [TN] See Thomas J.J. Altizer, *The Gospel of Christian Atheism* (Philadelphia: Westminster Press, 1966).

all the idea of a material force, a force which manifests itself visibly and outwardly and affirms itself by the use of external means, for such means indeed characterize the temporal power by very definition. On the contrary, spiritual authority, interior in essence, is affirmed only by itself, independently of any sensible support … If we can speak in this context of strength or force, it is only by analogical transposition."[5] What must be highlighted in this definition, which in my judgment is one of the most exhaustive, besides "interiority" (because sharing the same values prevents the hierarchical relationship that characterizes authority from being identified with the one between master and slave), is "independence from any sensible support." The question of authority is, in fact, the relationship between man and the invisible, the primacy of the invisible: such primacy can be discovered also in primitive societies,[6] confirming that the metaphysics of being is immanent within "common sense" – which is itself a distinctive assertion of this metaphysics.

As a matter of fact, the distinction between authority and power is very seldom understood in its deep significance, even when it is repeated verbally. Take, for example, the well-known book by Theodor Eschenburg *Über Autorität.*[7] We read that *auctoritas* prompts a spontaneous acceptance of another's will out of trust in the other's fully convincing superiority, so that authority becomes a particular form of dependence on *other men*, which is characterized only by the fact of being, originally, "interiorly accepted." It then "becomes a habit and generates permanent dependence."[8] Thus, authority is nothing but one of the forms of power: a thesis that is supported by Max Weber's very sociological and human notion of authority and by his distinctions between the authority of the "eternal past," the authority of the gift of personal grace or "charisma," and the authority of "legality."[9]

5 René Guénon, *Autorité spirituelle et pouvoir temporel* (Paris: éditions Véga, 1964) [TN: *Spiritual Authority and Temporal Power*, trans. H.D. Fohr (Hillsdale, NY: Sophia Perennis, 2001), 16–17].

6 See the very important book by Jean Servier, *L'homme et l'invisible* (Paris: Robert Laffont, 1964).

7 Theodor Eschenburg, *Über Autorität* (Frankfurt am Main: Suhrkamp, 1965), translated into Italian as *Dell'autorità*, trans. L. Malaguzzi Valeri (Bologna: Il Mulino, 1970). [TN: Apparently Eschenburg's book was never translated into English.]

8 [TN] Ibid., 9, my translation. The idea of authority as "accepted dependence" is attributed by Eschenburg to Horkheimer. He refers to Max Horkheimer et al., *Studien über Autorität und Familie: Forschungsberichte aus dem Institut für Sozialforshung* [Studies on authority and family: Research reports from the Institute for Social Research] (Paris: Alcan, 1936) 5: 24.

9 [TN] See Max Weber, "The Three Types of Legitimate Rule," *Berkeley Publications in Society and Institutions* 4, no. 1 (1958): 1–11.

As a matter of fact, the confusion between authority and power arises whenever the idea of authority is not linked to the metaphysics of the primacy of being over becoming and, as a consequence, the superhuman foundation of authority is not taken into account.

The philosophical consequences of the confusion between authority and power are immense. Indeed, only from the standpoint of their radical distinction can we speak of metaphysics as distinct from ideology. Conversely, if the idea of authority is absorbed into the one of power, it follows that general conceptions of reality are absorbed into ideology, understood as a practical act designed to legitimate, from the standpoint of being, some specific form of power, by calling being to fulfill this task. Accordingly, criticism takes the form of explaining religions and metaphysics[10] (necessarily understood in the plural) in terms of historical factors. Therefore, the belief that the concept of authority is reducible to the concept of power coincides with the "Marxian option," which is openly or silently accepted by a large part of contemporary culture. This is why today critical spirit is very often identified with Marxian or post-Marxian thought (in the sense that, having accepted all the negations of Marxism, it goes beyond), even by those who seemingly feel or profess no affinity for it. At the end of this process we find that science extended to the human sphere becomes the only valid form of knowledge.

4 The totalitarian phenomenon, in which the greatest extension of power led to the simultaneous denial of the idea of authority and the idea of freedom, motivated even scholars of a secular bent to formulate the question of the definition of authority in terms that differ from those that are customary in the Enlightened/radical literature.

Therefore, I will start from an essay by a writer who tackled the problem of authority after having explored the issues raised by totalitarianisms, Hannah Arendt.[11] This starting point is especially appropriate because Arendt's thought (she was a disciple of Karl Jaspers) is neither too different from nor completely similar to mine, which makes a discussion possible. According to Arendt, the obedience and the dependence (or even the discipline) required by authority are qualitatively different both from the idea of "persuasion" and from the idea of "forced

10 [TN] In Italian Del Noce uses the plural form "le metafisiche," meaning "the various metaphysical systems," referring to the widespread opinion that there is no such thing as a well-defined field of knowledge called metaphysics (which would be "la metafisica" in the singular).

11 Hannah Arendt, *Between Past and Future: Six Exercises in Political Thought* (New York: Viking Press, 1961).

coercion." Persuasion is subjective, egalitarian, and reached through a process of argumentation[12] (what nowadays is called "dialogue"). But after we have distinguished the concept of [authority from that of] persuasion, we must trace it back to the concept of *evidence*, recognizing that this *concept* is the great discovery of Greek metaphysics. The submission of the mind to evidence is more radical than submission obtained through force or persuasion;[13] but at the same time it has a liberating nature (from the pressure of lower or exterior forces). It is worth mentioning that this is the exact same view that was held by a too little known Italian philosopher, Carlo Mazzantini. Even though he did not discuss directly the concept of authority, he analysed the concept of evidence in terms that are strictly parallel to those that Arendt reaches by a different route. According to Mazzantini, the great discovery of Greek philosophy and the foundation of its lasting truth is that of *evidence*, understood not as force that constrains but as light that illuminates. It is necessary and does rule out its opposite, but without forcing the intellect.[14] He links this theme to the critique of both theological rationalism (and of "Christian philosophy") and voluntarism and arbitrarism (fideism, religious existentialism, empiricism), and so of modern philosophy in general, which keeps going back and forth between these two alternatives.

Thus, the idea of authority implies (a) that truth has a super-human character, so that dependence on it coincides with liberation from domination by other men; (b) that man not obey some arbitrary power; (c) on the other hand, that such dependence not be transferred into God Himself; in other words, that his "wisdom" not be understood as a norm to which his will is subordinated. Points (b) and (c) coincide, respectively, with Rosmini's criticisms of the systems of Occam and Leibniz and their various consequences.[15] Perhaps Rosmini's thought could be interpreted as an attempt to purify traditional Christian thought of the elements that lead to the opposite deviations represented by these two systems, at the boundary between orthodoxy and its rejection. Although Rosmini rarely uses the word authority, today his thought is exceptionally important in order to build a rigorous foundation for the theory [of authority], also because he is the philosopher of a Restoration, without

12 [TN] Ibid., 93.

13 [TN] Ibid., 107–8.

14 Carlo Mazzantini, *Il problema delle verità necessarie e la sintesi a priori del Kant* [The problem of necessary truths and Kant's a priori synthesis] (Turin: L'Erma, 1935), 41.

15 [TN] Antonio Rosmini, *Storia comparativa e critica de' sistemi intorno al principio della morale* [Comparative and critical history of the systems on the origin of morals] (Milan: Pogliani, 1837), 276–8.

any trace of "reaction" in the sense of idolizing a past historical order. Therefore, he regards theologically infused being, immanent in the dialectics of life, as the foundational element of order, so that order calls out for an authoritative presence of being and is an epiphany of being itself.

Having thus recognized that Plato's *nomos,* together with the particular form of obedience that it demands, is the metaphysical foundation of the idea of authority, if we then consider the historical circumstances that led to its affirmation (Socrates being convicted, and the hostility against philosophy on the part of the *polis*), we can discern from the genesis of its formulation that this idea is inseparable from the idea of freedom. The affirmation of the super-human is what frees man from dependence on other men. We also realize that the hierarchy inevitably associated with authority has an intrinsically interior character (because man discovers the order of being in the order of conscience): the freedom of what is specifically human, the rational component, requires the subordination of instinctual freedom.

Mentioning super-humanity leads us to connect the idea of authority with those of tradition and religion. But the idea of tradition is not compatible with any content whatsoever: in that case, it would reduce to faithfulness to and continuation of some *past.* It is in this sense that people speak of "national tradition," inverting the correct order and subordinating the "traditional spirit" to the philosophical position most opposed to it, namely pragmatism (the philosophical foundation of nationalism is indeed positivistic or pragmatistic). In this way, values are not respected – even if they are said to be supreme – inasmuch as they are considered only from the perspective of their civilizing function. Hence, the idea of tradition must be connected with the idea that truth is meta-historical. Traditional spirit means affirming the primacy of being, the primacy of the unchangeable, the primacy of intellectual intuition, or affirming the ontological value of the principle of non-contradiction (which, not by chance, appears in the fourth book of Aristotle's *Metaphysics* as the end point of the critique of sophistics). The meta-historical and super-human nature of the truth implies that its fixity includes the aspect of being ulterior to every possible way of expressing it, and thus of being inexhaustibly capable of expressing itself in yet-to-be-defined forms. However, this statement must be purified of all subjectivist aspects: it is the same identical truth which, because of its transcendence, is reached through an ascesis of conscience which necessarily has a historical character: it is a "personal perspective." This type of rediscovery recalls the Platonic theory of anamnesis. It is a knowledge that man has forgotten, even though somehow he still possesses it obscurely. Such knowledge is reawakened, not without great difficulty and effort, in the presence of the sensitive world. This theory stops being a myth if one understands the meaning of "sensitive world" in the more general sense, which includes the world of history.

The meta-historicity of the truth and its obscurity establish the connection between tradition and the sacred. It is the affirmation of the eternal within man, of the locus where the foundation of the human order and the foundation of being coincide; hence, "authority." At the same time, obscurely, so that authority must be realized as discipline in order to eliminate the elements of deceit which prevent the intuition of the truth (where the word intuition is used according to its etymology, in which "*intueri*" means "to see." The visual metaphor indicates that truth is not man's doing). The need to explain this obscurity is the reason why philosophy according to the traditional spirit is inseparable from the idea of a *fall*, of an original sin.

Participation in this uncreated wisdom is the foundation of the "world common to us all,"[16] which in the fallen creature finds residual support in "common sense" ("Human choice, by its nature most uncertain, is made certain and determined by the common sense of men with respect to human needs or utilities, which are the two origins of the natural law of the nations … [Common sense] is judgment without reflection, shared by an entire class, an entire people, an entire nation or the whole human race"[17]).

This analysis has extremely important consequences. The first is that the idea of authority, together with those of tradition and sacredness, is inseparable from the philosophy of the primacy of being. To summarize in a formula, we could say that in the philosophy of the primacy of being, authority is the foundation of power, whereas in the philosophy of the primacy of becoming power absorbs authority within itself, as can be seen in the ultimate outcomes of such a philosophy. It is not inappropriate to point out that today, at a time when judgments based on the philosophy of the primacy of becoming shape the dominant opinion (very often without any awareness of the first premises on which it is founded), not one day goes by without the publication of a new book about "power," while the literature dedicated to "authority" is negligible. This means that when the metaphysics of being has been utterly forgotten, the field is left open to all the disquisitions, as easy as they are banal, about the

16 [TN] Del Noce is again quoting Hannah Arendt, *Past and Future*, 90 and 178.

17 Giambattista Vico, *Scienza Nuova*, degnità 11 and 12 [TN: *The New Science of Giambattista Vico*, trans. Thomas Goddard Bergin and Max Harold Fisch (Ithaca: Cornell University Press, 1984), 63 (§141 and §142)].

"authoritarian syndrome." Thus, authority becomes associated with "authoritarian personalities," with frustrated people who want to reassert themselves by relying on what they call "absolute values," and on the claim that reality supports their desire to repress and oppress free personalities.

The core issue is still the relationship between "authority" and "evidence." Once we grasp this, we can understand the nature of the current fight against religion, which is even more dangerous because it is indirect.

One might certainly think that by now the philosophy of the primacy of being has permanently faded away and cannot be restored. In fact, the objection it must overcome is that it cannot account for history; the ideas of "progress" and "modernity" are brought up against it. Here we should discuss whether precisely understanding contemporary history – including the outcome of the form of thought that opposes the philosophy of the primacy of being – may not imply its rediscovery. Not coincidentally, the foundation of the philosophy of the primacy of being, the principle of non-contradiction, cannot be the object of a direct demonstration, but can only be proved via a negative route, through the self-refutation of the argument brought by its opponent. Today this argument is a philosophy that has become history: the contemporary world.

5 Thus, the ideal principle of authority must be sought in classical metaphysics. In general, however, historians of political thought focus mainly on Roman political doctrine. In it, authority takes the meaning of "faithfulness to the founding,"[18] which is why the authority of the living depends on the authority of the founders: the hereditary transmission of the authority of the ancestors (the *maiores*) to the *patres* who are members of the Senate; the ensuing distinction between *auctoritas* and *potestas*,[19] the sacred respect for old age because the elder was closer to the ancestors. But the connection to the foundation was understood as a bond with the will of the Gods (think of the task of the *auspices,* who reveal the divine approval or disapproval of human actions). Because of *pietas,* Roman political thought was able to converge with Greek philosophical thought.

Because of the collapse of classical metaphysics, the Roman faithfulness to the founding continued in an irreligious form (even when it is not openly stated as such), climaxing in the extreme trends of the

18 [TN] Arendt, *Between Past and Future,* 120ff.

19 "cum potestas in populo auctoritas in senatu sit" [since power resides in the people but authority in the senate], Cicero, *De Legibus* 3, 12, 38.

nationalist movements of our century. The manner in which these movements spoke about authority – making it their banner, but in the warped sense that I have described – is the source, even if only in part and because of a cleverly orchestrated operation, of the discredit that has been heaped on this word, as if the age of authority had found its full expression in the "Fascist age" that Europe experienced between the two world wars, and had burnt out completely and permanently in this totalitarian expression.

When Simone Weil speaks of the Romans as the "Nazis of antiquity,"[20] she is certainly wrong from the historical point of view. But she is correct in interpreting Nazism as a sort of *desacralized* analogue of the Roman world view.

6 Based on what has been said, the eclipse of the idea of authority is the defining characteristic of the contemporary world "as an epoch." Hence, our first task is to determine this "epoch" chronologically; that is, we have to identify the decisive event that determined a historical period that clearly differs from the one before in terms of prevalent categories of value. In this respect, the eclipse of authority presents itself as the true *result of the World War* (think of its uninterrupted advance, in the West, from 1945 until today, with a greater and greater acceleration after 1960). To be precise, it is the result of a historical judgment, uncritically accepted, about this war.

Indeed, I think that we should not speak of two world wars, but rather of two stages of one single world war, if we want to understand this war according to its specific characteristics, instead of simply listing it as one *species* within the *genus* war. Its distinctive feature is that it was set up from the start as a war-revolution against what was left in Europe of the "Middle Ages," the vestiges of the Holy Roman Empire and the Catholic Church. Unexpectedly, the Soviet Revolution came into the picture of this war, as an attempt to change it into a world revolution. The revolution and its after-shocks, which had the opposite political polarity but were subordinated to it in their opposition, originated the second stage, in which the war presented itself explicitly as a revolution. We should wonder whether this second stage marks the defeat of the transformation of the war into "revolution," since the revolution was transformed into a struggle for hegemony, and thus into a peace settlement which is not the establishment of justice but an outcome imposed by war. I mean that the

20 Simone Weil, *Écrits historiques et politiques* (Paris: Gallimard, 1960), 23ff. [TN: "The Great Beast" in *Selected Essays 1934–43*, trans. Richard Rees (London: Oxford University Press, 1962), 101ff.].

World War can be interpreted in two perfectly opposite ways: either as the creation of the conditions for a revolutionary process that is still unfinished, or as the proof of the defeat, one after another, of the revolutionary and anti-revolutionary projects of the 1800s, from Mazzini to Marx to the various other forms of revolutionary thought (like those that intend to combine liberalism and socialism, or those that seek an extreme break with every tradition, along the lines of the artistic avant-gardes and of Surrealism, or the one in which they merge, Marx-Freudism). So far, the first interpretation has prevailed, and the stages in the destruction of authority and tradition are strictly correlated with those toward the realization of the total revolution.

This prevalence has coincided with the perception of a *great break* such that the past – together with all its "authorities" and its "commandments," which claimed to be "eternal" – was supposedly swept away in that immense cosmic tragedy which, to use the gnostic terminology, marked the transition from one "eon" to another, or in the words of "revolutionary gnosis" from the "reign of necessity" to the "reign of freedom." The process through which authority disappears coincides with a shift in the focus of attention, due to the feeling of being in the middle of a revolution in which everything is being overturned. Equivalently, we have the well-known assertion that our age is characterized by the fact that the word "revolution" has become the "power-word" that guides us, so that, by directing our attention, it shapes almost all affective communications and, consequently, almost all judgments of value (in order to understand the word attention in the strong sense, think of what it means in the theory of free will of classical metaphysics and how it is formulated by St Thomas Aquinas). Therefore, we can fully agree with a recent statement by Carl Schmitt: "What was remarked by the historian of the French Revolution Auguste Mignet holds for a modern revolution: 'en temps de révolution, tout ce qui est ancien est ennemi.'[21] This means that what is new is legitimate because it is new, because it does not respect anything and devalues everything. It is the legitimacy of a raging process which produces directly and automatically an ideological superstructure as it produces itself."[22] The usage of the word revolution has to be clarified.

21 [TN] François-August Mignet, *Histoire de la révolution française: depuis 1789 jusqu'en 1814* [History of the French Revolution from 1789 to 1814] (Quedlinburg: Basse, 1868), 78.

22 From the preface to Carl Schmitt, *Le categorie del "politico"* (Bologna: Il Mulino, 1972), 25. It was written in August 1971. [TN: Italian translation of *Der Begriff des Politischen*, published in English as *The Concept of the Political*, trans. George Schwab (Chicago: Chicago University Press, 1996). Apparently Schmitt wrote this preface specifically for the Italian edition since it does not appear in the English editions].

To be precise, its meaning changes depending on whether it refers to the philosophy of the primacy of being or to the philosophy of the primacy of becoming, and to the transition in this latter from speculative philosophy to philosophy of praxis. According to the former, revolution means *risorgimento* of a more authentic tradition and authority[23] (many suggestions to this effect can be found in the works of Péguy). It is in the context of the second way of thinking that the radical opposition between authority (tradition) and freedom appears.

7 Thus, today's mentality is informed historically by the idea of the great break (accepted, by now, as the general framework inside which any legitimate discussion must take place) that supposedly marks the transition to the reign of freedom. In this sense, Revolution means replacing meta-physics with the ideal of a meta-humanity, in which mankind will acquire those powers that it already possesses potentially, but from which it alienated itself during the development of history, projecting them outside of itself in the act of creating God. As Voegelin accurately pointed out, the idea of the "superman" is already present in Marx in connection with the idea of "projection."[24] Hence, the idea of revolution as complete transformation implies the negation of every *dependence*, i.e., radical atheism, and also the negation of an unchanging human essence (and thus of eternal truths "worth" handing down) and of an unchanging "common sense." As a consequence, the total revolution can be carried out only by history (all ideas are de-sacralized, i.e., they are relative to a given historical situation; hence, it follows that the revolutionary absolute implies the critique of every metaphysical-religious absolute, even though this is not meant to imply a slide into positivism and relativism). However, revolutionary thought, in the unsurpassably consistent form it achieved in Marxism, maintains the idea of authority in its own way, by attributing it to history (hence the aspects of Communism as secularized religion, which are not just due to the fact that Communism fulfills the social, psychological, and emotional "functions" that were previously fulfilled by transcendent religion). Therefore, the *complete* crisis of authority follows after the crisis of revolutionary thought, in its aspect of being an attempt to restore authority after the end of the traditional conception thereof.

23 [TN] See the essay "Revolution, *Risorgimento*, Tradition" in this volume.

24 [TN] Elsewhere Del Noce cites, in this regard, Voegelin's essay "Apocalisse e rivoluzione" [Apocalypse and revolution] in the collection of lectures of the Unione Italiana per il Progresso della Cultura *1867–1967 un secolo di Marxismo* [1867–1967 a century of Marxism] (Firenze: Vallecchi, 1967).

Consider Marx's famous passage from the *The Economic and Philosophic Manuscripts of 1844*[25] where he formulates a form of atheism which is not the *conclusion* but rather the *precondition* of the whole system: "A *being* only considers himself independent when he stands on his own feet; and he only stands on his own feet when he owes his *existence* to himself. A man who lives by the grace of another regards himself as a dependent being. But I live completely by the grace of another … if he is the *source* of my life. When it is not of my own creation, my life has necessarily a source of this kind outside of it." We are not facing a theoretical proof of the non-existence of God, but an operation that leads to a moral prohibition to ask the question about God. From such a prohibition follows directly the promise, which claims the status of scientific certainty, of a new situation of mankind in which the problem of God will no longer arise (here, we understand why the total revolution must be literally understood, regarding its programmatic intention, as a "new creation").

Now, we ask: with respect to what idea of God is this option being formulated? As a matter of fact, Marx's text seems to be a mirror image, even in the choice of language, of some passages from Luther's *De servo arbitrio*,[26] the endpoint of the arbitraristic conception of God's will that had been reached by nominalist theology. Therefore some scholars, above all Thomists,[27] were correct when they emphasized the link between the Marxist option and Lutheran theology. Because of the form that the relationship of dependence takes in arbitraristic theology, the *aversio* can be interpreted only as complete corruption of human nature, so that there is a relationship of antithesis, of opposition, of irreparable division between God and man. In this way, the break with scholasticism becomes complete, in the sense that instead of finite participation in infinite Being we have a complete *aequivocatio* between the finite and the infinite. God is the *other* with respect to man. He is what man is not. The relationship with the transcendent becomes purely extrinsic. Therefore, and because the *aequivocatio* is based on the *aversio*, hostility and competition will dominate the relationship between Creator and creature. In this sense God is the absolutely other. At first sight, it seems that this absolute equivocation gives greater glory to the transcendent. But this is

25 [TN] Karl Marx, *The Economic and Philosophic Manuscripts of 1844*, trans. Martin Milligan (New York: International Publishers, 1964), 144.

26 [TN] Martin Luther, *On the Bondage of the Will*, in *Luther and Erasmus: Free Will and Salvation*, E. Gordon Rupp and Philip S. Watson, eds, (Louisville, KY: Westminster Press, 1969), 101ff.

27 See, for example, Georges Cottier, *L'athéisme du jeune Marx* [The atheism of young Marx] (Paris: Vrin, 1959), especially 46–7 [TN: my translation. To my knowledge Cottier's book was never published in English].

precisely what makes possible the Promethean option of rejecting dependence, since a relationship of competition has been established between God and creature, with the result that transcendence becomes separation and what is given to one is taken away from the other.

This apparent digression serves the purpose of showing that revolutionary atheism is the endpoint of a process that begins when in God the idea of power replaces the idea of authority (the Thomist *potentia ordinata*). It also intends to suggest that the only way to look for an alternative to the current eclipse of the idea authority is by understanding correctly (which is harder than one may think because the theses are interdependent; this is where the question of its "realism" arises) the Thomistic statement that metaphysical truths are relations founded upon eternal divine ideas (here one grasps better what was said earlier, that the question of the relationship between authority and power is perfectly symmetric to the question of the interpretation of evidence, either as light or as a fact, which has the coercive power of facts. From a rigorously philosophical standpoint, the problem of authority is part of the problem of evidence). Therefore, these relations are necessary also for God's intellect and God's will, not in the sense that God must obey a law but in the sense that God's nature is identical with a universal law that contains all other laws, so that what for the human intellect is a directive norm for the divine intellect is a constitutive essence. We are facing the great questions associated with the Thomistic understanding of natural law, which we cannot discuss here. What is important to keep in mind is that, due to the metaphysical necessity of eternal truths, authority differs from power because its essence is to set in order. In relation to the uncreated nature of order, the law does not exist because of sin, but rather precedes it and judges it. A decisive text on this point is found in *De malo*: "Est autem considerandum quod primo homini in sua institutione datum fuerat divinitus quoddam supernaturale donum, scilicet originalis iustitia, per quam ratio subdebatur Deo, et inferiores vires rationi, et corpus animae. Hoc autem donum non fuerat datum primo homini ut singulari personae tantum, sed ut cuidam principio totius humanae naturae, ut scilicet ab eo per originem derivaretur in posteros. Hoc autem donum acceptum primus homo per liberum arbitrium peccans amisit eo tenore quo sibi datum fuerat, scilicet pro se et pro tota sua posteritate" (see also *Summa Theologica*, 1, 2, XC–XCVII).[28]

28 [TN] "And we should consider that God had bestowed a supernatural gift, namely, original justice, on the first human being at his creation. And by that original justice, that human being's reason was subject to God, and his lower powers subject to his reason, and his body to his soul. And God had given this gift to the first human being both as an

8 I have briefly described the aspect of religious thought which is most vulnerable to revolutionary thought. What I have said is confirmed by the fact that today's many attempts to combine religious thought and theological thought – which are affected directly or, more often, indirectly by the revolutionary mindset – are accompanied by a decline of Thomism, or by its re-interpretation in forms that turn out to be incompatible with it.

Moving on, now, to the success of the idea of revolution, it can be explained as the ultimate outcome of certain presuppositions: that the historical development of thought moves toward an ever greater secularization, and that the idea of "modernity" has an axiological value; in brief, the themes of Enlightened-progressive culture. Thus, we have a peculiar situation: today's negations of authority and tradition betray a conservative attitude about the usual interpretations of history. As is well known, such interpretations were developed in the context of the historical reflection about the French Revolution. Cutting-edge culture seems to be avoiding most carefully the question whether they may have to be changed in order to understand contemporary history.

The identification of modern spirit with anti-traditional spirit has led people to describe the whole process of thought and civilization from the sixteenth century to the present in terms of critique of authority, so that its rejection today should be described as the *temporis partus masculus*, to use Bacon's expression. On the one side there is myth, which is unable to give reasons for itself and therefore generates dogmatism and its practical consequence, authoritarianism. On the other side there is the critical spirit, which proceeds from the abandonment of theology and speculative metaphysics and comes to discover the genesis of metaphysical and theological delusions. What today are called human sciences are, supposedly, the road to the fulfillment of this liberation in the spirit of the Enlightenment. Of course, this progress is not guaranteed because such optimism would require the dogmatic affirmation of an immanent providence. The danger of a counteroffensive by the authoritarian and reactionary spirit will always remain, and makes it necessary to protect and defend freedom.

9 Today, however, the progressive view of history faces serious difficulties, precisely regarding its ability to make sense of history, which seemed

individual person and as a source of the whole human race, namely, that he transmit the gift to his posterity by physical descent. And the first human being, when he by his free choice sinned, lost the gift in the same habitual condition in which he received it, namely, for himself and all his descendants," Aquinas, *De Malo*, 335.

to be its strongest argument. As a rule, progress in freedom was identified with the replacement of an authority that was previously regarded as despotic with a non-despotic authority. Thus, the inner authority of conscience was set in opposition to the authority of the Church; the authority of reason to the authority of Revelation, regarded as always exterior; and again, revolutionary thought included the idea of an authority of history, whose direction coincided with moral universality, which demanded the end of the domination of man by man. The conflict still involved two authorities, e.g., the one of faith and the one of reason, and normally rationalism believed that it could appropriate the elements of truth that were present in the opposite position (think of the notion of rational faith and similar ideas).

Now, on the contrary, today's permissivism replaces "freedom to" with "freedom from." It is a form of liberation in which every ascetic element, even in the most secular sense, is abolished. It is "libertarianism" replacing the liberal spirit (already Croce was very sensitive to the degeneration to which the ideal of freedom is vulnerable if it is separated from respect for tradition,[29] and he became even more aware of it as his thought developed. This is the source of the pessimistic aspects of the last stage of his philosophy). Liberation coincides with the *affirmation of instinctual freedom.* Going back to something I discussed before, the progressive-Enlightened mentality faces insurmountable difficulties as soon as it tries to explain the phenomenon of totalitarianism (which has not disappeared at all; it is its nature to take new and previously unpredictable forms), in which the negation of authority and the negation of freedom go hand in hand. These difficulties, I believe, are due to the fact that totalitarianism represents the greatest expansion of power in conjunction with the greatest rejection of authority: we can recognize in it the outcome of the revolution as contradictory to the program of universal liberation. But we have seen that affirming authority is the same as affirming the primacy of the invisible; the negation of the invisible, which characterizes the Enlightened-progressive mindset in its final stage, must erase the distinction between authority and power. This is why this mindset suffers from a peculiar type of compulsion: it must try to explain totalitarianism using the most assorted and strangest analogies with phenomena from the past (Asian despotism, ancient tyranny, medieval theocracy, dictatorship, and so on). Or it must present Soviet totalitarianism, for example, as a result not of Marx-Leninist doctrine but of a regression of Communism to some autocratic-Tsarist tradition.

29 [TN] See, for instance, the passage by Croce quoted on page 143 in this volume.

Or it must trace totalitarianism back to some residual religious aspect, by using the ambiguous expression (even though it can take a correct meaning) "secular religion." The political and practical consequences are exceptionally serious.

Focusing on the analogy with medieval theocracy, we must realize that the essential features of a totalitarian system are determined by its *secularist,* and not *religious,* character. Theocracy is founded on the idea that truth is eternal; on the contrary, totalitarian regimes regard everything that is not subject to empirical verification as ideology for the sake of power. Between theocracy and totalitarianism there is the most radical possible opposition, like that between affirming that truth is absolute and denying it.

Furthermore, the progressive conception is shaped by the idea that time moves in an ascending, irreversible line. Certainly, it does not deny that the journey toward freedom can run into obstacles. In fact, in the form of a new Enlightenment it abandons the idea of a necessary ascending process, granting that temporary setbacks may happen, and even admitting the possibility that barbarism may triumph. I have already observed that the idea of risk is what distinguishes this position from previous formulations; hence, it replaces optimism, which is regarded as a still-theological position, with meliorism. But whatever the value of this concession may be – because, in fact, progressives keep thinking in terms of opposition between the principle of authority, tied to metaphysics and to the religion of transcendence, and the affirmation of freedom, tied to the "modern" principle of immanence – the irreversible ideal of progress as liberation from dependence remains unchanged.

Now, the current situation calls back into question, instead, our picture of what is constant and what is cyclical in history. Limiting ourselves to the centuries of the modern age, radical criticism of authority along the lines we have described was formulated during the final stage of each of its major trends. After the failure of Bruno's revolutionary attempt (aimed at conquering the papacy), it appeared in the *libertinage* (all of whose essential themes are already found in the work of Giulio Cesare Vanini, who was the mediator between Italian irreligion, in the form it took after Bruno's defeat, and French irreligion).[30] At the end of the Enlightenment radical criticism of authority came up with the *philosophes* (along the line from Diderot to de Sade, which continued through Romanticism and reasserted itself in our century in the literary avant-gardes, especially in Surrealism). Today, it is found in the practical

30 [TN] Pen name of Lucilio Vanini (1585–1619), Italian freethinker and author.

implementation of both classical German philosophy, along the line from Hegel to Marx to Nietzsche, and Anglo-Saxon empiricism. We can say that libertinism, as mere opposition of freedom and authority, is constantly found in history whenever a philosophical process reaches an atheistic conclusion, and also that it always follows the defeat of a revolution: Bruno's revolution at the end of the Renaissance, the Jacobin at the end of the Enlightenment, and the Marxist today. Thus, what changes is not the arguments, which are all of a radically negative type, but rather the extension of the phenomenon, which in the 1600s affected the aristocracy and at the end of the eighteenth century the bourgeoisie, whereas in our time it has become a mass phenomenon. Hence the impression that today we are facing a fatal, irresistible process, and at the same time a new situation because, although one could easily detect premonitions of the eclipse of the idea of authority in earlier times, they were always accompanied by significant resistance which, at least, contained the process and limited it to determinate socio-cultural groups, always minorities of the population. But we should rather observe that negative thought seems to go through a cycle in which, after the idea of the revolution as "new creation" has faded, it must necessarily go back to its initial libertine position.

Therefore, it must be said that the crisis of authority does not undermine only religious-transcendent thought. It calls into question also the hopes of secular thought in the tradition of the Enlightenment, by raising a question that encapsulates why Nietzsche is still relevant today: whether nihilism might be the endpoint of the ascending line of the Western process of liberation. Indeed, it seems hard to think that we face a crisis of growth when we seem unable to envision any ideal, not even in the distant future. The eclipse of the idea of authority casts doubt on the two fundamental categories of the philosophy of the Enlightenment: modernity and progress. And not just on these two. According to a widespread opinion, the imposition of authority was associated with the promise of happiness. Despotic regimes could establish themselves by promising happiness in exchange for freedom. In this respect, just consider two classic texts, one from the time of the French Revolution and the other from the age of Restoration, which were widely read in the years immediately after the Second World War: the *Reclamation of the Freedom of Thought* by Fichte (1793),[31] as a critique of paternalism, and

31 [TN] Johann Gottlieb Fichte, "Reclamation of the Freedom of Thought from the Princes of Europe, Who Have Oppressed It until Now" in *What is Enlightenment? Eighteenth-Century Answers to Twentieth-Century Questions,* ed. James Schmidt (Berkeley: University of California Press, 1996), 119.

The Liberty of the Ancients Compared to That of the Moderns by Constant (1819),[32] as a critique of private happiness separated from the exercise of political activity. Certain mental habits that derived from this view are still with us, even if today they are seldom stated openly. Indeed, let us return to the opinion that claims that there is a symmetry between theocracy and totalitarianisms: supposedly, the authority of the former was founded on a promise of otherworldly happiness, the authority of the latter on a promise of worldly happiness, as a perversion of the modern spirit. Today, however, from the permissive point of view the "right to freedom," separated from any declaration of duties, and the right to happiness coincide, and happiness can be understood only in an individual sense, as full satisfaction of one's desires.

Finally, we should also not discount the fact that the eclipse of authority is taking place exactly along the lines already described by those who were its theoreticians. In recent years a passage from Plato's *Republic* about what today would be called "permissive democracy" has been cited often: "And does greediness for what democracy defines as good also dissolve it? – What do you say it defines that good to be? – Freedom – I said – for surely in a city under democracy you would hear that this is the finest thing it has, and that for this reason it is the only regime worth living in for anyone who is by nature free."[33] The description of the relationships that occur in this type of democracy, between children and parents, students and teachers, women and men, and of the resulting transition to a tyrannical government (or its present reality, because every despotism presupposes a system of forces, i.e., many non-unified sovereign wills among which one will or one group of wills becomes dominant by relying on such disorder) reminds us of our contemporary situation. This is important because it shows that traditional political thought is able to explain the outcome of such a situation, whereas the situation itself is not as well equipped for the same task.

10 The West is the epicentre of the crisis of authority. One must distinguish the ideas of Europe and of the West, which are completely different. The former refers to the continuity of a process of civilization that takes its first steps in the East. When we speak of West and East, instead, we want to express an opposition – between the activist, pragmatist spirit

32 [TN] Benjamin Constant, "The Liberty of the Ancients Compared with That of the Moderns" in *Constant: Political Writings*, ed. Biancamaria Fontana (Cambridge: Cambridge University Press, 1988), 309.

33 [TN] *The Republic of Plato*, trans. Allan Bloom (New York: Basic Books, 1991), 240 (Book VIII).

and the contemplative spirit. The present situation is characterized by *the replacement of the idea of Europe by the idea of the West.* We must remark that the fact that the eclipse of the *idea of authority* and the eclipse of the *idea of Europe* coincide is one aspect of this replacement. The emptiness of most discussions about Europeanism, which is so evident, is due to the fact that by Europeanism people actually mean Occidentalism. Thus, they intend to revivify and unite Europe precisely through the idea that is killing it!

But, how could the West become the locus of the sunset of authority? Notice that when people recall the etymology of the word West, "the land of sunset," this is all they actually mean.

We must refer one more time to the "guiding word," namely the revolution, understood as a "new creation" and thus first of all as total liberation from the past. As we have explained, its elevation to "sign of the times" was the result of the World War, a result that was passively received rather than turned into an object of reflection.

In front of the problem posed by the Marxist revolution, two paths were open: one was to rethink classical metaphysics in order to free it from the aspects that led to its crisis – which in their ultimate ideal motivations were also the cause of the world's troubles. The other path was to move beyond Marxism, having accepted its negations of metaphysical thought, and free it from the remnants of messianic and millennialist traditions – in response to the reconciliation with the past (of sorts) that had made possible the building of the new Russian state. What defines today's situation is the recognition of oppositions *that cannot be mediated*: on the one hand, by now the philosophy of the primacy of becoming has reached its ultimate consequences, *simply denying* the philosophy of the primacy of being and not trying to sublate it from a higher viewpoint. On the other, the representatives of the forms of thought and judgment that depend on classical metaphysics or presuppose it (as is the case of religious faith), have generally tried out forms of syncretism with aspects of the opposite position, which have always been very short-lived.

The fundamental intellectual mistake is the insistence on the thesis of "sublation."[34] Moving in this direction, one can only go toward ultra-Marxist positions, which complete and extend Marxism in the radical rejection of authority, tradition, metaphysics, religion, isolating Marxism's "secular" aspect by completely eliminating its "religious" aspect. Thus, starting in the 1960s, the revolution has been replaced by "secularization." One may wonder whether this replacement coincides

34 [TN] "Inveramento." See footnote 6 on p. 10.

with the replacement of the revolution by disintegration, or with the triumph of the bourgeois over the revolutionary spirit. The bourgeois spirit, which by nature is anti-traditional, anti-metaphysical, and implicitly anti-religious, always takes advantage of the revolution in order to reach the stage when it can manifest itself in its pure state.

If we now consider the moral situation of the West, we see that the Marxist revolution has been the precondition that allowed the moral features [of the bourgeois spirit] to come to the surface, while removing the circumstances that could bring about the revolutionary apocalypse. It seems that Marxism, instead of defeating the bourgeois spirit, enabled it to take a step further: viewed in the context of world history, it seems to have been the precondition that allowed the fundamental characteristics of Western civilization to achieve a complete break with the principle of traditional civilizations, in which "every society is aware of its celestial origin and is very careful not to magnify the initial imbalance, which was the cause of the fall; it tries to remain stable in order not to increase the distance from its archetype."[35]

11 The revolutionary sublation of Marxism, culminating in the most radical critique of authority, takes an obligatory form: that of a combination with the left-wing version of psychoanalysis. However, is psychoanalysis absorbed into Marxism or, on the contrary, is Marxism dissolved into psychoanalysis? One should not be fooled by the language, which is often extremely revolutionary. Since I cannot discuss this question in depth here, I will limit myself to the following comments: (a) by its very nature, theoretical Marxism cannot be combined with other philosophical positions; (b) these other forms may be from the left or from the right, but the outcome is always a form of revisionism, i.e., a subordination of the Marxist critique to the bourgeois hegemony. Old revisionism became subordinated to capitalism, the new one must become subordinated to neo-capitalism – regardless of how violently it attacks it – and, in the final analysis, to the same consumerist society that it claims to be fighting.

On this topic I should point out a great strength of the philosophy of Lukács, from the standpoint of Marxian consistency, namely its rejection of psychoanalysis viewed as a form of mystification in terms of bourgeois self-criticism which remains within the bourgeoisie. This could be confirmed by reflecting about the outcome of the students' rebellion, which expressed this thesis in revolutionary practice and certainly had very important consequences, but all in favour of the consolidation of the

35 Servier, *L'homme et l'invisible*, 390.

system that it was apparently fighting. Indeed, only through the rebellion was the "system" able to rid itself of a certain degree of commitment to traditional values, which before seemed to be forced on it as an unavoidable obligation.

To sketch an outline of such ultra-Marxist revolutionary movements, all centred around a radical critique of authority, we must turn our attention to Surrealism (as a particularly significant manifestation of the literary avant-garde), to the thought of Reich, and to the Frankfurt school.

12 Surrealism should not be regarded as an artistic phenomenon, in the sense in which art is distinct from other forms of spiritual life, but above all as a revolutionary phenomenon, characterized as such by totalizing categories; in fact, it intends to carry out not just a revolution *in* art, but a revolution *through* art. It differs from Marxism in the sense that it does not regard the transformation of man as a byproduct of social and political revolution. On the contrary, the society of free men will follow from the "remaking of the human intellect." Here we see already that Surrealism has to go against that last residual of authority that Marxism entrusts to history. An analysis of this point would be very important also in connection with the French origins of Surrealism, because this latter (following a strand of French philosophy that had religious origins, but is now completely secularized) denies the unity of necessity and freedom that was affirmed by classical German philosophy. In this respect, Surrealism's relationship with Communism is very interesting: it changed from initial adhesion, which led it in 1930 to change the title of the journal *La revolution surréaliste* into *Le surréalism au service de la revolution*, to dissent with Stalinism and to a quest to enter into an agreement with Trotsky. It ended in a break in 1947 due to the realization of Surrealism's different revolutionary character.

The declaration of the break, contained in the collective manifesto *Rupture inaugurale* published on the occasion of the International Surrealist Exhibit, is extremely interesting.[36] Essentially, it is about the inadequacy of Marxism for a "full-scale offensive against Christian civilization."[37] The Christian system, based on the necessity of the moral law, on the Decalogue, which remains the foundation of the common

36 "Rupture inaugurale" in *Le Surréalisme en 1947* (Paris: Maeght Éditeur, 1947) [TN: "Inaugural Rupture," in Michael Richardson and Krzystof Fijałkowski, eds, *Surrealism against the Current: Tracts and Declarations* (London: Pluto Press, 2001), 42–9].

37 [TN] "Pour une offensive de grande style contre la civilisation chrétienne" is the title of a preparatory essay by Henri Pastoureau, also published in *Le Surréalisme en 1947* (Paris: Maeght Éditeur, 1947), 78–83.

and constant profane right – and thus on the Commandments and on authority – supposedly established itself around 1000 AD when traditional elements from various sources merged together "in an alloy of various elements, malleable enough that St Thomas Aquinas, who moulded it some years later, was able to make it the most perfect expression of the doctrine that became universal at that time and has been ever since."[38] This Christian-Thomistic framework cannot be overturned by transforming economic relations. The bourgeois revolution has ended up reconciling with this pre-existing civilization and Marxism faces today the same danger. Interestingly, it is precisely Marxism's extreme lack of moral scruples that undermines its revolutionary power: it is the Leninist thesis that revolutionary action is exempted from all moral constrains, since there is no separation between ends and means, these latter being organically subordinated to the end that is dictated by the development of history. When this type of Machiavellianism is pushed to its extreme consequences, it allows, in practice, all kinds of "regressive" compromises, through which the revolution becomes captive to traditional morality A process develops, in the name of the need for order, of authority, of the restoration of the family, until nothing stands in the way of the restoration of religion. Because the criticism of authority has not been taken to the extreme, the Marxian fixity of the law of history risks bringing us back to the fixity of the moral law.

The Surrealists want to replace Communist "amoralism" toward today's morality with a moral intransigence of "immoralism" toward traditional values. The current moral law must always be violated, "but only in order to progress it."[39] I speak of "moral" intransigence in immoralism because the Surrealists refuse to envision the defeat of the Christian order as the automatic outcome of economic revolution; this statement would simply replace dependence on one idol with dependence on another idol, dependence on the transcendent God with dependence on the historical God. Hence the conclusion of the manifesto: "Let us return to morality, the most constant object of our preoccupations: it would be absurd to count on the political revolution alone to change them … These theoreticians [Marx's successors] have never denounced the current morality except when they saw an immediate political advantage in it. De Sade and Freud, on the other hand, opened the breach. Whatever the doctrine that must succeed Christianity, we see de Sade and Freud as the assigned precursors of its ethic."[40]

38 [TN] Pastoureau, "Pour une offensive," 79.
39 [TN] "Inaugural Rupture," 44.
40 [TN] Ibid., 45.

It is important to examine also the statements in which the greatest theoretician of Surrealism, André Breton, summarized his program shortly before his death: "To bring forever to ruin the abominable Christian notion of sin, of original fall, of redeeming love, to replace them without hesitation with the idea of the divine union of man and woman ... Morality based on the exaltation of pleasure will, sooner or later, wipe away the vile morality of suffering and resignation, preserved by forms of social imperialism and by the Church ... Tyranny by man will have to be replaced ... by a reign of the woman."[41] This passage is important for three reasons. First, the initial fall is mentioned. In my judgment, the dialectics of rationalism, understood as negation of the supernatural, starts from an original choice to deny without proof the initial fall.[42] Therefore, when it reaches its final conclusion in revolutionary thought (which is necessary in order to be consistent with this option, as rejection of dependence on authority), it must make historical outcome its criterion of truth. Second, an absolute antithesis is affirmed between Christianity and the new revolutionary morality. This latter does not "preserve" ("surpass," "sublate," etc.) but simply "denies"; therefore, the break with historical continuity is affirmed as decisive. Third, the sexual revolution is mentioned, viewed not just as a modification, radical as it may be, of a particular aspect of morality, but rather as a "revolution through the transformation of the meaning of sexual relationships." The Surrealist Manifesto of 1947 did not have much resonance, not only among politicians, who ignored it altogether out of false realism, but even among intellectuals. This happened in part because they tended to underestimate the ethical-political expressions of Surrealism, which they regarded as accessory elements of a poetic vision aimed at supporting baffling artistic expressions; and in part because at that time their interest was focused on Marx's philosophical thought – which had been poorly known in the West in the period between the two wars – and on its relationships with the forms of existentialism and personalism that had become successful in the years between 1930 and 1940. If we look back today, in the light of the immense transformation – not only of morals but also of judgments – that has taken place in the West since 1947, we cannot help being surprised by the prophetic nature of this document. The action of so-called "progressive" culture has turned out to be much

41 [TN] As far as I can tell, the attribution of this passage to Breton and the statement about when it was written are incorrect. It comes from Jean-Louis Bédouin's introduction to the anthology *André Breton* (Paris: Seghers, 1950), 63–4; my translation.

42 See my book *Il problema dell'ateismo* [The problem of atheism] (Bologna: Il Mulino, 1964).

more effective than political and economic action; and the history of the last few decades has moved exactly in the direction it wished for. We can say that the defeat or containment of political Marxism in the West has been the precondition for the success of what I have already called "ultra-Marxism." Cultural Marxism led the assault, but it would never have been able to maintain the breakthrough without the aid of these revolutionary forces that it regards as heretical. Conversely, these latter would never have been able to establish themselves without the break created by Marxism. In a sense we can say that Marxism and ultra-Marxism support each other, even though they cannot be reconciled.

Thus, what Surrealism envisioned (since its beginnings, actually) was a synthesis of Marxism and left-wing psychoanalysis as the only effective weapon against Christian civilization. That there would be attempts to develop this type of synthesis was a necessity inscribed in the order of things, so to speak. Marxism and psychoanalysis were competing explanations of the worldly origin of ideas. Therefore, it was completely natural that somebody (and very soon) would think of unifying them.

13 The first systematic attempt in this direction was made by Wilhelm Reich, an Austrian, in *The Sexual Revolution*.[43] This book already contains everything essential on the subject, and can well spare us the trouble of reading the countless novels or essays that the culture industry produces on this topic. They are literally only illustrations, i.e., concrete examples of the theses affirmed by this psychologist, who was heterodox with respect to mainstream psychoanalysis.

Given that it is a feature of every modern science to be accompanied by some type of utopia, Reich can really be considered the utopianist of psychoanalysis; and, as is the case for all utopias, his work is formally consistent. His thought is based on the premise, which of course is taken for granted and accepted without even a hint of a proof, that there is no order of ends, no meta-empirical authority of values. Thus, every trace is erased not just of Christianity but of idealism in the broadest sense of the word, or of any foundation of values in some objective reality, such as history for Marx. What is man then reduced to, if not a bundle of physical needs? When they are satisfied, when every repression is removed, he will be happy. Vital energy is identified with sexuality, in agreement with an ancient assertion. Through absolute, unlimited sexual freedom, man will free himself of neurosis and become fully capable of work and initiative. His psychological structure will be changed, and he will also be

43 [TN] Wilhelm Reich, *The Sexual Revolution*, trans. Theodore P. Wolfe (New York: Noonday, 1963).

freed from military and aggressive tendencies, and from sadist fantasies, which are typical of repressed people – as is illustrated, supposedly, by de Sade himself. But, what is the repressive institution *par excellence*? According to Reich, the traditional monogamous family, and from his point of view he is certainly correct. Indeed, the idea of family is inseparable from the idea of tradition, from a deposit of truths that we have to *tradere*, to "hand down." Hence, the family must be destroyed in order to achieve the abolition of every meta-empirical order of truths.

According to Reich, the need for a Freudian reform of revolutionary thought is demonstrated by the success of the Fascist movements, which refute the standard interpretation of historical materialism because it was precisely the impoverished masses who helped Fascism come to power, thus giving the impression that what is decisive at the practical-political level is not economic stratification, but rather the ideological aspect (hence the idea of a correlation between Fascist domination and Idealistic culture). Therefore, historical materialism must be completed by analysing the subjective factor of history, which Marx could not do because in his day scientific psychology did not exist. It is very easy to guess what this psychological complement should be: Fascism is the rebellion of the sexually repressed which takes a deviant, sadomasochistic, and destructive form because it failed to focus its criticism on the principle of repression itself.[44]

What is striking about Reich's thought is the weird mix of new and old elements. Certainly his moral theses are new with respect to the revolutionary tradition, which until then had been rigorously puritanical in the expressions that had really impacted history, from Robespierre to Lenin and Stalin. On the other hand, these theses look like a consistent reformulation of those of libertarianism. For instance, one could find a close relative of Reich's utopia in that of Cyrano de Bergerac, one of the most representative writers of eighteenth-century libertinism.

Let us investigate this point a bit more deeply because it reveals an antinomy of revolutionary thought. Undoubtedly, if revolution means a radical break with the past, any concession to the idea of the family constitutes the beginning of a reconciliation with tradition. On the other hand, the idea of a "new" order is essential to the idea of revolution: the revolution is not a negation of order but a transition to some kind of higher level. On the contrary, the domain of free sexuality is the *pure* present: one falls back into the sub-human, into animalism (think of Leibniz's *mens momentanea*). To avoid this situation one tries to escape

44 Wilhelm Reich, *Mass Psychology of Fascism*, trans. Vincent R. Carfagno (New York: Farrar, Straus & Giroux, 1970).

into "another reality," fantastic and utopian, where one can be free from the pressure of reality. This is the reason for the necessary link between widespread eroticism and the quest for "artificial paradises," ranging from drugs to a renewed interest in magic. Therefore, the "sexual revolution" marks the stage of the bourgeois involution of the revolution.

In fact, the history of Reich's thought is an extremely interesting document of this phenomenon. After his theses were condemned by Russian Communism, he judged that America was the most suitable country to incarnate his revolutionary ideal. And he was not mistaken because we can certainly speak of a "Western revolution," as long as we use the word simply to mean an inversion, from Puritanism to various forms of pansexualism. However, it is a "bourgeois" substitute for the revolution, in the fullest sense of the word. If by bourgeois society we mean a society defined by the primacy of the economic aspect, this society must periodically undergo qualitative leaps in order to survive, or actually to express its nature even better. Not by chance, the success of Reich's philosophy (Reich himself had died completely forgotten in an American jail in 1957) coincided with the initial rise of consumeristic and neo-capitalistic society. Definitely, there could not have been a better context to carry out a revolution of sorts, which however took place within the bourgeoisie, actually amplifying its characteristics. In fact, Reich had understood perfectly well that from his perspective the definition of revolution as a struggle against the bourgeois system had to be considered inadequate: "Soviet Russia, which owes its existence to a proletarian revolution, is today, in 1944, sex-politically reactionary, while America, with its background of a bourgeois revolution, is at least progressive, sex-politically."[45] Indeed, for him the classical Marxian categories become meaningless: the fight takes place between those who defend and affirm life and those who intend to repress and destroy it. Going back to an idea I have touched on before, Reich's attempt to secularize Marxism through psychoanalysis leads, instead, to the recognition of a veritable abyss between the two world views. According to Marxism there is an end, which is deduced from the development of history. Marx, being a Hegelian, thought that the absolute is not found at the beginning of history, but is its outcome. According to Reich, on the contrary, there is a primitive state from which we became removed through sexophobic morality and to which we must return by reinserting civilization into nature.

45 From the preface to the third edition (1944) of Reich, *The Sexual Revolution*, xviii.

Especially over the last decade, his theses have become enormously widespread. This is easily explained by recalling Sorel's statement[46] about the use of anti-clericalism by the radical bourgeoisie at the turn of the nineteenth century as a diversion from the revolution; this diversion has been replaced today by the erotic diversion. Just think of the widespread identification of authority with authoritarianism, repression, moralism, and even Fascism. This is just a repetition of Reich's stance when he spoke of the Communist "red Fascism,"[47] by which he meant not a common totalitarian background but rather a Puritan-repressive mindset that could take either a black or a red colour. Indeed, he articulated his pan-sexualism into a political proposal that was typically totalitarian: religion was not to be fought directly, but its criticism of the right to spread to the masses the attempts to secure sexual happiness would not be tolerated.[48] The outcome would be the disappearance of the religious sentiment, at least to the extent that it claims to have a supernatural origin. Unmistakably, this is the totalitarian approach to religious persecution.

14 It may seem strange that I have given Reich so much importance. And yet, simplistic as it is, his thought is consistent, so that it shows by contrast, like a watermark, the nature of authority. Revolution means radical liberation from authority, but such a rejection implies also the rejection of tradition, and the rejection of tradition implies the rejection of metaphysical-religious thought. The chain of ideas that I outlined earlier is perfectly confirmed.

If we consider the theses of the Frankfurt School, we are certainly moving to a much higher critical level. It is named after the Institute for Social Research which, having been founded in Frankfurt in 1924, achieved relevance after 1931 under Horkheimer's direction. After Nazism came to power, his collaborators kept up its activity, at first in France and later in the United States until 1950, when they were able to reopen the institute.

Their arguments, which arrive at opposite conclusions in Marcuse and in Horkheimer, are premised on an interpretation of contemporary history. Or more precisely on the fact, which their arguments intend to prove, that Marxism in its Russian-orthodox version is incapable of

46 [TN] I have not been able to identify the source of the statement by Sorel that Del Noce is referring to.

47 [TN] See Wilhelm Reich, *Reich Speaks of Freud* (New York: Macmillan 1967), 274–6; also, *People in Trouble*, trans. Philip Schmitz (New York: MacMillan, 1976), 11 and 205–7.

48 [TN] Reich, *The Sexual Revolution*, 265.

explaining contemporary history adequately. In any case, what makes them interesting is this lived connection with current history, and the meaning of the philosophical reassessment that is required in order to understand it.

In order to understand the context in which the school was born, we must look at the *revolutionary-libertarian mindset in Germany immediately after the First World War*, which led to the setting up of an opposition between "materialism," understood first of all as a philosophy of "happiness," and the various forms of Idealism, spiritualism, mysticism, and so on, which were all filed under the same label of philosophies aimed at defending the existing order. Therefore, the opposition progressive/ revolutionary thought vs conservative/reactionary thought absorbs the opposition between true and false. It is justified because, from the perspective of replacing "metaphysical" being with "social" being, liberation becomes the criterion of truth. This was the presupposition and the original flaw of the School, which however found its own critique in the development of Horkheimer's thought (and, at least partially, of Adorno himself, even though his thought can be interpreted in more than one way). This presupposition has the following implications.

- a Their revolutionary stance is a radical affirmation of the transition "from the reign of necessity to the reign of freedom," understood in the strongest sense. Thus, the disappearance of authority must be viewed as the end point of progressive thought, which, in fact, presents itself as a process of liberation from authority, theological or human, transcendent or empirical (where theological authority continues to be viewed as a reflection of human authority). The confusion between authority and power, which legitimates the criticism of order in the name of freedom, is typical of revolutionary thought; still, perhaps nobody had ever affirmed such a complete antithesis between authority and freedom. At the same time, we must say that perhaps there is no more interesting document in order to show the outcomes that result from the confusion between authority and power.
- b Hence the break between German critical Marxism and Russian dogmatic Marxism, which took place around 1930 and grew sharper and sharper afterwards. Regarding the polemic between Lenin and Kautsky, the Frankfurt group rejects Lenin's position, although this obviously does not mean that they embrace Kautsky's. Thus, their criticism targets Social Democracy as well as Russian Communism. The Russian Revolution is criticized because of its dictatorial and oppressive aspects, which must ultimately lead to a

process of reconciliation with tradition. The connection between the critique by the Frankfurt School and the critique by the literary avant-gardes is very clear. More generally, we can say that their thought expresses most rigorously, thus making possible a critical discussion, the quest to define an idea of European revolution (in the secular sense of the word "European") ulterior and superior to the Russian revolution.

c They observed the failure of Social Democracy and of the Weimar Republic. It was the failure of a constitution, which dealt only with rules of coexistence, whereas true life takes place outside such rules. In light of this critique of the Weimar Republic, their critique of Max Weber and the process that brought them back from Weber to Marx become fully pregnant.

d Meanwhile, Nazism triumphed to an unexpected extent. Whereas crude and dogmatic Marxism had won, critical Marxism was defeated and impotent in practice. The only alternative to abandoning the Marxian interpretive key was to integrate it with a psychological, actually psychoanalytical, factor. In order to explain Nazism, it was necessary to invoke psychological pathology, the "authoritarian syndrome" I have already mentioned.[49] Needless to say, we find here a connection with Reich's position, although in the form it had taken in Fromm. I have already argued that this position is unavoidable once the metaphysical nature of the idea of authority has been set aside without any proof. A separate critique ought to show that it is unavoidable if one chooses to stop at a reform of the Marxian interpretation of contemporary history without radically criticizing it.

e The transformation of psychoanalysis into revolutionary thought takes place through dialectics, viewed as the assertion that contradiction is necessary as a response to the objective contradiction of society. But it is dialectics without synthesis because otherwise it would lead to the perversion into "positive" ideology (where the word "positive" applies to metaphysics as well as to positivism) that characterizes dialectic materialism (a mere materialistic inversion of Idealistic dialectics) and forces it to reproduce the repressive structure of society.

The critique of authority is also what leads them to replace the link between dialectics and certainty with the link between dialectics and hope. A radical critique of authority really implies also abandoning the Hegelian and Marxian thesis that necessity and freedom

49 See the detailed discussion of this topic in Theodor W. Adorno et al., *The Authoritarian Personality* (New York: Harper & Row, 1950).

coincide, and that therefore there is an authority vested in a necessary process of history. In this connection, we have the rehabilitation of the word *utopia.*

f Their American experience led them also to criticize neo-positivism, pragmatism, and sociologism. It is here that the characteristic problem of the school emerges, namely, the coincidence – which cannot be maintained, as we shall see – of the critique of the metaphysical tradition and the one of positivism in its ancient and, above all, in its new forms. The critique of positivism and the polemics against the culture industry bring to the fore the same attitudes opposed to the Enlightenment and derived from counter-revolutionary thought that Marxism had already accepted and assimilated, although not openly. However, such attitudes come back in a very particular way, because they are separated from the "repressive" principle of the Logos that used to be their metaphysical foundation. Adorno's reflection about the principle of identity, interpreted as a law that expresses a prohibition, is especially interesting regarding the rejection of classical metaphysics.[50] Thus, some themes from tradition resurface, but they are completely de-sacralized, and such a de-sacralized recovery carries dangers. There is a sort of critique of modernity, but it takes place within a view of the historical development of philosophy that understands it as a process of liberation from all strands of thought which intended to open the way to adhesion to the super-natural.

The thought of this school can be viewed as a sort of irrationalization of Marxism (consequent to the rejection of Marxism-Leninism) in the form of a negative philosophy, which expresses the sum total of all the critiques it has accepted or formulated as a sort of syncretism of negations. Each negation is meant to prevent another form of thought with which it coexists from becoming absolute. A Russian scholar correctly said about Marcuse that "he fully deserves Marx's apt characterization of Proudhon: in his reading of Hegel he never got beyond simple negation."[51] As long as we add that also Proudhon is "turned upside down." In Marcuse the primacy of justice is replaced by the primacy of

50 Theodor W. Adorno, *Zur Metakritik der Erkenntnistheorie* (Stuttgart: Kolhammer, 1956) [TN: *Against Epistemology: A Metacritique,* trans. Willis Domingo (Boston: MIT Press, 1984)].

51 [TN] Yuri Zamoshkin and Ninel Motroshilova, "Is Marcuse's 'Critical Theory of Society' Critical?" *Russian Studies in Philosophy* 8, no. 1 (Summer 1969): 45–66; republished as "Man in the 'Industrial Society': Is Herbert Marcuse's 'Critical Theory of Society' Critical?" in *The Scientific and Technological Revolution: Social Effects and Prospects,* ed. Robert Daglish (Moscow: Progress Publishers, 1972), 262–79. They are two different translations

freedom understood as instinctual freedom. Because, if the Logos is regarded as "the origin of the logic of domination," it follows that "nature (its own as well as that of the external world) was given to the ego as something that had to be fought, conquered and even violated … The struggle begins with the perpetual internal conquest of the 'lower' faculties of the individual: his sensuous and appetitive faculties. Their subjugation is, at least since Plato, regarded as a constitutive element of human reason, which is thus in its very function repressive. The struggle culminates in the conquest of external nature, which must be perpetually attacked, curbed and exploited in order to yield to human needs."[52]

I have quoted this long passage because it clarifies, possibly like no other, the meaning taken by the words repression and permissiveness in Marcuse's work, which is still the most rigorous they have been given. At the same time, it reveals the typical confusion of the Frankfurt school, which regards Platonic purification and the modern idea of scientific-technical domination of nature as stages of the same process. Certainly, there is an abyss between Adorno and Horkheimer's *Dialectic of Enlightenment*[53] and the work by Marcuse I just mentioned. Reading the former, we are struck by a wealth of accurate observations about contemporary society, and also by the presence of a thesis that will lead by necessity to the development of a critique of the initial presupposition of the school, as we shall see. Nevertheless, the theme that is developed consistently in *Eros and Civilization* is also present. This book became the textbook of the students' movement and explains its huge misunderstanding: concretely, it became a rebellion, at the same time, against the technological society and the traditional spirit, i.e., against two opposites merged into one without making any distinction. This led to the unavoidable outcome of rediscovering the libertine position. By saying this, I also recognize its importance as a document: rebellion against authority must, *in contradiction with its own initial claim,* go through a cyclical process such that, at the end, *the revolution is turned upside down into libertine dissolution,* i.e., into disintegration of the existing order, through an anarchic-individualistic negation of every order. Hence, what happens in practice is the transition from positive and revolutionary atheism, aimed at the creation of a new reality, to negative and destructive atheism; thus, the revolutionary stage seems to have the function, within

of an article from the Russian journal *Voprosy filosofii* 10 (1968). I used the 1969 translation (p. 61), which reads better than the translation from 1972 (p. 275).

52 [TN] Herbert Marcuse, *Eros and Civilization: A Philosophical Inquiry into Freud* (New York: Vintage Books, 1962), 99–100.

53 [TN] Max Horkheimer and Theodor W. Adorno, *Dialectic of Enlightenment,* trans. John Cumming (New York: Continuum, 1972).

the cycle of atheism, of mediating the transition from aristocratic libertine atheism to today's libertine atheism as a mass phenomenon. Indeed, since there is no way of defining the transition from reality to utopia, the revolutionary action boils down to mere negation, which on the other hand (since it cannot be total negation) lets immediate existence become the only value.

15 Going back to the analogy with Proudhon, what we have here is Proudhon without the moral dimension, or without all the aspects that continue in Sorel; or, perhaps, Fourier's revenge against Proudhon. As for the critique of the scientific-technical mentality of the Enlightenment, we must describe it as a reversal of the process that moved from libertine thought to the Enlightenment.

If, according to revolutionary thought, the proof of the truth of a theory must be found in its historical results, and if, therefore, any internal criticism of such thought must concern the heterogenesis of ends to which it is subjected – or "the betrayal of the revolution necessary for its success," as it was argued especially by Ellul[54] – we can say that the attempt to carry out a Marcusian revolution was truly a baffling example of this phenomenon. It was also truly unique in its kind because the "betrayal" did not take place afterwards but was intrinsic to the revolution of the "great refusal." Indeed, it did not target the traditional values, which it regarded as already dead because they contradicted the process of development of bourgeois society,[55] but rather the positivistic system of the "one-dimensional man," which involved the neo-capitalist society just as much as Soviet-type Communism. As a matter of fact, no revolution was ever a tool of its enemies as much as the one promoted by Marcuse's philosophy, because its only victim was whatever remained of belief in the traditional values that the "system" had been unable to destroy. This task was carried out almost miraculously by the unexpected rebellion [of 1968]. The form of its failure enabled neo-capitalism to get rid of the onerous influence of the traditional values, which until then it had been forced to respect. Communism, on its part, achieved the result that philosophical Marxism came to be recognized as the discriminant factor of critical thinking, in the same way that Kantian thought had been regarded at the beginning of our century, i.e., as a position from

54 [TN] See Jacques Ellul, *Autopsy of Revolution*, trans. Patricia Wolf (New York: Alfred Knopf, 1971).

55 See, for instance, Herbert Marcuse, *L'uomo a una dimensione*, trans. Luciano Gallino and Tilde Giani Gallino (Turin: Einaudi, 1967), 77–8 [TN: *One-Dimensional Man* (Boston: Beacon Press, 1968), 58–9].

which one could move on, but after having accepted all its negations against the philosophies of the past. Thus, the Marxian[56] rebellion succeeded in creating the ideal conditions in which the system it was fighting could really establish itself in its novelty, and in which the truly oppressive nature of such a system – which Marxism denounced correctly – would no longer be perceived, since no real possibility was left to move beyond it. On the other hand, this was necessary: since Marcuse's adversary, within secular thought, was positivist thought, his defeat could only coincide with the victory of positivism (in the broad sense of the word he used), and thus of the kind of positivism that appropriated Marcuse's own arguments, turning them in its own favour.

We have observed that the formula "negation of tradition from within the system" applies to Reich's philosophy. Of course, Marcuse wants to distinguish himself from Reich, and rightly so. Indeed, he attributes the success of Reich's ideas to the fact that advanced industrial society grants the broadest sexual freedom, for the sake of "repressive desublimation,"[57] in order to turn it into a market value and a factor of social consumption. In practice, however, the popularization of the idea of the permissive society has marked a progressive deterioration, so that all that is left of Marcuse is what agreed with Reich. Thus, at the beginning of the Frankfurt School there is the acknowledgment of a practical defeat, that of critical Marxism by dogmatic Marxism. At its end there is another practical defeat, that of the sophisticated form of Marx-Freudism by Reich's elementary version.

16 In the school's first collective work, *Authority and Family*,[58] the part written by Marcuse is interesting not only for its radical statements (which at that time were agreed to by all the collaborators; see the introductory chapter by Horkheimer, which lays the theoretical foundations) but also for the historical-philosophical context that determines them. By itself, the idea of rejecting every form of subordination is a repetition of what had already been said by Marx in the passage I quoted earlier. What is interesting, however, is the humanistic emphasis which reminds us, in some respects, of Bauer's criticism of Marx. Objectivity, in the broadest sense, must not be understood as something to which human will and life have to conform; human activity is not

56 [TN] Based on the context, I suspect that here Del Noce meant to write "Marcusian" rather than "Marxian."

57 [TN] See Marcuse, *One-Dimensional Man*, 74–8.

58 [TN] Horkheimer et al., *Studien über Autorität und Familie* (Frankfurt: Institute for Social Research, 1936).

aimed at understanding the cosmos and, by understanding its order, at understanding the proper meaning of man. On the contrary, meaning is communicated to the world of objects to the extent that man takes them and makes them his own by means of his activity, changing them from things in themselves to "things for him." In this way, the objectivity of the world is not denied gnoseologically but rather axiologically. The world, nature, and in general whatever is not human exist, but their existence has no rational character; it does not express any order of which man is also part. Man's task is to negate this dead objectivity by reducing it to mere "raw material." What is most interesting is the historical excursus on which these statements are based, which confirms perfectly what I said before about the aspect of religious thought which is least resistant to the critique of authority. Marcuse's assertion is thus influenced by a set of interlinked theses that he accepts uncritically: the idea that Christianity, in its world-historical significance, coincides essentially with Protestantism – in this he follows the dominant trend of German thought, starting at least from Hegel's *Lectures on the Philosophy of Religion* – and the idea that the subsequent development of thought is a dialectical suppression of dualisms. It is natural for Marcuse to quote Luther's passage which says that a Christian is, on one hand, free from all things and subjected to nobody and, on the other hand, a slave to all things and subjected to everybody.[59] The question is how to overcome such a dualism of interiority and exteriority in order to affirm full human freedom.

This shows that the internal difficulties of revolutionary thought, as brought to light by the Frankfurt School, require that we call into question and criticize the usual rationalistic interpretation of the history of philosophy.

17 We have seen that the pro-Enlightenment and anti-Enlightenment aspects of Marxism coexist in the thought process of this school, both carried to the extreme. Because of this coexistence, Marcuse's philosophy does not represent at all the "climax of the critical theory of society," as has been frequently but incorrectly stated. On the contrary, Marcuse represents the attempt – which history itself has shown to be a mistake – to interpret as a revolution what is actually, in rigorous terms, a critique of the revolution. In this respect, the pessimism of Theodore Adorno (marked by aesthetic strands and ambiguities) and the religious pessimism of the final phase of the philosophy of the founder of the Frankfurt School, Max Horkheimer, are much more important. So much so that,

59 [TN] From Luther's *The Freedom of a Christian; see Martin Luther: Selections from His Writings*, ed. John Dillenberger (New York: Anchor Books, 1962), 53.

in my opinion, a rigorous study of the school should focus on the process of development of Horkheimer's thought.

Eclipse of Reason[60] by Horkheimer and *Dialectic of Enlightenment* by Horkheimer and Adorno appeared in the same year – 1947. Many of the ideas from the first book are presented, under a different form, in the second.

The first book argues that the emancipation of freedom from its objective and metaphysical foundations, and thus from authority, ends up in domination by "instrumental reason." It leads, in other words, to a world where everything is viewed under the category of "instrument," and thus to the greatest tyranny. The author rediscovers the old thesis that when subjective reason is emancipated from objective authority the necessary consequence is tyranny, which was regarded since antiquity as the effect of a subjective prevarication against the objectivity of law and tradition. However, going back to the old metaphysical systems (Horkheimer had in mind above all neo-Thomism, which was experiencing a successful revival in the US at that time) is impossible. Any attempt to restore metaphysics is based on pragmatic motivations, and so falls back within subjective reason. Hence, we experience the most complete pessimism. The progress of the Enlightenment is unstoppable, but it is accompanied not by liberation but rather by an ever greater suppression of freedom. The truth is that his vision had become broader through the encounter with American civilization. At the time of the polemic against authority his thought was focused on Nazism, in which he was inclined to recognize the incarnation of absolute evil; now, Nazism itself started to look to him like an aspect of a much more complex crisis. This is the thesis he stated in his last work.

However, in order to be consistent with negative thought itself, Horkheimer cannot stop at this type of pessimism. He must move on, toward a critique of the interpretation of negative thought as "revolution" and "utopia," and the necessary endpoint becomes negative theology (see his last writings *The Managed World*[61] and *The Longing for the Totally Other*[62]). When pessimism is thought in negative terms it turns into a religious philosophy, precisely in the form of a negative theology.

60 [TN] Max Horkheimer, *Eclipse of Reason* (New York: Continuum, 2004).

61 [TN] Max Horkheimer, *Verwaltete Welt: Gespraech zwischen Max Horkheimer und Otmar Hersche* [Managed world: A discussion between Max Horkheimer and Otmar Hersche] (Zurich: Verlag der Arche, 1970).

62 [TN] Max Horkheimer, *Die Sehnsucht nach dem ganz Anderen: Ein Interview mit Kommentar von Helmut Gumnior* [The longing for the totally other: An interview with commentary by Helmut Gunmior] (Hamburg: Furche, 1970).

He interprets along these lines also Adorno's major work *Negative Dialectics*[63]: the "Other" cannot be an object of analysis and description; however, the world can be interpreted only in reference to it, because any interpretation, in order to be critical and not justificatory, requires the awareness that the world of phenomena is not the only and ultimate reality.

This negative theology of sorts does not contradict the original assumption that the task of philosophy is to criticize the ideological legitimization of the existing order. What presented itself as hope for a total revolution became realized, and today revolutionary and progressive philosophy has the function of legitimizing a more oppressive and, in fact, totalitarian order, regardless of how it disguises itself. But the revolutionary idea started from the negation of the doctrine of original sin, inasmuch as it claimed that it could substitute politics for religion in the liberation of man. Therefore, it is easy to understand why Horkheimer encounters religion first of all in the doctrine of original sin: "The most grandiose doctrine in both religions, Judaism and Christianity – and here I am recalling a phrase of Schopenhauer – is the doctrine of original sin. It has shaped history until now, and it still shapes it for those who think. This doctrine is possible only under the presupposition that man was created by God endowed with free will."[64]

Hence, we are facing a religious development of Schopenhauer's thought that moves toward Kant and a form of Platonism: the very opposite of Marcuse's Hegelianism. It is also a religious form that stands in sharp contrast to the neo-Modernist trends, Protestant as well as Catholic, even if it is not tied to any orthodoxy.

Unquestionably, Horkheimer's religious affirmation is the final word of the critical philosophy of the Frankfurt School, and is faithful to the program of philosophizing in relation to our time, denouncing the masks of power. This can be proved in several ways. The first is by showing that it is not at all a late, senile stance, but the result of a process that began in *Eclipse of Reason*. Its development can be followed starting from the initial pages of *Dialectic of Enlightenment*: "Men pay for the increase in their power with alienation from that over which they exercise their power. Enlightenment behaves toward things as a dictator toward men."[65] Thus, at that time Horkheimer already regarded power, not

63 [TN] Theodor W. Adorno, *Negative Dialectics*, trans. E.B. Ashton (New York: Continuum, 1966).

64 [TN] Horkheimer, *Die Sehnsucht*, my translation from the Italian edition, *La nostalgia del totalmente altro*, Italian trans. R. Gibellini (Brescia: Queriniana, 2008), 78.

65 [TN] Horkheimer and Adorno, *Dialectic of Enlightenment*, 9.

freedom, as the opposite of authority. Next, if we consider his work *Zur Kritik der instrumentellen Vernunft*[66] which contains *The Eclipse of Reason* as its first part, we find in the second part, comprising a collection of essays written after coming back to Germany, all the elements necessary in order to trace the process that led him to his final statements. But, furthermore, let us recall that the opening act of the Frankfurt School had been the break with Marx-Leninism: hence, the fact that he ended by going back to the line of modern thought that had been most criticized by Lenin agrees with the logic of his formative process.

18 The partial truth discovered by the Frankfurt School and the necessity of their final outcome provide an occasion to shift our attention to René Guénon's analysis of contemporary reality. Guénon is a thinker very far from the Frankfurt School, and he has been ignored by professional philosophers. No matter how anti-academic the Frankfurters try to look, their background as German academics is quite visible; this also explains their success in academic circles, even at a time when universities are in crisis. On the contrary, Guénon's position is completely different, at least with respect to modern academia. Now, the task of the Frankfurt School could or should be viewed *de jure* as a "modern" introduction to this "anti-modern" thinker, something that future history may or may not confirm. If, setting aside some undeniable difficulties about his understanding of the relationship between metaphysics and religion, we focus on three of his books, *La crise du monde moderne* (1927),[67] *Autorité spirituelle et pouvoir temporel* (1930),[68] and above all *Le règne de la quantité et les signes des temps* (1945),[69] we face some disconcerting insights. For instance, in the last book I cited – a collection of essays already published in previous years and written without any concern to address current events – we find described in great detail the spiritual attitudes that would prevail in the following years, and today's situation. Everything non-banal that people wrote later on, regardless of their starting point and intuitions, even those most opposed to his, falls within the horizon that Guénon proposed at that time. Obviously, this is very significant:

66 Max Horkheimer, *Zur Kritik der instrumentellen Vernunft* (Frankfurt: Fischer, 1967) [TN: *Critique of Instrumental Reason*, trans. Matthew O'Connell (New York: Verso, 2013)].

67 [TN] René Guénon, *La crise du monde moderne* (Paris: Gallimard, 1927) [*The Crisis of the Modern World*, trans. Arthur Osborne (Hillsdale, NY: Sophia Perennis, 2004)].

68 [TN] Guénon, *Spiritual Authority*.

69 [TN] René Guénon, *Le règne de la quantité et les signes des temps* (Paris: Gallimard, 1945) [*The Reign of Quantity and the Signs of the Times*, trans. Lord Northbourne (Ghent, NY: Sophia Perennis, 2001)].

a true interpretation of contemporary history is possible only starting from the principles of classical transcendent metaphysics. This removes the usual argument that relegates such metaphysics to the "Middle Ages," inasmuch as it is supposedly incapable of understanding and explaining history.

According to Guénon, the crisis of the modern world is first of all metaphysical. It realizes the following sequence: rationalism – philosophy of the primacy of becoming – transition from the primacy of becoming to the primacy of action – coincidence of philosophy of the primacy of action and materialism – separation of the individual from the absolute and coincidence between the greatest extension of the idea of power and the relativistic conception of the individual – impotence and dissolutive crisis of Occidentalism. The negation of authority is not a stage or a consequence of rationalism; it is rather its *precondition*, as rejection of a super-human order (because the distinction between authority and power is established in relation to the idea of order) and of a cognitive faculty higher that individual reason (that is, of intellectual intuition, tied to the idea of an eternal truth). One could say, in the wake of this analysis, that it is not by chance that in its very last stage rationalism ends up becoming philosophy of praxis, since its original and determinant disposition is practical (based on a rejection without proofs).

Because much of Guénon's work aims at describing the logic of the "plan" that guides the modern world's progressive deviation, it clearly cannot be summarized, and I can only mention some intuitions that are especially stimulating. According to Guénon, the process that started from the rejection of authority leads in its final stages to "solidification" and then to "dissolution." Solidification is the stability associated with materialism, but is not a stage at which one can stop. It leads to a sort of impregnability similar to that of a mollusk, which remains shut inside its shell (hence the feeling of security on the part of the materialist). But when "an opening is made in this shell from below … subtle influences will at once make their way in, and they will do so all the more easily because, thanks to the negative work accomplished in the preceding phase, no element of a superior order will be able to intervene in such a way as to counteract them."[70] By way of this penetration and the unleashing of the subtle lower domain's insidious and destructive forces, the transition to dissolution really takes place: the deviation ends in "subversion," "a state diametrically opposed to the normal order."[71] When this stage has been reached, what is left of the old traditions that the "spirit"

70 Ibid., 170–1

71 [TN] Ibid., 197.

has deserted will be used in an "inverted" sense. The explanation of religious and metaphysical ideas through the subconscious must be viewed as the exact theoretical counterpart of the fissures through which the most evil influences from the subtle realm penetrate.[72]

This brief outline is enough to show the extent to which, in the 1930s, Guénon had already understood, better than anyone else, where history was headed, and without any explicit political reference. On the contrary, he regarded strictly political developments as sensible symbols of much deeper motivations. Indeed, consider: the satisfaction, stability, and safety inside the shell correspond to the materialist stage and to the first result of the materialist revolution; and certainly Marxism is the radical form that materialism can reach, as materialism able to understand history. However, materialism cannot endure, and the totalitarian age, symbolized by the materialistic shell, is followed by what earlier I called the age of secularization. Nobody has defined the meaning taken by the word dissolution as well as Guénon.

According to his thought, mankind has never been so far from "earthly Paradise" as it is now. However, it is precisely this distance that keeps us from giving in to despair, because the end of a cycle coincides with the beginning of a new cycle, so that the darkness of the present contains the possibility of a rebirth.

I said that Guénon's thought was purposely elaborated outside all political experiences. This would make even more interesting a comparison with the conclusions reached by Simone Weil, whose starting point was instead political, and whose philosophical context was initially the opposite of his. The analogies (on the ideas of force, progress, modern science, on Marxism, on psychoanalysis, etc.) are especially disconcerting precisely because there was no direct influence.

19 So far I have said that a reflection about the most important phenomena of contemporary history (world war, revolution, totalitarianism, disintegration) forces us to rethink the concepts of authority and freedom outside the schemes developed by the Enlightenment or by nineteenth-century philosophy, both in the direction of opposition and in that of reconciliation. Today's reality shows us that the eclipse of authority does not coincide at all with the advent of liberation, but rather with that of *power*, and totalitarian systems are the tangible expression of this substitution. Thus, the first consideration of this phenomenon must be from the philosophical, not from the juridical, standpoint. However, the

72 Ibid., 227ff.

habits of the past are so solidified that we still think of totalitarianism as the highest degree of authority. The practical consequence is that in non-totalitarian countries, freedom is interpreted as divesting the state of all ethical dimensions, replacing ethical principles with mere rules of coexistence. People also believe that the "wind of freedom" will push the countries still under authoritarian and totalitarian regimes toward a democratic evolution, which may be slow but is necessary. This position defines "contemporary democraticism." In order to realize how superficial such a view is, just think of what Simone Weil wrote about the "illusion of inward unity"[73] on which consensus in totalitarian systems is based.

I also mentioned the (necessary) bourgeois involution associated with the transition from the revolution to what I have called secularization. Both points are worth elucidating.

20 The widespread notion that the age of totalitarianisms ended with Hitlerism and Stalinism is completely mistaken. In fact, totalitarianisms are founded on the negation of the universality of reason, so that any form of opposition to established power (in the broadest sense), be it cultural or political, supposedly does not express rational concerns but conceals interests of class (according to Communism) or race (according to Nazism), regardless of the awareness of those who criticize. If one reflects about the relationship between authority and evidence, it becomes clear that, ultimately, negating these two notions must necessarily lead to the persecution, ending in elimination, of all dissenters. Weapons may change, and be either physical or psychological, but one should not assume that psychological persecutions are any less terrible.

Now, in the countries that claim to be democratic, even if nobody speaks any longer of race and few speak of social class, opponents are criticized on the grounds that their positions reflect the hidden "conservatism or reactionary spirit that characterize a repressed psychology," above all in the field of culture but more and more also in politics. The totalitarian spirit is already at work in these criticisms, even if the "materialism of the future" is replaced by a "materialism of the present." The materialism of the future still carries some religious tension, in the idea of an absolute good, and so of a mediator (the Leader) between the present and the good to come; such a mediator transforms evil, a necessary dialectical stage, into good. On the contrary, the materialism of the present banishes all absolutes, and thus all forms of verticalism. Such horizontalist totalitarianism is conservative, even if it is obliged to use a

73 [TN] See Simone Weil, *The Need for Roots* (Boston: Beacon Press, 1955), 246.

revolutionary language, not for purposes of political propaganda, but out of intrinsic necessity: indeed, the negation of tradition has reached its highest degree. Due to its conservative character, the manifestations of this totalitarianism differ from those of the past. But there is still a necessary contradiction between what it is and how it presents itself, with an unprecedented degree of persecution of the spirit and destruction of the soul, which definitely is never described adequately by the customary words alienation and reification.

Consider: accepting all the negations against metaphysics formulated by theoretical Marxism, and at the same time criticizing the remaining metaphysical aspects of Marxism, leads to the "totalitarian" view of science as the "only" true knowledge. According to this view, every other kind of metaphysical or religious knowledge expresses only "subjective reactions," which science, extended to the human world through psychological and sociological disciplines, is able or will be able to explain. Such scientific totalitarianism can be called scientism, but in a different sense from the naturalistic scientism of the last century, because it pretends to account for the human world. It is different, we might say, in the way that Marxian materialism is different from naturalistic materialism; therefore, it claims to overcome the criticism of scientism formulated by the most critical wing of Marxism. Now, an advocate of scientism, and a society based on his way of thinking, cannot help being totalitarian inasmuch as his conception of science – as exclusive of every other form of knowledge and, thus, of various aspects of reality that are declared to be either unknowable or non-existing – cannot be the object of any proof. Indeed, a scientistic thinker does not intend to elevate other forms of thought to a higher level (which is the attitude, for instance, of secular liberalism[74] toward religion), but he simply "denies them." Moreover, the metaphysical aspect of Marxism that the new scientism wants to eliminate involves the persistence of archetypes derived from messianism and biblical religion, i.e., the features that made it appear to be, in Berdyaev's words, "a doctrine of deliverance, of the messianic vocation of the proletariat, of the future perfect society in which man will not be dependent on economics."[75] These are the features that, historically, enabled Marxism to take roots in the Russian tradition. On the contrary, scientistic anti-traditionalism can realize itself only by dissolving the

74 [TN] I probably do not need to remind the reader that for a man of Del Noce's generation "secular (or "laic") liberalism" meant something completely different from what these words signify in the United States today: they referred to traditional European liberalism of the nineteenth and early twentieth century, as embodied in Italy by Benedetto Croce.

75 [TN] Nicolas Berdyaev, *The Origin of Russian Communism*, trans. R.M. French (Ann Arbor: University of Michigan Press, 1960), 132.

"fatherlands" where it is realized and becoming a "partisan" tool, by the very nature of science (which provides means but does not determine ends). As all higher values collapse, scientistic anti-traditionalism can be represented only by large-scale economic-bureaucratic organizations. The defining characteristic of totalitarianism is the extinction of the individual, by which I mean the individual inasmuch as he enters into relationship with the absolute, and through this relationship can become critical in the present – because, otherwise, what I have called "materialism of the present" can also be expressed as complete individualism (in the sense of denying any supra-individual ideal unity) and can be reconciled perfectly well with a formal endurance of democratic institutions. What matters is that the individual can subsist only to the extent that he "serves" the hegemonic power group. The essential element of totalitarianism, in brief, lies in the refusal to recognize the difference between "brute reality" and "human reality," so that it becomes possible to describe man, non-metaphorically, as a "raw material" or as a form of "capital." Today this view, which used to be typical of Communist totalitarianism, has been taken up by its Western alternative, the technological society. "Secularization" after the "revolution" destroys the last vertical element (toward the future) of Communism.

Since I cannot adequately discuss this idea that totalitarianism is a *direct* consequence of the negation of authority before being a consequence of the negation of freedom, here I will only quote some of the most acute interpreters of today's crisis of values.

Regarding the fact that scientism must necessarily promote a religious persecution, no matter whether directly or indirectly, the argument by one of the most promising young French philosophers of the 1930s, Benjamin Fondane, who died young in a concentration camp, deserves special attention. In his analysis of Freud's *The Future of an Illusion*[76] he highlighted the axiological aspect that shapes scientism and leads its proponents, even if they are scrupulous scientists, to extrapolate from science and embrace the most mythical and arbitrary constructions: *the hatred a priori against every form of transcendence.*[77] In other words, the *hubris* of science, or scientistic totalitarianism, originates from the fact that modern science knows only "horizontal causality," since it searches for laws as constant relationship between phenomena, i.e., it studies reality as a system of forces, not of values. From the standpoint of

76 [TN] Sigmund Freud, *The Future of an Illusion*, trans. James Strachey (New York: Norton & Co., 1989).

77 [TN] Del Noce is probably referring to Benjamin Fondane, *La conscience malheureuse* (Paris: Denöel et Steele, 1936).

absolute positivism, God cannot exist to the extent that his existence corresponds to a human aspiration. If his existence were indifferent, then he could exist.

If this vision is transferred to the field of ethical-political relationships, a choice will be made, in the name of the greater prosperity made possible by science, which will lead to that "ban of the questions" – even if they are rationally legitimate or even necessary – and to that conscious and deliberate "obstruction of reason" that are the characteristics of totalitarianism according to Eric Voegelin.[78] In every totalitarian system, what starts as persecution of *religion* mutates into persecution of *reason.* But the "lowest point" of totalitarianism – which is looming and is already partially realized in the West – consists in the primacy of the economic principle as legitimization of the obstruction of reason. This has several consequences. When one speaks of alienation or reification, it is hard to deprive these words of all ethical implications and all intimations of humiliation and suffering. Conversely, what is taking place today is an absolute generalization of the category of "instrument," which ultimately abolishes alienation (with respect to what?) and suffering (through widespread prosperity). The only value that scientism allows is vitality, which becomes negation of ethics when it is turned into an absolute. We cannot say, as a certain kind of vacuous argument would claim, that science brings about an organization of social life, while there exists another dimension, interiority, on which science has no jurisdiction. This would hold true if between the scientists and other people there was a "moral" agreement. On the contrary, we do not even have two moralities, determined by different contents. What disappears in a scientistic perspective is the very idea of "morals." We could say that the revolution, which was born to free man from subjection to the economic law, ends up in a system that consolidates its tyranny, bringing about precisely the primacy of the economic dimension.

However, what is pure power, when it is not subordinated to morals? Force. This brings us to the insights of Simone Weil, in a book[79] that was her final will and that is prophetic in all its parts: "For the last two or three centuries, people have believed that force rules supreme over all natural phenomena, and at the same time that men can and should base their mutual relations upon justice, recognized as such through the application of reason … Where force is absolutely sovereign, justice is absolutely unreal. Yet justice cannot be that. We know it experimentally.

78 Eric Voegelin, *The Myth of the New World* (Wilmington, DE: isi Books, 2001).

79 Simone Weil, *L'Enracinement* (Paris: Gallimard, 1949).

It is real enough in the hearts of men."[80] Thus, in her view, the end of the World War placed mankind in front of an absolute choice (in the sense of a *pari*) between scientism (elevating to an idol not really science but, in her exact words, modern science) and Platonism (the idea of justice, which coincides with authority in the sense I have explained). Modern times had tried in vain to avoid this *pari*. So far the choice has been in favour of modern science, viewed as an instrument of practical domination of the world, as if it automatically produced justice (but force, Weil goes on, "is not a machine for automatically creating justice"[81]). After all, it is understandable that the easiest path would be chosen. Modern science seems to spare us the ascetic element that is essential to morality. It is linked to utopia inasmuch as it looks for an automatic mechanism to live in harmony without sacrificing order and happiness. But force – Weil also says – "is a blind mechanism which produces indiscriminately and impartially just or unjust results, but, by all the laws of probability, almost always unjust ones. Lapse of time makes no difference: it doesn't increase in the functioning of this mechanism the infinitesimal proportion of results which happen by chance to be in conformity with justice."[82] Today's huge literature on power only confirms this thesis exactly: it goes back and forth between a form of cynicism that eliminates the idea of morality altogether and sometimes, in the better writers, incurable pessimism.

Horkheimer reaches very similar conclusions. He argues that from the positivist viewpoint it is impossible to develop any morality. Positivism makes impossible any criticism of the rule of force and thus eliminates the scandal in front of "the murderer triumphing over the innocent victim."[83] Hence, morality is founded on theology. Truth be told, a polemical attitude toward positivism was a constant theme of the Frankfurt School. But in its early period, and in the line of development that culminates in Marcuse, this polemic was part of the polemic against traditional philosophy as legitimization of the existing order. Thus, positivism seemed to be the last stage of traditional philosophy.[84] In Horkheimer this link is broken: positivism becomes the only enemy, into which revolutionary thought finally mutates. The question is how to

80 [TN] Weil, *The Need for Roots*, 241, 243.

81 [TN] Ibid., 243.

82 [TN] Ibid.

83 [TN] Horkheimer, *Die Sehnsucht*, my translation from *La nostalgia*, 75.

84 See, for example, the historical reconstruction in Herbert Marcuse, *Reason and Revolution* (New York: Humanities Press, 1968).

isolate and reject, through negative theology, the aspects of traditional thought that led to positivism or were unable to resist it.

Thus, the revolution and the confusion between authority and power (which lies at the origin of the revolution and shapes it) had the result of replacing the relationship of subordination between these two terms with one of opposition. With respect to the definition of authority stated at the beginning, this replacement coincides with the negation of the primacy of the invisible. But the negation of such primacy cannot but coincide with the greatest degree of positivism, i.e., with total surrender to facts as they are, as they impose themselves without referring to anything else, because they find in themselves and not in anything else their legitimization. But if this is the endpoint of the dialectics intrinsic to the negation of the idea of authority, it follows that today the problem of restoring the idea of authority originates in self-criticism of the idea of revolution, starting precisely from the moral instance on which it is founded. Both Weil's and Horkheimer's processes of thought are exemplary illustrations of the truth of this statement.

21 We have established a connection between extreme radicalization of the critique of authority, full expansion of power, scientism, complete secularization and irreligion, primacy of the economic aspect, abolition of values or their reduction to the mere category of vitality and eroticism (in this respect one can point out that today de Sade's views have been confirmed. His heroine, Juliette,[85] denied all idols except science; and de Sade's current popularity is certainly not coincidental: the new Enlightenment meets the old one precisely at its endpoint). On the one hand, the post-revolutionary process is irreversible; on the other hand, it must be said that the sexual revolution can be interpreted as the stage when the revolution falls back into the bourgeois spirit. This confirms a thesis that was already clearly outlined by Sorel. It also becomes clear that the resistance by Russian Communism against this type of liberation should not be regarded as conservative, regardless of what Western commentators say.

Now, is not the situation I briefly outlined precisely the one in which the bourgeois spirit reveals itself in its pure state? In other words, has the Communist revolution not ended up being also, at the world level, a stage in the progress of bourgeois hegemony? Or, actually, has it not been the historical condition that enabled the bourgeois *forma mentis*

85 [TN] Marquis de Sade, *Juliette*, trans. Austryn Wainhouse (New York: Grove Press, 1968).

to affirm its specific characteristics, freeing itself from all compromises with tradition?

Clearly, an adequate answer would require a phenomenology of the bourgeois spirit. This phenomenology, too, should be updated with respect to the traditional versions, in light of the rethinking of contemporary history. Even though, obviously, this cannot be the place to carry out such a task, we can nevertheless sketch a few lines using as a reference the theses of Jacques Ellul.[86]

Ellul focuses on two primary characteristics: the ideological one is the idea of happiness, the ontological one is the capacity to assimilate. The idea of happiness that has become dominant since the eighteenth century is completely different from the traditional idea of "beatitude," which indicates a correct relationship with being (a very important thesis because it demolishes the old thesis about the Puritan origins of the bourgeoisie). Because happiness is separated from such a relationship, it becomes individualized, that is, tied to the sensations, emotions, and desire of the individual. In this respect, the Marxian insistence on the individualistic and atomistic character of the bourgeois is certainly justified – but it highlights a derived character. This is also the origin of a deep-seated anti-Christianity: how can the Christian idea of the presence of "God's image" in other people still make any sense, given the possessive will of the bourgeois? And how can the idea of the initial fall still make any sense, given the "right to happiness" in this life? Clearly, the outlook of "a-religious individualism," which is typical of the bourgeois, generates an insatiable hunger for domination and prestige, which correspond to a primacy of "doing" over being and makes it impossible to think outside the category of instrument, which I already mentioned and which constitutes the form of thought of the *homo faber*.

The capacity to assimilate, i.e., to take, to transform, to make one's own, is a direct consequence of the instrumentalist disposition. Indeed, the bourgeois regards everything as relatively good because everything can be useful. There is no idea and there is no behaviour in which he cannot find some measure of good. But precisely because he thinks of everything as relatively good, there is no Truth, there is no Good; a reality in which everything is "useful" excludes the possibility of absolutes. On the one hand, then, the bourgeois cannot but profess to be democratic; on the other he is radically anti-Platonic. For him the transcendent must be brought down to man's level: religion can be allowed, too, but as a vitalizing experience. Truth must play second fiddle to life.

86 Jacques Ellul, *Métamorphose du bourgeois* (Paris: Calmann-Levy, 1967).

Thus, the evolution of the bourgeois spirit is driven by the revolutions, in the sense that it benefits from them to the extent that they reject some part of the tradition. To a partial revolution, like the French Revolution, corresponds a partial liberation from transcendence, in the sense of autonomous morals, of religion within the limits of reason, etc.; it is a forced compromise with tradition. Conversely, the total revolution and its defeat, or its "sublation," allow a total liberation. Hatred for tradition guides the bourgeois in choosing, in revolutionary thought and practice, between the negations of what he regards as the past condemned by "progress" and the affirmation of a new absolute. He cannot do otherwise, since his guiding idea – the possibility of happiness – forces him to believe in the natural goodness of man and in progress. As is often said, the bourgeois is the man of order and progress. In order for him to achieve complete success, order and progress had to be dissociated from both metaphysics and the revolution. Once every reference to metaphysical transcendence has been eliminated, the existing order is legitimized not in relation to absolute principles (the principles which made it possible to criticize such an order, but which a false form of spiritualism regarded instead as its foundation), but simply because it exists. The idea of revolution – characterized by the qualitative jump – is replaced by the idea of progress which, when it is made absolute (so that the word takes an independent meaning: it does not mean merely progress of science, of morality, and so on, but progress in general, which includes all the various progresses) means a quantitative and economic increase of the available goods. The acceleration of this progress is then identified with a new and superior form of revolution (industrial revolution, technological revolution, etc.)

It is now clear how the process of criticism of authority, which originally was directed against conservatism, against false consciousness, against mystification, etc., ends up reaching the greatest degree of conservatism and linguistic falsification ever known in history. It would be easy to illustrate from this perspective the new features displayed by the contemporary crisis: the collapse of faith in all ideals, to a degree never seen before; the resulting loss of hope; the falsification of love, almost always bestowed on something "far" in order to justify indifference or hostility toward what is near.

Only one aspect must be briefly considered: today's religious Modernism, as a critique of authority in the name of conscience, or in the name of a historical process thought to be providential and irreversible because willed by God, a process which eliminates every "fixism." Actually, all of this merely pays homage to the rationalistic vision of history, precisely when it is showing its difficulties to a macroscopic degree. Moreover, the

Modernist reconciliation is not with the revolutionary spirit, but rather with the bourgeois outcome of the process. We have already discussed Horkheimer's criticism of the new theology and what it means.

These words by Ellul are also worth meditating upon: "Teilhard is the culmination of bourgeois thought, pliable but absorbent. He is in the theoretical domain the same great assimilator that the bourgeois was in the practical one. He delivers complete spiritual and intellectual fulfillment and avoids all choices by reconciling everything."[87] It is true that Teilhard is neither the only nor the subtlest representative of the new religious thought. But his work represents the framework in which such new thought takes place.

22 Let us now return to the topic of the epochal character of the eclipse of the idea of authority, as the moral result of the World War. If we keep thinking of the historical process as a process toward immanence, secularization, demythologization, and so forth – a view which seems to be the current incarnation of the *pigra ratio*, but which, as such, finds strength in established and hard-to-uproot intellectual habits – we will end up reversing its original optimistic version; in fact, it will necessarily appear to us as a road toward nihilism. If we look deeper, if we are willing to interpret the expression "twilight of the idols" in a different or opposite sense from the usual one, we shall see instead that the crisis affects the attempts to provide a foundation to authority, or to reconcile authority and freedom, that were typical of the liberal age (1871–1914). This age was characterized by the persuasion that the end of the temporal power of the popes and the Commune of Paris had symbolically marked the end both of Catholicism and of revolutionary thought, where the former was viewed as an expression of authority without freedom, and the latter of freedom without authority.

That period embraced authority, in a way, but usually disconnected from a metaphysics of transcendence. Its foundation, as a general framework, was a critique of revolutionary thought, which extended to a critique of democracy and made it possible to establish various connections with the political positions of the Restoration. For example, there was continuity with that age's liberalism, because of the critique of Jacobinism and radicalism, and also with that age's traditionalism, because of that same aversion. The relationship between tradition and religion, however, was turned upside down, in the sense that it was not the latter that provided the foundation of the former, but rather it was the preservation

87 Ellul, *Métamorphose du bourgeois* [TN: My translation from the Italian edition, *Metamorfosi del borghese*, Italian trans. E. Ripepe (Milan: Giuffrè, 1972), 131].

of the former that implied that of the latter. This is the typical position of nationalism, which harbours an intrinsic contradiction.

From the more specifically philosophical viewpoint, there was a quest to preserve the aspect of the authority of the moral law, separated from its metaphysical-religious foundation by means of autonomous morality, whose model appeared to be Kantian ethics. In a rather unstable position, though, because it oscillated between a reduction of morality to sociology and the reaffirmation, in order to avoid such an outcome, of the metaphysical-religious foundation. Finally, there was the Idealist-subjectivist type of attempt.

Regarding the critique of the Jacobin mindset, Taine's work *Les origins de la France contemporaine* is decisively important.[88] Recent studies have documented its influence on Mosca and Pareto (whereas the work of the former seems undeniably outdated, the same cannot be said of the latter). Since Bayle was Pareto's favourite author, and the one to whom he would most have liked to be compared, we can observe a symmetry between Bayle's *Dictionnaire*[89] and the *Trattato di sociologia generale*.[90] However, this analogy must not be understood simply in the sense that both were keen on "tearing away the masks" in the spirit of the Enlightenment, which ends up depicting Pareto, as some people did, as an "atheist with respect to all religions." Actually, regardless of what may have been his awareness of the ultimate meaning of his work, we must distinguish between what he really thought and what he received passively from the cultural milieu regarding the assessment of theological-metaphysical thought. His importance lies only in his unsurpassable critique of the progressive mindset, and we have to wonder if this critique should not be extended in the sense of freeing it from all residual influences from Positivism and from the Enlightenment.

Comte, even more than Taine, is the reference point of Maurras, whose work was the most explicit and acute defence of authority during the initial decades of our century. His ideas deserve a detailed analysis, both because they greatly influenced the most original French political thinkers (including the writers who most criticized him later on) and, above all, in order to show the deviation due to the influence of Positivism. This deviation caused the relationship

88 [TN] Hyppolite Taine, *The Origins of Contemporary France*, trans. John Durand (New York: Holt, 1876–1894).

89 [TN] Pierre Bayle, *An Historical and Critical Dictionary* (London: Hunt and Clarke, 1826).

90 [TN] Vilfredo Pareto, *A Treatise on General Sociology*, trans. Andrew Bongiorno and Arthur Livingston (New York: Dover Publications, 1963).

between authority and tradition to take the form of "nationalism," which I have already discussed.

Unlike the authors I just mentioned, Croce started from a critique of Marxism. I talked about the importance of his criticism of activist libertarianism, which replaces the religiosity of freedom – like the devil acting as *simia Dei* – whenever freedom is separated from sacred respect for tradition. However, the lived sense of this unity is not given an adequate philosophical foundation. Indeed, in his theoretical speculation we have the highest degree of criticism of revolutionary thought that can be formulated *from within* a reformation of Hegelianism. But can this position be sustained? That it cannot is shown both by Gramsci's journey from Croce to Marx and, above all, by the fact that Gentile's Actualist philosophy is much more consistent as a reform of Hegelianism. Gentile's philosophy is extremely important because it is the most consistent attempt to preserve and, at the same time, to purify, through immanentism, the ideas of authority, tradition, and religion. Therefore, its defeat is the decisive proof of the impossibility of reconciling the idea of authority with philosophical immanentism, even in the form of philosophy of immanent divinity.

Since Gentile's investigation is carried out in strictly philosophical terms, we recall that politics faces the same problem as metaphysics, namely how to realize the opposite poles of the one and the many, without confusing them and without suppressing them. But for Gentile this connection assumes a particular significance because it means surpassing speculative philosophy or, as he often says, intellectualism, into philosophy of praxis (i.e., he poses the same philosophical problem as Marxism, but he intends to solve it through absolute Idealism). The reductionist tendency that characterizes metaphysical rationalism is pushed to the extreme (multiplicity is reduced to the absolute and exclusive unity of the act), while at the same time the critique of intellectualism leads to the affirmation that philosophy is an essentially political endeavour.

Resuming the line of thought of the *Risorgimento*, above all in its Giobertian form, secularized along Hegelian lines by Bertrando Spaventa,[91] Gentile intends to reconcile the terms authority and freedom. These two must be linked, because freedom without authority ends

91 [TN] Bertrando Spaventa (1817–83) was a professor of philosophy at the University of Naples and one of the earliest and most influential advocates of Hegelian philosophy in Italy.

in anarchy, and authority without freedom in despotism.[92] Subsequent reconciliations (people and government, general will and individual will, law and personal autonomy, conservation and progress) must refer back to this first reconciliation. Idealism enables us to use the idea of reform (hence, of a new form assumed by the tradition) to replace both the idea of conservation and that of revolution, which according to Gentile are both naturalistic: conservatism representing the materialism of the status quo, and revolutionary thought the materialism of utopia. The spirit is conceived as perpetual self-making, and thus as continuous opposition of what ought-to-be vs what is; authority (the ought-to-be) is thus brought inside the spirit itself. In other words, Gentile wishes to continue the Hegelian claim of going beyond Spinozism by thinking totality no longer as a substance, but as a subject, thus realizing the "Christian philosophy." What really happens is that his thought combines the difficulties both of metaphysical rationalism and of the philosophy of praxis, even though it formulates decisive arguments against both. The interiorization of authority leads to the idea that the state is found *in interiore homine* rather than *inter homines*. Except that the transition to authority coincides for Gentile with the affirmation of the unique transcendental I, and we cannot speak of any form of transcendence such that this subject would be some sort of "normal subject" to which finite individualities would have to conform. In this way, the Spinozian theme that only God exists is carried to its extreme logical consequences, but when it reaches these consequences it assumes a peculiar aspect because of an inextricable confusion – which is objectively so – between God and the human subject. According to a formula that Gentile uses often, the will is "free as it makes itself free; it is subjected to the law that it unceasingly keeps creating."[93] This means that his philosophy ends up making God, the free creator of the truths, immanent. This God/Human-Subject, though, cannot acknowledge other souls beside himself; therefore, the consciousness of the individual is transformed into God, but into a "thingifying" God, so that all other souls are reduced to bodies (to objects, instruments). Others *qua* others are nature, matter, instruments of creation. But, conversely, every subject is nature, matter, instrument of creation, etc. for the other. Or again: if the purpose of Gentile's thought is to realize a universal will that may surpass and unify

92 See his political essay on Gioberti of 1919, later included in Giovanni Gentile, *I profeti del Risorgimento italiano* [The prophets of the Italian *Risorgimento*] (Florence: Vallecchi, 1923).

93 [TN] Giovanni Gentile, *Sommario di pedagogia come scienza filosofica* [Compendium of pedagogy as a philosophical science] (Bari: Laterza, 1922), 44.

the will of the individuals, the outcome is, instead, the greatest exaltation and at the same time the greatest humiliation of the individual. No matter how often it is said that we want to understand authority as a superior will that can discipline the associated wills, bringing them together in a common law, in reality what is missing is precisely such a unitary principle. In summary, Gentile's philosophy is the proof that within immanentistic thought authority cannot really be distinguished from force, and is suffered by each individual as force. This topic would be fully elucidated if one studied the point-by-point coincidence between the contradictions of Gentile's philosophy and those of Fascism.

The critique of democracy during the initial decades of our century developed in close relation with what was called the "Idealistic reaction against science."[94] Gentile's philosophy represents the final point of this "reaction" (the term is inappropriate) and also its most intentionally religious version, because it intends to achieve the transition from the transcendent God, which is regarded as a myth, to the immanent God. This is peculiar and confirms again, going back to my previous thesis about the weakest spot of religious thought, that the immanent God reproduces the features of the God of theological arbitrarism, taken to the extreme.

Remaining in Italy, I should mention two books published after the First World War which challenged the dominant culture, that is, Croce's and, above all, Gentile's forms of Idealism. The first book was *Filosofia dell'autorità* by Giuseppe Rensi.[95] From the theoretical standpoint, it can be viewed as a naturalistic-skeptic inversion of Actualism. If one looks at the results of Gentile's philosophy from the viewpoint of nature and of multiplicity, instead of the unity of the act, they lead to a kind of Protagorean skeptical conservatism. Rensi's book is interesting because it is possibly the last in which the idea of authority is tied to philosophical skepticism, producing a form of conservatism that is no longer connected with the idea of tradition and the religious-metaphysical foundation. Even though Mosca and Pareto are not cited, Rensi's work can be considered the philosophical endpoimt of the positivist side of their works. Today, this book gives an impression of inner consistency but at the same time of being outdated and old. Skepticism presupposes the idea of an absolute, although unattainable, truth – which is demonstrated by

94 [TN] Del Noce is referring to the book by Antonio Aliotta *La reazione idealistica contro la scienza* (Palermo: Optima, 1912), translated into English as *The Idealistic Reaction against Science*, trans. Agnes McCaskill (London: Macmillan, 1914).

95 Giuseppe Rensi, *Filosofia dell'autorità* [Philosophy of authority] (Palermo: Sandron, 1920).

Rensi's whole philosophical experience, which was tormented and restless. The new positivism wants to base itself precisely on the negation of this idea, and as a result it abolishes skepticism in favour of "relationism."

The other book is *Riflessioni sull'autorità e la sua crisi* by Giuseppe Capograssi.[96] It did not have a large impact in its time and is still not well known, whereas it deserves the greatest attention, since it is one of the best works ever written on this subject. In those uncertain years, Capograssi already grasped perfectly what was being lost in the collapse of the idea of authority, and displayed an exceptional awareness both of modern thought, which has to be criticized in order to restore that idea, and of the tradition, which has to be rediscovered for this task: Rosmini, Vico, St Thomas. At that time these thinkers were considered different from or even opposed to each other. Capograssi was the first who was able to see the continuity among them in a truly rigorous fashion, rediscovering it through the analysis of the idea of authority and its metaphysical implications. There is no need to say how much what I am proposing agrees with these assertions. Lack of space prevents me from discussing many other thinkers from that period and from the next who are worthy of attention. However, another brief comment on Max Weber is indispensable, since his example illuminates well the transition from the liberal age to the next phase. The fact that the social sciences do not formulate judgments of value did not mean for Weber anything comparable to some of today's positivist positions. On the contrary, it expressed the need not to confuse, not to contaminate what ought to be with what is. Therefore, in 1905 he wrote that "The reason why I denounce with such extraordinary fervour ... the confusion between 'ought' and 'is,' is not because I undervalue the problem of the 'ought,' but just the opposite: because I cannot bear problems of world-shaking importance, of immense ideal proportions, in a sense the highest problems that can move a human being – I cannot bear these problems being turned into a technical 'question of productivity,' and discussed here as if they were within the province of a specialized discipline like economics."[97] After the war, this distinction between judgments of value and judgments of fact was regarded (see Lukács and the beginning of the Frankfurt School)

96 Giuseppe Capograssi, *Riflessioni sull'autorità e la sua crisi* [Reflections on authority and its crisis] (Lanciano: Carabba, 1921), republished in *Works*, vol. 1 (Milan: Giuffrè, 1959).

97 [TN] Max Weber, *Gesammelte Aufsätze zur Soziologie und Sozialpolitik* [Collected essays in sociology and social politics] (Tubingen: Mohr, 1924), 419. This passage is quoted by Herbert Marcuse in "Industrialization and Capitalism," *New Left Review* 1, no. 30 (1965): 3. I used the English translation of Weber's sentence on page 4 in Marcuse's article.

as the foundation of an indirect consensus with the existing order. Judgments of value truly perform such a function if they are separated both from metaphysics and from science. The point of agreement between revolutionary thought and metaphysical thought is the rejection of autonomous morality, which is founded on the distinction between the two types of judgments. In passing, observe that this explains the significance of the Frankfurt School, provided that we recognize Horkheimer as its most representative figure. We find in it all the essential steps: critique, through Weber, of the period 1870 to 1914; revolutionary thought; critique of revolutionary thought; re-proposal of metaphysical-theological thought.

23 Thus, we have come to recognize that the theme of authority, traced back to the one of evidence, is the form taken today not just by a particular philosophical problem [but by the philosophical problem] as a whole, after philosophy tried, with Marxism (which is, in this writer's opinion, the endpoint of rationalism), to become the world or – to use the problematic language that is the only possible one in this context – after the crisis of revolutionary thought and praxis. Therefore, the form in which the problem of authority has manifested itself in our century coincides with the question of understanding contemporary history. This has imposed some constraints on the method of this study. First and foremost, it has forced us to focus primarily on the characteristics of its disappearance and on how to interpret them. This is why the choice of the authors to be discussed was determined, even more than by the rigour of their research, by how much they represented various stages of a process and how much their positions provide examples that illuminate this history. For instance, if anybody asked why Maritain was omitted, we should answer that this whole entry has centred on the meaning of Thomism and on the present significance of its distinctive features, as a rejection of both theological rationalism and arbitrarism. I have taken as already known that Maritain has been, among today's Thomists, one who has most reflected on and written about the topic of authority, motivated both by the desire to understand this fundamental theme of Thomism and by his sensitivity to recent historical events. However, I chose not to talk about him explicitly because in a few lines it was impossible to distinguish between the many positive elements of his thought and some inadequate aspects, and above all to identify the reasons for the latter.

A few words of conclusion must emphasize what *is no longer in question* about the interpretation of the age of totalitarianisms: that the problem of authority has to be discussed in a radically different way with respect to the approach that has been common throughout the centuries of the modern age, especially since the Enlightenment. In fact, the habit of setting in opposition primacy of freedom (West, progress, modernity, dynamic and innovative spirit, etc.) and primacy of authority (East, Middle Ages, despotism, past, immobility, etc.) dates back to that time. This habit still survives, and in the most dangerous form because it keeps shaping the standard ethico-political and historical judgments, even if their first premises are seldom recalled and made the object of a rigorous critical examination. Because of this, the idea of authority has been tied to the image of an exterior force capable of coercion, using the idea of despotism as mediator. Hence the affirmation of the primacy of freedom as the great modern conquest. Then, there were attempts to justify the role of authority, lest freedom degenerate into *arbitrium.* We find images that stipulate conditions of this kind at the origins of religious Modernism (for example, in Laberthonnière, a typical thinker who starts from images and emotional reactions[98]). Gentile was undoubtedly the one who formulated this position most rigorously.

The age of the revolution gave up on searching for unity, and accepted a sharp opposition. The *ideal* endpoint is identified with liberation from authority, from the reign of force and necessity. However, what has happened so far suggests, rather, that the rejection of authority, understood in its metaphysical-religious foundation, leads instead to the fullness of "power." In other words, the opposition authority vs freedom and the problem of their synthesis (whether it is possible or not) must be replaced by the opposition authority vs power, where the former has a liberating character and the latter an oppressive one. In fact, it is hard to deny, at least on the basis of our current experience, that the *real* endpoint (regardless of the intentions) of the process of revolutionary liberation leads to the complete dependence of man on society. It does not matter much that this dependence is concealed behind words like communitarian spirit, altruism, and so on. The reality is, on the contrary, that we are approaching a time when it will be normal to think that man is entitled to exist inasmuch as he is socially useful, i.e., inasmuch as *others* judge him to be so. One gets the impression that today's proclaimed altruism is merely the perversion of the idea of solidarity. A famous passage from Kierkegaard's *Journals* comes to mind, as a transition to religious metaphysics after the self-refutation of rationalism: "Only a wretched and mundane conception of the dialectic of power holds that it increases in proportion to its ability to compel and to make dependent. No, Socrates knew better; the art of power lies precisely in making

98 [TN] Lucien Laberthonnière (1860–1932), French philosopher and religious thinker.

free ... it needs to be emphasized again and again that it is the highest: it is something only omnipotence truly succeeds in";[99] "one human being cannot make another wholly free, because the one with the power is himself captive in his possession of it and is therefore continually coming into a false relationship with the one he wants to make free."[100] This text is interesting because of the relationship it brings up between the exigencies that move Greek anti-sophistic metaphysics since its origins and its fulfillment in theological thought.

All of this may end up turning upside down the very idea of "criticism." Until yesterday criticism meant a process of liberation from the last dogmatic remnants of classical metaphysics (whose advocates, anyway, experienced such a sense of inferiority that they tried to tamper with its theses, mixing them with the results from the latest "critical" positions, with easily predictable results). Today, on the contrary, the "political occasion" may (we keep thinking in terms of possibility, in the sense described before) lead to the inversion of this meaning, and to the quest to define precisely the inadequate expression of classical metaphysics, as infidelity to its own beginning, that can explain the rise of the mistaken view that has manifested itself in the present crisis.

99 [TN] Søren Kierkegaard, *Papers and Journals: A Selection*, trans. Alastair Hannay (London: Penguin, 1996), 235.

100 [TN] Ibid., 234.

12

A "New" Perspective on Right and Left

ONE OF TODAY'S MANY CLICHÉS says that dialogue between so-called right-wing and left-wing Catholics is absolutely impossible. Supposedly, the opposition is as radical as that between "static and closed" religion and "dynamic and open" religion. These are old words, certainly, whose success dates back to 1932, to the too-famous book by Bergson *The Two Sources of Morality and Religion*,[1] which arguably marked the rebirth of religious Modernism. But today's left is not especially fond of originality or novelty of language, for the simple reason that repetitions are not in the least boring; they are actually welcome, to the extent that one likes what they say. Now, non-believers are extremely pleased to hear about this impossibility to dialogue because, supposedly, it proves that Catholicism is finished. Today's new believers are just as pleased; they think that the word of God can be interpreted only in radically new ways, since the *recentiora tempora* swept away almost all the ancient theological questions.

FEAR OF HISTORICAL TRANSCENDENCE

Indeed, dialogue implies the recognition that the argument of the other side may contain an aspect of truth. But, according to a fashionable cliché, the Catholics who for a long time have been called "integralists" regard religion as a component of what they call a "Christian" civilization. Therefore, in their view the old civilization and the old forms

This chapter was first published as "Un discorso 'nuovo' su destra e sinistra," *L'Europa* 4, no. 10 (1970): 24–8. Republished in *Rivoluzione Risorgimento Tradizione* (Milan: Giuffrè, 1993), 171–86.

1 [TN] Henri Bergson, *The Two Sources of Morality and Religion*, trans. R. Ashley Audra and Cloudesley Brereton (London: Macmillan, 1935).

of religious life are inseparably connected. Thus, any attempt to distinguish between a theological/philosophical/moral right and a political/social right is in vain. Builders of "dams" and "bastions" are condemned by history because they must steadfastly curse a changing world and perform the impossible task of keeping it in the exact same state in which they found it. Supposedly, the primary motivation for their attitude is political, even though often it is not shaped by specific economic interests: it is fear of historical transcendence – another cliché.

But, is this really a "proven" truth? At a time when experimentalism is so fashionable, diffidence about abstract definitions should be a plausible attitude. This is why it is an important event that a Catholic writer who is considered to be on the right, Thomas Molnar, and Mounier's successor as editor of *Esprit*, Jean-Marie Domenach, have agreed to engage in dialogue.[2] All the more so because their dialogue starts precisely where it is not supposed to, according to the definition I mentioned: from politics and from the question of the definition of the idea of the left.

The record of this discussion is important not only because of the results it already implicitly achieved – as we shall see – but also because it can be a starting point. Observe that neither one of the participants sidestepped their most serious disagreements out of a misguided sense of politeness. If anything, they could be criticized for the opposite reason: arguably they did not criticize enough the clichés that from the start put Catholics on the two sides in a irritated disposition, which is the psychological obstacle to dialogue. In fact, these clichés remain, as Molnar points out in his reply.[3] Now, in my reflections, I would like to show that in this discussion we can also find what is needed to criticize these clichés. This will allow us to gauge, on the one hand, the "difficulty" of the dialogue, which is real but of a psychological nature, and on the other, its "necessity," which is metaphysical.

Describing these obstacles is all too easy. In the thirties, when European intellectual youth was starting to rediscover leftist ideas, one could often hear the following statement: "Interests are on the right (mystified as values), ideals on the left" (this brief sentence contained in advance the whole way of thinking that has become prevalent over the last twenty-five years, did it not?). Supposedly, a true man of the right is characterized by

2 [TN] Their exchange was originally published in *Esprit* in the July–August 1969 issue [Thomas Molnar and Jean-Marie Domenach, "L'impasse de la gauche," *Esprit* 7–8 (1969): 44–67]. The Italian translation was published the following year, together with the present essay by Del Noce, in the volume *Il vicolo cieco della sinistra* [The dead end of the Left] (Milan: Rusconi, 1970).

3 [TN] Molnar and Domenach, "L'impasse de la gauche," 66–7.

a cynical attitude: if he wins, it is because he exploits the naïveté of generous *hidalgos*, deluded fighters – no matter how sincere their faith may be – against what they think is Marxist atheism and materialism, in the name – so they believe – of man's freedom and dignity. Therefore, there is a glaring contradiction between what a man of the right says and what he does. His discourse is "moral": he constantly appeals to an eternal order of values, and he could not do otherwise. On the contrary, his actions are driven exclusively by economic factors, in the broadest sense. The proclamation of eternal values becomes a tool to defend the existing order, and actually the strongest interests within this order. But let us stop here, since today all the blather about "false consciousness" and the demystification of ideologies can be found even in the mass media.

Conversely, the defining characteristic of a man of the left was said to be generosity, unwillingness to come to terms with mystification and evil. He was a man of hope, even if sometimes hope could make him too optimistic about when and how ideals would be realized. Can we deny that even in this recent intervention Domenach paid homage to these worn out stereotypes? In this regard, one only needs to read the final words of Molnar's reply.[4]

A RADICAL DETACHMENT FROM REALITY

Molnar also, however, sometimes insists on aspects that, strictly speaking, should make dialogue impossible. In his view, the left is characterized by the utopian mindset, which expresses philosophically a radical detachment from reality. But, at the same time, it is dominated, contradictorily, by a frenetic lust for power. It is easy to understand by what dialectical process utopianism is destined to become a cover and a justification for the most unscrupulous and realistic political action if it is brought to bear on real life. The complete absorption of morality into politics – which leads to persecutions, terror, and, ultimately, the selfishness of a new ruling class, which is the endpoint of all revolutions – could never be achieved without the utopian component, which promises that humanity will reach peace, happiness, and security after such turmoil. In this sense, the often-repeated statement that only the Leninist revolution could

4 [TN] "What irritates me, however, in Domenach's proposal … is the arrogance of sticking the labels 'socialism' and 'left' on every human self-surpassing, on generosity, on justice … In front of such a bundle of all virtues, the man of the right is truly reduced to being just a member of a gang of consumers and power fanatics … What is then the usefulness of discussing with him?" (Ibid., 67 [my translation]).

reach the highest degree of Machiavellianism – by relying on the alternative "either Communism or complete barbarism" – is true.

Let us now make a theoretical consideration. If we insist one-sidedly on either one of these critiques, "dialogue becomes indeed impossible." We have to say that the moral scandal of the man of the left is perfectly justified, and the moral scandal of the man of the right is equally justified. It would be useless to try to water them down and to seek some middle ground. They are, instead, partial truths that must be surpassed into a higher synthesis. We should apply to them the old thesis that "choice" is the essence of heresy. And this observation would be quite appropriate, because both of these Catholic positions are at risk of ending in heresy if they are made fully consistent, to the point that all their implications become explicit. No historical period has verified Proudhon's famous line "at the bottom of politics there is always theology"[5] as well as ours.

TODAY'S POWER WORD IS "DEMYTHOLOGIZATION"

Hence, both the left and the right need a parallel process of self-criticism. Where will it lead? Perhaps, to a unified Catholic view of contemporary history; here, I wish to present a first sketch of this thesis.

Domenach is fully convinced that such self-criticism is necessary. One cannot but be surprised by the beginning of his contribution: "Who can miss the fact that in Europe the left has failed?"[6] Apparently, at the level of values, everything seems to say the opposite. If by "right" we mean faithfulness to the spirit of tradition, meaning the tradition that talks about an uncreated order of values, which are grasped though intellectual intuition and are independent of any arbitrary will, not even the divine one;[7] and if by "left" we mean, on the contrary, the rejection not merely of certain historical superstructures but of those very values,

5 [TN] Pierre-Joseph Proudhon, *Les Confessions d'un Révolutionnaire* (Paris: Bureau du journal La Voix du Peuple, 1849), 61.

6 [TN] Molnar and Domenach, "L'impasse de la gauche," 53.

7 Each one of these words must be emphasized, lest we simply confuse tradition with "what has been" or "what is disappearing." In fact, the crisis of the idea of tradition and the beginning of the secular spirit coincided precisely with the negation of the uncreated order of values, which characterizes theological arbitrarism. On the other hand, it is extremely difficult to understand exactly the relationship between the divine mind and the order of values, and I think that such a correct understanding is what makes Thomism exceptional. Therefore, I also think that the teachers of the 1930s, Gilson and Maritain, must still be regarded as the guides in order to rethink today the metaphysical conditions for the political action of Catholics.

which are "unmasked" to show their true nature as oppressive ideologies, imposed by the dominant classes in order to protect themselves, well, then it seems that in no other historical period has the left advanced so dramatically as during the last quarter of a century. The power word of contemporary intellectuals is "demythologization": in their view, social progress will go hand in hand with the progress of demythologization and will be shaped by it, in terms of both ideas and morals. This is the faith of progressive intellectuals, and in this respect secular and Catholic intellectuals are indistinguishable.

And yet, one has to say that Domenach is right: if by "right" we mean "management technique at the service of the strongest,"[8] regardless of what ideologies are used to justify this management, we have to say that its victory has never been so complete, because it has been able to completely turn the culture of the left into its own tool. Even Marxist culture: in this regard, it is somewhat striking to hear the editor of *Esprit* declare that it is now unquestionable that "Communists have become accomplices and victims of an empire that destroys spiritual freedom and puts nations in chains."[9] A new oppressive power has established itself using leftist culture as its foundation, and it is much more powerful and dangerous because it is able to manage effectively the "common well-being," which is something completely different from the "common good."

Everything would be quite simple if this were a betrayal, if we could, for instance, blame Stalin as usual, say that "the revolution was betrayed," and so on. But the crisis of the left goes deeper: if the left can be defined most rigorously as an alliance between "a rebellion and a science," in Domenach's words,[10] what must be called into question is precisely the culture that claims to interpret it. The left is important for a "metaphysical reason"; therefore, reflecting about its crisis leads to the "question of being."[11] Having formulated the problem in these terms, what is Domenach's diagnosis?

> The characteristic disease of the left is its passion for the limitless … this obsession about an alienation whose boundaries are poorly defined, which makes individuals and nations crazy and pushes them to search hysterically for some "Being" that has escaped them, that has been lost, about which we have only elusive, even if exciting, clues … Freedom, identified with a vague notion of nature, unfolds in a vacuum, and toward what ends? Rest, happiness, friendship.

8 [TN] Molnar and Domenach, "L'impasse de la gauche," 64.
9 [TN] Ibid., 53
10 [TN] Ibid., 56.
11 [TN] Ibid., 57ff.

These are the first fruits of Being, but they are utopic and ineffectual because they are not ordered to any hierarchy of values. In truth, Being is not a hidden treasure that will free itself ... by exploding the crust of a repressive society. Being is an ascending totality within which human relationships are articulated: among humans, with nature and with the supernatural. If Being is not affirmed as an order of values, it is pushed into the realm of dreams; being formless, it is confused with the impossible delights of a lost world or an imaginary world.[12]

THE TRANSITION TO SUPER-HUMANITY

I will now try to build on Domenach's analysis using my own arguments, which, however, agree completely with what he wrote, as far as I can tell. In the extreme left, the alliance between power and the intellectuals has been expressed through the idea of the total revolution. For a true revolutionary, the revolution is no longer a mere transformation of juridical institutions, which will create the conditions in which everyone will be able to realize himself as a person, so that no individual will any longer perceive his life as a tool used by others to support a given social order, but will be able instead to perceive himself also as an end of the whole social order. Instead, revolution means that mankind will recover the powers from which it supposedly alienated itself, by projecting them outside of itself, when it created the Godhead. Thus, it is a transition to a super-humanity, to a surreality. Consistently, history until today must be regarded as "prehistory," as Marx said.[13] The idea of super-humanity is not found only in Nietzsche. It belongs to the whole branch of atheism that is usually called "positive" in order to distinguish it from pessimistic atheism (today this latter is out of fashion. Historically, it followed a trajectory that necessarily led it to the threshold of Christianity. Some people regarded Leopardi as a secular version of Pascal, but the history of modern pessimism developed according to a process that from Leopardi went back to Pascal[14]). Moreover, positive atheism is always inseparable from the idea of total revolution. Supposedly, there is a qualitative jump in the process of evolution which will lead from man to superman, and today this is about to take place. Are the press and the popular literature

12 [TN] Ibid., 58–9.

13 [TN] In the 1859 preface to *A Contribution to the Critique of Political Economy.*

14 [TN] On this topic, see Augusto Del Noce, "Giuseppe Rensi tra Leopardi e Pascal ovvero l'autocritica dell'ateismo negativo in Giuseppe Rensi" [Giuseppe Rensi between Leopardi and Pascal, or the self-criticism of negative atheism in Giuseppe Rensi], in *Filosofi dell'esistenza e della libertá* (Milan: Giuffrè, 1992), 469–540.

not full of such notions, in many different flavours, either pseudo-theological or pseudo-scientific, which claim that after thousands of years of history man is about to take a new form?

The usual pseudo-realists will object that this is an intellectual interpretation of the revolution, which has little to do with real political problems. Be careful! Within the left, politics and culture cannot be separated, and today the idea, shared by Marx and Freud, that transcendent reality is a projection of our unsatisfied and unconscious needs is very widespread among intellectuals. In its derivations, this idea has saturated today's common opinions, as can be verified simply by observing the huge change in ideas and morals that has taken place over the last twenty years.

If we now define the left in terms of subordination to this culture, it becomes possible (1) to understand the nature of its crisis and (2) to see why Domenach and Molnar are bound to meet each other if they develop their ideas consistently.

Domenach speaks of "passion for the limitless." This brings to my mind the sentence used by Engels in order to define the teaching of dialectical thought: "Everything that exists deserves to die."[15] It is certainly not one of his best-known statements, and yet no other seems to me as effective in expressing the essence of revolutionary thought as a "negative philosophy." Indeed, according to this phrase not even Communist society, i.e., the full reconciliation between man and nature and between human existence and human essence, can be regarded as the end to which the historical process is ordered. One must say so ideologically, in order to motivate the masses. For that purpose, one has to depict for them a final stage of mankind, marked by the end of all conflicts. One must use utopia.

But, rigorously speaking, revolutionary thought is not utopian thought, nor its development.[16] We can describe its deep essence, as Molnar does following Maritain, as hatred for reality in the name of what "is not,"

15 [TN] *Ludwig Feuerbach and the Outcome of Classical German Philosophy* (New York: International Publishers, 1941), 11. In fact, Engels himself is quoting the words of Mephistopheles in Goethe's Faust: "Alles was entsteht, ist wert, dass es zugrunde geht."

16 The rejection of what is for the sake of what "will be" has different characteristics in utopia and in revolutionary thought. According to utopian thought, what will be is a future that "must" become present, because "it is right" for it to be. According to revolutionary thought we must speak of an eternal "will be," which is the criterion to deny the value of the present. In other words, utopia has a "moral" measure. Revolutionary thought has a "metaphysical" nature, and it was born as such, even if in its epilogue it protests against "metaphysical alienation."

which will be designated through symbolic expressions that can change depending on historical circumstances and can be evaluated in terms of their practical efficacy.[17] In short, revolutionary atheism represents a sort of horizontal transcription of negative theology. Being remains beyond what we can say about it; however, it is not God, but rather the limitless and the formless. This definition, though, applies to pure revolutionary thought, not to the left in the generic sense of the word.

But, what does negative thought deny? It denies every order of values, reducing it to ideology. It denies any continuity with the past because, once the idea of handing down values is eliminated, the past takes the appearance of the dead trying to suffocate and kill the living.

At that point, having been pushed to the extreme, negativity itself dissolves. It flips upside down and turns into acceptance of empirical reality as it immediately appears, wrongfully elevating it to an ideal. It turns into acceptance of a reality that presents itself as raw power. Thus, the task of the politician changes, by a dialectic metamorphosis, into that management technique at the service of the strongest that I mentioned earlier. Today's technocratic right is precisely the outcome of this crisis of the left. The separation between the ruling class and the masses becomes extreme because the members of the former know that every argument in terms of values is merely ideology as an instrument of power (even if it is not openly declared as such).

UTOPIA AND POSITIVE THOUGHT

Still, the two authors did not fully understand each other, to say the least. Just think of Molnar's reply, especially the final lines. It is important to understand why this happened.

In my opinion, Molnar's fault is that he defines the left in terms of its utopian goal, which, however, must not be confused with revolutionary thought, for the reasons I stated. A utopianist hopes in a final state of mankind, and therefore utopia is still an instance of positive thought. On the contrary, the principle of revolutionary thought is the acceptance that things constantly die, as a constant negation of their finiteness (and on this point we must say that Marcuse was correct, in his old book on *Reason and Revolution*[18]). It is true that these two positions mix together, but it seems to me that today the idea of negation is prevalent. Generally speaking, every thesis is accepted because of what it denies (of what it destroys, of what it rejects). The "what we want" part is left

17 [TN] Molnar and Domenach, "L'impasse de la gauche," 46.

18 [TN] Herbert Marcuse, *Reason and Revolution* (Boston: Beacon Press, 1960).

undefined, and is chosen provisionally, just to delineate the contours of "what we deny." Now, Molnar's aversion to utopia as "perennial heresy" goes so far that it leads him to write a sentence that I find rather unfortunate: supposedly, the typical characteristic of utopianism is the impossible search, by the left, for the "coincidence between what is and what ought to be."[19] But such a quest has nothing to do with "perfectism" (which, according to Rosmini's definition, is "the system which believes in the possibility of perfection in human affairs and sacrifices present benefits for some imagined future perfection"[20]) and with utopia. The perfectist delusion is the idea that evil can be eliminated at its root. But the certainty that in history evil is a constant, and constantly destined to be reborn in new forms, does not contradict the fact that evil can be beaten, or at least minimized, at a specific moment in time and in a specific place, in each of the forms it takes; and that a politician's task is to establish the best conditions to facilitate such a struggle. Do we need a very simple example? Eliminating world hunger certainly will not extinguish evil. Nevertheless, who could regard that as a good reason not to make any effort today toward this goal? Certainly, anti-utopianism is not necessarily linked to a narrow and passive conservatism (but is the influence of utopianism strong today? I would say not, even if it can be detected in a certain type of scientism). However, the two attitudes often go together. I certainly do not intend here to impute to Molnar such narrow conservatism. Nevertheless, some of his sentences are too sharp, and it is easy to see that they caused Domenach's irritation, with whom we certainly cannot disagree when he defends the best meaning of the left, as "the refusal to separate politics from the ideal in order to turn it into a management technique."[21]

A DEAD END

Moreover, opposing the left today in the name of the typical pessimistic realism of conservative thought – which essentially turns politics into a

19 [TN] Molnar and Domenach, "L'impasse de la gauche," 47: "l'ambition de la gauche consiste alors à compléter la réalité, à rechercher l'impossible coïncidence de ce qui est avec ce qui devra être."

20 [TN] Antonio Rosmini, *The Philosophy of Politics*, trans. Denis Cleary and Terry Watson (Durham, UK: Rosmini House, 1994), 1: 74. Since in Italian Rosmini himself uses the form "perfettismo" (as opposed to the standard Italian word "perfezionismo"), I translated it as "perfectism" (as opposed to "perfectionism"). This has the advantage of distinguishing the philosophical position Rosmini wants to describe from a mere psychological inclination.

21 [TN] Molnar and Domenach, "L'impasse de la gauche," 63.

technique at the service of the "lesser evil" – is a dead end. On top of everything else, this kind of right has no political space because it is suffocated by the new technocratic right, which inexorably opposes it, being itself the epilogue of the left. The technocratic right, founded on the philosophy of the primacy of action and on the instrumentalist conception of ideas – which is the outcome of the revolution that took place over the last fifty years, first of all at the moral level – is much more crudely oppressive than the old right inspired by the philosophy of the primacy of contemplation and of the idea of participation. One of its intrinsic features is the abolition of any distinction between strength (at the service of an ideal principle) and violence (which denies every ideal principle). After all, this abolition is dear to the new intellectual avant-gardes and agrees perfectly with the mindset of the new economically dominant groups (in the broadest sense of the word "economic"). Because of the culture that inspires it, the technocratic right is mortally opposed to traditional thought as I briefly defined it earlier. In fact, the alliance between technocratic right and cultural left is there for everyone to see. Molnar points to it when he talks about the "respectably progressive" press,[22] opening an urgently needed discussion.

On the other hand, a limitation of Domenach's analysis is his delusion about the revolutionary awakening of May 1968. It seems that the greatest barrier between the two interlocutors is in Molnar a psychological aversion to the word utopia, and in Domenach a sympathetic resonance at the sound of the word revolution.

Actually, what characterized the May movement in France was that revolutionary negativism manifested itself in its pure state. Obviously, at the political level, the revolutionary left cannot impact reality except through adaptations that ultimately end up distorting it. Domenach points out correctly that one of the aspects that best expresses the crisis of the left is the abandonment of internationalism.[23] Communism broke off from Socialism after and because of the failure of the Second International to deal with European nationalisms. However, did the Third International meet a better fate? The left's first compromise with factual reality takes place at the national level, and it is easy to add that this is the beginning of a process that leads the left to face its greatest historical enemy, imperialism, a new analysis of which is needed – as Domenach points out quite correctly.[24] To start from the beginning, and recalling truths that must not be forgotten just because they are obvious,

22 [TN] Ibid., 49.
23 [TN] Ibid., 61.
24 [TN] Ibid., 60.

think of how Lenin was able to triumph over Kerensky. If we read again the writings by intellectuals and politicians in the Western countries during that distant year 1917, we will see that Kerensky's rise to power was welcomed with extraordinary enthusiasm by the democratic factions of the *Entente*. Was it not a scandal that the most autocratic of the great powers, Russia, was part of an alliance whose ideal justification was to fight for the freedom of nations? The February revolution had brought reality into sync with ideology. But from this perspective, Russia was bound to join the democratic nations as a Johnny-come-lately. By adopting Lenin's Communism, on the contrary, it could take the role of first-born nation in the world revolution. This was an ancient dream: Russia's destiny was not to follow in the footsteps of Europe, borrowing its values and norms, but rather to carry out a redemptive action in favour of a by now incurably corrupt Europe. According to the Slavophiles, this salvation of the world was supposed to come from Russian Christianity. Lenin succeeded by taking up the same idea but with the opposite sign. This is objectively what happened, regardless of how much the protagonists of the drama were aware of it. Perhaps this is also the ultimate explanation of the massacre of the imperial family: Lenin had to erase every trace of Tsarism because he was taking up the task assigned to it by the Slavophiles. Kerensky's escape was not very important, but the destruction of the imperial family was essential. In this respect, Stalin merely continued Lenin's work – through socialism in one country, linguistics, and so on – obeying the reality principle. From the extreme revolutionary perspective such obedience may well be regarded as a betrayal, because of the essence of the revolutionary idea, but on the other hand it is a necessity.[25]

"REVOLUTIONLESS REVOLUTION"

We must remember that in the years immediately after the war somebody stood up against this necessary adaptation of the revolution to reality: the Surrealists. For instance, let us read again the collective manifesto titled *Rupture inaugurale* (from Marxism), "a declaration approved on June 21 1947 by the group in France in order to define its

25 It may be superfluous to remark that this would be the place for a precise assessment of Trotsky's position. It is a fact that he formulated all the criticisms of Communism as it became realized in practice. What he failed to grasp was that his critique had to apply to revolutionary thought itself. Since such thought is born from a separation from reality, it can find an accommodation with reality only by accepting the betrayals that Trotsky described, in the order in which he described them.

position against any partisan politics," published on the occasion of the International Surrealist Exhibit.[26] It remarks that the Communist Party's lack of political scruples allowed "regressive practices," and expresses a concern that Marxism, through a sequence of compromises, might end up letting the "age-old enemy" of the revolution survive. This enemy is described as the "Christian-Thomist framework," which has been able to change shape infinitely many times, in order to survive the successive disappearance of various exploitative classes. Then the manifesto concludes: "Let's return to morality, the most constant object of our preoccupations: it would be absurd to count on the political revolution alone to change them ... These theoreticians [Marx's followers] have never denounced the current morality except when they saw an immediate political advantage in it. De Sade and Freud, on the other hand, opened the breach. Whatever the doctrine that must succeed Christianity, we see de Sade and Freud as the assigned precursors of its ethics."[27]

The French "May Revolution" was marked precisely by the hybridization of Marxian themes with Freudian themes and themes inspired by de Sade. Therefore, it cannot be interpreted as a revolt that has not yet found its form or as a quest, even if necessarily unfinished, for a new revolutionary model. The ethics described by the Surrealist manifesto dominated for twenty-two years almost unchallenged, almost unnoticed by those who were supposed to fight it, through a continuous escalation, in literature and in art, and especially in popular literature and art. This had to produce its effects. I do not know to what extent the groups that promoted such ethics were aware of the Surrealist teachings, but I consider extremely likely that what was called a "revolutionless revolution" – meaning that it lacked a program – because it could not bring to power any new social class and because it completely conformed to revolutionary negativism, will be remembered in history as the "Surrealist Revolution." This formula implies a complete divorce from reality, pure negation, and at the same time extreme desecration (Richard Wagner, during his revolutionary stage, had already said, "All that is must collapse in front of what it must become," where according to him "what it must become" was "life, always rejuvenated and always taking new shape"[28]).

26 "Rupture inaugurale" in *Le Surréalisme en 1947* (Paris: Maeght Éditeur, 1947) [TN: "Inaugural Rupture," in Michael Richardson and Krzystof Fijałkowski, eds., *Surrealism against the Current: Tracts and Declarations* (London: Pluto Press, 2001), 42–9].

27 [TN] "Inaugural Rupture," 45.

28 [TN] As quoted in Giovanni Cattaui De Menasce, *Contestazione e metanoia* [Student protests and metanoia] (Rome: A.V.E., 1969), 16. The quotation in De Menasce's book is actually a collage of sentences from the article *Die Revolution* [The revolution] from the 8

ADAPTATION TO REALITY AND UNREALISM

In fact, the crisis of the left takes the form of a split into two opposite developments. One is adaptation to reality, which ultimately leads to submission to the "reality principle." Reality, however, is no longer ordered toward values but rather coincides with pure power. The other is pure unrealism, which, however, objectively becomes an accomplice of the first attitude in the global rejection of all values.

This is not Domenach's view, at least based on what he wrote: "When I hear the protesters cry 'we need action, not a theory' I share in their anger against the decomposition of the language of the left, but I respond that those who want to act need theory more than those who only want to think."[29] I am inclined to reply to him that, given the internal logic of their position, the protesters are perfectly correct. And I do not rule out the possibility that further reflection might lead Domenach to agree with me, because it is the natural consequence of what he writes.

Can we get to some conclusions? In the 1950s people insisted, especially Catholics (and I think I remember some very strong statements by Domenach), that politics, metaphysics, and religion must be kept rigorously distinguished. Today this insistence is even more widespread, which is not surprising given the Catholic world's habit of falling behind the curve. Supposedly, we should try to mention God as little as possible in political discussions, because by mentioning Him we turn Him into the God of the conservatives and the *bien-pensants,* who hampers human advancement and the growth of life, against whom blasphemies and denials are justifiable.

I disagreed, from immediately after the war, as anybody who reads my book on the problem of atheism can verify. How could I not be glad that today Domenach inclines to agree with me? Because how else could we interpret his statement: "The left simply believes that in man there is always something more. And therefore its politics must be effectively oriented toward Being, or else it will get lost in the delirium of the limitless"[30]? This means: whereas he and many other Catholics felt and feel attracted – especially today, I think – by a philosophically neutral left, guided only by the ethical presupposition of the equal dignity of every human person, today he acknowledges that in our century the left

April issue of *Volksblätter,* Dresden, 1849. This article was published anonymously, but its authorship is universally attributed to Richard Wagner.

29 [TN] Molnar and Domenach, "L'impasse de la gauche," 57.

30 [TN] Ibid., 64.

was underpinned by a particular metaphysics, and that the reason for its crisis lies in this metaphysics.

CATHOLICS BETWEEN RIGHT AND LEFT

During the whole course of our century Catholics have been divided – and today this division has reached its climax – between men of the left (advancement of the human condition in the name of ideals) and men of the right (preservation of principles). Now the crisis of the left, precisely as it has been described by the editor of the journal that for many years was its most significant expression, suggests to philosophy that politics cannot be based on ideals without making reference to a fundamental principle of traditional thought. How shall I formulate it? I read in a recent article by Cattaui de Menasce, "Things do not 'receive' value, but contain 'in themselves' something that 'demands, deserves to be acknowledged by intelligence.' When I formulate a judgment of value … I affirm, at the same time, the existence of being and a hierarchy of beings."[31] I cannot emphasize enough how much I agree with this statement, and I will merely offer a brief comment in order to highlight its importance. Usually people have thought that making such an assertion is the essence of the right. According to common opinion, one cannot be "progressive" without rejecting this view of the world (as far as the Catholics are concerned, the most moderate among the *engagées* choose at the very least not to talk about it, lest they lose access, they think, to the "cultural continent" of our age). After reading this debate, if we look at what is essential and leave aside a few accidental polemical stings, we conclude that this perspective is utterly false.

31 [TN] Cattaui De Menasce, *Contestazione e metanoia*, 19–20.

Appendices

APPENDIX A

The Story of a Solitary Thinker

An interview with Augusto del Noce, by Massimo Borghesi and Lucio Brunelli

Professor, how did you become interested in philosophy?
You are asking me for a serious memory effort, because I have to go back more than fifty years, to the time when I finished high school in 1928. I can say that what I was facing at the time was essentially a moral question. I was looking for a sense of direction, in front of a world that was changing rapidly and a system of values that I did not share and that, for complex reasons, I did not like. In short, I simply was not happy with the world.

Did your family environment somehow affect this uneasiness?
In part, yes. My family had fallen into decline and basically was oriented toward the values of the past. Therefore, on the one hand, I was attached to those values; on the other, I sensed that they lacked a foundation. This is at least one of the reasons that led me to philosophy. Yes, you can say that my starting point was properly moral, rather than gnoseological, metaphysical, or epistemological.

Therefore, your choice to devote yourself to philosophy matured without hesitation during your years as a student at the University of Turin –
No, not without hesitation, also because Giorgio Falco,[1] my professor of medieval history in the humanities department, strongly advised me to

Originally published as "Storia di un pensatore solitario" in *30Giorni*, no. 4 (April 1984): 63–7; reprinted in Massimo Borghesi, *Augusto Del Noce: La legittimazione critica del moderno* (Genova: Marietti, 2011).

1 [TN] Giorgio Falco (1888–1966) was a distinguished medievalist. He was persecuted by the Fascist regime because of his Jewish background. In 1938 he had to leave his job at the University of Turin and move to Rome, where in 1939 he converted to Catholicism. His best-known book (and the only one to have been translated into English) is *The Holy Roman Republic*, trans. K.V. Kent (New York: A.S. Barnes & Co., 1964).

study history, and the Latin scholar Augusto Rostagni[2] tried to direct me toward classical philology. Perhaps I should have followed their advice … who knows, but at that point I was too interested in philosophy. More seriously, I should mention that in the 1930s and 40s my initial moral motivations were complicated by the addition of political reasons –

Those were the years of Fascism. According to the historian De Felice, they were the years when the regime enjoyed its greatest "consensus." What was your position as a young intellectual?
My position was what I would call "isolated" anti-Fascism. You see, anti-Fascists were a small minority among the young, and in Turin this small minority was generally driven by a liberal-socialist political philosophy, inspired by Pietro Gobetti's[3] ideas and by the initiatives of the Giustizia e Libertà group.[4] That was the school of thought that later would generate the Partito d'Azione.

How relevant was Communist anti-Fascism in that same period?
As I just said, among young intellectuals anti-Fascism had mainly a liberal-socialist orientation. The Communist presence was minimal, and I think not just for obvious reasons of police repression. In fact, the intellectuals who became Communists in the 1940s came from so-called "left-wing Fascism," at least generally speaking.

Could you elucidate in what sense your position was "isolated" anti-fascism?
I was isolated because I was Catholic. The anti-Fascist intellectuals close to the positions of Giustizia e Libertà had a largely secular, anti-Catholic outlook. Almost all my anti-Fascist university classmates, from Leone Ginzburg[5] to Norberto Bobbio,[6] shared this liberal-socialist orientation.

2 [TN] Augusto Rostagni (1892–1961), Italian classical philologist and professor of Latin Literature at the University of Turin from 1930 until his death.

3 [TN] Pietro Gobetti (1901–26), Italian journalist and intellectual. Gobetti was an early and uncompromising anti-Fascist, and advocated a radical form of liberalism.

4 [TN] Italian anti-Fascist resistance movement founded in Paris in 1929 by a group of Italian political refugees. In 1942 some of its members founded the Partito d'Azione, a liberal-socialist political party that advocated radical social change while rejecting Communism. The party disbanded after being defeated in the 1946 election, but its ideas were deeply influential on post-Second World War Italian culture and politics.

5 [TN] Leone Ginzburg (1909–44) was an Italian writer and anti-Fascist activist. He co-founded the Partito d'Azione and edited its newspaper *L'Italia Libera*. He was arrested in Rome by the Fascist police in February 1944 and died after being tortured.

6 [TN] Norberto Bobbio (1909–2004) was an Italian historian of political thought and political philosopher. He was probably the best-known academic representative of the Italian liberal-socialist tradition. Bobbio and Del Noce were classmates both in high school

What about the official Catholic side?
In a way I was "isolated" also in the organized Catholic world of the time. In fact, it is hard to identify a clear anti-Fascist position among young Catholic intellectuals of the 1930s.

Therefore, contrary to the majority of today's Catholic establishment, your cultural formation did not take place in the FUCI (Italian Catholic University Federation) of Msgr Montini[7] or in the cultural environment of the Catholic University of Fr. Gemelli.[8]
No. I was a member of FUCI, but I did not participate. I was always Catholic, but actually my formation remained rather extraneous to the world of Catholic intellectual associations. I must add that the presence of FUCI in the School of Humanities of the University of Turin was rather limited.

Let us put aside for a moment the political aspect and let us talk about the cultural environment at the University of Turin. Do you recognize anybody as a true "teacher" in your philosophical formation?
In a certain way my teacher was Carlo Mazzantini,[9] who is not well known outside of Turin but whom I consider the best Italian Catholic mind since the end of the First World War.

And besides Mazzantini?
I think I owe a lot to the French school. You see, at that time the Italian intellectual world was dominated by Gentile's Idealistic philosophy, which felt totally foreign to me. Thus, it was not coincidental that I became, so to speak, a "private" student of the Sorbonne. Since I had chosen as my dissertation topic the religious interpretation of Descartes – particularly in Malebranche's philosophy – I came in contact with

---

and at the University of Turin and remained friends throughout their lives, in spite of their philosophical differences.

7 [TN] Msgr Giovanni Battista Montini (1887–1978) in 1954 became Archbishop of Milan and in 1963 was elected Pope Paul VI. From 1925 to 1933 he served as director of FUCI (Federazione Universitaria Cattolica Italiana), which at that time was the most important organization of Italian Catholic university students.

8 [TN] Fr Agostino Gemelli, OFM (1878–1959) was an Italian Franciscan friar, physician, and psychologist. He also founded the Catholic University of the Sacred Heart in Milan and served as its first rector.

9 [TN] Carlo Mazzantini (1895–1971) was an Italian philosopher and a professor at the University of Turin.

personalities like Henri Gouhier,[10] the author of a beautiful philosophical history of the religious sentiment in France,[11] Étienne Gilson, and Jean Laporte.[12]

Was this encounter with French philosophy an opportunity to come in contact also with Jacques Maritain?
At the time Maritain was a fashionable author, at least among Catholics. I started by reading his *Reflections on Intelligence*,[13] published in the early twenties, and then I followed all his works starting from *Three reformers*[14] to *Anti-modern.*[15] However, the book by this French philosopher that struck me the most, to the point that I learned it almost by heart, was *Integral Humanism.*[16] I read it in 1936, when it had just been published in France ... I think I was one of its very first Italians readers.

Were you as interested in the later Maritain?
I must say that I liked less the later Maritain, with the exception of works like *Moral Philosophy*[17] and *The Peasant of the Garonne.*[18] In *Integral Humanism,* besides the political aspects, I was interested in the vision of the history of modern philosophy that Maritain proposed.

10 [TN] Henri Gouhier (1898–1994), French philosopher, historian of philosophy, and literary critic.

11 [TN] Whereas Gouhier wrote many books on the history of philosophy and religion in France, no single work of his seems to fit Del Noce's description. However, Del Noce owned several volumes of Henri Brémond's monumental *Histoire littéraire du sentiment religieux en France* [Literary history of the religious sentiment in France] (Paris: Bloud et Gay, 1916–36). It is possible that in the course of the interview Del Noce suffered a memory lapse and either mixed up the two authors or neglected to mention Brémond's name explicitly.

12 [TN] Jean Laporte (1886–1948), French philosopher and historian of philosophy, he is especially remembered for his groundbreaking works on Cartesianism, e.g., *Le rationalisme de Descartes* (Paris: Presses Universitaires de France, 1945).

13 [TN] Jacques Maritain, *Réflexions sur l'intelligence et sur sa vie propre* (Paris: Nouvelle Librairie Nationale, 1924).

14 [TN] Jacques Maritain, *Three Reformers: Luther, Descartes, Rousseau* (New York: Charles Scribner's Sons, 1929).

15 [TN] Jacques Maritain, *Antimoderne* (Paris: Éditions de la Revue des Jeunes, 1922).

16 [TN] Jacques Maritain, *Integral Humanism: Temporal and Spiritual Problems of a New Christendom,* trans. Joseph W. Evans (New York: Charles Scribner's Sons, 1968).

17 [TN] Jacques Maritain, *Moral Philosophy: An Historical and Critical Survey of the Great Systems,* trans. by Marshall Suther et al. (New York, Charles Scribner's Sons, 1964).

18 [TN] Jacques Maritain, *The Peasant of the Garonne,* trans. Michael Cuddihy and Elizabeth Hughes (New York: Holt, Rinehart and Winston, 1968).

In any case, philosophy and politics are constantly intertwined also in your intellectual journey. If I am not mistaken, starting in the mid-1930s your anti-Fascist position evolved –
Yes. In those years my anti-Fascism led me to a Communist-Catholic position. It was almost inevitable, given the liberal-socialist cultural context in which my opposition to the regime had matured when I was in Turin.

How did you reconcile yourself to the atheism present in Communist philosophy?
Essentially, I was starting from the idea that Communism was not against religion per se, but against bourgeois Christianity. This judgment reflected a typical human atmosphere shared by many young intellectuals of my generation, more than deep reflection. It was an atmosphere that Maritain himself undoubtedly helped create.

In what sense?
In the sense that two different positions coexist in *Integral Humanism*: on the one hand, there is the correct perception that atheism is an essential constitutive element of Marxism, which affects all its aspects; in short, the perception that atheism is not a mere "superstructure" in Marx's thought. On the other hand, there is the idea that Marxism fights a false God whom supposedly the bourgeois world and also a certain Catholic world use for the sake of power. In the years from 1936 to 1940 I found this second theme of Maritain's convincing. Later on, instead, I was more convinced by the first theme.

What caused this change of position?
This change was mostly due to the experience of the Italian "civil war" in the early 1940s. Or, rather, to how the Communists conducted that war, in a way that dissolved ethics into politics and, as a consequence, led to totally unscrupulous politics.

Once again your human and intellectual itinerary seems unusual. Whereas for so many Italian and European intellectuals, the Resistance marked the time of greatest closeness and, in many cases, of adhesion to Marxism, for you –
For me it marked the moment when I was least interested in Marxism and I distanced myself from it. Yes, in fact my experience is the very opposite of that of many other intellectuals.

Excuse us, Professor, but were you opposed to "every" notion of anti-Nazi/anti-Fascist Resistance?
No, I approved the idea of purely defensive resistance. You see, my anti-Fascist position had been deeply influenced by my friendship with

pacifist Aldo Capitini.[19] I still think that Capitini's early work *Elements of a Religious Experience*[20] truly represents the highest expression of Italian anti-Fascism. To me the concept of "anti-Fascism" was so tightly connected to that of "non-violence" that the Resistance, as it was conducted by the Communists, seemed a distortion of the truest anti-Fascist spirit. It felt like being betrayed by somebody I had fallen in love with –

Could we say that after these events and the related crisis of the Communist-Catholic experience, you rediscovered the other side of Maritain's thought, the one that ties deeply together Marxism and atheism?
Yes. I reached a new judgment about Marxism, which I elaborated for the first time in an essay published in 1946.[21] Those theses of mine have been confirmed today by the analysis of Vittorio Strada, a distinguished scholar who over the last few years has studied the relationship between Marxism and real socialism.[22] But at that time those ideas were unusual, to say the least.

What was the key idea behind your interpretation?
That Marxism is the *subject* of contemporary history. More precisely, contemporary history is *at the same time* the story of its success and its failure. I stress the words "at the same time" because, on the contrary, most critics of Marxism focus either on its realization (now few people do, actually!) or on its failure. Whereas Marxism did realize itself, but by realizing itself *at the same time* it negated itself.

This is the idea of the "suicide of the revolution," which gives the title to one of your most famous works[23] –
Yes. Marxism negated itself in the sense that it decomposed.

19 [TN] Aldo Capitini (1899–1968), Italian philosopher, politician, anti-Fascist, and poet, was one of the first proponents in Italy of Gandhi's philosophy of nonviolence.

20 [TN] Aldo Capitini, *Elementi di un esperienza religiosa* (Bari: Laterza, 1937).

21 [TN] Augusto Del Noce, "La 'non-filosofia' di Marx e il comunismo come realtà politica" [Marx's "non-philosophy" and Communism as a political reality] in *Il materialismo storico. Atti del I congresso internazionale di filosofia* [Historical materialism. Proceedings of the 1st International Conference on Philosophy] (Milan: Castellani, 1947), 357–88, republished in *Il problema dell'ateismo* [The problem of atheism] (Bologna: Il Mulino, 1964), 213–66.

22 [TN] Vittorio Strada (1929), Italian scholar of Russian history and literature.

23 [TN] Augusto Del Noce, *Il suicidio della rivoluzione* [The suicide of the revolution] (Milan: Rusconi, 1978).

In the context of this brief overview, what is the connection between the crisis of Marxism and the advent of a new type of nihilism?
Once upon a time, forty years ago, existentialism was described, not altogether incorrectly, as the "patient of the crisis."[24] Today the patient of the crisis is nihilism. Marxism succeeded in denying that values are absolute, and the nihilism that dominates the Western world reflects this "success-failure" of Marxism. On the other hand, the world's political situation, dominated by two giants that are unable either to reconcile or to destroy each other, finds its philosophical "counterpart" precisely in this inability to attain a superior value. However, today nihilism is no longer the tragic nihilism of Nietzsche or, in part, of Dostoevsky; it is "accepted" nihilism, so to speak.

In what sense is your formulation of the problem of atheism in contemporary society unusual, with respect to those found today in Catholic culture?
Consider the case of the "new theologies." Their thought is based, at least unwittingly, on an interpretation of contemporary history coming either from Marxism or from "progressivism." According to this interpretation, in the twentieth century we saw the final battle between two opposing historical trends, the "Progressive" and the "reactionary." After the First World War and the Russian Revolution, the "reactionary" form lost its remaining "respectable" aspects and embraced the barbarism that is generically called "Fascism." Also according to this interpretation, the Church allied itself with the reactionary forces up to the pontificate of Pius XII. All the "new theologies" rely on this view of contemporary history, and "liberation theology" most openly so.

There is also another interpretation of contemporary history, which I consider more adequate, that identifies "secularism" as the radical disease of our century.

24 [TN] The description of existentialism "as a *patient*, not an *agent*, of the current crisis" is due to Marxist philosopher Galvano Della Volpe (1895–1968). It is found in *Discorso sull' ineguaglianza* [Discourse on inequality] (Rome: Ciuni, 1943), 12, republished in *Opere* [*Works*], vol. 3 (Rome: Editori Riuniti, 1973), 271. Many Italian intellectuals, including Norberto Bobbio, shared the idea that existentialism was primarily a reverberation of the European crisis of the 1930s, rather than a viable, self-sustaining theoretical effort. Del Noce and Della Volpe knew and respected each other, although their philosophical journeys were very different. Whereas Del Noce moved past his youthful Marxist temptations, Della Volpe started as a neo-Idealist but then embraced Marxism in a radically materialistic, anti-Idealistic, and anti-existentialistic form. Della Volpe regarded Del Noce as one of the foremost Italian experts on Marx, and offered him a position as his assistant at the University of Messina [Enzo Randone, private communication].

Undoubtedly, this is a minority interpretation in the Catholic world –
This is not an exclusively Catholic interpretation. If I had to come up with some names, I would immediately think of Simone Weil and Aleksandr Solzhenitsyn. However, I wish to emphasize that this is absolutely not a pro-Fascist or "reactionary" interpretation. It actually regards Fascism and Nazism as the tragic outcomes of a secularization process that historically precedes them, as two dramatic manifestations of the age of secularization.

How does the crisis of Marxism affect the current orientations of Catholic progressivism?
Marxism being out of fashion, today Catholic progressivism seems to favour the "Enlightenment-modern" interpretation, in its democratic-progressive version. Thus, it arrives at "neo-bourgeois" positions. This trajectory could not have reached a more peculiar and paradoxical endpoint: today Catholic progressivism has become a tool at the service of the new business-oriented bourgeoisie –

In 1968 you wrote an essay on the condition of young people.[25] *How would you describe today's youth, if you were to write it again today?*
I think that the young people of the 1980s bear the burden of the previous generation's problems … a generation they meet in school, in their teachers, when they reach the critical age of eighteen or twenty. However, they seem less ideological –

But maybe also less alive, less committed –
True, but we also need to ask ourselves: what kind of ethical-political proposals are offered to them in this society? In his own way Khomeini offers some answers.

Right! Islam –
Today Islam, surprisingly in its most traditionalist version, seems to be the only worldwide force capable of mobilizing young people, to the point of pushing them to the slaughter, to the front line. Conversely, there seems to be nothing left for Western youth except for cynical desire for a career and an outlook on the future so pessimistic that it is reflected, for example, in a clear will not to have children.

25 [TN] Augusto Del Noce, "Appunti per una filosofia dei giovani" [Notes for a philosophy of young people] in *L'epoca della secolarizzazione* [The Age of Secularization] (Milan: Giuffrè, 1970).

Let us go back to your scholarly endeavours. Some time ago you promised to complete your history of modern philosophy, which for the time being has stopped at Descartes –
I do not think I will be able to … we shall see. Instead, these days I am writing an introduction[26] to Dante's *De Monarchia.*[27] It is a work that contains very interesting ideas which apply to today's situation, among them a definition of "secularity" which I think is unsurpassable.

And after this work?
I would like to prepare a collection of my political essays, in order to leave a general interpretation of contemporary history … a sort of historical-political will. Yes, if I can I would like to write two wills, one historical-political and one philosophical.

One final question. As this conversation confirmed, yours has been in all respects a solitary journey, both within and without the Church. What helped you most to remain faithful to your convictions?
If I recall correctly, the English writer Chesterton said that it was the positivist Spencer who pushed him, by contrast, toward Catholicism.[28] Similarly, I would say that secular ideas, both liberal and Marxist, are what kept me in it. Since I was born Catholic, I would have needed some "reasons" to leave, but these reasons, proposed by many sides, never convinced me.

26 [TN] Del Noce never published the work he mentions. Various manuscripts exist, some of them unreadable and others fragmentary. A group of these texts was published in Flavio Silvestrini, *Attualità della tradizione: Dante politico in Augusto del Noce* [The relevance of tradition for our time: Dante as a political thinker in Augusto Del Noce] (Rome: Edizioni Nuova Cultura, 2010). [I thank Professor Enzo Randone for this reference].

27 [TN] *The De Monarchia of Dante Alighieri* (Boston and New York: Houghton, Miflin & Company, 1904).

28 [TN] "It was Huxley and Herbert Spencer and Bradlaugh who brought me back to orthodox theology. They sowed in my mind my first wild doubts of doubt … when I had finished reading Herbert Spencer I had got as far as doubting … whether evolution had occurred at all," from G.K. Chesterton, *Orthodoxy* (New York: Doubleday, 2012), 85.

APPENDIX B

Notes on Secularization and Religious Thought

THE TERM "SECULARIZATION" IS MEANINGFUL if it is used in reference to Marxism, considered in its origin – the Hegelian Left's critique of religion, which concluded in Marxism – and in its only faithful historical consequence, namely Leninism and what came out of it (even if, obviously, Marx did not foresee the effects of his doctrine). Consider that Marx's philosophical position can only be defined as an effort to think *man's liberation from every dependence*; first of all from God, image of the "Lord." And it is undeniable that Marx pushed this position – which was shared by much of nineteenth-century philosophy, inasmuch as it came after the French Revolution and interpreted it – further than anybody else, going from immanentism (*Deus manet in nobis*) to materialism and atheism.

Somebody may object that the definition "rejection of every dependence" should rather apply to anarchism, which Marx and later the Communists constantly and forcefully opposed. But the Marxist critique boils down to the statement that anarchists ignore, or even choose to ignore, the course of history and its laws, so that the intransigent approach that they display is actually a cover for acquiescence, for servility to the status quo (Stirner[1] the *petit bourgeois*!). The goal of *rejecting dependence*, as the soul of both forms of thought, remains the same. It implies a total negation of creation (a sign of such dependence) and yet *faith*, changed from faith in the beyond to faith in the future, but still, in

This chapter was first published as"Note sulla secolarizzazione e il pensiero religioso," *Il Nuovo Aeropago* 2, no. 3 (1983): 66–79, reprinted in *Verità e ragione nella storia*, ed. A. Mina (Milan: Rizzoli, 2007), 310–28.

1 [TN] Max Stirner, pen name of Johann Kaspar Schmidt (1806–56), German post-Hegelian philosopher who advocated anarchism and radical individualism. Del Noce is referring to the scathing criticism of Stirner by Marx and Engels in *The German Ideology*.

its own way, a *religion*, even if (or rather because) it is linked with a complete negation of the transcendent and the supernatural. In the first decades of the twentieth century both Mussolini in his revolutionary stage and Gramsci spoke of socialism as the "religion destined to kill Christianity."[2] The word "secularization" certainly takes a full meaning in the context of such a transposition of religion to this world.

Why, then, has this word cast for many years (today, fortunately, a little less) some sort of spell on the minds of many Christian theologians and thinkers? The explanation is simple. Just recall Hegel's famous phrase, which is valid also beyond Hegelianism, that philosophy is "its own time comprehended in thought."[3] These theologians are convinced, in the words of Sartre in his 1960 *Critique of Dialectical Reason*,[4] that Marxism is unsurpassable because it is the "philosophy of our time" and the "most radical attempt to clarify the historical process in its totality." Hence the idea that "there is no turning back from Marx," and the attempts to reconcile Marxism with Christianity through various routes, often by invoking biblical philology as a mediator (what is unfortunate is that the real thought process, which is actually motivated by very recent historical events, too often is concealed; these theologians should be invited to respect the intelligence of their readers). The reasoning is simple: if history is "sacred," guided by Divine Providence, and if "Marxism is the philosophy of our time," we must try to reconcile it with Revelation, as was done long ago with the philosophies of Plato and Aristotle.

THEOLOGY OF SECULARIZATION

Now, it definitely makes sense to say that Marxism is "untranscendable" from the perspective of any philosophy that denies the supernatural and the transcendent, even if we cannot dwell on this point and on its specific meaning. It is perfectly true that it was the protagonist of the twentieth century, and that no subsequent political phenomenon can be understood without referring to it. It must be said that the Communist

2 [TN] Antonio Gramsci, "Audacia e fede" in *Avanti!*, 22 May 1916.

3 Georg W.F. Hegel, *Elements of the Philosophy of Right*, ed. Allan W. Wood, trans. Hugh B. Nisbet (Cambridge: Cambridge University Press, 1991), 21.

4 [TN] Jean Paul Sartre, *Critique of Dialectical Reason*, trans. Alan Sheridan-Smith (New York: Verso, 2004). However, the sentences quoted by Del Noce come from the prefatory essay "Question de Méthode," which was printed at the beginning of the first French edition of *Critique de la raison dialectique* (Paris: Gallimard, 1960) but not in the subsequent American editions. "Question de Méthode" was published separately in English as *Search for a Method*, trans. Hazel E. Barnes (New York: Alfred A. Knopf, 1963). The quotations in question are found there on pages 29 to 30.

revolution took place as a worldwide event and not just in underdeveloped countries. But it led to the greatest heterogenesis of ends ever seen in history. I will quickly summarize the essential points:

1 In Eastern Europe it gave rise to the "Soviet Empire," which is precisely the "secularization" of Tsarism. Yet, it must be said that its rise is not in the least a "betrayal" (in the Trotskyist sense) either of Marxism or of Leninism, but their unforeseen necessary outcome.
2 In the West it acted as negation of all immutable and absolute values, producing a new bourgeoisie that pushes the bourgeois characteristics to the extreme and that Marxism is totally incapable of overthrowing.
3 Marxist thought – according to the statement already formulated by Lenin in 1903 in "What Is to Be Done?"[5] – can be brought to the working class only "from without," by intellectuals capable of comprehending the direction of the historical movement in its entirety.[6] Essentially, this says that Marxist doctrine is exempted from the economic-social conditioning that historical materialism describes theoretically, and that a "philosophical" and not "economic" view of history is necessary in order to preserve the revolutionary substance of Marxism.
4 The Communist revolution could only be conceived as world unifying, and instead provoked its greatest division.

The two criticisms that democratic writers usually present as self-standing, namely the one about the "new class"[7] and the one about "totalitarianism," are significant, instead, only in connection with the four I described. In fact, a revolution without a ruling class is unthinkable, and a total revolution aimed at creating a "reign of freedom," radically different from the previous "reign of necessity," cannot develop according to the rules of democratic evolution.

These premises are necessary for the brief remarks that follow. I want to propose the idea, of course without discussing it exhaustively, that the same heterogenesis of ends that affects the Marxist revolution occurs also in the revolutionary microcosm of the theology of secularization.

The push by Catholics toward modernization – which was so strong in the two decades from 1960 to 1980 – and the propensity to give witness

5 [TN] V.I. Lenin, "What Is to Be Done?" in *Collected Works*, trans. Joe Fineberg and George Hanna (Moscow: Progress Publishers, 1960), 5: 422.

6 [TN] An almost verbatim quotation from the *Communist Manifesto*, chapter I.

7 [TN] Milovan Djilas, *The New Class* (New York: Praeger, 1957).

to it on the part of everybody who was tempted by it – almost as a public confession of a tendency that previously had to be kept secret – has made the literature on this topic as huge as it is useless, because of countless repetitions or clumsy attempts to "say in different words." Therefore, in this initial presentation I will try to reconstruct it a priori, explaining why it became widespread and focusing in particular on the non-religious and actually secular foundations on which it stands.

Essentially, I think that it can be boiled down to the following eleven theses.

1 The Kerygma (revealed message) transcends all civilizations and all cultures. This thesis is stated in another form by saying that faith is not culture, or that faith and religion must be kept separate, because religion supposedly is the corruption of faith that consists in presenting it in the objectivistic form of a world view.

   This implies that the "objectivistic form" – metaphysics, in short – is always relative to a given time, and whoever speaks of the "eternal truths" of metaphysics is a "reactionary." The history of the Catholic University of Milan bears the marks of this evolution, from the strenuous affirmation of metaphysics in the 1930s to today's situation. But it is only a small example.

2 Modern culture and civilization *qua* secular originate from Christianity. This statement is based on the principle that "the world needs to be completely worldly in order for God to be completely divine." Supposedly, the world's complete worldliness conjoined with God's complete divinity is expressed by the principle of a transcendent creator God. Therefore, God's transcendence, the elimination of any trace of pantheism, is the foundation of the world's atheization, demythologization, and desacralization. The secularization of the world supposedly follows from the affirmation of the principle of creation in its fullness. The new secular categories are more authentically Christian or biblical than the previous categories because the new secular Christianity – and this is said to be the exact formulation – is the child of modernity, which in turn was the child of Christianity, inasmuch as it continues its work of desacralization and demythologization of the world.

3 Supposedly the great misunderstanding of the centuries of the modern age has been the failure to recognize the Christian origins of secular civilization. The consequence has been "secularism," i.e., the interpretation of "secularization" as associated no longer with creationistic theism but with a process that ultimately leads to atheism. However, the responsibility for this misunderstanding lies

primarily with Christians and their interpretation of religion's presence in society in the form of closed religion and society.

4 The transition to a fully worldly world coincides with the transition from the "cosmocentric" to the "anthropocentric" conceptual structure – what is usually called "dehellenization."

5 This anthropocentric perspective, in which man is no longer subjected to fate, but is rather the creator of a "new world," leads to the affirmation of the future as the primary category, and to the devotion of one's efforts to it and not to the other world. Precisely because of divine transcendence, faith lets the world be *this world;* precisely as faith, it is openness to the non-absolute, non-divine reality of the world as such, and thus it allows the world to be viewed radically as man's world.

6 From this follows the idea of a fulfillment that "lies in front of us, not above us."

7 The future implies the idea of an absolute *novum,* which is not just an evolutionary extension but an "unthinkable" future world toward which we progress through a permanent revolution.

8 As a result, speculative philosophy, based on the primacy of contemplation and on the subordination of practice to a super-sensible objective order, is replaced by the philosophy of the primacy of becoming (of action, of praxis).

9 Hence the radical critique of metaphysics, on the grounds that it is characterized by an essential concealment of the future (of what is not yet).

10 Theology is developed explicitly as eschatology, in the sense that eschatology is the form of every theological statement, because the world manifests itself as history only in the theological context of hope.

11 Since creative hope refers essentially to the world as society and to the forces that transform it, the theology of the world is above all a political theology.

The connection with the Hegelian-Marxist theme of philosophy as reflection about one's own age explains why the intransigently theistic themes found in Gogarten[8] grew progressively weaker in later theologians, heading toward pantheism not as *Deus sive natura* but as *Deus sive historia.* It also explains why secularization ended up meaning above all

8 [TN] Friedrich Gogarten (1887–1967), German Lutheran theologian.

the realization of God's kingdom in the political and social world; or, at least, the emphasis shifted in that direction.

Viewed in this general context, secularization may be interpreted in two different and incompatible ways. We would like to define these two extremes – which rarely appear in a pure state – between which the thought of the theologians of secularization generally oscillates. I think that the core thesis of any future book on the religious literature of secularization, if anybody wants to take the trouble to write one, should be that these oscillations are inevitable. Regarding the first extreme, we must mention the peculiar success that Bloch's work has enjoyed among theologians.[9] This peculiarity is actually easy to explain: Bloch's "heresy" with respect to real socialism is a return to original Marxism, analogous to Christian heresies. According to the first interpretation, the two returns, to primitive Christianity and to original Marxism, coincide. Clearly, we have here a sacralization of politics as the true way of participating in divine life, which actually ends up dissolving religious faith into politics. Ultimately, we have the absorption of Christianity into Marxist-inspired utopianism, and in this framework the unbeliever necessarily prevails over the Christian and in the end cannot but make him like himself. The idea of total revolution means replacing the search for metaphysical truth and the resulting moral obligation, as conformity to the order of being, with the search for a meta-humanity, meant as a future to be realized, about which we know above all that it will radically reject the existing society in its founding metaphysical first principles. Here, one should discuss a question about the Hegelian premises of the theology of secularization that has been brought up many times but never adequately addressed, as far as I know. Does this theology presuppose the transfiguration of Christian dogmas that already took place in Hegel? Such a transfiguration has been mentioned often in connection with the theme of original sin, but other themes should also be linked to it and read in its light, particularly the theme of God's death, rediscovered as the dialectic engine of secularization. The designation "secularization theology" is the definition of the task it fulfills as an adaptation to the transcendental condition of today's crisis. For this purpose, it constructs a sort of "German patrology" (Hegel, Feuerbach, Marx, Nietzsche, Freud) and makes the atheist liberation from fetishes, idols, and taboos an aspect of de-divinization carried out in God's name. Of course, the new patrology erases the old one and the traditional teachers are eclipsed. St Augustine,

9 [TN] Ernst Bloch (1885–1977), German Marxist philosopher. One of his most influential books was *Atheism in Christianity*, trans. J.T. Swann (New York: Herder and Herder, 1972).

as the Doctor of Grace, is almost never mentioned. St Thomas is occasionally cited, but he is given an "anthropocentric" interpretation, very different from the "cosmocentric" one which supposedly held captive all scholars, including the most recent.

POLITICAL RELIGION

In fact, the idea that the essentially political nature of secularized religion must lead to a complete metamorphosis of the Christian religion has been advocated by the most advanced trends of secularization theology. As an example, I will refer to the writings of Dutch scholar Sperna Weiland,[10] not for being particularly authoritative but because he has the ability to express this theology's common ideas in the most banally clear form. In his opinion, Christianity embraced metaphysics, moving away from its Hebrew origins, under the influence of Hellenism. Therefore, it is only natural that today many people regard the decline of metaphysics as the collapse of Christianity, and it is not surprising that many Christians have started a crusade against secularization. In a sense, it is a collapse because it marks a transition from metaphysical to non-metaphysical Christianity; this transition redefines Christianity not in metaphysical terms but as a project of freedom and justice in the historical, social, human, and finite world. Or, to use the general definition by Sperna Weiland himself,[11] secularization is the transition from a metaphysical interpretation of reality to an experience and an interpretation of reality in which the historical, social, human, and finite world represents the horizon of human responsibility and destiny. More briefly, secularization is a process during which all the worlds beyond have disappeared, leaving only the historical, social, human, and finite world.

Clearly, few people can comfortably embrace these extreme positions. The fact that the dissolution of religion into revolutionary thought is untenable legitimates a completely different attempt, based on the full distinction of the temporal and the spiritual. Thus, we go from the extreme form to the very opposite, the most moderate one. The overarching themes are still the adult man and the secularity of the modern world. But supposedly this secularity reflects the need to distinguish nature and grace, so that the peculiar character of this thesis is to affirm supernatural life, given by grace and therefore distinct from what belongs to man as created nature. We are tempted to spot a degree of

10 [TN] See Jan Sperna Weiland, *New Ways in Theology*, trans. N.D. Smith (New York: Newman Press, 1968).

11 [TN] Ibid., 7–9.

hypocrisy in this religious defence of the gratuitousness of the supernatural, when the focus of attention is actually political and social life. But let us further outline this attempt, which, in any case, is not very original. It starts from a standard thesis, typical of secular textbooks. Supposedly, the centuries after the 1600s were marked by man's reclamation of his dignity as creature, of his ability to develop autonomously. So far, this really cannot be said to be an especially original view. The novelty is that, in contrast with the traditional Catholic perspective, an "internal" truth is found in this reclamation, which can manifest itself in all its significance in a different context.

Indeed, what supposedly happened was that those who felt most deeply these legitimate needs interpreted them in an immanentistic and worldly sense, the so-called secularist interpretation. Catholic thought bears the primary responsibility for this misunderstanding. Why? Actually, as I have already said, I am a little hesitant even to describe this view, because this way of presenting secularization is based on a historical interpretation that really lacks originality. It is all too easy to recognize in it the last vestiges – reduced to a scheme and accepted unproblematically – of the views advanced by the great philosophies of history of the nineteenth century. The ancient world entered a great crisis, after which, due to well-known historical circumstances, the progress of civilization could take place only through the crucial contribution of the Church, which acted as a substitute. The Church took over a task that should rightfully belong to man as such. This historical fact was bound to have theoretical repercussions: it manifested itself in the conviction that society and Christianity coincide, which is the belief that inspired and continues to inspire most Christian thinkers, even those who claim to be most open, Maritain included.

Speaking of Maritain, it must be said that these political theologies have appeared in close correlation with a decline of his fortune; so much so that today we can speak, to some extent, of a comeback of his ideas corresponding to the current crisis of the theologies of secularization. Indeed, Maritain criticized atheism and irreligion for being ultimately subservient to that "false God that is history."[12] Conversely, the positions I described almost divinize history, so that sin is the refusal to join the present movement wherein reality finds its meaning. Therefore sin is the anti-history, which is also anti-liberation.

Thus, on the one side, there is the identification, by most Catholic thinkers, of the ideal of Christian society with the ideal of a particular

12 [TN] See Maritain's "On the Meaning of Contemporary Atheism," in *The Review of Politics* 11, no. 3 (1949): 267–80.

historical age, the age that in this interpretation recovers its original meaning of "middle age." On the other side, secularists, who identify Catholic thought with the theocratic ideal in its medieval form, share this incorrect persuasion. Therefore, there is also the idea of a connection between religiosity and a situation in which nature is not mastered, and the reduction of religiosity to a feeling of fear of the external world, which one would like to turn into a sense of dependence on an absolutely good divinity. Supposedly, such a divinity reassures us about the ultimate and final triumph of goodness, which is shifted to the beyond since the present world is depicted and lived as immobile. Hence the need also for an authority that guarantees certain knowledge of the divine will; hence the importance given to the Church's authority and institutional aspect; hence, and this inference is all too easy, the inflexible, immobile, and fixed way in which the historical incarnations of these principles and values were understood. This explains why the recovery of human and rational autonomy took the form of secularism, in the sense of radical rejection of religious transcendence, vis-à-vis Church policies or a Catholic culture that was inclined to preserve a given historical order and that identified with a pre-modern civilization.

As everybody can see, this view of secularization presents two problems: (1) a particular conception of the relationship between nature and grace; (2) a conception of modern history as liberation of the Church from a role as a political substitute; religious conservatives (reactionaries, integralists) misjudged this liberation as a step back for the Church, leading to a process of de-Christianization, whereas they should have seen it as the mature fruit of faith, which had to suffer its role as a substitute in times when humanity was not yet adult and not yet able to exercise in full its rational capacity.

Regarding the first point, the objection that can be raised is that this way of thinking implies abandoning the entire Catholic theological-philosophical tradition in its essential core.

Having described the first of the two forms of secularization as a revolution, we must do likewise for the second, which is, even more evidently than the first, a political theology and a politicization of theology. In fact, think of what is unquestionably recognized as one of the fundamental principles of Thomism: "Gratia perficit naturam, non tollit."[13] Here, on the contrary, it seems that nature sustains grace. Nature is capable of fully autonomous self-realization, to which grace would be *added* as a free

13 [TN] Thomas Aquinas, *Summa Theologiae* I, I, 8 ad 2.

divine gift; but grace itself could be received as such only after nature's autonomy has been fulfilled.

In particular, Saint Augustine's thought is completely reversed and viewed, we can say, as the emblematic expression of the time when, because of the historical situation, the Church had to substitute for civil authority. This view could be described as the complete revenge of Pelagius over Saint Augustine, in the sense of trusting human nature. In fact, Pelagius's ghost has already been evoked (for example by Leo Moulin[14]) as a prefiguration of the ideology and the sensibilities of the left: of its very strong sense of human power and freedom and of its Promethean trust in man's future capabilities; so much so that one may think that the left's criticism of inheritance is itself an aspect of the rejection of Augustine's inheritance of sin. The position I outlined is a sort of "secularized" Pelagianism, because historical Pelagianism was indeed a defence of nature, but still for the sake of eternal salvation. Secularization lets Pelagius win over Saint Augustine, but on terms that Pelagius could not have accepted.

But let us even set aside the fact that this process of thought does not develop any pre-existing potentialities of Catholic thought, but is rather a process of inversion. Where this interpretation of secularization truly faces insurmountable obstacles is in its conception of grace as something *added on*. If secularity is interpreted as self-sufficiency of human nature, it is hard to see how religious truths can enter our spirit and have any meaning.

So, secularization theory oscillates between two forms of disappearance of religion, and therefore of capitulation to the modern world as secularly defined: one is the dissolution of religion into politics, and the other is a separation which de facto leads to the marginalization of properly religious culture and behaviour, or to a form of separation which is the same as exclusion.

Regarding the much emphasized distinction between secularization and secularism, I think we have to say that secularization inevitably yields to secularism in the two forms that this latter can assume and that I have already discussed in my 1964 book on *Il problema dell'ateismo*: the first is voluntarism and absolute subjectivism, the second technological physicalism-scientism.[15] The two forms of secularization yield, respectively, to the first and second form of secularism.

14 [TN] Leo Moulin, *La gauche, la droite et le péché originel* [The left, the right, and original sin] (Paris: Librairie des Méridiens, 1984).

15 [TN] Augusto Del Noce, *Il problema dell'ateismo* [The problem of atheism] (Bologna: Il Mulino, 1964.

This brings us to a question best expressed by the following words of Hans Urs von Balthasar: "He who fails to examine his own premises falls prey much more surely to some crude ideology; for example, the one of 'modern man' … 'modern man' (truly a mythical creature!) is raised to be the criterion of what God's word can and cannot say."[16] "Any theological interpretation that reduces Christology to anthropology, God's love to man's love, charity to morality, that empties the cross regarding it as a myth, an analogy, a symbol, that reduces the pair love-death to a literary model, is the negation of Christianity."[17]

But what are these premises? A secularization theologian is a theologian who wants to speak to "modern man." Therefore, analysing the idea of secularization leads us first of all to analyse the idea of modernity. Here we face the same view that we heard expressed in the words of Sperna Weiland I quoted earlier, repeated in a thousand ways. Apparently, doubt can be cast on everything except on the fact that history demonstrates that philosophy and civilization move irreversibly from metaphysical transcendence to immanence. Also Bonhoeffer's thought, his idea of the "adult man," is based on the thesis, taken as an axiom, that secularization is a movement toward the autonomy and autonomous responsibility of man in the world, a movement that, according to him, already started in the thirteenth century.[18]

MODERN RELIGION

Yesterday, anti-modern Catholic philosophy of history viewed secularization as a road to catastrophe. Today's new development is that a large number of Catholic thinkers view the final stage of secularist thought as the moment of reconciliation, when Christianity breaks away from metaphysics, from Greek captivity. In doing so, it is helped by Marxist criticism, even if this latter must take a further step and self-criticize, breaking away from a metaphysical involution.

16 [TN] Hans Urs von Balthasar, *Who is a Christian?* (London: Burns & Oates, 1969), 31–2.

17 [TN] Del Noce is quoting the introduction to Hans Urs von Balthasar's *Cordula ovverosia il caso serio* (Queriniana: Brescia, 1968), 10 (my translation) – the Italian translation of *Cordula oder der Ernstfall* (Einsiedeln: Johannes Verlag, 1966), published in English as *The Moment of Christian Witness* (New York: Newman Press, 1969). However, the sentence is not really by von Balthasar; apparently, Del Noce did not realize that the introduction to the Italian edition of *Cordula* was written by the editor, Enzo Giammancheri.

18 [TN] See Bonhoeffer's letter to Eberhard Bethge of 8 June 1944, in *Letters and Papers from Prison*, trans. Reginald Fuller, Frank Clark, et al. (New York: Touchstone, 1997), 324–9.

Thus, at the core of secularization theologies we find the attribution of an axiological value to the idea of modernity, viewed as the historical proof that thought and civilization move irreversibly from transcendence to immanence. It seems so evident that this is the only possible organizing principle for the history of philosophy that such proof is usually not emphasized. Whereas history of philosophy arose, in its first great model, as the historical confirmation of Hegel's philosophy, its role today has been reversed after historicism and the positivist critique of evidences, i.e., after we have consistently come to the point of rejecting meta-historical truths. By now, such an ability to understand and promote history is the only argument available to a rationalist thinker. But we may wonder if today we face a reversal, in which the idea of modernity reveals its dogmatic side, and in order to live critically we must scrutinize such rationalist dogmatism.

Here, I have to outline briefly what I wrote elsewhere.[19]

The idea that the philosophy of the modern age moves irreversibly toward complete immanence is internally consistent only within the Idealistic perspective that viewed the process toward immanence and the end of a transcendent God either as a purification of the idea of God into divine immanence or as a restoration of the divine in terms of immanence. In order to affirm such a perspective, here in Italy we would have to return to the times of Croce and Gentile. I have nothing against these philosophers; actually, I think that they should be rescued from the oblivion into which they have sunk today. However, I also think that they cannot be made relevant again. The philosophy of divine restoration, which wants to preserve the religious contents in divine form, is forced to erase from the history of philosophy all atheistic episodes; it must erase them in the sense of regarding them as inchoative attempts at defending worldly reality, but in a crude materialistic way, because directed against a God depicted as spatial exteriority. Supposedly, atheism as materialism is an aspect of the same naturalism that gives rise to the idea of God as a transcendent being. The supporters of God's transcendence and his materialistic deniers share the same naturalism, so that these two positions have to be surpassed by a philosophy that does not deny the divine, but the transcendence of the divine. The elders among us, who grew up at the time of Idealistic culture, know what little space was given to either Marx or Nietzsche in history of philosophy as it was taught at that time. But this did not happen only in Italy: it is enough

19 [TN] In the book *Il problema dell'ateismo* and also, more concisely, in the essay "The Idea of Modernity" in this volume.

to think of the histories of philosophy by either Brunschwicg[20] or Bréhier[21] to realize that the situation in France was not different.

Elsewhere I tried to show that precisely the introduction of the phenomenon of atheism at the final point of the three fundamental modern trends that affirm the sublation of religion into philosophy – namely, at the end of Renaissance philosophy with Libertinism, at the end of the Enlightenment, and at the end of classical German philosophy in the period from Hegel to Nietzsche – undermines the standard notion of a unitary process of modern philosophy.[22] I showed, instead, that modern philosophy includes two incompatible lines, one from Descartes to Nietzsche and one, we can say at least approximately, from Descartes to Rosmini, which aimed at recovering and refining metaphysical and religious thought.

The key role that the historical scheme of modernity has played for secularization theologies would be inexplicable apart from a particular interpretation of contemporary history, which supposedly sweeps away the "anti-modern" perspective that previously dominated Catholic philosophy of history as it originated from de Maistre, de Bonald, and Descartes (Donoso Cortés). This perspective was expressed in the 1920s (think of the book-manifesto *Antimoderne* by Maritain[23]) and, basically, during the pontificate of Pius XI. The "anti-modern" was linked, to a large extent, with the revival of Thomism. According to a common interpretation – which, however, is refuted by the most recent historical research, even by secularist scholars (leftist Catholics are by definition latecomers) – the vision of religious life and of the role of the Church in society that marked the historical period from the pontificate of Leo XIII to the entire pontificate of Pius XII made necessary the alliance between the Church and Fascism as a *true* alliance, because of essential similarities (defence of order and of the past; aversion to historical transcendence) and common enemies. The "anti-modern" could only become historical reality precisely by accepting Fascism and being involved in its catastrophe.

20 [TN] Léon Brunschwicg, *Le progrès de la conscience dans la philosophie occidentale* [The progress of conscience in Western philosophy] (Paris: Alcan, 1927).

21 [TN] Émile Bréhier, *The History of Philosophy*, trans. Joseph Thomas (Chicago: University of Chicago Press, 1963).

22 [TN] Del Noce, *Il problema dell'ateismo.*

23 [TN] Jacques Maritain, *Antimoderne* (Paris: Éditions de la Revue des Jeunes, 1922).

This view presupposes a judgment which is as simple as it is widespread: that "we are living through a revolution," the greatest known to history. This revolution must involve the Church itself, according to the very simple judgment pronounced by a certain post-Vatican II mentality. In fact, secularization theology, viewed in its overall manifestation, is the form that the revolutionary idea must take within religious thought, even though, unquestionably, it gives secularists the impression of a euthanasia of religion carried out by writers who, even if they are resigned to the onset of a post-Christian age, still do not want to leave the Church and think she may still have a role, even in the new age.

In fact, the judgment that "we are living through a revolution" is not as obvious as it may appear. If we look at today's situation, instead of the development of the revolution we seem to be looking at its ruins. Indeed, in one part of the world we find the technology of power, as a consequence of having made the political aspect absolute and reduced the whole human experience to an instrument of political power. In the other part we see the Western libertarian phenomenon, which can only be explained as the other side of the decomposition of the revolutionary idea.

In Communism, however, a trace of the messianic aspect remains, even if it is confined more and more to the background. This trace is what is erased by Western libertarianism, which in this way is able to create the most complete vacuum of any dependence on the values of the past. What is left, if not a human being disconnected from the past and without hope for the future, deprived of a community based on values, so that we can speak, as a general form, of an individual without a person?

We seem to be moving toward the victory of a physicalist-scientistic-technological culture, to which corresponds a form of morality that reverses Kant's imperative and thus sounds like "think of what is human in yourself and in others as a means, not as an end." Even in yourself, because your so-called self-realization (to use a current formula) requires that you make yourself a means. "What I relate is the history of the next two centuries. I describe what is coming … *the advent of nihilism*."[24] Thus spoke Nietzsche in one of his last fragments. And perhaps one of the possible definitions of what today is called nihilism is the inversion of the Kantian imperative. Based on a mistaken interpretation of the history of our century, or of modernity in general, secularization theology accompanies the transition from the revolutionary idea to

24 [TN] Friedrich Nietzsche, *The Will to Power*, trans. Walter Kaufmann and R.J. Hollingdale (New York: Vintage, 1968), 3.

the scientistic-technological society. Providing solutions is certainly beyond the scope of this brief work, which only intends to stimulate reflection. But this we can say: from the secularist perspective, the end of Christianity could only be envisioned precisely in the form in which the theologians of secularization intend to achieve it, regardless of their degree of awareness.

APPENDIX C

Eric Voegelin and the Critique of the Idea of Modernity

Demythologization, in the usual sense, means criticizing tradition in the name of the "spirit of modernity." This book by Voegelin turns this notion upside down.[1] What must be demythologized is the *forma mentis* behind ordinary demythologization, namely the "spirit of modernity" itself or, to be more precise, the "mystique of the new man," the idea of a transfiguration of human nature through a process of self-redemption (in which the Revolution replaces grace). His critique must necessarily take the form of an investigation of the origins of this idea. From Feuerbach to Freud, irreligious thought has focused on genetic analysis as its only argument, and it is precisely on this ground that it can be defeated, by turning its arguments around. Thus, Voegelin outlines for us a subterranean history of the Western spirit. It is the history of forces that have emerged to full light in today's world after a very long period of incubation. Our world is marked by the greatest development both of science and technology and also of the mythical spirit, a contradiction which is only apparent: Nazism's unity of fanaticism and technology goes to show that there is no contradiction. However, after so many years, in so many publications, and in so many studies of Nazi fanaticism, I believe there has been no particular effort to study the crucial issue of its alliance with technology. The prejudice that the advent of science and technology marks the end of *homo credulus* is too well established.

But, what meaning should be attributed to this formula: spirit of modernity? The standard periodization of history is well known: after ancient philosophy and medieval Christian thought, which are viewed as

"Eric Voegelin e la critica dell'idea di modernità," originally published as the introduction to Eric Voegelin, *La nuova scienza politica* (Turin: Borla, 1968), the Italian edition of *The New Science of Politics* (Chicago: University of Chicago Press, 1952).

1 [TN] Eric Voegelin, *La nuova scienza politica* (Turin: Borla, 1968).

now concluded, there is modern thought, in which the Christian transcendence of man is preserved but the supernatural is rejected, so that transcendence takes a purely worldly meaning. This picture is in no way the result of empirical observation, nor is it devised merely as a scheme to organize facts, based on a study of what particular attitudes prevailed at different times. Rather, as this book makes clear, it plays the roles of a category that illuminates the development of history and of an ideal to be fulfilled. Modernity in this sense can be represented in two ways, the one of Romanticism and the one of the Enlightenment. They differ in their stance toward the idea of tradition. The former is concerned about continuity with the past, about preserving the old values in a new form. The latter is sharply critical of tradition and seeks liberation from all myths, viewed as masks hiding reality. During the initial forty years of our century, the Romantic interpretation prevailed, at least in Western Europe. Conversely, the period after the Second World War has been marked by a growing prevalence of the mindset of the Enlightenment, in a renewed and extreme form. This process cannot be explained merely in terms of dialectics of ideas. The decisive factor was *a fact*, the Second World War as the tragic epilogue of the Fascist movements. The reaffirmation of the world view of the Enlightenment, as the only one that can defend man from "totalitarianism," was the result of an interpretation of Fascism, understood as a "reactionary" movement. Indeed, it is an elementary observation that, in general, the categories of today's moralists always posit "Fascism" as the paradigm of evil. It is Fascism elevated to a general essence, in which all so-called "reactionary" positions are absorbed. Given this attitude, they necessarily reach a general definition that says that evil lies in "fear of transcendence," where by transcendence they mean the ability, which is part of man's essence, to "go beyond" and to radically change human arrangements and relationships.[2] Fears of "novelty," of "freedom," of "risk," of "responsibility" are all synonyms of this fear. If the ability to go beyond is man's essence, all moral vices are easily derived from this fear, ranging from the private vices of envy and

2 These words were used by Ernst Nolte in *Der Faschismus in seiner Epoche* (Munich: Piper, 1963), starting from p. 515 [TN: Ernst Nolte, *Three Faces of Fascism* (New York: Holt, Rinehart and Winston, 1966), 430ff.]. He has been the only scholar so far who has studied Fascism as a transpolitical phenomenon, using an approach that is both historical and philosophical. I believe that his thesis is essentially incorrect. Nevertheless, it is a work of very great value because, by being itself rigorously developed, it stimulates rigorous criticism. I must add that Nolte intends to do the work of a historian who only wants to understand, not of a moralist. However, the definition he uses expresses perfectly the moral judgment about Fascism by radical intellectuals, even if he does not reach it starting from a presupposed political judgment.

resentment to general hatred of human nature, expressed as a spirit of oppression and violence. When such hatred enters the political dimension it produces totalitarian phenomena, which are viewed as pathological attempts to bring back forms from a distant past, charged with a different meaning because they are used against the modern conquest of freedom and openness to progress. These are macroscopic examples of evil, but their germs are found in romantic attachment to the past, in traditionalism that mistakenly regards as eternal and sacred structures and norms whose significance is purely historical. Thus, starting from anti-Fascism the progressives rediscover the Enlightenment. Therefore, today's man can commit only one sin: *to look backwards*. Or, as is often said, to oppose the *direction* of the movement of history, the constant invention of new forms, the progressive humanization of nature.

I must point out that this position is unavoidable if modern thought, as I described it, is regarded as a position from which there is no return. Within the spirit of modernity, the victory of the Enlightenment's interpretation over the Romantic one is irreversible. A more extended discussion would also clarify, in connection with this process, the distinction between anti-Fascism and Resistance, which lately has been much emphasized. Anti-Fascism still moved within a romantic framework, as a healthy form of Romanticism opposed to morbid Romanticism. It was pessimistic about vitality, which it considered a threat to spiritual values. The Resistance marked, instead, the rediscovery of revolutionary thought as the idea of an active reason. As such, it included vitality, with its world-changing power.[3] The philosophical development of the last two decades has been characterized, in its dominant trend, by the quest to free revolutionary thought from its romantic residues.

Voegelin's views could not be more opposed to this "progressive" diagnosis of the ethical-political ills of our time. However, his vision differs from other positions because it could never be accused not only of Fascism or racism, but even of having a reactionary tone.

Let me say why he is worth listening to. Nobody could reasonably accuse the new generation of not having taken to heart the diagnosis I described. Aversion against the traditional spirit has never been so strong and widespread, and reverence for the "so-called" eternal values has never been mocked so much, reaching the highest degree of desecration. But what have been the results? Empirical observation casts doubt on the efficacy of the cure, so that even radical intellectuals become perplexed.

3 The works of Giaime Pintor, collected in the volume *Il sangue d'Europa* [Europe's blood] (Turin: Einaudi, 1950), are extremely significant documents in order to understand how this process took place among young Italian intellectuals around 1940.

As I get ready to write these pages, I am reading a column by a radical writer in an Italian newspaper about the "escalation," the faster and faster pace of the "taste for violence," for destruction, for erotic perversion, for the exaltation of callousness, "brutality and cynicism" as the typical characteristics of the "heroes of our time."[4] The de-humanization process that characterized the totalitarian regimes did not stop; it has actually become stronger. "We cannot see its endpoint," Adelfi writes.[5] But it is easy to draw the implicit consequence of his analysis: given that every society reflects the people who form it, we are threatened by oligarchies and persecutory systems that would make Nazism and Stalinism look like pale images, although, of course, [these new oligarchies and persecutory systems] will not present themselves as a new Nazism or a new Stalinism. On the other hand, it would be simply ridiculous to explain the present process of de-humanization as a residual or a regurgitation of the Fascist period. Even leaving aside the fact that past forms of totalitarianism do not come back, or that young people have a very poor recollection of what Fascism or Nazism or Stalinism were like, lingering habits would not explain the escalation. But a radical intellectual can only stop at registering the facts, and cannot go any further. He cannot make the transition to the explanatory level, for which Voegelin's book provides indispensable tools.

Let us quote what he himself said during a recent conference in Milan:

In his book *Being and Nothingness*, in the chapter on "insincerity," Sartre paid special attention to the fact that in order to live in the particular state of mind that is typical of ideologues, one must develop a special ability to ignore the facts that contradict the delusions that he entertains about reality. This phenomenon is precisely what he calls insincerity. The problem of insincerity … is typical of the attitude of twentieth-century ideologues, whereas it was not a problem, for example, for Schiller or Engels because they did not know more about history than what they showed that they knew … Hence the new phenomenon of insincerity, and all the resulting negative mental and psychological effects due to the fact that people who live insincerely know, of course, that they are living insincerely and are aware of all the difficulties, which nevertheless they want to ignore and whose existence they refuse to admit … Sartre's chapter on insincerity is

4 [TN] Nicola Adelfi, "Troppo sangue" [Too much blood], *La Stampa* 102, no. 5 (6 January 1970): 3.

5 [TN] Nicola Adelfi was the pen name of Italian reporter and columnist Nicola De Feo (1909–87).

extremely interesting, precisely because Sartre himself lives in the most absolute insincerity regarding his own attitude toward Communism.[6]

On this matter, I can only add that Voegelin attributes to Sartre a degree of originality that he does not deserve, and that the very fact of quoting Sartre is not in good taste. Why not refer to the classical theory of attention, upheld by all religious thinkers, which already said what is essential about the phenomenon of insincerity, but with much greater depth? There is really nothing new in Sartre except a rediscovery, but in a warped form, of the classical theory about the relationship between freedom and attention.

But – why does one lie? Obviously in order to possess other people, not to persuade them. Thus, the idol that is broken is the very idea of truth, in the name of the will to achieve power and success. All the features that I mentioned earlier come together. Thus, for instance, within the general attitude of striving to possess, love degrades into eroticism and must go down the road that de Sade brilliantly described. The spirit of novelty expresses itself as a spirit of destruction. The progressivist rediscovery of the Enlightenment has taken the road going from Diderot to de Sade, who today are, not by chance, two of the most read authors. Here in Italy, the rediscovery of Diderot was the alternative that non-Marxist secular progressivism devised vis-à-vis Gramsci's line of development "from Croce to Marx." But one cannot start down a road without going through certain unavoidable steps. Moreover, even though these two lines started differently, today they are actually indistinguishable, as Croce already pointed out.

Thus, the persuasion that the "reactionary" human type is the obstacle to the world's natural evolution toward order, philanthropy, and peace had the effect, by eliminating the "closed" spirit of tradition and conservation, of making more overt a process of both desecration and dehumanization. The manifestations of this phenomenon in the totalitarian systems of the past did not exhaust it. Given this empirical observation, Plato's distinction between philalethes,[7] lovers of truth, and philodoxers,

6 Eric Voegelin, "Apocalisse e rivoluzione" [Apocalypse and revolution], in the UIPC collection of lectures *1867–1967 un secolo di Marxismo* [1867–1967 a century of Marxism] (Florence: Vallecchi, 1967), 131–2.

7 [TN] Actually, to my knowledge, it is not in Plato that we find the adjective φιλαλήθης – transliterated as "philalétes" – but in Aristotle, *Nicomachean Ethics*, 1127b.1. See also Plutarch's *Caius Marius*, chapter 28, and Diodorus Siculus, *Bibliotheca Historica*, Book I, chapter 76.

sophists, comes back. Let the latter embrace the formulas that they find useful, changing them according to the "direction of history." Philalethes will find in Voegelin's book deep intellectual stimulation, whether they agree with it or not. Also because nobody, even those most opposed to the theses it proposes, will find that it serves any value other than the soul's openness to the truth.

Nothing is more relevant to our age than to meditate anew on the contrast between Saint Augustine's view of history and that of Joachim of Fiore. According to Saint Augustine, the two cities, the heavenly and the earthly, will exist side by side and fight each other until the end of time: they will be separated only at the final judgment. This is the most radical possible criticism of millennialism, which maintains that the ideal city will replace the earthly city in time. At the time, this view found support in a well-known passage from the Book of Revelation ("With such violence the great city of Babylon will be thrown down, never to be found again … Then I saw 'a new heaven and a new earth,' for the first heaven and the first earth had passed away, and there was no longer any sea. I, John, saw the Holy City, the new Jerusalem, coming down out of heaven from God."[8]).

But apparently the tendency to project in time the coming of the kingdom of God is ingrained in the human spirit, and so in the twelfth century Joachim of Fiore divided human history into three periods corresponding to the three persons of the Trinity, and prophesied the upcoming Kingdom of the Spirit. Thus, he replaced again coexistence of the two cities with temporal succession. Certainly, according to his prophecy greater fullness within history would not be produced by an "immanent eruption," but by a new "transcendent irruption" of the divine spirit. Nevertheless, Joachimite thought provided the background for the rise and ultimate success of the process of "secularization," through a long process that can be described, roughly speaking, by the usual formula "from humanism to the Enlightenment," although this increase in the significance of history became a completely worldly phenomenon, without "transcendent irruptions," only in the eighteenth century, with the idea of progress. Regardless of the historical form in which it propagated itself, certainly Joachim's Trinitarian eschatology created the symbolic system through which modern man interprets history.

Just think of the standard periodization of history in its various versions (Hegel, Marx, Comte) and of the idea that the history of modern thought is a unitary process toward radical immanence. Usually this

8 Rev. 18: 21 and 21:1–2.

thesis is taken to be so obvious that the problem shifts to "whether what calls itself modern is really so," in the sense of being really free from theological and transcendent presuppositions. Still, is the question truly so obvious? Is it so clear that Joachim is right against Saint Augustine? Indeed, it is obvious, even if nobody ever points it out, that an Augustinian conception of the history of philosophy could never accept that a sequence of periods corresponds to higher degrees of truth, but should rather affirm a constant struggle, through various ages, between the religious view and the worldly one.

The influence of Joachimite thought is very well known. On this topic, Löwith's book about the theological origins of the philosophy of history has been one of the most widely read books in history of philosophy of the last few years.[9] However, Voegelin's viewpoint is completely different and leads, or at least opens the way, to completely different results. Indeed, his research is not primarily about philosophy of history but about modern political societies. It is a history of experiences, of lived attitudes more than ideas, and its looks completely different because it introduces a reflection about the political factor, as a determining factor and not as a derived one.

Löwith's project is to criticize the idea and the forms of the philosophy of history by showing that they always contain a theological residue: they result from the disintegration of the religious world view and are marked by it. In spite of some misunderstandings to which his writings may have lent themselves, his thought moves entirely within the "spirit of modernity," even though for him the thinker "before whom we cannot go back" is neither Kant, nor Hegel, nor Marx, but rather Nietzsche. According to Voegelin, on the contrary, the question of the meaning of history is an error – inasmuch as the course of history in its totality in not an object of experience – due to the immanentization of the Christian eschaton. This question does not arise within the soteriological vision of Christianity, because eschatological super-nature is not a nature in the philosophical sense. Although he stays at a purely descriptive level, his critique leaves Christian thought perfectly intact, whereas it applies to all the philosophy that calls itself "modern," in the sense of being free from any dependence on a supernatural revelation.

Here comes a crucial question: is what is still clear to Löwith – that it is impossible to go back to a theoretical-transcendent view – really so clear from the standpoint of critical reason? Recent religious thought has established what I would like to call an ecumenical idea, in the sense that

9 Karl Löwith, *Meaning in History: The Theological Implications of the Philosophy of History* (Chicago: University of Chicago Press, 1949).

all, or nearly all, religious thinkers agree with it: "faith cannot be demonstrated, and yet faith alone makes it possible to explain existence rationally, while at the same time it is concretely verified by it in terms of reason and experience."[10] Does rationalism not start, likewise, from an unprovable option, *which however is not declared as such?* And does not its history put it to the test, with the result that its initial contradiction manifests itself in its inability to organize life rationally?[11]

Voegelin's book provides precious evidence to support this thesis.

The spirit of modernity, which is the foundation of modern opinions and political movements, is thus the immanentization of the Christian eschaton. In his judgment, the driving factor of this evolution is Gnosticism, so that the evolution of the spirit of modernity coincides with the one of Gnosticism. Certainly, the use of this word can raise serious concerns. One must carefully distinguish between an ancient gnosis and a post-Christian gnosis, and this would require an investigation to determine whether they can be regarded as varieties, or developmental stages, of the same essence. I think that the answer could *only be negative.* According to the precise definition by H.W. Bartsch, "ancient gnosis is characterized by a radical dualism which, for the first time, is not within the world but rejects the world in its entirety, both the Greek Cosmos with its gods and the Eastern world with its planets, placing them on the side of evil and separated from a unique, good, distant God. This world view is expressed in several mythologies, all of which can be recognized as Gnostic because of the break that separates the world from God."[12] Therefore, ancient gnosis atheizes the world (by denying that it was created by God) in the name of divine transcendence. Post-Christian gnosis atheizes it in the name of radical immanentism. We can certainly find a common feature in the quest to escape the miseries of life,[13] but highlighting this common element helps better illuminate the crucial difference between pessimism and optimism (or meliorism, as people

10 I am quoting the words used by Sergio Cotta in his important introductory essay to the Italian translation of Reinhold Niebuhr's *Faith and History: A Comparison of Christian and Modern Views of History, Fede e storia,* trans. Franco Giampiccoli (Bologna: Il Mulino, 1966), xvii.

11 Regarding the characteristics of the atheistic option, see my book *Il problema dell'ateismo* (Bologna: Il Mulino, 1964).

12 Hans Werner Bartsch, "Gnostiches Gut und Gemeindetradition bei Ignatius von Antiochen" in *Beiträge zur Förderung christlicher Theologie,* 2nd series, 44 (1940): 6.

13 In both cases what is being sought are rules to escape from the world as it is. However, whereas in ancient gnosis this is achieved by destroying the spirit of power within oneself, and by freeing the soul from the world, in post-Christian gnosis the exact opposite takes place.

tend to say today, implying such a radical secularization that it eliminates all secular counterparts of divine providence). The Gnostic quest is about rules to free the soul from the world; conversely, post-Christian immanentism searches for rules to build an absolutely new world. The former has an aristocratic character; for the latter, appealing to the masses – or, in fact, the very rise of the idea of mass, in its precise meaning – is essential. The remark about optimism and pessimism shows that we are dealing with opposite, timeless essences. It would be easy to show that so-called ancient gnosis never disappeared, and that its themes have been rediscovered in the history of modern pessimism.[14] Perhaps, we could even say that immanentism has the effect of prompting in pessimistic dualism a revision process of the feature they share in common, the idea of a form of knowledge that should replace faith; this is a process that could lead to openness to Christianity.

Nevertheless, *a new gnosis* – where "new" means at the same time "post-Christian" or "decayed" or "degenerate," as we shall see – is the only possible formula that can be used to describe the process that led to the myths of modernity and of the Revolution (regardless of what adjective is used to specify it: political, scientific, technological) as a historical break that will make possible to transition to the "new man." Indeed, it cannot be replaced by the term millennialism, even if this word would indicate nicely that in today's world there is an archetype that seems as far removed as it could be from the scientific mindset. The reason is that, in the forms of thought that are usually called millennialistic, man's condition in the world is transfigured through a divine intervention, whereas the essential feature of the immanentization of the Christian eschaton is the transition to the idea that man is capable of self-redemption, i.e., of achieving salvation through action.[15] It is the conviction that the advent of the reign of perfection on earth will be fulfilled by a human initiative. As for Rosmini's term "perfectism" ("the system which believes

14 Let me cite two works of mine about the Italian pessimists Piero Martinetti ("Martinetti nella cultura italiana e piemontese" [Martinetti in Italian and Piedmontese culture] in *Giornata martinettiana* (Turin: ed. di Filosofia, 1964)) and Giuseppe Rensi ("Giuseppe Rensi tra Leopardi e Pascal, ovvero l'autocritica dell'ateismo negativo in Giuseppe Rensi" [Giuseppe Rensi between Leopardi and Pascal, or the self-criticism of negative atheism in Giuseppe Rensi] in the proceedings of the *Giornata Rensiana* (Milan: Marzorati, 1967)). In its final stage the thought of the latter is *defenceless* against Pascal's position. But above all, what matters is the experience of Simone Weil, as the rediscovery of Gnostic pessimism starting from the crisis of the years after 1930. In her, this rediscovery was precisely the beginning of a process of conversion to Christianity, which was real even if it remained imperfect.

15 [TN] Voegelin, *New Science of Politics*, 121.

in the possibility of perfection in human affairs and sacrifices present benefits for some imagined future perfection"[16]) or meta-Christianity, they are appropriate to describe the outcome of this process but not the process itself. Neither should we speak of "laicism,"[17] because there are also forms of laicism, for instance Croce's, that are characterized by its opposition to Gnosticism,[18] although one can raise the question whether the new Gnosticism can be successfully resisted from within laicism. I think that it would not be hard to answer this question (Croce is an example!).

Within the new Gnosticism, *the activist and revolutionary version is destined to prevail over the contemplative version.*

At the empirical level this is all too easy to see. Just consider the relationship between Regalism and Marxism, or the dominant trends of contemporary philosophy. But what matters is to understand why.

I spoke of a degenerate gnosis, and I believe that this adjective might be acceptable to Voegelin. Indeed, why is a new Gnostic blind to the obvious fact that men lack cognitive tools to define the meaning and the end of history? Because he has lost his faith, and he is looking for a surrogate to save himself from the abyss of desperation and nothingness. "The more people are drawn or pressured into the Christian orbit, the greater will be the number among them who do not have the spiritual stamina for the heroic adventure of the soul that is Christianity; and the likeliness of a fall from faith will increase when civilizational progress of education, literacy and intellectual debate will bring the full seriousness of Christianity to the understanding of ever more individuals."[19] He can find such a surrogate only in "experiential alternatives, sufficiently close

16 [TN] Antonio Rosmini, *The Philosophy of Politics* (Durham, UK: Rosmini House, 1994), 1: 74. About Rosmini's usage of the term "perfettismo" and its English translation, see note 20 on page 255.

17 [TN] In France and Italy the word "laicism" [laicisme, laicismo] is used in a sense very similar to the English "secularism." Its emphasis, however, is more specifically on keeping religion out of the public sphere than on affirming an irreligious world view in a broader sense.

18 Such is, after all, the nature of his polemics against the philosophy of history. If we consider Croce's thought from this perspective, what today is possibly his most disparaged work, "Perchè non possiamo non dirci cristiani" [Why we cannot not call ourselves Christian], *La critica* 55 (1942): 289–97, becomes more significant. It is not just a wartime piece that must be linked to the framing of the Second World War as a religious war between Christianity and neo-paganism. There is also a presentiment of the type of meta-Christianity (anti-Christianity as meta-Christianity) that prevailed afterwards, and its rejection.

19 [TN] Voegelin, *New Science of Politics*, 123.

to the experience of faith that only a discerning eye would see the difference, but receding far enough from it to remedy the uncertainty of faith in the strict sense. Such alternative experiences were at hand in the gnosis which had accompanied Christianity from its very beginnings."[20] About this search for a surrogate, we can truly speak of "fear of transcendence," but of transcendence in the theological sense. It would be much better to speak of "fear of the supernatural" instead of "fear of transcendence," since by now this word has taken too often the worldly meaning that I discussed at the beginning. And this has happened for a reason, because when transcendence is separated from the supernatural, it does indeed tend to take this new meaning.

What Voegelin does not say, but nevertheless seems to be implicit in his discussion, is that ancient gnosis affirmed a truth, whereas the new gnosis arises in order to satisfy a practical need. Therefore, the transition from the former to the latter cannot be described as a development. However, having neglected to say this explicitly can lead to an extremely serious misunderstanding, which is the foundation of neo-Modernism: the idea that gnosis is a *unitary* phenomenon, in its Christian and post-Christian versions. Two examples will suffice to convey the seriousness of this question. In 1953, a young philosopher, Claude Tresmontant, started a series of volumes aimed at re-understanding all of Christian thought in light of Teilhard de Chardin's evolutionism. Inevitably, he had to go back to Laberthonnière's thesis that Christian thought and Greek thought are opposed to each other. However, whereas Laberthonnière ended up rejecting completely Thomism and almost all of classic Christian philosophy, Tresmontant thought that he would be able to develop an interpretation of Thomism that would agree with neo-Modernism. Now, here is what he wrote: "At each step during this work we have run into gnosis, which has presented itself to us as the opposite metaphysics of biblical metaphysics, its adversary. Gnosis has faithfully accompanied Christian metaphysics over the course of its history: gnosis is the anti-Christian philosophy. *We can legitimately speak of gnosis as a single metaphysics*: behind the variations introduced by each individual Gnostic we actually keep finding a constant metaphysics, certain original options and shared tendencies that define the perennial gnosis."[21] This is

20 [TN] Ibid.

21 See Claude Tresmontant, *Études de métaphisique biblique* (Paris: Gabalda, 1955), 229. It is true that more recently Tresmontant himself seems to have changed his mind, at least in part: see his work "Le Père Teilhard de Chardin et la théologie" in *Lettres*, no. 49–50 [September–October 1962]: 1–53.

perfectly correct in the context of Tresmontant's formulation: in order to harmonize Christian thought with Teilhardian evolutionism we must indeed separate it from a "constant metaphysical structure," which can only be denoted by the word gnosis. But this confirms precisely that *one cannot simply oppose biblical thought and Gnosticism without arriving at modernism.* The next best proof is the fact that the official representative of "dialogic" Marxism, Roger Garaudy (who wants to replace the "method of persecution" with the method of "dialogue," but without taking anything away from Marxist atheism), welcomed enthusiastically the idea that what is specifically Christian in Christianity has been swamped by Gnostic corruption. In his recent book *De l'anathème au dialogue, un marxiste s'adresse au Concile,* he recast this narrative (by appealing not only to Teilhard but also to Bultmann, Robinson, and Rahner) in terms of a syncretistic ideology with Hellenistic roots, in which cosmic religions, mystery religions, and stoicism supposedly merged confusedly, creating the Gnostic "myth about the destiny of the soul."[22] It included the original fall, which originated the resignation that made possible the "Constantinian tradition," which in turn turned Christianity into the "opium of the peoples." Hence, today Christianity has both the opportunity and the duty to redeem itself by getting rid of this Gnostic superstructure. Supposedly, an alliance with the Marxists is possible because for them atheism is not a principle but an "outcome," although Christianity would join a revolution whose "outcome" would be the end of theism. Once again, we must point out that Garaudy is just drawing the consequences of the pure anti-Gnostic position, as it was actually formulated by religious thinkers and theologians. How many times have I read in recent Catholic authors that the dogma of the incarnation means the rehabilitation of matter against the Gnostic anathema? The logical endpoint is the incarnation without the cross and without redemption from sin. Logically, the outcome must be a dialogue between two similar positions: Marxism and a "new Christianity" like the one, essentially, of Saint-Simon.

It is true that Voegelin's argument is always focused on the new gnosis. And certainly the new and the old share a common feature, the idea of a form of knowledge superior to the *cognitio fidei.* This leads them to deny the idea of Christian philosophy as a philosophy that arises within faith.[23]

22 [TN] Roger Garaudy, *From Anathema to Dialogue: A Marxist Challenge to the Christian Churches,* trans. Luke O'Neill (New York: Herder and Herder, 1966), 101.

23 Regarding the notion of Christian philosophy, see the chapter "Philosopher dans la foi" in *Introduction à la philosophie chrétienne,* by Étienne Gilson (Paris: Vrin, 1960), 13–15.

But this common aspect must not be emphasized one-sidedly, lest we fall into a pure opposition of Christianity and Gnosticism, within which the Modernists are right. In that case his book would be at risk of being less effective. Actually, the difference between the two forms of gnosis is *qualitative*.

Because it is post-Christian, the new gnosis must attribute to man the power to create. Therefore, the very idea of a meta-Christianity – the edification through human power of a "third kingdom" coming after Christianity – was destined to lead to radical anti-Christianity, which indeed is manifesting itself at the final stage. It was destined to take a position that does not preserve Christianity by "sublating" it, but simply denies it, in its dogmas as well as in its morality.[24]

This is a consequence of replacing redemption by God with the idea of self-redemption. The denial of original sin lies at the root of the new Gnosticism, and its history goes to show that once this denial is accepted, the whole edifice of Christianity is destined to crumble.

Therefore, Voegelin is perfectly correct when he remarks that the idea of the "superman" is already present in Feuerbach and Marx: God is the product of a projection by the human spirit, and man will find his essence again by taking back what he "alienated" himself from.

Now, let me offer a brief reflection. What could be logically weaker than the theory that God is a projection of human needs? Supposedly God does not exist because his existence reflects human exigencies. This argument presupposes that *God could exist only if man did not need Him.* What could be more absurd? But then, why is this idea so widespread? In the Milan conference I mentioned, Voegelin stated that in the United States all intellectuals agree about this theory. This may well have been a verbal exaggeration. Nevertheless, it is still true that certainly most American intellectuals subscribe to it, at least tacitly or by accepting its consequences.

Thus, this idea is logically weak and very persuasive at the same time. It owes its power to the fact that it is truly irrefutable from within the neo-Gnostic system, as its ultimate consequence. Indeed, think about it: a system which begins by projecting the ideal city into the world, as a reality that can be built by man, can only logically conclude to the divinization of man himself. The theory of projection expresses precisely this divinization. Then, the religious notion of sin is completely reversed: the creation of the idea of God is the sin from which man can free himself.

24 In this respect, one should reflect about the rise of Marx's activist gnosis after Hegel's contemplative gnosis. Its rise and its success are consistent with the nature of the new gnosis.

If we put together the weakness of the argument and its irrefutability within the system, we realize the *non-rational* character of the new Gnosticism. And perhaps this is the deeper meaning of Nietzsche's proclamation that God has been killed. Nietzsche must definitely be regarded as the thinker who lived most deeply the tragedy of modern gnosis, even if he was unable to escape it. His folly is a philosophical fact, which symbolizes a threat hanging over the world as the final outcome of the new gnosis.

This non-rational origin also explains why the new order, which is described theoretically in terms of freedom and fulfillment, can be realized, in its final outcome, only as totalitarian oppression. Two essential elements of this new order are the symbolic value of modernity and the axiological value attributed to the standard periodization of history. Supposedly, the Middle Ages were followed by a modern age that freed itself from the shackles of various forms of authority and that seeks the truth in human reason itself (a common formula which expresses the deeper idea of human self-redemption).

Of course, the process of elaboration of post-Christian Gnosticism has been very slow: its theoretical definition has emerged only during the last century, and its practical effects only over the last fifty years. In its early stages it could present itself, and be perceived by its advocates, as a Christian spiritualization of worldly reality. An especially interesting aspect of Voegelin's book is the illustration of the way in which a neo-Gnostic mentality and totalitarian attitudes grow together.

This is why one of the most remarkable chapters is the one dedicated to the "Puritan case" – viewed as the first wave of post-Christian Gnosticism – and to the incalculably valuable typological analysis of Puritanism that was formulated by its adversary Richard Hooker (who had a Thomistic background but is usually viewed, very incorrectly, as a precursor of Locke).[25]

Clearly, the idea of a third kingdom, inasmuch as it is a work to be carried out by man himself, implies the re-divinization of the temporal sphere of power, in opposition to its de-divinization by Christianity, and consequently the absolutization of the political aspect. Indeed, if we immanentize the eschaton, evil coincides with the past; it is projected outside ourselves, in the institutions, and a new form of government will be the cure for all evils. Now, Puritanism provides a uniquely important example showing how Gnostic themes are superimposed on Christian

25 [TN] Voegelin, *New Science of Politics*, chapter 5. In the next two paragraphs Del Noce goes over the main argument in this chapter, repeating verbatim some of Voegelin's expressions.

themes, because political and revolutionary action is promoted in the name of scripture. Certainly, man is not divinized, yet, but somehow he has already taken the place entrusted to the Angel in the Book of Revelation.

However, no passage in the New Testament legitimates the revolutionary mindset. The leaders of the movement had to link their doctrine to some passages and words from scripture, and to mould the minds of their followers so that this link would become automatic. But, how did they justify in front of themselves the choice to expunge the scriptural passages that contradicted their doctrine? By claiming a special illumination from the Holy Spirit, which enabled them to discover in the texts what others could not see. Thus, a group of elect individuals is established, whom common people must follow. Having been "indoctrinated" in this way, these common people are then presented as those to whom the voice of Christ has been primarily communicated, and who have been given the task of destroying Babylon in order to raise Jerusalem. Given these presuppositions, every opposing argument, even when saintly theologians advance it, can be rejected by describing it as coming from "the world's side." The quest for the truth is replaced by the quest for a psychologically ironclad attitude directed at a political goal. In this way, the social function of persuasion is destroyed: the conviction of having received a special illumination, for the sake of a task assigned by God, leads not only to the refusal to discuss, but also to the placing of a taboo on all instruments of critique through social boycott and political defamation. In the case at hand, a taboo on classical philosophy and scholastic theology, with huge consequences for English thought that can be fully observed today. Adversaries were declared to be "enemies of the people of God" and a pamphlet from 1649 by the extreme wing of Puritanism, the *Queries*, says that the only course of action will be "suppressing the enemies of godliness fore ever."[26]

Who can fail to recognize in these positions, even if at that time they were couched in religious language, the paradigms and the attitudes that are necessary to every totalitarian experience – or the paradigms that have been rediscovered today by progressive religious thought? The Puritans justified their attitude by invoking an illumination by the Holy Spirit. But are the Marxists doing anything different, when they place a taboo on the arguments of their adversaries by calling them "classist"? Is the nature of the relationship between the leading elite and its followers not the same in both cases? Is the appeal to the masses – which have been

26 [TN] "Certain Queries Presented by Many Christian People, 1649," in *Puritanism and Liberty*, ed. A.S.P. Woodhouse (Chicago: University of Chicago Press, 1951), 241–7.

indoctrinated, even if later they are described as the voice of God or of history – not identical as well? In all its forms, the new Gnosticism must reject the universality of reason and its foundation in the theory of the Logos. This is due to a structural necessity, which its advocates have not invented but by which, one could say, they are "acted upon." The practical option at the origin of the new Gnosticism leads them, depending on its various versions, either to despise reason or to attribute to it worldly origins and an instrumental character.

Dictatorship is forced on them by the following contradiction: on the one hand, the followers of degenerate gnosis replace religion with politics as the road to human liberation; on the other, they cannot hope to succeed through persuasion because the immanentization of the eschaton is a theoretical fallacy. No matter what form of Gnosticism will prevail, believers in the ancient values will be ostracized and sentenced to the hell of social oblivion, precisely because of their morality and sincerity. And the sentence will be pronounced in the name of a new religious interpretation or of an unverifiable meaning of history (or of both at the same time). Such a sentence is a form of violence, because it strikes those who think in terms of truth – it destroys the truth of the soul, as Voegelin says[27] – in the name of myth. Because the word myth takes its full meaning in connection with the immanentization of the Christian eschaton, due to the genetic process I described.

I am tempted to propose the following definition of totalitarianism: a regime that persecutes the "philaletes" in the Platonic sense of the word. This is what distinguishes it from all past forms of authoritarianism, including eastern despotism, medieval theocracy, and absolute monarchies.

Thus, Voegelin's book concludes by drawing the picture of a cycle of the history of civilization, whose detailed exploration would require a huge amount of work. The climax of this cycle is marked by the coming of Christ. The great pre-Christian civilizations form its ascending arc, inasmuch as they progressed in recognizing the soul as the *sensorium* of transcendence. Conversely, Gnostic civilization in the modern sense moves in the opposite direction, and accordingly it must be called regressive, even if it invented the idea of progress.[28]

• • •

Let us return briefly to the points I mentioned at the beginning.

27 [TN] Voegelin, *New Science of Politics*, 163.
28 [TN] Ibid., 164.

I said that Voegelin's interpretation is completely opposed to the one that says that totalitarian movements had a reactionary origin. I believe that his analysis is also able to support the opposite thesis, and this makes it particularly powerful. The new gnosis is founded on not recognizing reality, and it creates a dream world. This world can attain effective reality only by compromising with traditional elements. For instance, Communism could never have succeeded without establishing an alliance with the idea of a primacy of Russia and of its special task for the liberation of the world, i.e., without absorbing, not just with Stalin but already with Lenin, elements of a mindset that originally was extraneous to it. It is through this process that revolutions, which initially present themselves as servants of the universal cause of mankind, produce in concrete reality nations with hegemonic claims. The interpretation of the totalitarian movements as reactionary is born out of confusion between their original principle and a necessary stage of their implementation. As for Nazism, it was born in response to Russia's westward expansion, and therefore it was bound to display symmetric but ideologically opposite characteristics with respect to Stalinism. Hence, it is no wonder that initially it recruited its followers from social groups threatened with decline. But Nazism itself cannot be explained by its association with these groups. The fact that it, too, is a neo-Gnostic movement is revealed by the very symbol of the Third Reich and by the idea of the thousand years.[29]

The second remark is about the growing process of de-humanization and de-sacralization. Voegelin's research gives us an extremely useful line of attack in order to understand the developments of the last few years. Indeed, let us reflect about the original insincerity that he exposed in the immanentization of the eschaton. The quest that characterizes the degenerate gnosis is not, as we have seen, a quest for truth but *a quest for power.* This characteristic, which is inscribed in its beginnings, becomes manifest in its final stages in a symmetrically reverse order with respect to its genesis. Marxism is certainly a decisive document of this phenomenon, because in it we find at the same time, and interconnected, the affirmation of the primacy of action, atheism and the super-humanistic character, and the permanent break with Christianity. Later on, the primacy of action mediated the transition from an activist philosophy of

29 Regarding the subordination of Nazism to Marxism, as an ideological inversion, it is important to reflect about Hitler's exaltation of nature as a struggle that makes possible a higher and higher evolution, of obedience to its law, and of natural institutions. It is the exact opposite of the Marxist humanization of nature, which is viewed as an "anti-natural" position. Hitler met Nietzsche as the antithesis of Marx starting from this opposition.

history to totalitarianism, which subordinates the intellectuals to the politicians. Last, the decline of the intellectuals leads to replacing truth with successful mendacity, as the final stage of the degenerate Gnostic experience. In fact, let us consider the spiritual process of the last twenty years. It is unquestionable that theoretical Marxism has lost ground, but in favour not of Christianity but of scientism. Now, it is a fact that scientism – which means the interpretation of science in terms of a new gnosis – leads to a greater degree of de-humanization than Marxism as a political praxis.

No matter how scant are the details provided by Marx and Engels about the situation that will come about after the transfiguration of mankind, we can discern that ultimately they thought that individual conscience would be absorbed within a universal conscience (otherwise how could have they talked about abolishing the state?). Therefore, in the classless society religion also will end, inasmuch as its role will become superfluous because it will have been replaced.

On the contrary, this aspect is completely lacking in scientism. Science, at least in the sense of modern science, is completely unlinked from the idea that the order of being is revelatory, and cannot provide values. Hence, from a purely scientistic perspective, what is left is mere self-fulfillment, selfishly understood (or the fulfillment of associations, in groups, of selfish individuals). Other people are viewed as mechanisms that can be used. Adorno pointed out correctly that de Sade's Juliette[30] "believes in science ... She operates with semantics and logical syntax like the most up-to-date positivism."[31]

Thus, should we really be surprised by the escalation in the spirit of violence? In this respect, the products of the recent culture industry certainly take a symbolic significance, by revealing a morbid curiosity about how to break apart man's psycho-physical mechanism.

• • •

Voegelin published this book in 1951. He wondered about the possibility of an anti-Gnostic reaction, since Western society is not completely dominated by the spirit of modernity. Rather, modernity is, within it, one movement that develops in opposition to the classical and Christian tradition. The years that went by certainly did not paint an encouraging

30 [TN] Marquis de Sade, *Juliette*, trans. Austryn Wainhouse (New York: Grove Press, 1968).

31 [TN] Max Horkheimer and Theodore W. Adorno, *Dialectic of Enlightenment*, trans. John Cumming (New York: Continuum, 2001), 96.

picture. Did we not see the spirit of the degenerate gnosis penetrate even into the core of the resistance, into a large section of the clergy? And did we not witness the rise of the theology of the "death of God," tied to the idea that today religion must focus on renewing the realities of the world?

Nevertheless, the connection between the process of de-humanization and the process of de-sacralization in the name of novelty is so evident that it may prompt the question whether a certain diagnosis about contemporary history was inadequate. And we can already glimpse the germs of new attitudes.

I conclude with two thoughts that have been prompted by reading this book. Everybody knows the theses of Saint Augustine's *City of God.* Strangely enough, it seems that during the last few centuries religious thinkers themselves forgot them. Certainly, one should not be surprised by the fact that the Joachimite scheme, in its secularized form, has dominated the rationalist philosophy of history since Lessing and has shaped the history of philosophy. What is surprising is to observe that actually it has also permeated Catholic historical thinking.

The only exception is Rosmini and his admirable critique of perfectism. The historical vision of Catholic reactionary thinkers, instead, has been completely dominated by the secular view of history and has in fact accepted the three-fold scheme of historical periodization, merely changing the sign of its value from positive to negative. As a result, all Catholic-reactionary interpretations of history ended up (since the time of Lamennais) turning into Modernism,[32] this extraordinary folly that would like to adapt Christianity to meta-Christianity (and then, by necessity, to its atheism, whether one wants it or not. The theological trend of the "death of God" is not just a bizarre accident). This is happening at the very moment when secular thinkers are baffled by its final outcomes.

From this standpoint the teaching of Voegelin's book is an admonishment that we have to climb back up a steep hill and an assurance that it can be done. But steep hills are not easy to climb and so we cannot be too optimistic. Even if the ideal essence of the new Gnosticism has fully manifested itself by now, it has created countless theoretical and historical habits that shape current opinions, without any awareness of their origin. The end of its philosophical development has coincided with a climax in its practical power, which is very far from being exhausted.

32 It is significant that, to my knowledge, there has been no exhaustive study of such a connection between the reactionary and the Modernist positions. Nor has anybody adequately highlighted that Rosmini is, in this respect, the only exception.

The second thought goes back to the difference I have already pointed out between the interpretations of Löwith and of Voegelin, and to the fact that the former has run out of steam. Because everybody can see the downward trajectory in Löwith's work, from *From Hegel to Nietzsche*[33] in 1935 to his more recent writings, which give the impression – *absit iniuria* – of a stroll among the ruins. Emphasizing that at the origins of what is usually called secular thought there is a non-rational choice and an option for politics and power can also explain the partial truth of Marxism. Historical materialism is valid, but precisely only as an explanation of the secular forms of thought and of their sequence.

33 [TN] Karl Löwith, *From Hegel to Nietzsche*, trans. David E. Green (New York: Holt, Rinehart and Winston, 1964).

Index